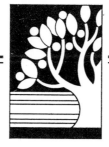

In Honor of
The Marriage of
Mr. & Mrs. Morton H. Bauer

Presented by

Mr. & Mrs. Robert H. Folk

to

New Cumberland Public Library

2005

D1413842

The Encyclopedia of
NORTH
AMERICAN
BIRDS

MICHAEL VANNER

This is a Parragon Publishing Book
First published in 2002

Parragon Publishing
Queen Street House
4 Queen Street
Bath, BA1 1HE, UK

Text © Parragon
For details of photograph copyrights see pages 382/3

Produced by Atlantic Publishing
Designed by Judy Linard

Hardback isbn 0 75258 733 1
Paperback isbn 0 75258 734 X

Printed in China

CONTENTS

wing linings

leading edge
of wing

wing tip

primaries

trailing
edge of
wing

secondaries

crown   eye ring   nape

forehead

back

throat

wing bar

rump
(under wings)

breast

under tail
coverts

side

upper tail
coverts

belly

tail

INTRODUCTION

The pursuit of finding and identifying birds is an ideal way to get back in touch with nature, to move away from the stressful and trivial worries of modern life. Birds can be an endless source of delight and are everywhere to be seen and birding for many people is primarily for enjoyment, something that can easily be done on a casual basis and with the minimum of equipment. North America has an abundance of bird life - more than 900 species either breed there, visit regularly or drop in occasionally. However, quite a few of these are found only in far-flung regions, are extremely rare or live much of their life far offshore and not even the most experienced birder has seen all of them.

Being able to identify an individual species with confidence gives a great sense of satisfaction, and this book has many features that will help anyone interested in nature to make an informed identification of most of the birds to be found in North America. Each major species is illustrated with a clear picture to help with identification, and the text gives detailed descriptions of size, habitat, plumage, nesting habits, preferred food and interesting information about behavior. It also notes other similar birds that might be mistaken for the species in question, and highlights the features to look for to make a firm identification. Range maps for each bird not only show the areas it inhabits, but also indicate whether this is in summer, winter, all year or only during migration.

Identifying Birds

The best time to look for most birds is early in the morning, when they tend to be more active - and for some species also in the early evening. However, it is possible to see a few birds throughout the day - particularly hawks and other birds that soar high in the sky. Birding is an all-year activity, since different species are seen at different times of the year. Although even the backyard or local park will usually have some interesting birds to watch, quite similar types of birds often prefer widely differing habitats, so try to look in a variety of places. The main field marks - or physical characteristics that can be picked out in the wild - to identify a bird species are listed in a separate box below the species name. They are as clear as possible, but sometimes using a technical term is unavoidable, although this has been kept to the minimum. The exact parts of a bird that these terms refer to are shown on the diagram on page 8. Many birds have different breeding plumages, or the males have different coloring to the females, and as much detail as possible about this has been given. However, juvenile birds, faded adults late in summer - and sometimes molting birds - can often look very odd and be extremely hard to identify. Each bird is also an individual, so it may not match the pictures in this book exactly. Therefore it is important to concentrate on shape and pattern rather than specific markings, and to use more than one field mark to identify each bird. Similar-looking species can also cause confusion, so any other birds that closely resemble a particular species are also listed, along with notes of any major differences.

Size

Size is another important factor - if an all-black bird is only glimpsed fleetingly, its size will tell you immediately if it is more likely to be a member of the

blackbird family or one of the much bigger crows. If a bird is particularly likely to be seen in flight, its wingspan is also given. At first, it may be difficult to estimate size at a distance, but constant practice will help.

Habitat

The kind of habitat that a bird prefers may also be a big clue to identifying a particular species. The Swamp Sparrow and the Rufous-crowned Sparrow can look very similar and parts of their ranges overlap, but the Swamp prefers wet places while the Rufous-crowned likes rocky hillsides. Habitat is also important in a wider sense, since many birds can only thrive in certain conditions so it is essential that their habitat is protected or the species may die out.

Range Maps

The same birds are not found everywhere, and some birds are only found in certain areas at specific times. Each bird pictured in this book has a range map, which is color-coded to show when the birder is most likely to see it. Although birds do wander out of their set ranges and storms sometimes blow

	summer range
	winter range
	all year round

them off course during migration, the maps will show the most likely candidates within a particular area. Sometimes the range map will identify a bird conclusively - the Black-capped Chickadee and the Carolina Chickadee are almost identical, but each has its own very distinct range.

Common and Scientific names

Different species of birds are organized into families that have the same characteristics. Some families have only a few members, others have many - for instance Pelicans form a small family in North America with only two examples, while Warblers form a much bigger family with more than 50 species. In addition, each individual bird not only has a common name, but also a Latin scientific name. The first part of this is known as the genus, and indicates a group within a family that is closely related. The second part identifies a particular bird. Within the family of Warblers the *Dendroica pinus* is the Pine Warbler - *Dendroica* is the genus, pinus identifies the individual bird. The Blackpoll Warbler is *Dendroica striata* so the two birds belong to the same genus and are closely related. Sometimes a bird will have a third part to its Latin name, which identifies a sub-species, but the differences cannot usually be easily identified in the wild. One advantage of the Latin names is that they are the same in any language, so birders all round the world can recognize the same bird.

The American Ornithologists' Union (AOU) Checklist

The American Ornithologists' Union (AOU) is a committee of experts who not only standardize the names and classification of birds, but also set the order in which the families are listed. Traditionally, the most primitive birds are at the beginning and the most highly-developed at the end. This book follows the official AOU list in general, but birds that are extremely rare or are only casual visitors to North America have been omitted - unless they are locally very common. For information, the full official list is as follows:

Loons	Shearwaters, petrels
Grebes	Storm-petrels
Albatrosses	Tropicbirds

Gannets, boobies
Pelicans
Cormorants
Anhingas
Frigatebirds
Herons, egrets
Ibises, spoonbills
Storks
American vultures
Flamingos
Ducks, geese, swans
Hawks and eagles
Falcons
Chachalacas
Grouse
American quail
Coots, rails
Limpkins

Cranes
Plovers
Oystercatchers
Stilts, avocets
Jacanas
Sandpipers
Gulls, terns, jaegers
Auks
Pigeons, doves
Parrots
Cuckoos
Barn owls
Typical owls
Nightjars
Swifts
Hummingbirds
Trogons
Kingfishers

Woodpeckers
Flycatchers
Shrikes
Vireos
Crows, jays, magpies
Larks
Swallows
Chickadees, titmice
Verdins
Bushtits
Nuthatches
Creepers
Wrens
Dippers
Bulbuls
Kinglets
Gnatcatchers, Old
World warblers

Thrushes
Wrentits
Mockingbirds,
thrashers
Starlings
Pipits, wagtails
Waxwings
Silky-flycatchers
Olive warblers
Warblers
Bananaquits
Tanagers
Sparrows, towhees
Cardinals, buntings
Blackbirds, orioles
Finches
Old World sparrows

Birding Ethics and Conservation

Birders must be very aware of their behavior when out watching - and this is even more essential as more and more people take it up. Always bear in mind that the welfare of the bird must be more important than any other consideration and avoid causing any kind of disturbance - particularly when the birds are nesting or roosting. Never do anything that might compromise the habitat of a bird. Several birds have disappeared from North America over the last century - and some have even become extinct - purely because their habitat has been damaged or destroyed by human intervention. Bird feeders will bring many species right into the backyard, but it is important to keep them scrupulously clean to avoid spreading diseases through the bird population.

It is also polite, and will help others coming along later, if the rights of landowners and other members of the population are considered and observed. Never trespass or cause any damage to private property.

Keeping Track of Sightings

Most birders like to keep some sort of record of the birds they have seen. Rather than just ticking off the names on a list, many keep a notebook recording the name of the bird, the date and place, and information about its habits and field marks. If a rare bird is spotted, this information will be essential to have the sighting verified. Rare birds are not only spotted by experts - the informed amateur has just as much chance of seeing one if he is well-prepared and knows what to look for. Knowing what to expect is also important - before visiting a new area, check what species are likely to be found there.

Many local and national birding organizations work to preserve important habitats that are under threat and to protect individual species, and amateur birders can usually become involved. It is also often worth contacting these organizations since they will be able to offer information on good observation places. However, don't become too involved in how others think it should be done - birding should always be enjoyable, so the best approach to birding is always the one that suits you.

RED-THROATED LOON *(below)*

Scientific name:	*Gavia stellata*
Length:	25 inches
Habitat:	Arctic lakes, coastal areas
Identification:	Small seabird. Slender upturned bill, gray back with white spots, white throat
Similar species:	Often confused with the Arctic Loon, particularly in winter when the red throat turns white, because of the white plumage on its flanks that extends upwards in a similar way. However, the Arctic Loon is an Old World species that is only seen in America in western Alaska. Distinguished from grebes by a longer body and quite a short neck

This is the smallest and most slender of the loons, with a thin bill that turns up slightly at the tip; it also tends to hold its head angled slightly upwards. In the summer breeding season the mature adult has dark brown upperparts - without the white checker-pattern seen in other loons - a gray head and brick-red throat that is often hard to see and can look quite dark in flight. Since the red throat only appears during the mating season while the birds are in their Arctic breeding grounds, this species will probably be more familiar in its winter plumage, which is much paler. The throat becomes white and there are extensive white areas on the face, while the gray back is dotted with a profusion of small white spots. The juvenile bird is gray-brown, sometimes with dull red markings on the throat. Nesting and breeding in the Arctic take place on the banks of ponds or lakes. Migration along both east and west coasts is in loose groups or sometimes single birds - this loon never travels in organized flocks. The Red-throated Loon flies with its head drooping slightly, unlike the other species of loon, and is often seen on the Great Lakes in winter, and occasionally inland in western areas. Loons are wonderful divers and very strong swimmers, but they find it difficult to walk on land and appear very clumsy. They catch fish to eat by diving and pursuing them under water.

PACIFIC LOON

Scientific name:	*Gavia pacifica*
Length:	26 inches
Habitat:	Arctic lakes, coastal areas
Identification:	Medium seabird. Straight bill, dark back, white throat in sharp contrast to dark nape
Similar species:	Similar to the Common Loon, but has a much thinner bill and less white around the eyes in winter plumage. In flight, it has smaller feet and head. Also very like the Arctic Loon, but has no white extending upwards onto its flanks and is seen across a much wider area

A medium-size loon, with a slim and straight bill; it holds its smooth, rounded head very level and has a shorter neck than the Red-throated Loon. At one time this bird was thought to be identical to the European Arctic Loon, but they are now considered to be two distinct species. In the summer breeding season the mature adult has a black back with a white checker-pattern and a pale gray head. The throat has an iridescent dark purple-green patch that is very difficult to see and can look black, with a series of white stripes on each side. In winter its plumage is much paler; the throat turns white with a clean straight edge against the darker nape and a thin brown "chin-strap"; the back is plainer without the white checkered markings. In all plumages, there is no white extending upwards onto the rump. The juvenile bird is paler in color than the adult, with a "chin-strap" that can be very faint. Nesting and breeding take place in the Arctic on the banks of ponds or small lakes, and can extend to the east as far round as Hudson Bay. Migration along the west coast is in small organized flocks. The Pacific Loon is rare inland, but is sometimes seen on the east coast. It is more often seen over open ocean or far out in bays, much preferring to be flying above deep water. Like the other species of loon, the Pacific Loon feeds mainly on small fish, occasionally also eating crustaceans and insects.

COMMON LOON

Scientific name:	*Gavia immer*
Length:	32 inches
Habitat:	Forest lakes, coastal areas
Identification:	Medium seabird. Thick neck and bill, dark plumage, white checker-pattern to back in summer
Similar species:	Resembles the other loons in winter plumage, but has larger head and feet. In summer is like the Yellow-billed Loon, except for the yellow bill. However, the Yellow-billed is much larger and heavier and is rarely seen south of Canada

A large loon, with a thick bill that has a slightly curved upper edge. In the breeding season the mature adult has a distinctive plumage of black back with an extensive white checker-pattern, black head and bill and a black-and-white vertically striped collar and small "chin-strap". In winter the back is much plainer, with the crown and nape rather darker, the nape coloring extending round to the sides of the neck in an uneven line, while the striped collar and "chin-strap" disappear leaving the throat plain white. The bill turns a paler blue-gray although the upper edge still remains very dark. The juvenile bird has coloring similar to the winter adult, but the scapulars have a white scallop pattern, unlike the plainer adult bird. Nesting and breeding take place on large lakes, and this species is still fairly common across both Canada and northern America in summer, although due to pollution and the destruction of the natural wilderness that is its main habitat, its population is declining. Migration is both overland and along the coast, with this species generally flying much higher than the other loons. The Common Loon winters around both the east and west coasts and on any large inland lake that remains free of ice. It can dive down to more than 150 feet in search of fish, and stay below the surface for long periods.

HORNED GREBE

Scientific name:	*Podiceps auritus*
Length:	$13\frac{1}{2}$ inches
Habitat:	Lakes, ponds, coastal bays
Identification:	Waterbird. Gray plumage with black cap. Turns chestnut-red in summer, with gold feather "horns" on a black head
Similar species:	In winter plumage, looks much like the Eared Grebe, but has white cheeks, a pale spot in front of the eye and a thicker bill. Also resembles the Red-necked Grebe in winter, but is smaller, has a shorter bill and red eyes

The Horned Grebe summers in northern America, and migrates across the country to spend the winter on salt water in coastal bays, or on large ice-free lakes. It is occasionally found in small groups of breeding pairs, but more often in single pairs. The summer plumage is very eye-catching, with a chestnut-red neck and gold feather "horns" on a black head. In the winter months it is rather plainer, with white cheeks and throat, a dark crown and nape and no "horns". Its bill is straight and short, thinner than that of the Pied-billed but thicker than the Eared Grebe's, and its head is larger and flat-topped. The Horned is also slightly heavier and larger than these two species, with a thicker neck. All species of grebe have lobed toes, which makes them very strong swimmers. The Horned Grebe prefers to spend most of its time on water, but is often seen in flight during migration. Its nest is a floating raft of plants, anchored in reeds to stop it drifting away. The chicks are strong swimmers but are often carried on their parents' backs. The Horned Grebe feeds mainly on small fish and tadpoles, which it catches by diving.

RED-NECKED GREBE

Scientific name:	*Podiceps grisegena*
Length:	20 inches
Habitat:	Shallow lakes, coastal areas in winter
Identification:	Medium-sized waterbird. Gray neck and face with white crescent ear patch. In summer, red neck, black crown and a gray face edged in white
Similar species:	In winter plumage, looks similar to the Horned and Eared grebes, but is bigger than both and has a long, tapered yellow bill and black eyes. In summer resembles the Western and Clark's grebes, but can be distinguished by its red neck

The Red-necked Grebe is not common, but it is seen in summer on marshy ponds and shallow lakes in the northwest. It spends the winter in small groups around coastal bays or on deep open water, particularly if food is plentiful, but it is more often a solitary bird. Afloat it looks stocky, with a short body and a large head. In summer its plumage is handsome, with a red neck, black crown, a gray face edged in white and a tuft of black feathers giving the head a triangular shape. In winter the red neck turns pale gray, with a crescent of white running from under the chin round the rear of the face. Its bill is almost as long as the head, heavy, tapered and yellow in color. The juvenile bird has a striped head. Like other grebes, the Red-necked is not built for walking on land or long flights and spends most of its time on water. The Red-necked Grebe feeds mainly on small fish and tadpoles and newts, which it catches by diving. It also often swallows feathers - as do the other species of grebe - probably to enable it to strain out fish bones and other undigested material and regurgitate this unwanted matter.

PIED-BILLED GREBE

Scientific name:	*Podilymbus podiceps*
Length:	13½ inches
Habitat:	Freshwater ponds, marshes, lakes
Identification:	Diving waterbird. Drab brown plumage, black bill ring and throat in summer
Similar species:	Sometimes seen with other waterfowl, but its black striped bill in the summer months makes it unmistakable

Over much of its range the Pied-billed Grebe is a permanent resident and is very common, although it is usually seen on its own or in pairs rather than in flocks. It occasionally mixes with other waterfowl, but in general is somewhat secretive and elusive. A compact bird with a short neck, its plumage is a rather drab brown throughout the year, although in winter the lower throat has a reddish tint. In the summer, its thick bill turns white with a distinctive white ring, while its white chin and upper throat become black. The juvenile bird has very similar plumage to the winter adult, but the neck is streaked with brown and white. The Pied-billed Grebe is rarely seen on land or in flight, preferring to spend most of its time on water. When threatened, it can sink below the surface of the water with only its head showing, like a submarine with the periscope up, or dive completely beneath the surface. Its nest is a floating raft of marsh plants, anchored to reeds or bushes in the water, and young hatchlings are carried and fed on either parent's back. Although this species breeds across America, the birds in northern areas retreat south to spend winter on open water with no danger of ice. Like many other grebes, the Pied-billed feeds on fish, crustaceans and insects.

WESTERN GREBE

Scientific name:	*Aechmophorus occidentalis*
Length:	25 inches
Habitat:	Freshwater lakes, inshore coastal areas
Identification:	Large long-necked grebe. Black above, white below, long thin yellow bill
Similar species:	So similar to Clark's Grebe that they were once considered one species. Can be told apart only by the Western Grebe's yellow-green bill and its black cap that extends down round the eyes. Also similar to loons in winter plumage, but have a much longer neck and bill

The Western Grebe, North America's largest grebe, is an elegant bird that is seen on freshwater lakes in western America and winters around the west coast on sheltered bays and open inland waters. It covers roughly the same area as Clark's Grebe, but is far more numerous in the north and east. Its neck is long and slender, its bill long, thin and a dull yellow-green. The head, neck and body are black above and white below, and the black cap on its head extends down below the eyes. It performs a spectacular courtship dance, each pair racing across the water, diving and then rearing up out of the water in a mirror image of each other; several hundred birds may display together. It migrates in loose flocks, that spread out to feed during the day. When leaving the floating nest to reach the feeding grounds, the adult birds dive and swim underwater to get past the defended territory of other nesting pairs. Both parents care for the eggs and feed the chicks. The Western Grebe feeds on fish, insects and small crustaceans and can be badly affected by chemicals that have accumulated in their food, and also by oil spills.

CLARK'S GREBE

Scientific name:	*Aechmophorus clarkii*
Length:	25 inches
Habitat:	Freshwater lakes, coastal areas
Identification:	Large long-necked grebe. Black above, white below, long thin yellow-orange bill
Similar species:	Very like the Western Grebe, and once considered one species. Clark's Grebe has a yellow-orange bill and its black cap finishes above the eyes. Also similar to loons in winter plumage, but has a much longer neck and bill

Clark's Grebe is a close relative of the Western Grebe and they were once considered to be one species. They cover much the same area, but Clark's is much less common in the north and eastern parts of their range. Clark's Grebe inhabits freshwater lakes in western America during the summer and migrates to winter around the west coast on sheltered bays, inlets and open inland water. The adult has a slate-black cap that stops just above the eyes, and a slate-black neck and upperparts with white below. The neck is long and slender, the bill long, thin and yellow-orange. Clark's Grebe is as large as the Western, and performs the same kind of courtship dance, each pair of birds mirroring each other as they race across the water. Several hundred birds may gathered together, so the display can be quite a show. Clark's also migrates in loose flocks, but spreads out while feeding. Both parents care for the eggs and feed the chicks on the floating nest; after they hatch, the young birds are often carried on their parents' backs. Clark's Grebe feeds mainly on fish, insects and small crustaceans and, like the Western, can be badly affected by chemicals and by oil spills.

EARED GREBE

Scientific name:	*Podiceps nigricollis*
Length:	12½ inches
Habitat:	Freshwater lakes
Identification:	Small grebe. Gray plumage with black cap, white crescent ear patch. In summer, black neck and feathery gold "ears" on either side of black head
Similar species:	In winter plumage, looks much like the Horned Grebe, but has black cheeks, no pale spot in front of the eye and a thinner bill that is upturned rather than straight

The Eared Grebe is often very common, nesting in colonies on freshwater lakes in western America and wintering in the south in large flocks, but it is rarely seen in the east. Its summer plumage is distinctive, with a black neck and feathery gold "ears" on either side of its black head, and a black back with red below. In the winter months the feathery tufts disappear and its dark cheeks contrast with a whitish throat and chin, which extends up in a crescent round the cheeks; the back remains dark but the red beneath becomes white. Its bill is long and thin and curved upwards, and its head is rather round with a peaked crown. The Eared Grebe prefers to spend most of its time on water, but rides higher in the water than some of the other grebes, exposing its white undertail. Its nest is a very untidy floating raft of marsh plants at the edge of water but with little apparent attempt at concealment; the parents may build several before settling on the final version. Both parents incubate the eggs and feed the chicks. The Eared Grebe migrates during the night, and feeds mainly on insects as well as small crustaceans. In the late 19th century its summer plumage was a highly-prized fashion accessory and many thousands of nesting birds were destroyed, but now it is under protection.

GREATER SHEARWATER

Scientific name:	*Puffinus gravis*
Length:	19 inches, wingspan 44 inches
Habitat:	Off the Atlantic coast
Identification:	Medium-sized seabird. Thin black bill, dark gray-brown and white plumage
Similar species:	Cory's Shearwater has similar coloring, although smudgier and less defined and with a yellowish bill, but Cory's prefers warmer water so is rarely seen off America. The Greater Shearwater is often also confused with the Black-capped Petrel, which has a smaller black cap, more white on collar and rump, a longer tail and a black bar on its underwing.

The Greater Shearwater moves into offshore waters along the Atlantic coast during spring through fall, and is rare during the winter months. It is most common during spring in the south and in summer off eastern Canada - although it prefers open ocean and is seldom seen from shore. It nests in colonies in the South Atlantic, mainly on remote islands. Its plumage is sharply contrasting, with a distinct black cap against a white face and throat, dark brown above with a white band above the tail and often also at the nape, white below with black marks under the base of the wing and a blurred dark patch on the belly. Its bill is thin and black and it has straight, narrow, pointed wings. Greater Shearwaters often soar just inches above the surface of the water as they search for small fish and crustaceans to eat and are one of the few shearwaters that will dive into the water after food. They often follow fishing boats for scraps tossed overboard, and when this happens their graceful flight descends into a melee of flapping wings and slashing bills as dozens of birds fight for the best portion.

PINK-FOOTED SHEARWATER

Scientific name:	*Puffinus creatopus*
Length:	19 inches, wingspan 43 inches
Habitat:	Off the Pacific coast
Identification:	Medium-sized seabird. Pinkish bill with black tip, gray-brown and white plumage
Similar species:	The Sooty Shearwater has similar coloring, but is smaller, has darker underparts and a black bill, and flies with faster wingbeats. The Black-vented Shearwater also has the same coloring, but is a much smaller bird

This shearwater appears from spring through fall off the west coast of America, although it is rare during the winter months. It is most common in fall, when thousands can congregate in a few favorite feeding places - although it prefers the open ocean and is seldom seen from shore. It nests in colonies in the southern hemisphere, mainly on the smaller islands off the Chilean coast. About the size of a gull, the Pink-footed Shearwater is dark gray-brown above and white below, has white underwings with dark borders, and a pinkish black-tipped bill and pink feet. The pink feet and the pink on the bill are both quite distinctive at close range. Both sexes have the same coloring, but during May to July this species may undergo a rapid molt, which can result in odd wing shapes, unusual white wing bars and white patches. Unlike other light-bellied shearwaters along the west coast, the Pink-footed flies with slow wingbeats followed by a long glide - often staying close to the surface of the water as they search for small fish and crustaceans to eat. They catch these by alighting on the water and dipping their bills, and also occasionally by diving.

NORTHERN FULMAR

Scientific name: *Fulmarus glacialis*
Length: 19 inches, wingspan 42 inches
Habitat: Offshore, coastal cliffs
Identification: Medium-sized seabird. Rounded yellow bill, gray and white plumage
Similar species: Often mistaken for a medium-sized gull, but has longer wings and the bill is shorter and has distinctive nostril tubes. Gulls tend to fly with a steady flapping, while the Fulmar's flight consists of rapid wingbeats alternating with a stiff-winged glide

The Northern Fulmar is related to the shearwater family and is common and increasing, but spends much of its time far out to sea. It can sometimes be seen following fishing boats for scraps, or looking for food around harbors and piers. Otherwise the fulmar only comes into land to nest on the cliffs of northern islands and along the Arctic coast, where it lays just one egg in a shallow depression lined with a thin layer of soil or a few blades of grass. Its coloring is very variable; the darkest birds are a dark smoky-gray all over, with just a lighter patch at the base of the primaries; the lightest ones are very light gray above and white beneath, and there are many intermediate color versions. Darker birds tend to predominate on the Aleutians and off south Alaska, while the lighter version is more common around the Bering Sea. The lighter birds do look very similar to gulls, but their stiff-winged flight style and way of banking and skimming low over the water is very different. Above the stubby, hooked, yellow bill, the nostrils are encased in a tube and work in conjunction with special glands to filter out excess salt, to allow the bird to drink seawater. When disturbed, the Northern Fulmar can regurgitate an unpleasant and smelly oil, which was once collected both to fuel lamps and as a cure for various illnesses.

SHORT-TAILED
SHEARWATER *(above)*

Scientific name:	*Puffinus tenuirostris*
Length:	17 inches, wingspan 41 inches
Habitat:	Offshore
Identification:	Medium-sized seabird. Rounded head, short black bill, dark gray-brown plumage
Similar species:	The Sooty Shearwater has similar coloring, but has a longer bill, tapering forehead and a silvery-white patch on the underside of the wing

This shearwater is often one of the most abundant to be seen off the Pacific coast, appearing from spring through fall - although only rarely during the winter months except very occasionally off California. Like the Sooty Shearwater, it is most common in the summer, when flocks of millions of birds can congregate in one place - mainly around British Columbia and Alaska - and it is one of the few shearwaters that can usually be seen from the shore. It nests in colonies deep in the southern hemisphere, mainly in Tasmania and on islands off the Australian coast. The Short-tailed Shearwater is generally a uniform dark gray-brown all over, although some birds may have a pale throat and a darker cap. It has a rounded head, short tail and a short black bill. Both sexes have the same coloring. Like other shearwaters, the Short-tailed is rather clumsy on land but flies very gracefully, gliding and planing close to the surface of the water as it searches for small fish and crustaceans to eat. When migrating north after breeding it flies halfway round the world, first moving up towards Japan, then across to Alaska, returning south along the Pacific coast of America, crossing the Fiji Islands and then returning to Tasmania.

BLACK-VENTED
SHEARWATER

Scientific name:	*Puffinus opisthomelas*
Length:	14 inches, wingspan 34 inches
Habitat:	Offshore
Identification:	Small-sized seabird. Black bill, gray-brown and white plumage
Similar species:	The Pink-footed Shearwater has very similar coloring, but has pink feet and bill, rather than black, and is a much bigger bird. Could also be mistaken for Audubon's Shearwater, although Audubon's is smaller, has more defined coloring and is an east coast species

The Black-vented Shearwater is not a world traveler like some of the other shearwaters. It is seen along the Californian coast from August to May, but it moves farther and in much bigger flocks during years when the water is warmer. Although it likes the open ocean, it tends to stay close to the coast and is quite often seen from the shore. It returns south to nest on the islands off the Baja peninsular in June and July. It was formerly considered a sub-species of the Manx Shearwater, a bird of the eastern Atlantic that is sometimes seen along America's east coast. The Black-vented Shearwater is dark brown above and white below, with dark undertail coverts. The face and throat have variable dark mottling, which extends down the side of the breast and sometimes across the front, and this species has a black bill and feet. Both sexes have the same coloring. Unlike other light-bellied shearwaters along the west coast, the Black-vented flies with fast wingbeats, gliding and turning above the water. It usually plucks its food from the surface but occasionally dives after a particularly tasty morsel.

SOOTY SHEARWATER

Scientific name:	*Puffinus griseus*
Length:	18 inches, wingspan 41 inches
Habitat:	Offshore
Identification:	Medium-sized seabird. Thin black bill, dark gray-brown plumage, white underwing
Similar species:	The Pink-footed Shearwater has similar coloring, but is larger, has white underparts and a pink, black tipped bill, and flies with slower wingbeats. The Short-tailed Shearwater also has similar coloring, but has a smaller bill, rounder head and lacks the silvery-white patch on the underside of the wing

This shearwater is often one of the most abundant off the Pacific coast and is also common on the Atlantic, appearing from spring through fall but not during the winter months except off California. It is most common in summer, when millions of birds can congregate in gigantic flocks - it is one of the few shearwaters that can be seen regularly from shore. It nests in colonies deep in the southern hemisphere, mainly on the smaller, more isolated islands. The Sooty Shearwater is a uniform dark gray-brown all over, except for a silvery-white area on the underwings, and has a tapering forehead and a thin black bill. Both sexes have the same coloring. The Sooty flies in a typical shearwater way, gliding and planing close to the surface of the water as it searches for small fish and crustaceans to eat. Since shearwaters fly great distances when migrating, they have developed a technique of both picking up thermal currents and riding the wind itself, which means they can fly for hours on almost motionless wings - although when the air is still they are forced to sit on the water and wait for a passing breeze.

AUDUBON'S SHEARWATER

Scientific name:	*Puffinus lherminieri*
Length:	12 inches, wingspan 28 inches
Habitat:	Offshore
Identification:	Small seabird. Black bill, white spot in front of eye, black-brown and white plumage
Similar species:	The Black-vented Shearwater is very similar, but is slightly bigger, has more smudgy coloring and is a west coast species seen at somewhat different times of the year. The Manx Shearwater has quite close coloring, except for a white tail covert, but prefers cold water so is rarely seen in the southern Atlantic

Audubon's Shearwater is commonly seen along the southern Atlantic coast from May through October and prefers warm water. During the winter months, it returns south to its nesting grounds on islands in the Caribbean. It nests in colonies, creating a mass of grass among rocks or in dense vegetation to hold the single egg. Both parents care for the young, which stay in the nest for about 10 weeks after hatching. Audubon's is the smallest American shearwater; its plumage is very dark brown to black above and white below, with dark undertail coverts and a long tail. The wings are relatively short, with the undersides of the primaries dark, the white throat extends up into the face and there is a white spot in front of the eye. Both sexes have the same coloring. Audubon's Shearwater flies with very fast wingbeats and quite short glides low above the water. It eats squid and fish, but is one of the few shearwaters that is not seen following ships.

WILSON'S STORM-PETREL *(below)*

Scientific name:	*Oceanites oceanicus*
Length:	7 inches, wingspan 15 inches
Habitat:	Offshore
Identification:	Ocean bird. Dark plumage, square tail. In flight feet extend beyond tail, broad white band on rump, shallow fluttering wingbeats
Similar species:	Identification of the different types of storm-petrel is often very difficult. Wilson's and Leach's storm-petrel are very similar, but Leach's has longer and more sharply angled wings, a forked tail, and flies with deep strokes, while Wilson's has short, fluttering wingbeats

Wilson's Storm-Petrel is very common off the Atlantic coast between May and September, can very occasionally be seen off the Gulf coast, and is very rare off California in the fall. A bird of the open sea, which nests in colonies on islands well down in the Southern Hemisphere, it can sometimes be seen during deep-water fishing trips. During the summer it is active during daylight hours, but is nocturnal at its nesting grounds. It lays one egg in a rocky crevice or in a burrow in soil, which is incubated by both birds. The plumage of this storm-petrel is mostly black, with lighter areas in the center underwing and on the tips of the wing coverts and a bold white band across the rump that extends underneath across the undertail coverts. Its flight is distinctive, with rather shallow, fluttering wingbeats and its feet trailing behind, often extending beyond the tip of the tail. One of the smaller seabirds, it tends to hover quite close over the surface of the water when feeding, with its wings held upwards in a V, and pattering its feet on the surface as it plucks up small fish and plankton. It also sometimes takes refuse thrown from ships.

LEACH'S STORM-PETREL

Scientific name:	*Oceanodroma leucorhoa*
Length:	$8\frac{1}{2}$ inches, wingspan 18 inches
Habitat:	Offshore
Identification:	Ocean bird. Dark plumage, long forked tail, pointed wings, deep wingbeats
Similar species:	Identification of the different types of storm-petrel is often very difficult. Wilson's and Leach's storm-petrel are very similar, but Leach's has longer and more sharply angled wings, a forked tail, and flies with deep strokes, while Wilson's has short, fluttering wingbeats

Leach's Storm-Petrel is fairly common off both the east and west coasts of American in the summer, but is very rare towards the southern Atlantic and round the Gulf. It prefers the open sea, and nests in colonies on offshore islands, but is more usually seen as a single bird following a boat. It is nocturnal at its nesting grounds and lays one egg in a burrow dug by the male, which is incubated by both birds. The plumage of this species of storm-petrel varies in different areas. It is mostly brown-black, with a lighter band along the tips of the wing coverts. All the Atlantic birds and those in the north Pacific have a bold white band across the rump, but those further south than California on the Pacific coast often have a dark rump. However the white is not visible when the bird is sitting. Its flight is very distinctive and erratic, with deep strokes of its pointed wings; its wings are quite long and it holds them rather sharply angled. Although slightly larger than Wilson's Storm-Petrel, it is still one of the smaller seabirds. Leach's Storm-Petrel feeds by plucking up small fish and shrimp from the water, while hovering just above the surface. It also sometimes follows ships to take the rubbish that is thrown overboard.

Fork-tailed Storm-Petrel

Scientific name: *Oceanodroma furcata*
Length: 8½ inches, wingspan 18 inches
Habitat: Offshore
Identification: Ocean bird. Pale gray plumage, forked tail
Similar species: Among storm-petrels, the Fork-tailed is quite distinctive, as it has quite pale gray-colored plumage. However it could be confused with the Red Phalarope, which spends time out at sea, although this has a longer, pointed bill and white round the face and throat

The Fork-tailed Storm-Petrel prefers to be over cold water and is seen only along the northern Pacific coast of America, being fairly numerous off Alaska and western Canada. It nests in colonies on offshore islands, but visits the nest only at night. It is rather stocky and broadwinged and is comparable in size with other storm-petrels. Its plumage is a striking blue-gray above and smooth pearly-gray beneath, with much darker underwing coverts and eye-patch. The tail is quite long and forked, and the bird carries it upswept in flight. It flies in a fairly straight line with quick and shallow wingbeats; often followed by a short glide, but adverse weather conditions can affect this pattern quite considerably. The Fork-tailed Storm-Petrel feeds by plucking up small fish, shrimp and plankton from the surface of the water as it flies along, but also sometimes makes shallow dives beneath the surface.

WHITE-TAILED TROPICBIRD

Scientific name:	*Phaethon lepturus*
Length:	30 inches (including tail streamers), wingspan 37 inches
Habitat:	Offshore
Identification:	Tropical seabird. White plumage with long tail streamers, black stripe across upper wing, black tip to wings
Similar species:	The Red-billed Tropicbird is similar coloring, but much larger and lacks the distinctive black stripe along the edge of the upperwing coverts. Royal Terns are sometimes mistaken for tropicbirds, but they have a less direct and more bouncing flight pattern and lack tail streamers

This tropical seabird is common in Bermuda, but is only an occasional visitor to North America - although it is sometimes seen in summer in the Gulf Stream off North Carolina and off Florida, and sometimes off the southeast coast. It nests on tropical islands, where it lays its single egg in a rock crevice or a cave, or sometimes just under vegetation near the shore. The young chicks hatch after around 40 days and stay in the nest for about nine weeks. The White-tailed Tropicbird is the smaller of the two species that are commonly seen. Its plumage is mostly white, with tail streamers that are as long as the bird again - although these are sometimes missing. The tip of the wing is black, there is also a distinctive black stripe across the upper wing, and a small black patch around the eye; its rather short bill is orange or yellow. The juvenile bird lacks the distinctive wing stripe and its back is roughly barred, so it can very easily be mistaken for a Red-billed Tropicbird. The White-tailed flies steadily and high, with quick, flicking wingbeats. It sometimes rests on the sea and floats well out of the water with its tail streamers raised up into the air. It feeds on fish, squid and crustaceans, which it catches by suddenly plunging into the water from the air.

RED-BILLED TROPICBIRD

Scientific name:	*Phaethon aethereus*
Length:	40 inches (including tail streamers), wingspan 44 inches
Habitat:	Offshore
Identification:	Large seabird. White plumage with long tail streamers, black tip to wings, red bill
Similar species:	The White-tailed Tropicbird is similar coloring, but much smaller, has a distinctive black stripe along the edge of the upperwing coverts and a yellow-orange bill. Royal Terns are sometimes mistaken for tropicbirds, but they have a less direct and more bouncing flight pattern and lack tail streamers

The Red-billed Tropicbird is a tropical species that is an occasional visitor off the coast of southern California in summer and fall, and is sometimes seen off the southeast coast. It nests in the Caribbean and along the Pacific coast of Mexico, where it lays its single egg in a burrow or cave near the shore. The young chicks hatch after around 44 days and stay in the nest for about 12 weeks. The Red-billed Tropicbird is considerably larger than the White-tailed. Its plumage is mostly white, but its back is finely barred in black and it has black primary coverts and a small black patch around the eye; its red bill is larger than that of the White-tailed. The tail has white streamers as long again as the body of the bird - although they are sometimes missing. The young bird lacks the tail streamers and its bill is yellowish, and the juveniles of both species can very easily be mistaken for each other. The Red-billed flies quite high, with relatively fast, steady and shallow wingbeats. When resting on the water, both species float high with tail streamers raised up into the air. The Red-billed Tropicbird feeds on fish and squid, which it catches by diving from the air into the water.

BROWN BOOBY *(right)*

Scientific name:	*Sula leucogaster*
Length:	30 inches, wingspan 57 inches
Habitat:	Offshore
Identification:	Large seashore bird. Chocolate brown, sharply defined pure white belly, pointed yellow bill, bright yellow feet
Similar species:	When flying close to the surface of the water, Brown Boobies may be mistaken for the darker shearwaters, but they dive for fish, rather than dipping for food

A tropical seabird, but found at sea off southern Florida and around Dry Tortugas in summer and very occasionally off the southern Pacific coast. The Brown Booby is often seen perching on channel markers, navigational towers and sometimes trees. It breeds in the Southern Hemisphere; the adult does not build a nest but lays 1-3 eggs on bare ground or rocks, often very near the edge of a cliff. Both birds incubate the eggs, which takes about 6 weeks, with the hatchlings staying in the nest for around 15 weeks. The Brown Booby is smaller than the Masked but has the typical booby shape. Its plumage is a uniform dull chocolate brown, with a sharply defined contrasting pure white belly, a heavy, pointed yellow bill and bright yellow feet. Its pointed wings are relatively short, with white on the underwing, and its tail is quite long - although this is not necessarily very evident. The female has the same general coloring as the male, but has a yellow face similar to the bill color. The juvenile bird has a brown mottled belly, or may be an even brown all over. The Brown Booby flies with strong swift wingbeats, sometimes diving straight down into the sea from a height, but also flying low over the water and entering in a low-angle dive.

NORTHERN GANNET

Scientific name:	*Morus bassanus*
Length:	37 inches, wingspan 72 inches
Habitat:	Offshore, rocky cliffs
Identification:	Large seabird. Snow-white plumage, yellow tint to back of head, long, black-tipped wings, pointed white tail
Similar species:	The mature adult is like the Masked Booby, but is bigger, has much less black on the wings, a white tail, no black mask and a yellow tinge to the back of the head. First-year birds can be very similar to immature Masked Boobies

The Northern Gannet is the biggest seabird found off the Atlantic coast; it prefers to be out at sea, but can be seen from the shore during migration and in winter. It nests in dense colonies on isolated rocky cliffs or islands around the Gulf of St Lawrence, but in winter can spread as far south as the Gulf of Mexico. The adult lays a single egg in its large nest of seaweed and debris, and both birds incubate the eggs. The Northern Gannet sometimes rests on the water, but is never seen on land except at the breeding site. Its plumage is predominantly pure snow-white, with a yellow tint to the back of the head, long, black-tipped wings and a pointed white tail. Its gray bill is sharp and pointed. The juvenile bird is gray-brown all over, with white uppertail coverts and white speckles that gradually increase until it achieves mature plumage after around 3-4 years. The Northern Gannet makes spectacular dives to catch fish - it can dive from more than 100 feet and reach a similar depth below the surface.

MASKED BOOBY

Scientific name:	*Sula dactylatra*
Length:	32 inches, wingspan 62 inches
Habitat:	Offshore
Identification:	Tropical seabird. White plumage, black mask, black tail; much black on wings, large pointed yellow bill
Similar species:	The mature adult is like the Northern Gannet, but has more black on the wings, a black tail, black mask and yellow bill. When flying close to the surface of the water boobies may be mistaken for shearwaters, but otherwise their flight pattern is different

A bird of tropical seas, but a regular visitor to American waters that is usually seen off the Gulf of Mexico in summer and sometimes offshore from the southern Atlantic coast. It nests in the Southern Hemisphere, but there is also a breeding colony on Dry Tortugas, Florida. The adult lays 1-3 eggs on bare ground or rocks, and both birds incubate the eggs. Unlike the Brown Booby, when resting the Masked Booby sometimes perches on the ground. Its plumage is predominantly white, but with a black mask, quite short black tail and a great deal of solid black along the trailing edge of the wings. Its yellow bill is relatively large and pointed. The juvenile bird has a dark head and wings, but a white collar, chest and underneath - they can look a lot like young gannets, except they have more white on the underwing. Boobies fish from high in the air, making spectacular dives into the water to catch fish. Sometimes Frigatebirds harass them in flight, forcing them to drop their catch which the Frigatebird then grabs as it falls.

AMERICAN WHITE PELICAN

Scientific name:	*Pelecanus erythrorhynchos*
Length:	62 inches, wingspan 108 inches
Habitat:	Seawater, large lakes
Identification:	Large waterbird. White plumage, black on trailing edge of wings, large yellow pouched bill
Similar species:	The shape of the pelican and its huge bill make it almost unmistakable, although in flight its wing pattern might look similar to the Wood Stork

With its nine-foot wingspan, the American White Pelican is a massive bird, which can be seen in many areas of North America at different times of the year. A sociable waterbird, it is often found in flocks either along the coast or on large lakes. It nests near water, building a large nest mound to hold its two eggs. The chicks have no feathers when they hatch, so the parent bird must protect them from the sun's rays. The mature adult's plumage is mostly white, with black along the trailing edge of the wings, which is only evident when the bird is flying. The huge, flat bill is bright orange, and during the breeding season a fibrous plate grows on the upper mandible, which is shed after the eggs are laid. The breeding adult also has a yellowish crest, which again vanishes after the eggs are laid; the crown and nape turn a gray-white while the adult is still caring for its chicks. The juvenile bird has a brownish tint to the head, neck and back. The pelican is rather ungainly on land but is handsome in flight; flocks often fly together, soaring high in unison. It eats fish, which it scoops up in its bill, filling its huge throat pouch as it swims along the water. The bill and throat pouch can hold nearly 3 gallons of water - which is more than twice the capacity of its stomach. Flocks may also hunt together, lining up in a row to drive fish into the shallows where they cannot escape.

BROWN PELICAN

Scientific name:	*Pelecanus occidentalis*
Length:	50 inches, wingspan 84 inches
Habitat:	Seawater
Identification:	Large waterbird. Gray-brown plumage, white head, large gray pouched bill
Similar species:	The shape and coloring of the Brown Pelican, and its huge bill, make it unmistakable

Unlike the American White Pelican, the Brown Pelican is a sea bird, which very rarely finds its way inland. It can be found in the south, down both the Atlantic and Pacific coasts of America - although the east coast birds tend to be smaller than the west coast. A sociable bird, it tends to stay in flocks and can be seen flying in a single file over water. It builds a bulky nest of sticks lined with fresh green plants near water, to hold its 2-3 eggs. The mature adult's plumage is gray-brown, with a white head sometimes washed with yellow and a darker belly. The huge, flat bill is gray, and the throat pouch is normally a gray-brown, although during the December to August breeding season that of the Pacific coast birds turns bright red. On both coasts, the back of the neck in the breeding adult changes color to a dark chestnut-brown, while a yellow patch appears at the base of the throat. The juvenile bird is grayish-brown, with off-white underparts and it does not achieve its full adult plumage until the third year. In flight, the Brown Pelican alternately flaps and glides with its broad, powerful wings. It eats fish, which it catches by making a spectacular twisting headfirst plunge of up to 30 feet into the sea, grabbing the fish in its bill. It comes to the surface to eat, tossing the fish into the air to swallow it headfirst. Unfortunately, it sometimes loses its lunch at that point to a cheeky gull, which darts by and snatches the fish in mid-air. Once severely threatened by pesticides, the Brown Pelican made a comeback after DDT was banned.

GREAT CORMORANT
(left)

Scientific name:	*Phalacrocorax carbo*
Length:	36 inches, wingspan 63 inches
Habitat:	Seawater, bays, rocky coasts
Identification:	Waterbird. Hook-tipped bill, black plumage, broad white band across throat, yellow throat pouch. In breeding season large white patches on each flank, wispy white plumes on head
Similar species:	The Double-crested Cormorant has very similar plumage, but is smaller and the breeding bird has an orange throat pouch and lacks white patches on its flanks. Cormorants are occasionally mistaken for loons, but have longer tails, a different bill and fly with shallower wingbeats

A bird that is widespread in the Old World, the Great Cormorant is also found in northeastern North America. It is seen in large flocks just offshore, but a few single birds also venture inland. Some birds breed in colonies on the east coast of Canada, building nests of sticks and seaweed on remote, rocky ledges. The 4-5 eggs are incubated for around 30 days, by both adult birds, and the young chicks stay in the nest for around 7-8 weeks. The adult bird is large and bulky, with a short tail, a large, squarish head and a thick, hook-tipped bill that is held pointing upward when it swims. Its plumage is black, with a broad white band across the throat behind a lemon-yellow throat pouch; during the breeding season it develops large white patches on each flank and wispy white plumes on the head. The juvenile bird is brown, with a darker brown back and white belly, and its throat pouch is dull yellow. The Great Cormorant tends to fly in long lines or in V-formation. It feeds on fish, which it catches by diving down from the surface of the water. Like other cormorants, it sometimes swims submerged up to its neck.

NEOTROPIC CORMORANT

Scientific name:	*Phalacrocorax brasilianus*
Length:	26 inches, wingspan 40 inches
Habitat:	Marshy ponds, shallow inlets, lakes
Identification:	Waterbird. Hook-tipped bill, black plumage, yellow throat pouch. In breeding season pouch edged in white
Similar species:	Similar coloring to the Double-crested Cormorant, but is smaller, has a longer tail and the smaller, pointed throat pouch does not extend round the eye

The Neotropic Cormorant is found in the American tropics, and is common in Texas and elsewhere in the southwest. It was previously known as the Olivaceous Cormorant. It often nests in the same areas as the Double-crested, in colonies in trees near lakes, ponds or marshes. Unlike other cormorants, it can easily perch on slender branches. The nest is a mass of sticks up to 20 feet above the ground, with 3-6 eggs. The adult bird is slender, with a noticeably long tail, a small head and a shorter bill than other cormorants. Its plumage is black, with a small yellow throat pouch that goes to a point behind the bill and is bordered with white in the breeding season. The juvenile bird is brown, including its breast and neck, with a darker brown back. Like the Double-crested Cormorant it tends to fly high in long lines or in V-formation. When flying, the Neotropic Cormorant holds its neck straight; the neck is about the same length as the tail. It holds its bill upwards when swimming, and eats fish, frogs and aquatic insects.

BRANDT'S CORMORANT *(left)*

Scientific name:	*Phalacrocorax penicillatus*
Length:	35 inches, wingspan 48 inches
Habitat:	Seawater
Identification:	Waterbird. Hook-tipped bill, black plumage, buff patch around throat pouch, pouch cobalt blue in breeding season
Similar species:	Can be mistaken for Pelagic Cormorant, but Brandt's is bigger, its head and bill are larger and it is more likely to be seen over open ocean. Also similar to the Double-crested, but is darker and lacks orange throat pouch

A very common bird along the Pacific coast of America south of Alaska, this species prefers being out over the open ocean and rarely comes inland. Brandt's Cormorant is extremely gregarious and is often seen in flocks of several hundred birds, flying in long, straggling lines low over the water. They breed in large colonies, building nests of seaweed and grass on offshore rocks or on flat rocky surfaces on islands and laying 3-6 eggs. Quite stocky and dark, the plumage of the adult bird is glossy black, with a buff-colored patch around the throat pouch. In the breeding season the throat pouch turns cobalt blue, but is quite difficult to see, and the bird develops slender white plumes on face and back. Immature birds are dark brown above and slightly paler beneath. Like other cormorants, Brandt's eats fish and sometimes small crustaceans, which it catches by diving. Several birds often dive together in unison, creating a "net" to catch fish.

PELAGIC CORMORANT *(above)*

Scientific name:	*Phalacrocorax pelagicus*
Length:	26 inches, wingspan 39 inches
Habitat:	Seawater, steep cliffs, rocky coasts
Identification:	Waterbird. Slim bill with hook at tip, black plumage, white patch on flanks in breeding season
Similar species:	Pelagic Cormorant is very similar to Brandt's, but is smaller, prefers coastal waters to the open sea, and the breeding bird has two small crests on crown and nape at close range. In flight, it has a smaller head and a longer tail. The Red-faced Cormorant has a larger area of bright red facial skin and a yellow bill

The smallest cormorant along the Pacific coast of America, this species is found all round the west coast of Alaska and as far south as California and into the Bering Strait. Like Brandt's, it rarely comes inland but also does not venture far out to sea. Less sociable than many cormorants, it is seen alone or in small flocks. It breeds in small colonies, building a nest of seaweed and grass on a ledge of a steep cliff and laying 3-7 eggs. The ledge is often so narrow that the bird has to take off and land facing the cliff face. The adult is slim, with a long, slender neck and a thin, dark bill. Its plumage is glossy black with an iridescent green tint; a dark red patch on the face is very difficult to see. In the breeding season white patches develop on the flanks and fine white plumes on each side of the neck, and the head has small tufts on crown and nape. Immature birds are dark brown, similar to young Red-faced Cormorants. The Pelagic Cormorant dives to catch fish and small crustaceans.

DOUBLE-CRESTED CORMORANT *(opposite)*

Scientific name:	*Phalacrocorax auritus*
Length:	32 inches, wingspan 52 inches
Habitat:	Seawater, inland lakes, rivers
Identification:	Waterbird. Hook-tipped bill, black plumage, orange throat pouch. In breeding season small tufts on head. When flying holds its neck in distinctive kink
Similar species:	The Great Cormorant has very similar plumage, but is larger and the breeding bird has a lemon-yellow throat pouch and white patches on its flanks. Also similar to Brandt's Cormorant, but Brandt's coloring is more uniform and it lacks an orange throat pouch

This is the most widespread cormorant in North America, common in many areas - especially inland. It often nests in colonies near large areas of deep water, either high up in trees, on cliff edges or on the ground on an island. The nest is a mass of sticks or seaweed and the 2-9 eggs are incubated for around 25 days, by both adult birds. The adult is around the size of a goose, with a long tail and a straight, hook-tipped bill that is held pointing upward when it swims. Its plumage is black, with an orange throat pouch, the orange also extends up the face and in front of the eye. During the breeding season it develops small tufts on each side of the head that are black in southeastern birds and whitish in north and west. The juvenile bird is brownish, with a darker back and lighter breast and neck. The Double-crested Cormorant tends to fly in long lines or in V-formation, but holds its neck with a slight kink just behind the head. When foraging, it dives and swims underwater for fish.

RED-FACED CORMORANT

Scientific name:	*Phalacrocorax urile*
Length:	31 inches, wingspan 46 inches
Habitat:	Seawater, steep cliffs
Identification:	Waterbird. Glossy black, bright red patch on face extending up onto forehead, white patch on flanks in breeding season, white plumes on neck, crests on crown and nape
Similar species:	The Red-faced Cormorant is very similar to the Pelagic, but has wings slightly lighter in color than its body, a larger area of bright red facial skin and a yellow bill

This cormorant is only found round the coast of Alaska and is a permanent resident of some Alaskan islands. More sociable than the Pelagic, it is seen in smaller flocks and breeds in small colonies, building nests of seaweed and grass on the ledges of steep coastal cliffs and small islands. It lays 3-4 blueish eggs and both male and female take care of the young; when the birds change over on the nest, the incoming parent goes through an elaborate display. The adult is a stocky bird, with a relatively short neck and a pale-yellow bill. Its plumage is glossy black with lighter brown-black wings, and it has a bright red patch on the face that extends up onto the forehead. Like the Pelagic, in the breeding season the mature Red-faced Cormorant develops white patches on its flanks and fine white plumes on each side of the neck, and the head has small tufts on crown and nape. Immature birds are brownish and look very similar to young Pelagic Cormorants. The Red-faced Cormorant eats fish and small crustaceans, which it catches by diving down from the surface.

ANHINGA

Scientific name:	*Anhinga anhinga*
Length:	35 inches, wingspan 45 inches
Habitat:	Swampland
Identification:	Tropical waterbird. Black plumage, white spots and streaks on wings and upper back, long slim neck, swims with only head and neck out of water. Female's neck buff-colored
Similar species:	Can be confused with a cormorant, but is told apart by the white markings on the upper part of its wings, its thin, narrow, pointed bill, long elegant neck and fan-shaped tail

The Anhinga is a tropical bird, so those found in the southern swamps of North America are at the northern edge of their range. They nest in colonies, along with egrets and other birds, building a small mass of twigs and sticks lined with green leaves up to 40 feet above the ground, either in trees or bushes - they sometimes take over an old heron's nest. They lay 1-5 eggs, which are incubated for 25-28 days by both parent birds. The mature adult has a mainly glossy iridescent black plumage, with extensive white spots and streaks on its wings and upper back, a very long, slender neck, a long thin pointed bill and a fan-shaped tail. The female has a buff-colored neck and head. Both sexes of the juvenile bird have less white on the wings and a buff head and neck; they look alike until the third winter, when the male's neck and head plumage turns black. The Anhinga often swims with only its head and neck above the surface of the water, earning itself the nickname of "snakebird". It spears fish, frogs and small crustaceans with its dagger-like bill, before surfacing fully to toss them up in the air and swallow them head first. It can often be seen perched on stumps or branches with its wings spread out to dry. When flying it can soar to great heights, gliding on warm air currents on its long, pointed wings for hours on end.

40

MAGNIFICENT FRIGATEBIRD

Scientific name:	*Fregata magnificens*
Length:	40 inches, wingspan 90 inches
Habitat:	Offshore
Identification:	Tropical seabird. Long narrow angular wings, deeply-forked tail, long hooked bill. Male is glossy black, orange-red throat pouch sometimes inflated in display. Female is blackish-brown, white chest
Similar species:	No other birds are really similar, the Swallow-tailed Kite is much smaller

A large, tropical seabird, the Magnificent Frigatebird can be seen in the Gulf of Mexico, along the Florida coast and occasionally along the Californian coast. It does sometimes venture inland, or finds itself there after tropical storms, and there is a breeding colony on the Dry Tortugas islands off Florida. When resting, the Magnificent Frigatebird never sits on the water but perches on isolated sea cliffs or on bushes. It nests in bushes or on rocky ground, building a cup of sticks and grass to hold 1-2 eggs. Both parent birds incubate the eggs, for more than 50 days, and the chicks stay in the nest for a further 5 months after hatching. The adult bird has long, narrow, angular wings, a long, deeply-forked tail and a long, hooked bill. The male is a glossy black, with an orange-red throat pouch which is sometimes inflated in display during the breeding season (*above*). The female is a blackish-brown with a white chest. The juvenile has a white head and underparts and takes around 4-6 years to achieve its full adult plumage. The Magnificent Frigatebird eats fish, squid and small crustaceans, sometimes snatched from the surface of the water, but also stolen from other species of seabird after spectacular aerial chases.

GREEN HERON

Scientific name:	*Butorides virescens*
Length:	18 inches, wingspan 26 inches
Habitat:	Woodland streams, ponds and marshes
Identification:	Small wading bird. Bright orange legs in breeding season, greenish blue-gray plumage, chestnut-brown on neck, white to center of throat. Crown feathers raised in crest if bird is alarmed
Similar species:	No other birds have a similar size and coloring, but if the juvenile bird has very brown plumage it can be mistaken for the Least Bittern

A small, chunky and secretive bird, the Green Heron is common across much of southeast America. It has quite short legs and a long, straight dark bill. Unlike many of the other herons, it is a very solitary bird - it not only fishes alone, but breeding pairs nest in a tree by themselves, building a nest of sticks in dense bushes or in a tree, which holds 3-6 eggs. Young herons often wander far from their breeding area, so they may return to a different place to breed themselves the following year. The adult bird has quite dark coloring, with deep chestnut-brown on the back and sides of the neck, greenish blue-gray upperparts, and white to the center of the throat and neck. The green-black feathers of the crown are sometimes raised in a crest, particularly if the bird is alarmed; it also flicks its tail. In the breeding season, the dull yellow legs of the male turn a bright orange. The immature bird is browner and its white throat and underparts are streaked with brown. The Green Heron fishes in fresh water with woodland cover, perching on a convenient branch and crouching over the water.

LITTLE BLUE HERON

Scientific name: *Egretta caerulea*
Length: 24 inches, wingspan 40 inches
Habitat: Freshwater ponds, lakes, marshes, saltwater wetlands
Identification: Long-legged, long-necked wading bird. Slate-blue plumage, blue bill with black tip
Similar species: The immature Little Blue Heron is all-white and is very easily confused with the juvenile Snowy Egret, except the Snowy has a black bill and mostly dark legs

The Little Blue Heron is common across the southeast, but is rarely seen in the west. Small and trim, it is a solitary bird when fishing, but nests in colonies. It builds a shallow cup or platform of sticks high above the ground in a bush or a tree, in which it lays 3-7 eggs. Both parents incubate the eggs, which takes 20-25 days, and the young birds leave the nest after around 6 weeks. The adult bird is mostly slate-blue, with a dark-purple tint to head and neck, a blue bill with a black tip and dull green legs and feet. In the breeding season, the head and neck become more red and legs and feet turn black. The juvenile bird is pure white, like the young Snowy Egret, but has dull yellow legs and feet and a thicker gray bill. Gradually it molts, becoming patchy white and blue - which is known as its "calico" phase - until it eventually acquires the adults' darker coloring. The Little Blue Heron feeds in both salt and fresh water, wading very slowly and methodically or standing perfectly still with its neck extended and its bill pointing down, waiting to spear a fish. It will also eat frogs and small reptiles.

TRICOLORED HERON

Scientific name:	*Egretta tricolor*
Length:	26 inches, wingspan 36 inches
Habitat:	Salt marshes, mangroves
Identification:	Wading bird, long-legged, long-necked. Dark blue with white belly, white stripe up front of the neck, yellowish facial skin and base of bill turn bright blue in breeding season
Similar species:	No other birds have a similar coloring

The graceful Tricolored Heron is a slender bird and is common in the coastal salt marshes and mangrove swamps of the southeast; it is also sometimes seen inland and to the west and has bred in North Dakota and Kansas. It was previously called the Louisiana Heron. Like the Little Blue, it is a solitary bird when fishing, but nests in colonies - sometimes with other heron species. It builds a nest of sticks either on the ground or high in a bush or a tree, in which it lays 3-7 eggs. Both parents incubate the eggs, which takes 21-25 days, and the young birds leave the nest after around 5 weeks. The adult bird is mostly dark blue, with a white belly and a white stripe up the front of the neck, and with a yellowish color to the facial skin and at the base of the bill. In the breeding season, the yellowish areas turn bright blue. The immature bird has chestnut-brown on the back of the neck instead of blue, and chestnut-brown markings on the wings. The Tricolored Heron stands motionless with its neck extended and looking intently down into the water, waiting to spear a fish. It also eats frogs, small reptiles, worms and insects.

GREAT BLUE HERON

Scientific name:	*Ardea herodias*
Length:	46 inches, wingspan 72 inches
Habitat:	Wetlands, still water
Identification:	Large, long-legged, long-necked wading bird. Blue-gray plumage, white head with black stripe ending in black plumes behind eye. In breeding season, gray plumes on upper chest
Similar species:	Sandhill Crane is similar size and coloring, but has a much shorter neck and very different body shape. In Florida, there is an all-white version of the Great Blue Heron that looks very similar to the Great Egret, but is a much bigger bird

The most widespread and familiar heron across much of the country, the Great Blue is also the largest heron in North America. It is a solitary bird and single birds are often seen flying slowly overhead - although they tend to nest in colonies that can contain hundreds of birds. The nest is an untidy-looking platform of sticks, either in trees or bushes, or on cliffs, that is built up to 100 feet above the ground. The 3-7 eggs are incubated for around 28 days, by both adult birds. The chicks leave the nest about 8 weeks after they hatch. The mature bird is huge, with a very long neck and a heavy yellow bill. It has mainly blue-gray plumage, white underparts with black streaks, and a white head with a black stripe that goes into black plumes behind the eye. In the breeding season, gray plumes develop on the upper chest. The juvenile is more gray-brown and has no plumes. In Florida, an all-white version was previously thought to be a separate species and known as the Great White Heron, and there is also one with gray plumage and a white head that is sometimes known as "Wurdemann's Heron". The Great Blue Heron can fly 10-15 miles to where fish are plentiful, and then stand patiently in the water or on the bank waiting to spear a catch. They also sometimes eat frogs, snakes and small mammals.

AMERICAN BITTERN

Scientific name:	*Botaurus lentiginosus*
Length:	28 inches, wingspan 42 inches
Habitat:	Marshland and grassy shores
Identification:	Short-legged wading bird. Brown plumage striped in darker brown, black streaks on neck, pointed wings tipped with black
Similar species:	Juvenile looks similar to juvenile night-herons, but is larger, has longer bill, and in flight has black wingtips, more pointed wings and a faster wingbeat

A master of camouflage, the shy American Bittern is usually very hard to spot, although the male may be seen performing his courtship display out in the open during March and April. Part of the heron family, it is widespread across much of America but lives deep in inaccessible marshy areas and bogs. The breeding pair find an isolated spot and select their territory, which is then defended by the male while the female builds a platform of reeds and grass in heavy cover near to the water's edge. The 2-3 eggs are incubated by the female only, which takes about 29 days; the young birds leave the nest after around 6-7 weeks. The plumage of the adult bird is a rich brown, striped in subtly darker brown and with black streaks on the neck, and the rather pointed wings are tipped with black. The juvenile bird has no black neck streaks. When disturbed, the American Bittern freezes in position with its bill pointed upwards, blending into the vertical stalks of the marsh grass, or suddenly flies up with rapid wingbeats. It eats fish, frogs, small eels, water snails and insects.

LEAST BITTERN

Scientific name:	*Ixobrychus exilis*
Length:	13 inches, wingspan 17 inches
Habitat:	Freshwater marshland with dense cover
Identification:	Small, short-legged heron. Brown plumage, large buff-colored patches on wings visible both in flight and when perching; dark cap, black back with pale stripes
Similar species:	The juvenile Green Heron can look similar if its plumage is very brown, but lacks the large buff patches on the wing that are noticeable both in flight and when the Least Bittern is perched

The tiny Least Bittern is the smallest American heron. It is widespread across much of southeast America but is very secretive and hides away in dense cover in marshy areas. It nests in isolated pairs or in loose colonies, building a platform of dried plants just above the water, or sometimes taking over the disused nest of another bird. The 4-5 eggs are incubated by both parents, which takes about 25 days; the young birds leave the nest around 25 days after hatching. The plumage of the adult bird is mainly brown, with large pale buff-colored patches on the wings that can be seen both in flight and when the bird is perching; the male has a black cap and a black back with two pale stripes, the female a chestnut brown cap and back, also with lighter stripes. The juvenile bird is like the female, but has deeper brown streaks on its back and breast. Like the American Bittern, when alarmed the Least will freeze in position with its bill pointed upwards, mimicking the vertical lines of marsh grass. Rather than flying, it will clamber through grass and reeds at the top of their stout stalks. It lives on fish, frogs and tadpoles.

BLACK-CROWNED NIGHT-HERON *(above)*

Scientific name:	*Nycticorax nycticorax*
Length:	25 inches, wingspan 44 inches
Habitat:	Wet woodlands, marshland
Identification:	Nocturnal, short-legged heron. White body, black cap and back, gray wings, long white plumes at nape
Similar species:	Adult unmistakable, juvenile distinguished from juvenile Yellow-crowned Night-Heron by darker brown back with bolder white spots and thicker neck; in flight, the feet barely extend past the tip of the tail. Young bird is also like the juvenile American Bittern, but the Bittern is larger, has longer bill, and in flight has black wingtips, more pointed wings and a faster wingbeat

A stocky heron with a short, thick neck, the Black-crowned Night-Heron is a mainly nocturnal bird that is found across much of America. It roosts in groups during the day, perching in a hunched-up posture in trees or under shady cover in marshes. At night, it comes out to hunt alone, looking for fish, frogs and sometimes crustaceans. It breeds in colonies, building a ramshackle construction of sticks, reeds and twigs up to 160 feet above the ground in trees, in which it lays 2-6 eggs. These are incubated by both parent birds, which takes 24-26 days; the young birds leave the nest after around 6-7 weeks. The adult bird has a white body, gray wings and tail and a green-black back and crown, with three long white plumes at the nape; it also has quite large red eyes. The juvenile bird is two-toned brown above with bold white spots, pale buff with darker streaks below and has pale yellow-orange eyes and a yellowish bill. The young bird's plumage blends in very well with the background, making it almost invisible.

YELLOW-CROWNED NIGHT-HERON

Scientific name:	*Nyctanassa violacea*
Length:	24 inches, wingspan 42 inches
Habitat:	Wet woodlands, swamps
Identification:	Mainly nocturnal, short-legged heron. Gray plumage, striking black and white face, three long white plumes at nape, feet extend past tail in flight
Similar species:	Adult unmistakable, juvenile distinguished from juvenile Black-crowned Night-Heron by less conspicuous white spots on back, longer legs and thicker black bill. In flight, the feet extend further past the tip of the tail

Like the Black-crowned, the Yellow-crowned Night-Heron is mainly a nocturnal bird, but it does also hunt during the day. It is seen mainly in southeast America, very rarely venturing into the western states. It is not particularly gregarious, hunting alone and nesting in isolated pairs or in small colonies. It builds a very sturdy cup of sticks, reeds and twigs 15-50 feet above the ground in a tree, in which it lays 2-8 eggs. These are incubated by both parents, which takes 21-25 days; the young birds leave the nest after around 25 days. The adult bird has gray plumage, with a striking black and white face, quite large red eyes, and three long white plumes at the nape; its pale yellow crown is not very noticeable. The juvenile bird is two-toned brown with small white spots on the back and distinct streaks on the breast, a thick all-black bill and has pale yellow-orange eyes. The young bird's plumage blends well with the background, making it difficult to see, and this species will often freeze rather than fly away when surprised. In coastal areas, the Yellow-crowned Night-Heron eats crabs, but it will also take fish and frogs. When foraging, it walks very slowly, but strikes with speed when it spots something edible.

GREAT EGRET

Scientific name:	*Ardea alba*
Length:	39 inches, wingspan 51 inches
Habitat:	Lakes, marshes, wetlands
Identification:	Large, long-legged, long-necked wading bird. White plumage, long thin yellow bill, black legs
Similar species:	Its large size distinguishes the Great Egret from most other white herons. Its black legs set it apart from the all-white version of the Great Blue Heron

The Great Egret is the largest and the most widespread egret in America. Most egrets are white, and their population was endangered in the late 19th century by hunters killing them for their feathers, which were highly prized in the millinery industry. Now the birds are in danger from the draining of their wet habitats. The Great Egret is a sociable bird and nests in large colonies, either in reeds or more usually in trees. It builds a large, sturdy platform of sticks - old nests are often repaired and reused - and lays 3-5 eggs. These are incubated for 23-36 days by both adult birds, with the chicks staying in the nest for 6-7 weeks after hatching. The plumage of both adult birds is pure white, and they have a long, thin, yellow bill and black legs and feet. Breeding birds have long lacy white plumes extending from their back, reaching further than the end of the tail. Immature birds are also white, but a rather duller color and have no plumes. The Great Egret wades elegantly through shallow water, stalking its prey slowly and methodically; it eats fish, frogs, water snakes and insects.

SNOWY EGRET

Scientific name:	*Egretta thula*
Length:	24 inches, wingspan 41 inches
Habitat:	Wetlands, freshwater lakes
Identification:	Medium-sized , long-legged, wading bird. White plumage, small plumes on head, long thin black bill, long black legs, yellow feet
Similar species:	Similar to Cattle Egret and immature Little Blue Heron, but has black bill. Cattle Egret also has thicker neck, shorter bill and legs, young Little Blue Heron has blue-gray tips to its wings

A medium-sized egret, the Snowy Egret is common in the wetlands of southern America. Like the Great Egret, it is a sociable bird and

nests in colonies. It builds a large, sturdy platform of sticks - either in reeds or more usually 5-12 feet up in trees - and lays 2-6 eggs. These are incubated for 22-26 days by both adult birds, with the chicks staying in the nest for around 4 weeks after hatching. When changing over on the nest, the arriving bird greets its partner with several deep bows. The plumage of both adult birds is snow white, with small plumes on the head, a long, thin, black bill, black legs and yellow feet. Breeding birds have particularly long lacy white plumes extending from their back, which curve upwards and were highly prized by feather hunters in the late 19th century. Immature birds are also white, but have a yellowish stripe down the back of the legs and no plumes. The Snowy Egret hunts in shallow muddy water, probing and stirring up the bottom with its bright yellow feet and startling fish and frogs, which are promptly speared with its sharp bill.

CATTLE EGRET

Scientific name:	*Bubulcus ibis*
Length:	20 inches, wingspan 36 inches
Habitat:	Fields among livestock, marshes, swamps
Identification:	Compact and stocky heron. White plumage, pale orange plumes on crown, back and chest, short yellow bill
Similar species:	Similar to Snowy Egret, but has shorter yellow bill, or red-orange in breeding season, shorter legs and thicker neck. When flying, the Cattle Egret beats its wings deeper and faster than the Snowy

A rather stocky bird, the Cattle Egret originally came from the Old World but spread to Florida via South America and continues to spread northwards across America. It is a very sociable bird and nests in huge colonies, which often contain many hundreds of birds. Its nest is a cup of sticks and twigs, either at the water's edge or 5-12 feet up in a tree, in which it lays 2-6 eggs. These are incubated for 22-26 days by both adult birds, with the chicks staying on in the nest for around 4 weeks after they have hatched. The plumage of both adult birds is white, with pale orange plumes on crown, back and chest. The relatively short bill is yellow, but turns red-orange in the breeding season; the yellowish legs also turn reddish. Immature birds are like the adult, but very young birds have a black bill that only begins to turn yellow during the first year. The Cattle Egret is often seen in fields full of livestock, feeding on the insects and earthworms stirred up by the animals' hooves - unlike other species of heron, it never wades in water when foraging.

WHITE IBIS

Scientific name: *Eudocimus albus*
Length: 25 inches, wingspan 38 inches
Habitat: Coastal salt marshes, swamps, mangroves
Identification: Medium-sized, long-necked, long-legged wading bird. Long, decurved bill, white plumage, black tips to wings. Holds neck extended in flight
Similar species: The immature White Ibis looks similar to both the Glossy Ibis and White-faced Ibis, but can be distinguished by its white belly

White Ibis are quite common all year round in wetlands around the southern coasts of the United States, and have been recorded breeding as far north as Virginia. They are gregarious birds and live in small colonies, building nests of sticks and twigs in trees or reed beds. The female lays 2-5 eggs, which are incubated for 21-23 days. The chicks take a further 28-35 days to fledge. Both the adult male and female bird have white body plumage, with black tips to the outer primary wing feathers. The bill and facial skin are a reddish-pink, and the legs are red. The immature bird has a brown head, neck, back and wings, with a white belly. Its bill and facial skin are both orange and the legs are a dull brown. The White Ibis is closely related to the Scarlet Ibis, a South American species which has either escaped or been introduced to Florida. The two species have interbred in this area, leading to offspring in various shades of pink and scarlet. When feeding, adult birds wade through shallow water catching fish and aquatic invertebrates with their long, curved bills. They have also been known to eat small reptiles and amphibians.

WHITE-FACED IBIS

Scientific name: *Plegadis chihi*
Length: 23 inches, wingspan 36 inches
Habitat: Freshwater marshes
Identification: Medium-sized, long-necked, long-legged wading bird. Long, dark gray decurved bill, red eyes. Holds neck extended in flight
Similar species: Mature White-faced Ibis can be distinguished from Glossy Ibis by their red eyes, and in breeding plumage also by their red legs and white feathered border to red facial skin

White-faced Ibis spend spring and summer in their breeding grounds in the freshwater marshes across central North America.

They are rare in the mid-west, but are sometimes found on the east coast as far north as New England. Some birds spend all year round in southern Mexico. They may frequent brackish areas and will also feed in flooded fields. The female lays 2-7 eggs, which are incubated for 21-22 days. The chicks take around 28 days to fledge. At most times of the year, both male and female adult birds have red eyes, gray facial skin, gray-green legs and gray-brown feathers with the head and neck streaked with white. In the breeding season, the plumage of both becomes an iridescent purple-red, with wings and tail an iridescent green. The legs turn red and also the facial skin, which becomes entirely ringed with an even band of white feathers. Adult birds feed almost exclusively on aquatic invertebrates, which they catch with their long, curved bills while wading through shallow water. The birds that breed in central North America move south for the winter, to areas around the Gulf of Mexico.

GLOSSY IBIS

Scientific name:	*Plegadis falcinellus*
Length:	23 inches, wingspan 36 inches
Habitat:	Freshwater and saltwater marshes
Identification:	Medium-sized, long-necked, long-legged wading bird. Long, dark gray decurved bill, brown eyes. Holds neck extended in flight
Similar species:	Mature White-faced Ibis can be distinguished from Glossy Ibis by their red eyes, and in breeding plumage also by their red legs and white feathered border to red facial skin

The Glossy Ibis is to be found in the freshwater and saltwater marshes of Florida and the Atlantic coast, and its range is expanding north along the east coast. These birds rarely go inland, but have been seen as far west as Colorado. They roost in trees, and nest either on the ground or up to 10 feet above in a tree, building a platform of sticks. The female lays 2-7 eggs, which are incubated for 21-22 days by both parent birds. The chicks take around 28 days to fledge. At most times of the year, both male and female adult birds have brown eyes, gray facial skin bordered with a bluish line, gray-green legs with red joints, chestnut body and greeny-brown wing feathers. In the breeding season, the plumage of both becomes an iridescent purple-red, with wings and tail an iridescent green. The immature bird is very similar to the young White-faced Ibis, only being distinguished by having a blue line edging the face rather than white. The Glossy Ibis congregates in flocks to feed, eating crayfish, insects and frogs which they catch with their long, curved bills while wading through shallow water.

WOOD STORK

Scientific name:	*Mycteria americana*
Length:	40 inches, wingspan 61 inches
Habitat:	Wet meadows, swamps, ponds, coastal shallows
Identification:	Large, long-necked, long-legged wading bird. Long, thick, down-curved bill, naked gray head, white plumage, black on tail and wing
Similar species:	In flight can resemble the American White Pelican, but has more black on its white wings and flies with its head straight out, rather than tucked back

The Wood Stork is the only native American stork; it is seen in Florida throughout most of the year, although during the summer it spreads much further through the southwest. It nests in large colonies, building a flimsy-looking platform of sticks and twigs in trees, sometimes as much as 80 feet above the ground. The 3-4 eggs are incubated by both parent birds for 28-32 days, and the young chicks leave the nest around 50-55 days later. The adult bird is large, with long legs, a bald, leathery, black-gray head and neck and a long, thick, down-curved bill. Its body plumage is mainly white, with black tail feathers and black along the trailing edge of the wing. The juvenile bird is similar, but its head has grayish-brown feathers and its bill is yellow. The Wood Stork walks slowly and sedately through shallow water, with its head down, feeling with its bill for fish, frogs, reptiles and insects. Flocks of storks often soar high into the sky, flying with slow, deliberate wingbeats and with head and legs extended. Their population has been endangered by the draining of their habitat in recent years.

ROSEATE SPOONBILL

Scientific name: *Ajaia ajaja*
Length: 32 inches, wingspan 50 inches
Habitat: Marshes, lagoons, mangroves, mudflats
Identification: Large, long-necked, long-legged wading bird. Long, spatulate bill, pink plumage,. Holds neck extended in flight
Similar species: Flamingos are similar size and coloring, but no other bird has the distinctive spoonbill

These beautiful birds are very gregarious and are often seen feeding or flying in flocks around the Gulf of Mexico and in the southwest. They nest in small colonies, often with varieties of heron. Their courtship ritual is elaborate, with flying displays and clapping of bills. The Roseate Spoonbill mates for life and the pair construct a nest of twigs and sticks, usually in bushes, trees or reeds, but sometimes on the ground. They lay 2-3 eggs in one clutch, which they incubate for 22-23 days. The chicks take a further 35-42 days to fledge. The adult male and female look very similar, with a white neck with a pink back and wings highlighted in red. The head has no feathers and is greenish in color, while the distinctive spatulate bill is pale gray with darker gray-black mottling. The eyes are red, the legs are red with dark feet. The immature bird has yellow eyes and a yellowish bill, with white head feathers, and its body is white or a very pale pink. When feeding, the adults swing their distinctive spoon-shaped bills back and forth through shallow water to catch small fish, crustaceans and aquatic invertebrates. They also sometimes eat plant material. Roseate Spoonbills were once hunted for their plumes, which were used in the millinery trade, but now - despite the destruction of their habitat in some areas - their numbers in America have increased.

MUTE SWAN

Scientific name:	*Cygnus olor*
Length:	60 inches
Habitat:	Ponds, lakes, parks
Identification:	Very large, long-necked waterfowl. White plumage, orange bill with black knob at base. Tends to hold neck in S-curve
Similar species:	The juvenile Mute Swan looks very similar to the juvenile Trumpeter, but tends to hold its neck in more of a curve

The Mute Swan is an Old World species that was introduced into North America and is found mainly on the east coast and around the Great Lakes - it likes to be near people. Populations are increasing, displacing native birds, so in some areas they are being removed. It is often silent, although it sometimes hisses or grunts, but when flying its wingbeats produce a loud rhythmic hum. Like other swans it breeds near water, building a large mass of plant material in which it lays 4-6 eggs. Incubation is done by the female bird, and takes around 34-38 days. The young birds leave the nest very soon after hatching, but stay with the parent birds for a further 4 months. The Mute Swan has white plumage, a long pointed tail and a very long slender neck, which it tends to hold in an S-curve. Its bill is orange with a prominent black knob at the base and it quite often swims with its wings held up over its back in an arch. The immature bird has a pinkish-gray bill and its plumage is a dull brownish-white, which it retains through until midwinter. The Mute eats aquatic plants, which it dislodges with its powerful bill - a blow from it can break a man's arm.

TRUMPETER SWAN

Scientific name:	*Cygnus buccinator*
Length:	60 inches
Habitat:	Wooded ponds, rivers
Identification:	Very large, long-necked waterfowl. White plumage, black bill. Tends to hold neck straight upward
Similar species:	Very similar to Tundra Swan, but is bigger and has longer bill with no yellow. The juvenile Trumpeter looks very similar to the juvenile Mute Swan, but tends to hold its neck straight rather than in a curve

The other major North American race of swan, the Trumpeter, is a huge bird that is found in the northwest but is being introduced further east. At the beginning of the twentieth century the species had almost died out, after hunters slaughtered it for its down and skin, and swans' eggs had become sought-after by gourmets. After protection was introduced, the population rose and is still slowly increasing. The Trumpeter Swan breeds near water, building a large mound of plant material in which it lays 2-13 eggs. Incubation is done by the female bird, and takes around 33 days. The young birds leave the nest very soon after hatching, but stay with the parent birds until the following spring. The Trumpeter Swan has white plumage and a very long slender neck, which it tends to hold straight upwards. Its straight bill is black and it has black facial skin which comes down in a deep V on the forehead. The immature bird has a pinkish bill and its plumage is a dull gray-brown, which it retains through the first spring. This species eats aquatic plants and insects; they use their long necks to reach food on the bottom.

TUNDRA SWAN

Scientific name:	*Cygnus columbianus*
Length:	52 inches
Habitat:	Shallow ponds, lakes, marshes, rivers
Identification:	Large, long-necked waterfowl. White plumage, black bill, yellow spot in front of eye. Tends to hold neck straight upward
Similar species:	Similar to other swans, but is smaller than Trumpeter Swan and has shorter bill; most Tundras have a yellow spot in front of the eye. Adult can be distinguished from the adult Mute Swan by having a black bill rather than orange

A North American race that was formerly known as the Whistling Swan, the Tundra Swan is found in summer on Arctic tundra but comes further south in the winter. It tends to return to old haunts and is usually seen in flocks; its call is quite musical. It breeds near tundra ponds, building a large mound of leaves and grass in which it lays 2-7 eggs. Incubation is done by the female bird, and takes around 32 days. The young birds leave the nest very soon after hatching, but stay with the parent birds until the following spring. The Tundra Swan is the smallest American swan; it has white plumage and a relatively long slender neck, but it tends to hold its neck straight upward. Its slightly concave bill is black; it has black facial skin with a rounded border across the forehead and most birds have a small yellow spot in front of the eye. The immature bird has a pinkish bill and its plumage is a dull gray-brown, but it turns white much sooner than the juveniles of other swan species. Most birds feed on both land and water, eating aquatic plants and small mollusks.

CANADA GOOSE

Scientific name:	*Branta canadensis*
Length:	25-45 inches
Habitat:	Ponds, marshes, grassland, open farmland
Identification:	Medium waterfowl. Black head and neck, white "chin strap", dark back, white undertail coverts. In flight, shows dark wings and white U-shaped rump band
Similar species:	Smaller birds could be mistaken for Brant, but in Canada Goose the black of the neck stops above the chest and it has a broad white "chin strap"

The most common and distinctive goose in America, which can be found across the entire country at different times of the year. Its nest is a large hollow lined with plant matter and soft down, in relatively open areas near water. It lays 2-12 white eggs, which are incubated by the female only for around 25-30 days. The male defends his mate and offspring very fiercely - warning intruders away at first, but not hesitating to attack even much larger suspected enemies. The young birds are downy and leave the nest soon after hatching, but stay with the parents until the following spring. The plumage of the mature adult can vary quite considerably, but it generally has a black head and neck, with a distinctive white "chin strap" from ear to ear, dark back, white undertail coverts. In flight, it shows dark wings and a white U-shaped rump band. Eastern birds are generally paler, western birds darker, but the difference can be hard to see. Northern birds tend to be smaller than those in the south. The Canada Goose flies in V-formation when migrating, stopping often to feed. It eats aquatic plants, grain, grass and small aquatic animals. This species is currently spreading into city parks and golf courses and populations are increasing.

BRANT

Scientific name:	*Branta bernicla*
Length:	25 inches
Habitat:	Shallow bays, marshy coasts
Identification:	Medium waterfowl. Black head, neck and chest, whitish patch on either side of neck, dark back, white undertail coverts almost concealing black tail
Similar species:	Could be mistaken for Canada Goose, but generally smaller, darker and stockier, black of neck extends further onto chest and lacks broad white "chin strap"

Primarily a sea goose, which breeds on high Arctic tundra and spends the winter mainly along the west coast, a few are found on the east coast but it is very rare inland. Its nest is a hollow lined with plant stems, down and feathers in which it lays 1-7 eggs. Incubation is done by the female bird, and takes around 22-26 days. The young birds leave the nest very soon after hatching, but stay with the parent birds until the following spring. The mature adult has a black head, neck and chest, with a whitish patch on either side of the neck, dark back and white undertail coverts almost concealing the black tail. Eastern birds have a white belly, western birds have a dark belly, but the difference can be hard to see. Juvenile birds have pale bands across the back and often lack the white neck patch entirely. The Brant flies in low, ragged formations of 20-50 birds, its quite long and pointed wings beating rapidly. It eats aquatic plants, insects and crustaceans and can be seen in winter on marshy coasts or grazing on open fields near the seaside.

ROSS'S GOOSE

Scientific name:	*Chen rossii*
Length:	23 inches
Habitat:	Marshes, open fields
Identification:	Medium waterfowl, short-necked. White with black wingtips, short pinky-red bill
Similar species:	Snow Goose is larger, has longer neck and flatter head, bill has black "grin patch", in flight wingbeats are slower. The darker form is very distinct from the darker form of the Snow Goose, as it has a white belly

A very common bird in some parts of the south in winter, sharing much the same range and migration patterns as the Snow Goose and often seen with it - usually in large flocks. It nests in colonies on islands in Arctic tundra, making a shallow depression lined with grass, plant stems and down in which it lays 2-6 eggs. Incubation is done by the female bird, and takes around 21-24 days. The young birds leave the nest very soon after hatching, but stay with the parent birds until the following spring. The mature adult has a round head and is mostly white; in flight it has a gray-blue tint to the wing coverts and primary feathers are black. Its pinky-red bill is short and triangular, and it has quite a short neck. A very rare color variation has a mostly white head, a brown back, variable amounts of white underneath and more black on the wings. The juvenile bird is white but has some grayish tinting to its head, back and flanks, the juvenile of the darker form is overall a dark gray-brown, with white face and belly. Ross's Goose eats aquatic plants, young shoots, grain and insects and can often be seen in grasslands and grainfields.

GREATER WHITE-FRONTED GOOSE

Scientific name:	*Anser albifrons*
Length:	28 inches
Habitat:	Freshwater wetlands, farmland
Identification:	Large waterfowl. Grayish-brown, black bars underneath, pinky-orange bill with whitish tip and broad white stripe at base, orange feet and legs
Similar species:	Juvenile is almost identical to Bean Goose, but Bean has black bill, sometimes with a yellow-orange band and is rarely seen in America. Juvenile of the darker form of the Snow Goose is very similar overall, but has darker legs and lacks white face band

A very common bird in some parts of the west and mid-west, the Greater White-fronted Goose is named for the distinctive white band at the base of its bill. Like other geese it nests in colonies near water, making a shallow depression lined with down in which it lays 4-7 eggs. Incubation is done by the female bird, and takes around 28 days. The young birds leave the nest very soon after hatching, but stay with the parent birds until the following spring. The mature adult is mostly grayish-brown, with variable black bars underneath; in flight it has a gray-blue tint to the wing feathers and a U-shaped white band on the rump. Its pinky-orange bill has a whitish tip and a broad white stripe at the base, and it has orange feet and legs. The adult bird varies greatly in size and in coloring; tundra breeders are smaller and paler, with heavier barring; taiga breeders are the largest, darker with less barring; Greenland breeders are medium size, darkest in coloring and have an orange bill. The juvenile is very similar overall, but does not acquire the face band until its first winter and black

barring until second fall. The Greater White-fronted Goose eats aquatic plants, grain and insects and can often be seen grazing in fields. When migrating, it is sometimes seen in flocks of many thousands of birds.

Snow Goose

Scientific name:	*Chen caerulescens*
Length:	28 inches
Habitat:	Grassland, grainfields, coastal wetlands
Identification:	Large waterfowl. White with black wingtips, pinky-orange bill with black "grin patch"
Similar species:	Ross's Goose is smaller, has shorter neck and rounder head, bill lacks black "grin patch", in flight wingbeats are faster. Juvenile of the darker form is very similar overall to Greater White-fronted Goose, but has darker legs and lacks white face band

A very common bird in some parts of the south in winter, and seen in large flocks of hundreds of birds over specific routes when migrating from its breeding grounds on Arctic tundra. It nests in colonies near water, making a shallow depression lined with grass, plant stems and down in which it lays 3-8 eggs. Incubation is done by the female bird, and takes around 22-25 days. The young birds leave the nest very soon after hatching, but stay with the parent birds until the following spring. The mature adult has a flattish head and is mostly white; in flight it has a gray-blue tint to the wing coverts and primary feathers are black. Its large bill is pinky-orange with a black "grin patch", and it has quite a long neck. In summer, rusty markings appear on the face. Another color variation, which was formerly known as the Blue Goose, has a mostly white head, a brown back, variable amounts of white underneath and more black on the wings. The juvenile bird is grayish, with a dark bill, the juvenile of the darker form is overall a slaty gray-brown, very similar overall to the Greater White-fronted Goose but has darker legs and lacks white face band. The Snow Goose eats aquatic plants, grain and insects and can often be seen in winter grazing in fields.

BLACK-BELLIED WHISTLING-DUCK

Scientific name:	*Dendrocygna autumnalis*
Length:	21 inches
Habitat:	Marshes, tree-lined shallow ponds, flooded woods
Identification:	Medium waterfowl, long-necked. Gray face with white ring round eye, red bill, chestnut neck, back and chest, black belly, rump and tail
Similar species:	Adult is unmistakable, because of its goose-like shape and distinct coloring

The Black-bellied Whistling-Duck is increasingly common; it is mainly found around the Mexican border, but is also established in Florida and is spreading into Texas. Its nest is usually built in a cavity of a tree, up to 30 feet above the ground, or is sometimes on the ground hidden in vegetation. It also quite often uses nest boxes if they are near water. The nesting place is lined with plant matter and usually holds 12-16 eggs, which are incubated for 25-30 days by both adult birds. The young chicks are downy and leave the nest soon after hatching, but do not fly for 8-9 weeks. The adult bird has a gray face with a white ring round the eye, bright red bill, chestnut neck, back and chest, and black belly, rump and tail. Its wings have black along the trailing edge and underneath and a broad white stripe above, which shows as a white patch on the side of a resting bird. The juvenile bird is paler, with a gray bill. Active at dawn and dusk, this species often forages at night, looking for seeds, grain, insects and snails.

GREEN-WINGED TEAL

Scientific name:	*Anas crecca*
Length:	14½ inches
Habitat:	Marshland
Identification:	Dabbling waterfowl. Male has chestnut head, green ear patch outlined in white, gray sides with white vertical line in front of wing, gray-brown back
Similar species:	Almost identical to the "Eurasian" or "Common" Green-winged Teal, which is a rare visitor to the northwest and northeast - the male of this species only differs in having a white horizontal stripe on the body and having no vertical white bar on side, the female cannot be safely distinguished from other female teals, although it has a smaller bill than some others

The smallest of the American dabbling ducks, the Green-winged Teal is found in marshes across North America, breeding in the north and spending winter in the south. Its nest is a hollow of grass lined with down, hidden in vegetation near water. It holds 10 or more eggs, which are incubated by the female bird for around 24 days. The downy young chicks leave the nest soon after hatching and fly at about 6 weeks. The adult male (*left*) has a chestnut head and cheeks, with a dark green ear patch outlined in white, a buff breast with darker speckles, gray sides with a white vertical line in front of the wing, and a gray-brown back. The female is light brown speckled with darker brown with mainly white undertail coverts. In flight, the wings of both adults have a green patch. On its winter grounds and at staging areas the Green-winged Teal gathers in flocks of hundreds of birds, which often fly in tight formation, describing complicated maneuvers in the air. On the water the flock breaks up into smaller groups to feed on insects and aquatic plants.

WOOD DUCK *(above)*

Scientific name:	*Aix sponsa*
Length:	18½ inches
Habitat:	Woodland swamps, ponds and rivers
Identification:	Waterfowl. Male has glossy green and purple head, long crest, black and white face pattern, chestnut breast, buff flanks, black back. Female is gray-brown, teardrop white patch round eye
Similar species:	Male's coloring and crest are distinctive, but female resembles the female Mandarin Duck, except for large teardrop-shaped eyepatch

The Wood Duck is widely regarded as one of America's most beautiful water birds. It is widespread across much of the country at different times during the year, although it is rarely seen in its breeding grounds during the winter. One of the few ducks to roost high up in trees, it makes its nest up to 50 feet above the ground, lining a cavity in the tree with soft down; it also uses nesting boxes. The nest holds 8-14 eggs, which are incubated by the female bird for 28-32 days. The young birds leave the nest soon after hatching, dropping down from the nest to follow their mother to water, although they are not able to fly until around 7 weeks. The male adult has a glossy green and purple head with a long, downswept crest, bold black and white face pattern, chestnut breast, buff flanks and a black back. The female is gray-brown with paler spots on the flanks, a small crest, dark back and a teardrop-shaped white patch around the eye. The juvenile resembles the female. The Wood Duck eats aquatic plants, nuts, fruit, insects, small fish and crustaceans.

FULVOUS WHISTLING-DUCK

Scientific name:	*Dendrocygna bicolor*
Length:	20 inches
Habitat:	Marshes, shallow waters, rice fields
Identification:	Medium waterfowl. Bright tan, white stripe on flanks, gray bill, dark back with chestnut stripes, blue-gray legs and feet. In flight, wings mainly black, white crescent above the black tail
Similar species:	Adult is unmistakable, because of its goose-like shape and distinctive coloring

The Fulvous Whistling-Duck is locally common in the south and often wanders farther north; it prefers wide-open areas. Its nest is usually on the ground hidden in dense vegetation, or rarely built in a cavity of a tree, up to 30 feet above the ground. The nesting place is lined with plants and usually holds 10-20 eggs - although sometimes more than one pair seem to use the same nest at the same time. They are incubated for 24-26 days by both adult birds. The young chicks are downy and leave the nest soon after hatching, but do not fly for 8-9 weeks. Both adult birds are mainly bright tan, with a white stripe on the flanks, white streaks on throat, dark gray bill, dark back with bright chestnut stripes, and blue-gray legs and feet. In flight, the wings are mainly black and a white crescent can be seen above the black tail. More active during the night, the Fulvous Whistling-Duck can often be seen flying in flocks at dawn and dusk. It eats seeds and grain and commonly forages in rice fields, often diving for food.

MALLARD

Scientific name:	*Anas platyrhynchos*
Length:	23 inches
Habitat:	Freshwater shallows, tidal marshes
Identification:	Dabbling waterfowl. Male has green head, white collar, yellow bill, gray body. Female is sandy brown, orange bill marked with black. Wings have bright blue patch on upper side, bordered with white
Similar species:	Male easily identified by its metallic green head and neck, female looks very similar to other species but has an orange bill marked with black

The Mallard is probably the most abundant and familiar wild duck in the Northern Hemisphere, and is the ancestor of most domestic ducks. It is common across much of America, not only in the wild but also in semi-wild state around cities and in parks. It nests near water in vegetation, lining a hollow with grass, stems and down, which holds 5-14 eggs. These are incubated for 26-29 days, by the female bird only, and the downy chicks leave the nest soon after hatching but do not fly until 8 weeks later. The male bird (*above*) has a glossy green head and neck with a narrow white collar, yellow bill, chestnut breast and gray body. The female is mottled sandy brown, with an orange bill marked with black. Both have a white tail, and in flight the wings have a bright blue patch on the upper side, bordered on each side with a white stripe, and white wing linings. The juvenile bird resembles the female, but its bill is dull olive. This species also dabbles, tipping tail-up to forage for aquatic plants, snails, insects and small fish.

MOTTLED DUCK

Scientific name:	*Anas fulvigula*
Length:	22 inches
Habitat:	Coastal marshes
Identification:	Dabbling waterfowl. Sandy-brown, yellow bill, wings have blue-green patch on upper side, white wing linings
Similar species:	Both sexes look similar to American Black Duck, but have a paler body, plainer throat and face and a blue-green wing patch. Mottled differs from female Mallard by having darker plumage, no white in tail and no black on bill

A warm-weather species, the Mottled Duck is found regularly in Florida and along the Gulf coast but has been introduced in some other areas and sometimes ventures quite far inland. It remains in the same area all year round and prefers remote marshes, so its population is relatively stable. It nests in vegetation near water, lining a hollow with grass, reeds and down, which holds 8-11 eggs. These are incubated for 26-28 days, by the female bird only, and the downy chicks leave the nest soon after hatching but do not fly until much later. The adult bird's plumage is mainly a rich sandy-brown, with paler head and neck; both sexes have a yellow bill, although that of the female is duller. In flight, the wings have a blue-green patch on the upper side and white wing linings. This species is also a dabbling duck, eating submerged plants, snails, frogs and seeds.

AMERICAN BLACK DUCK

Scientific name:	*Anas rubripes*
Length:	23 inches
Habitat:	Woodland lakes and streams, freshwater and tidal marshes
Identification:	Dabbling waterfowl. Sooty-brown, yellow bill, wings have violet patch on upper side, white wing linings
Similar species:	Both sexes look similar to the female Mallard, but have a darker body and gray head

The American Black Duck is common in the northeast, but its population is declining inland to the west, where it is being replaced by the Mallard. These two species also often interbreed, so hybrids are often seen. The American Black prefers woodland ponds and coastal salt marshes and is a very wary bird, flying away instantly and at great speed if disturbed. It nests in vegetation near water, lining a hollow with grass and stems to hold 5-17 eggs. These are incubated for 26-28 days, by the female bird only, and the downy young leave the nest soon after hatching and are flying 9 weeks later. Despite its name, the American Black Duck is not black; its plumage is a rich sooty-brown, with paler head and neck; the male has a yellow bill and the female olive-green, sometimes mottled with black. In flight, the wings have a violet patch on the upper side and white wing linings. This species rarely goes hungry, dabbling in spring to eat submerged plants but happy to add worms, snails, frogs and seeds to its diet.

GADWALL

Scientific name:	*Anas strepera*
Length:	20 inches
Habitat:	Shallow ponds
Identification:	Dabbling waterbird. Male is gray, white belly, black tail coverts, chestnut on wings. Female is brown, white belly, steep forehead, gray bill with orange sides
Similar species:	Male is unmistakable, female resembles female Mallard, but has white belly, steeper forehead and bill is gray above and orange below

Fairly common, especially in the west, the Gadwall is quite a plain duck and can often be overlooked. It prefers open areas of shallow water, where it gathers in large flocks. Its nest is a hollow of grass lined with plants and some down, built near water and often on an island, holding 7-15 cream-colored eggs. The female incubates the eggs for 25-28 days, the young chicks leave the nest soon after hatching and begin to fly at 7-9 weeks. The breeding plumage of the male (*left*) is mostly gray, with a sandy-brown head, white belly, distinctive black tail coverts and pale chestnut on the wings. The female is mottled brown and resembles the female Mallard, except for a white belly, steeper forehead and gray bill with orange sides. Both sexes have a square white patch on the trailing edge of the wing that is evident in flight, and sometimes shows as a small white patch on the side of a swimming bird. The Gadwall floats quite high in the water, often picking up food from near the surface. It eats aquatic plants and seeds, with some insects and mollusks.

AMERICAN WIGEON

Scientific name:	*Anas americana*
Length:	19 inches
Habitat:	Fields, marshes, shallow water
Identification:	Dabbling waterbird. Male has white crown, green face patch on grayish head, small blue-gray bill. Wings mainly white on upper surface, green patch
Similar species:	Coloring makes both sexes unmistakable

Very common in the west and fairly common elsewhere, the American Wigeon is often seen in flocks on land near water, including semi-urban areas like parks and golf courses. Its nest is a hollow of grass lined with plants and a great deal of down, built in tall reeds often some distance from water, holding 6-12 cream-colored eggs. The female incubates the eggs for around 25 days, the young chicks leave the nest soon after hatching and begin to fly at 7-8 weeks. The plumage of the male (*left*) is mostly brown, with a white belly, grayish head and throat, white crown - hence its nickname, "baldpate" - and long green face patch running back from the eye. In flight, the wings have a green patch and extensive white areas on the upper surface and mainly white wing linings beneath. The female resembles the male, but has no white on the head and no green face patch. Both have a rather small blue-gray bill. Wigeons and diving ducks often winter together - the Wigeon is a dabbler that feeds on aquatic plants, with some insects and mollusks, but the diving ducks reach much further down to dislodge food from the bottom. When its food is scarce, the Wigeon simply steals from the other birds when they come to the surface.

NORTHERN PINTAIL

Scientific name:	*Anas acuta*
Length:	20-26 inches
Habitat:	Marshes, open ponds, lakes
Identification:	Dabbling waterfowl. Male has white breast with thin white stripe to brown head, gray body, long black tail feathers. Female is buff-brown, long tail, grayish bill. Both sexes have metallic brown-green patch on upper wing and white band on trailing edge
Similar species:	Male is unmistakable because of its coloring and long thin tail. Female is similar to many other female ducks, but is larger than most

A lean, elegant dabbler, the Northern Pintail is found across much of America, breeding in the north and wintering in the south. It prefers open areas and is more common in the west than in the east. Its nest is a hollow of plant material, lined with down and holding 6-12 eggs. These are incubated for around 26 days by the female, and the young chicks leave the nest soon after hatching and fly at about 7 weeks. The male (*below*) has a chocolate-brown head, white breast and neck with a thin white stripe running up onto the head, mainly gray body, and black central tail feathers extending beyond the rest of the tail. The female is mottled buff-brown, with a paler head and neck, longish pointed tail and grayish bill. In flight, both sexes have long, pointed wings, and a metallic brown and green patch on the upper wing, with a white band on the trailing edge. The immature bird is similar to the female. The Northern Pintail prefers shallow water as it dabbles for food, foraging on the bottom for snails, small fish and crustaceans and also eating insects and seeds. Like other dabblers, it does not need to run across the water to get airborne, but can simply leap up from the surface into flight.

BLUE-WINGED TEAL

Scientific name: *Anas discors*
Length: 15½ inches
Habitat: Marshes, open ponds, lakes
Identification: Small dabbling waterfowl. Male has violet-gray face, white crescent before eye
Similar species: Coloring makes male unmistakable, female distinguished from female Green-winged Teal by larger bill, more heavily spotted undertail coverts, yellowish legs, and from female Cinnamon Teal by grayer plumage, smaller bill

Very common east of the Rockies, the Blue-winged Teal hates cold weather more than most ducks. It is happy on any water, no matter how small, landing with precision even on what is little more than a large puddle. Its nest is a hollow of grass lined with down, built in dense vegetation near water, and holding 6-15 white or cream-colored eggs. The female incubates the eggs for around 24 days, the young chicks leave the nest soon after hatching and begin to fly at about 6 weeks. The breeding plumage of the male (*above*) is mostly speckled brown, with a violet-gray face and a white crescent in front of the eye. The female is mottled grayish-brown, as is the male during the winter. In flight, the wings have an obvious pale blue patch, and mainly white wing linings beneath. Juveniles are an overall pale brown, with yellowish legs, and they cannot be distinguished from those of the Cinnamon Teal. The Blue-winged Teal filters mud with its bill and eats seeds, aquatic plants, snails and insects, but rarely up-ends like other dabbling ducks, merely dipping its head below the surface of the water. This species was once decimated by hunters, but now the hunting season opens after most of the birds have already migrated.

CINNAMON TEAL

Scientific name:	*Anas cyanoptera*
Length:	16 inches
Habitat:	Marshes, ponds, lakes
Identification:	Small, dabbling waterfowl. Plumage bright cinnamon brown, red eyes
Similar species:	Coloring makes male unmistakable, female distinguished from female Blue-winged Teal only by larger bill, browner plumage. Juveniles cannot be distinguished from those of Blue-winged Teal

A close relative of the Blue-winged Teal, the Cinnamon Teal is more common in marshes and shallow ponds in the west and rarely seen in the east. Its nest is a shallow cup of grass lined with down, hidden in dense vegetation a short distance from water, and holding 10-12 white or buff-colored eggs. The female incubates the eggs for around 25 days, the young chicks leave the nest soon after hatching and begin to fly at about 7 weeks. The breeding plumage of the male (*left*) is mostly a bright cinnamon brown. The female is mottled brown, as is the male in winter - but it can be distinguished by its red eyes. In flight, the wings are very similar to those of the Blue-winged, with an obvious pale blue patch, and mainly white wing linings beneath. Juveniles are an overall pale brown, with yellowish legs, and are almost identical to those of the Blue-winged Teal. The Cinnamon Teal filters mud with its bill and eats seeds, aquatic plants, snails and insects.

NORTHERN SHOVELER

Scientific name:	*Anas clypeata*
Length:	19 inches
Habitat:	Marshes, ponds, bays
Identification:	Dabbling waterfowl. Male has green head, white breast, chestnut-brown sides, white in front of black tail. Female is mottled brown, big gray and orange bill
Similar species:	In winter plumage, the male has a white crescent like that of the Blue-winged Teal; in breeding plumage it has a green head like the Mallard, but with a white breast. Both sexes can be distinguished by the large, spatulate bill that is longer than the head

The Northern Shoveler is common to abundant in the west and is increasing in the east. Its nest is a hollow of grass lined with down and concealed in dense vegetation near water, holding 6-14 greenish or buff eggs. The female incubates the eggs for around 26 days, the young chicks leave the nest soon after hatching and begin to fly at about 7 weeks. The breeding male (*right*) has a green head, white breast, chestnut-brown sides and white in front of a black tail. The female and juveniles are a drab mottled brown. In winter the male's head and breast turn grayish, with a whitish crescent in front of the eye. Both sexes have a large, spatulate bill that is longer than the head, that of the breeding male is grayish, otherwise it is tinged with orange. In flight, the wings are very similar to those of the Blue-winged, with an obvious pale blue patch, and mainly white wing linings beneath. The Northern Shoveler needs shallow open areas where it can sieve the water with its large bill for crustaceans, insects, mollusks, seeds and aquatic plants.

COMMON EIDER

Scientific name:	*Somateria mollissima*
Length:	24 inches
Habitat:	Shallow bays, rocky shores, tundra ponds
Identification:	Diving sea duck. Female is brown. Male has white back, neck and breast, black below, white head, black cap, orange bill
Similar species:	Male is distinctive, female similar to female King Eider, but is larger, with even bars on sides and back

The largest sea duck in America, the Common Eider is abundant in the far north, and is seen around the Great Lakes and on the east coast as far south as New England. It breeds on tundra ponds, usually in colonies, but prefers the open ocean in other seasons. Its nest is a hollow lined with plant stems and large amounts of down, usually out in the open away from the water on rocky islets, where eggs and chicks are safe from predators. It lays 4-7 greenish or buff eggs, which the female incubates for around 24-27 days. The downy young chicks leave the nest soon after hatching, but do not fly until about 8 weeks. The breeding male (*above*) has a white back, neck and breast, black below, white head with light green nape, black cap, orange bill. The female varies in color from rusty-brown to gray, with darker fine barring on sides and back. Juvenile males are dark and attain mature plumage by their fourth winter. Both sexes have a short neck, sloping forehead and a long sloping bill, which gives them a distinctive profile. The Common Eider eats mollusks, starfish, crustaceans and fish. The down from the female's breast is used for sleeping bags, pillows and down coats but is collected from the nest, which does not involve killing the bird.

KING EIDER

Scientific name:	*Somateria spectabilis*
Length:	22 inches
Habitat:	Tundra ponds, coastal waters, Great Lakes
Identification:	Diving sea duck. Female is brown with darker crescent markings. Male has orange shield over orange bill, blue-gray head, white breast and wing patch, black body
Similar species:	Male is distinctive, female similar to female Common Eider, but is smaller, has more rounded head and crescent-shaped bars on sides and back

Smaller than the Common Eider, the King Eider occupies a similar territory. It is common in the far north, increasing on the Great Lakes and can be seen on the east coast as far south as Virginia. It breeds on tundra, but winters at sea - often far north in openings in the pack ice. Its nest is a flattened hollow lined with large amounts of down, usually near the water, in which it lays 4-7 greeny-buff eggs, which the female incubates for around 23 days. The downy young chicks leave the nest soon after hatching. The breeding male (*right*) has a distinctive orange shield over its orange bill, blue-gray head, white breast and wing patch, and a mainly black body. The female is a rich brown, with darker crescent-shaped barring on sides and back. The juvenile male has a brown head, pinkish bill and brownish body, and attains mature plumage by its third winter. The King Eider dives down up to 180 feet to find mollusks, starfish, crustaceans and fish. Eiders dive down from the surface of the water, propelling themselves downward and then back up with their wings - literally flying underwater.

HARLEQUIN DUCK

Scientific name:	*Histrionicus histrionicus*
Length:	16½ inches
Habitat:	Rocky coasts, swift mountain streams
Identification:	Sea duck. Favors turbulent water. Female is dark with white patches on head. Male is slate blue, bright chestnut flanks, white markings outlined in black
Similar species:	Male is distinctive, female similar to female scoters, but is smaller and has a much shorter bill

The Harlequin Duck is usually found in small flocks and prefers very turbulent water on rocky coasts, moving inland to swift mountain streams for breeding. It is regularly seen on the east coast as far south as Virginia but is rare around the Great Lakes. Its nest is a hollow lined with grass and down, concealed in thick vegetation or under boulders near rushing water, in which it lays 5-10 buff eggs. The female incubates them for around 27-33 days and the downy chicks leave the nest soon after hatching, flying about 6 weeks later. Even very young chicks can dive swiftly and negotiate turbulent water with ease. The breeding male is slate blue with bright chestnut flanks, and has bold white markings on head and wings outlined in black. The female and non-breeding male are dark brown, with two or three small white patches on the side of the head. The Harlequin Duck dives to the bottom, using both feet and wings, to forage for snails, crabs, small fish and aquatic insects.

RING-NECKED DUCK

Scientific name:	*Aythya collaris*
Length:	17 inches
Habitat:	Freshwater marshes, woodland ponds, small lakes
Identification:	Diving duck. Male has black back and head, white vertical bar between gray sides and black chest, two vertical white bars on blue-gray bill. Female is gray-brown, dark crown, white eye ring, pale area at base of bill
Similar species:	Can be mistaken for Tufted Duck, the male of which has white sides instead of gray and a long tuft on the back of the head. Female scaup is similar coloring but has more contrasting white patch at base of bill

The Ring-necked Duck prefers sheltered fresh water, but is sometimes seen in coastal marshes in the south during winter. Its nest is a hollow of grass and down, in vegetation near water, in which it lays 6-14 greenish eggs. The female incubates them for around 26 days and the downy chicks leave the nest soon after hatching, flying about 7-8 weeks later. The breeding male (*right*) has a black back and head, a white vertical bar separates its pale gray sides from a black chest, and there are two vertical white bars on its blue-gray bill. The dark chestnut-brown neck-ring is rarely apparent. The female is gray-brown, with a dark crown, white eye ring, and a pale area at the base of its bill. When flying, both sexes have a gray stripe along the trailing edge of the wing. The Ring-necked Duck dives to probe the bottom for aquatic plants and crustaceans and also eats insects and snails. Although considered very edible, it is rarely hunted because it does not gather in large flocks in winter.

TUFTED DUCK

Scientific name:	*Aythya fuligula*
Length:	17 inches
Habitat:	Seashore, sheltered ponds, coastal lagoons
Identification:	Diving duck. Male is black with white sides, round head with long black tuft, gray bill with dark tip. Female is gray-brown, white at base of bill, white under tail
Similar species:	Can be mistaken for Ring-necked Duck, but male has white sides instead of gray and a long tuft on the back of the head, female does not have pale cheeks. In flight has white to trailing edge of wing and can resemble Greater Scaup

An Old World species, the Tufted Duck is a regular visitor to Alaska and in winter along the east coast to Maryland and the west coast to southern California. It prefers coastal areas, but is also very rarely seen around the Great Lakes. Its nest is a down-lined hollow of grass and stems, in vegetation near water, in which it lays 6-10 buff or greenish eggs. The female incubates them for 23-28 days and the downy chicks leave the nest soon after hatching, flying about 7 weeks later. The breeding male is mainly black, with white sides, a round head with long black tuft, and a gray bill with dark tip. The female is dark brown, with paler brown flanks, white at the base of the bill and under the tail, and often a short tuft on the back of the head. When flying, both sexes have a white stripe along the trailing edge of the wing. The Tufted Duck dives to forage for aquatic plants and mollusks and also eats insects and frogs.

GREATER SCAUP

Scientific name:	*Aythya marila*
Length:	18 inches
Habitat:	Wet tundra, lakes and rivers, coastal bays
Identification:	Diving duck. Male has black head, breast and tail, white below, light with wavy gray lines above. Female is gray-brown, white face patch at base of bill
Similar species:	Almost identical to Lesser Scaup, but Lesser has peak at back of crown and smaller bill, in flight less white on wing

A coastal bird, the Greater Scaup is less common inland but may be seen as it migrates south from its breeding grounds in the north. Its nest is a hollow lined with plant matter and down, near water in dense vegetation, in which it lays 7-10 green eggs. The female incubates them for around 24-28 days; the young leave the nest soon after hatching, and first fly about 5-6 weeks later. The Greater Scaup has a rounded head, higher toward the front and sloping down at the back and quite a large blue-gray bill. The breeding male (*right*) has black head with a green sheen, black breast and tail, and is white below and light gray with wavy darker gray lines above. The female and non-breeding male are gray-brown, with paler sides and a white face patch at base of bill; in spring and summer the female may also have a white crescent ear patch. When flying, both sexes have a long white stripe along the trailing edge of the wing. The Greater Scaup is often seen with other diving ducks, foraging for aquatic plants and crustaceans.

LESSER SCAUP

Scientific name:	*Aythya affinis*
Length:	$16\frac{1}{2}$ inches
Habitat:	Marshes, small lakes, ponds, sheltered bays, inlets
Identification:	Diving duck. Male has black head, breast and tail, white below, light with wavy gray lines above. Female is gray-brown, white face patch at base of bill
Similar species:	Almost identical to Greater Scaup, but has peak at back of crown and smaller bill, in flight less white on wing

The Lesser Scaup is very common inland in winter but may also be seen in coastal waters; like the Greater Scaup, it breeds in the north. Its nest is a hollow lined with some grass and down, not too far from water in tall vegetation, in which it lays 9-12 olive-brown eggs. The female incubates the eggs for around 27 days, covering them with down when she leaves the nest. The young leave the nest soon after hatching, and first fly about 7 weeks later. The Lesser Scaup has a rather pointed head with a peak at the back, and a slightly smaller blue-gray bill than the Greater Scaup. The breeding male has a black head with a purple sheen, black breast and tail, and is whitish below and light gray with wavy darker gray lines above. The female (*right*) and non-breeding male are gray-brown, with paler sides and a white face patch at the base of the bill; in spring and summer the female may also have an indistinct white crescent ear patch. When flying, both sexes have a white stripe along part of the trailing edge of the wing. The Lesser Scaup is often seen in large flocks, foraging for aquatic plants and crustaceans.

REDHEAD

Scientific name:	*Aythya americana*
Length:	19 inches
Habitat:	Marshes, ponds, lakes
Identification:	Diving waterfowl. Rounded head, short blue-gray bill with black tip. Male has chestnut head and neck, pale gray back and sides, black chest and tail. Female is brown, darker crown
Similar species:	Like Canvasback, but has shorter two-color bill, rounder head, contrasting pale stripe on wing

Very similar in coloring to the Canvasback, but smaller, the Redhead is found across much of south and western America. It breeds in marshes, building a nest of reeds sparsely lined with down, concealed in dense vegetation near deep open water. It lays around 12 eggs, but then often goes on to lay more eggs in the nests of other ducks. The female incubates the eggs for around 24 days and the chicks leave the nest soon after hatching, flying at around 8-10 weeks. The male (*above*) has a rounded chestnut head and neck, black chest, pale gray back and sides, and black under the tail. The female is uniform brown with darker crown. The bill of both birds is shortish, blue-gray with a black tip, and in flight they have a contrasting pale stripe on the trailing edge of the wing. The Redhead mainly eats the foliage and seeds of aquatic plants, insects and mollusks. It was once much more numerous but draining of its habitat has caused a sharp decrease in population, so hunting is now banned in some areas.

CANVASBACK

Scientific name:	*Aythya valisineria*
Length:	21 inches
Habitat:	Prairie marshes, lakes, bays
Identification:	Diving waterfowl. Long black bill and sloping forehead give distinctive shape to head. Male has chestnut head and neck, whitish back and sides. Female is brownish-gray, pale brown head and neck
Similar species:	Like Redhead, but has longer black bill, sloping forehead, no contrasting pale stripe on wing

One of the largest diving ducks, the Canvasback is found across much of America, sometimes in large flocks. A wary bird, it tends to stay towards the center of large lakes or bays, rarely coming ashore except to breed in the marshes of the northwest. Its nest is a solid cup made of grass and lined with down, concealed in tall vegetation near deep open water. It lays 7-9 greenish eggs, which are incubated for 24-27 days by the female bird. The chicks leave the nest soon after hatching and fly at around 10-12 weeks. The Canvasback has a long black bill and a sloping forehead, which give a distinct shape to the head. The male (*right*) has a chestnut head and neck, with whitish back and sides. The female is brownish-gray with pale brown head and neck. The Canvasback mainly eats the roots and tubers of aquatic plants. A favorite with hunters; it was once much more numerous but draining of its habitat has caused a sharp decrease in population, although this now seems to have stabilized.

OLDSQUAW

Scientific name:	*Clangula hyemalis*
Length:	16-22 inches
Habitat:	Great Lakes, tundra ponds, shallow seas
Identification:	Medium-sized sea duck. Male has very long tail, mostly white, with dark brown back and breast, pink band on stubby bill. Female has shorter tail, dark bill, plumage paler. Swift careening flight, noisy three-part yodeling call
Similar species:	Long tail is similar to Northern Pintail, but patterning and coloring different

Sometimes known as the Long-tailed Duck, the Oldsquaw likes cold water and stays offshore when not nesting. It winters in small groups on the ocean along both northern Pacific and Atlantic coasts, preferably over a sandy bottom, and breeds on tundra ponds. Its nest is a hollow of grass and down, concealed in vegetation or among rocks near water, which holds 6-11 olive or buff eggs. The female incubates these for around 23-25 days and the chicks leave the nest soon after hatching, flying at around 5 weeks. The male bird's very long tail is obvious in flight, but can be hidden underwater when it is swimming. In winter and spring the male (*right*) is mostly white, with dark brown back and breast, and a pink band on a stubby bill. By early summer, it has become mostly dark, with pale gray face patch, and later acquires a pale crown. The female has no long tail, bill is dark, plumage whiter overall in winter, darker in summer. Oldsquaws can be identified in flight by their swift, seemingly uncontrolled flight, dark wings and noisy three-part yodeling call. They dive up to 200 feet below the surface to forage for aquatic plants, shrimp and mollusks.

SURF SCOTER

Scientific name:	*Melanitta perspicillata*
Length:	20 inches
Habitat:	Tundra, woods near water, coastal waters
Identification:	Medium-sized sea duck. Female is dark with pale cheek patches. Male is black with white patches on forehead and nape, large bill with white, black and red-orange markings
Similar species:	Male is distinctive, female similar to female White-winged Scoter, but has no white wing patches

The Surf Scoter is common along the coast much of the year, especially on the Pacific. It can usually be seen some distance offshore, but also floats in small groups near jetties. It breeds on tundra and forest bogs in Alaska, but spends only a short period there. Its nest is scraped out of bare ground and lined with grass and down, often some distance from water on marshy ground. The down not only insulates the eggs from the cold earth, but is also used to cover the eggs when the female goes off to feed. The 5-8 buff or pinkish eggs are incubated by the female bird only and the young chicks leave the nest soon after hatching. The adult male (*right*) is black with white patches on forehead, nape and round the eye, and a large bill with white, black and red-orange patterning. The female is dark with black crown and pale cheek patches, the mature female often has a white patch on the nape. Juvenile birds are similar to the female but have a whitish belly and often white face patches. The Surf Scoter dives for crustaceans and aquatic plants. Courtship displays from several males around a single female can be seen in winter in sunny weather, until the female chooses her partner.

WHITE-WINGED SCOTER

Scientific name:	*Melanitta fusca*
Length:	21 inches
Habitat:	Inland lakes, rivers, coastal waters
Identification:	Medium-sized sea duck. Female is dark with light cheek patches. Male is black with white "comma" shaped patch round eye, both sexes have white wing patch
Similar species:	Male is distinctive, female similar to female Surf Scoter but has white wing patches and no black crown

The largest of the scoters, the White-winged is common in coastal areas in winter and on inland lakes and rivers in the breeding season, but is rarely seen in the south. Like other scoters - and often with them - it can be seen floating in groups on the water, and such a gathering is known as a "raft". The White-winged prefers sandy rather than rocky shores in winter and breeds in northern forest areas. Its nest is a hollow in bare ground lined with grass and down, sometimes exposed and sometimes concealed in thick vegetation. The 6-14 pinkish eggs are incubated by the female bird only for around 28 days and the young chicks leave the nest soon after hatching and fly at around 9-11 weeks. The adult male (*right*) is black with a white "comma" shaped patch round the eye, and both sexes have a white wing patch that shows in flight and also sometimes on the side of a resting bird. The female is dark with white cheek patches, which can be indistinct. Juvenile birds are similar to the female but have more distinct face patches and a whitish belly. The White-winged Scoter eats crustaceans, mollusks, sand dollars and aquatic plants.

BLACK SCOTER

Scientific name:	*Melanitta nigra*
Length:	19 inches
Habitat:	Tundra, woodland waterways, Great Lakes
Identification:	Medium-sized sea duck. Female is dark with pale face and throat and black cap. Male is black with bright orange spot on upper bill
Similar species:	Male is distinctive, female similar to female Surf Scoter, but has paler foreneck, rounder head, smaller bill

Scoters are often found in mixed flocks, but the Black Scoter, previously known as the Common Scoter, has a smaller range than the other two species commonly found in North America. It breeds in coastal areas in western Alaska and in some areas of northern Canada, migrating to winter on both the west and east coasts of America - although it rarely makes it very far south. Its nest is a hollow of grass and down, concealed in vegetation near water, in which it lays 5-8 buff or pinkish eggs. The female incubates them for around 27-31 days and the young chicks leave the nest soon after hatching, although they are not able to fly until about 6 weeks later. They do not mature enough to breed until the third summer after they hatch. The adult male is entirely black, except for a bright orange knob at the base of its bill. The female (*above*) and the immature male are dark, with much paler face and foreneck, and a black cap. The Black Scoter can dive down to 100 feet or more beneath the surface of the water, to forage for mollusks, crustaceans and aquatic insects. It is particularly fond of blue mussels, which are found on both the east and west coast.

COMMON GOLDENEYE

Scientific name:	*Bucephala clangula*
Length:	18½ inches
Habitat:	Lakes, rivers, coastal waters
Identification:	Medium-sized diving duck. Male has white spot before yellow eye, green-black head and back, white chest and sides. Female has chocolate brown head, gray body
Similar species:	Barrow's Goldeneye has smaller bill, steeper forehead, male has white crescent instead of spot before eye, more black on back

The Common Goldeneye is found across much of America, usually in small flocks. It breeds around lakes and bogs near coniferous forests, spending the winter in coastal areas or on inland lakes and rivers. Its nest is high up in a tree - it often takes over an abandoned woodpecker's nest - and sometimes quite far from water. The cavity is lined with down and holds 6-15 greenish eggs, which the female does not start to incubate until the last is laid. Once begun, incubation takes 27-32 days and the chicks leave the nest soon after hatching, dropping up to 60 feet to the ground since they cannot fly until around 8-9 weeks. The adult bird has a large, rather triangular head, with sloping forehead and long bill. The male (*left*) has a round white spot before its yellow eye, a black head and back, and white chest and sides. The female has a chocolate brown head on a gray body; its dark bill is sometimes yellow near the tip. In flight, the wings make a whistling sound, giving rise to this species' nickname of "Whistler".The Common Goldeneye mainly eats aquatic plants and insects, mollusks and crustaceans.

BARROW'S GOLDENEYE

Scientific name:	*Bucephala islandica*
Length:	18 inches
Habitat:	Lakes, ponds, rivers, coastal waters
Identification:	Medium-sized diving duck. Male has white crescent before yellow eye, purple-black head, black back and sides, white chest, row of white spots on side. Female has chocolate brown head, gray body
Similar species:	Common Goldeneye has larger bill, sloping forehead, male has white spot instead of crescent before eye, less black on back. Females not safely distinguished apart

A diving duck which prefers cold water, Barrow's Goldeneye is found across western America, with a few also in the northeast. It is much rarer than the Common Goldeneye but they are sometimes seen together in small flocks. Barrow's breeds around open lakes and small ponds, spending the winter in coastal areas or on inland lakes and rivers. Its nest is high up in a tree - often an abandoned woodpecker's nest - and sometimes quite far from water. The cavity is lined with down and holds 9-10 greenish-white eggs, which the female does not start to incubate until the last is laid. Once begun, incubation takes 32-34 days and the chicks leave the nest soon after hatching, dropping up to 50 feet to the ground since they cannot fly until around 8 weeks. The adult bird has a large, oval head, with a steep forehead and a shortish bill. The male (*right*) has a crescent-shaped white spot before its yellow eye, a purple-black head, black back and sides, white chest and a row of white spots on each side. The female has a dark-brown head on a gray body; its dark bill is pinkish-yellow. Like the Common, in flight the wings make a whistling sound. Barrow's Goldeneye mainly eats aquatic insects, mollusks and crustaceans.

BUFFLEHEAD

Scientific name:	*Bucephala albeola*
Length:	13½ inches
Habitat:	Woodland lakes and ponds, sheltered bays, rivers
Identification:	Small diving duck. Male has a white patch on black head, black back, white chest and sides. Female has gray head with white ear spot, gray back, white chest and belly
Similar species:	Has similar coloring to Goldeneye, but is smaller. Hooded Merganser has similar head pattern, but different body coloring

The smallest of the diving ducks, the Bufflehead is common across much of America at different times of the year and is often seen in small flocks. It breeds around lakes and shallow ponds, spending the winter in coastal areas or on inland lakes and rivers. Its nest is in a tree, often an old woodpecker's nest or other cavity. The hole is lined with feathers and down and holds 6-12 buff eggs, which the female starts to incubate when the last is laid. Incubation takes 29 days and the chicks leave the nest soon after hatching, dropping up to 20 feet to the ground as they cannot fly until 7-8 weeks. Once they are all down, the female looks after them alone until they can fly with her to join the males. The adult bird has a relatively large head, with a short bill. The male (*right*) has a white patch like a headscarf on a green and purple glossed black head, black back, white chest and sides. The female has a gray head with an oval white spot behind the eye, dark gray back, white chest and belly. The Bufflehead flies fast and usually close to the water; when disturbed the flock often rises but settles back into its original place. This species dives to forage for aquatic insects and plants, snails and crustaceans.

RUDDY DUCK

Scientific name:	*Oxyura jamaicensis*
Length:	15 inches
Habitat:	Freshwater wetlands, lakes, bays, salt marshes
Identification:	Small diving duck, long stiff tail feathers. Male has chestnut-brown body, dark cap, white cheeks, bright blue bill in breeding season. Female brownish with pale cheeks crossed by single dark line
Similar species:	Coloring and stiff tail feathers make this species distinctive

The Ruddy Duck is a small diving bird that is common in many areas across America and is often seen in large flocks. It breeds in freshwater wetlands, spending the winter on lakes, bays and salt marshes. Its nest is a floating woven mass of vegetation anchored in dense reeds and lined with feathers and down, which holds 5-17 large whitish eggs. The female incubates the eggs for 24 days, but both parent birds care for the ducklings. The chicks leave the nest soon after hatching, but cannot fly until 6-7 weeks. The adult bird has stiff tail feathers, which are often carried on or below the water surface, but can be raised in display. The breeding male has a bright chestnut-brown body, black cap and tail feathers, white cheeks and belly, and bright blue bill. The female (*right*) and the winter male are gray-brown with pale cheeks, the cheek of the female is crossed by a single dark line, both have a gray bill. The Ruddy Duck flies close to the water, with rapid beats of its rather short wings. It is a deep water diver, mainly eating the seeds and foliage of aquatic plants. Even the hatchlings dive to feed, unlike other species which start by picking off the surface.

HOODED MERGANSER

Scientific name:	*Lophodytes cucullatus*
Length:	18 inches
Habitat:	Woodland ponds, rivers, backwaters
Identification:	Diving duck. Male has white crest with black border that can open up like a fan, black back, white below, cinnamon sides. Female is brownish with paler crest
Similar species:	Similar head pattern to male Bufflehead, but different body coloring

The smallest of the North American mergansers, the Hooded is common in the east but uncommon in the west. It prefers fresh water near the coast birds the winter and in the breeding season is found on woodland ponds, rivers or backwaters in small flocks. Its nest is in a tree cavity or old log, lined with a mass of down and holding 8-12 white eggs. The female incubates these for 28-32 days and the chicks leave the nest soon after hatching and begin to fly at 9-10 weeks. The adult bird has a long, flat head, with a dark bill. The male has a white crest with black border that can open up like a fan in display, giving the head a rounded shape, a black back, white below, and cinnamon-colored sides. The female (*above*) is brownish, with a paler, bushy crest, and is smaller than other mergansers. At the start of the breeding season, the male performs an exciting courtship dance, then swims round and round the chosen female in a further display. The Hooded Merganser flies with rapid wingbeats and both sexes show a small white patch on the inner wing. It eats aquatic invertebrates, small frogs, newts and small fish.

COMMON MERGANSER

Scientific name:	*Mergus merganser*
Length:	25 inches
Habitat:	Woodland lakes and rivers
Identification:	Large diving duck. Male is mostly white, with a black back and green head. Female is gray with a rusty-red head and white throat
Similar species:	The male Mallard and Northern Shoveler also have green heads, but different shape and body coloring. Female is like female Red-breasted Merganser, but contrast between head and neck coloring is sharper. Also like male Redhead, but lacks black chest

The largest of the North American mergansers, the Common can be found across much of North America at different times of the year - sometimes in quite large flocks. It is mostly seen on fresh water, preferring wooded lakes and rivers in the breeding season. Its nest is in a tree cavity, old log, or among rocks, lined with a mass of down and holding 6-12 pale buff eggs. The female incubates these for 28-32 days and the chicks leave the nest soon after hatching and begin to fly at 9-10 weeks. The adult bird has a long body and sits low in the water. The male (*right*) is mostly white, with a black back, green head and red bill. The female is gray with a bright, rusty-red head and a white throat. Like other mergansers, the Common Merganser has a long, narrow bill with serrated edges and a hooked upper mandible - they are called "sawbills" by hunters. It dives to pursue its prey underwater; it eats aquatic invertebrates, small frogs, newts and small fish.

RED-BREASTED MERGANSER

Scientific name:	*Mergus serrator*
Length:	23 inches
Habitat:	Woodlands near water, sheltered coastal areas
Identification:	Diving duck. Male has gray sides, white collar, dark red breast, black back and green head with shaggy crest. Female is gray with a pale rusty-red head and whitish throat
Similar species:	Male is darker than male Common Merganser, and has crested head. Female is like female Common Merganser, but paler and lacks contrast between head and neck coloring.

Unlike the other mergansers, the Red-breasted prefers brackish or salt water in winter, and is found all along both North American coasts around jetties and beaches. In the summer breeding season, it migrates to woodlands near lakes and rivers in the north. Its nest is a hollow in dense vegetation or among rocks, lined with grass and down and holding 8-10 olive-buff eggs. The female incubates these for 28-35 days and the chicks leave the nest soon after hatching and begin to fly at about 8 weeks. The male has gray sides, a white collar, dark red breast, black back and green head with shaggy crest. The female (*right*) is gray with a whitish throat that blends into a pale rusty-red head. The Common Merganser flies very fast and low over the water and the adult male shows a white patch at the top of the upper wing, crossed with two black bars. This species eats mainly small fish, but also aquatic invertebrates, small frogs, and newts.

TURKEY VULTURE

Scientific name: *Cathartes aura*
Length: 27 inches, wingspan 67 inches
Habitat: Open country, woodlands, farms
Identification: Large carrion-feeder. Black-gray plumage, gray edging to wings, bare red head, yellow feet. In flight, has long wings, glides with wings held in a shallow V
Similar species: Black Vulture has gray head, short tail, black wings tipped in white, flies in short glides with wings held flat, punctuated with several rapid flaps. Juvenile Turkey Vulture has gray head, but long tail and flight pattern are distinctive

The Turkey Vulture is much more widespread than the Black Vulture, being found as far north as southern Canada. It glides all day over open country, looking for food which it finds by scent. It often roosts in flocks, and many birds will converge to feed at a carcass. It prefers the meat to be quite ripe, which makes it easier to strip off the bones - hence its bare head, as feeding can become quite messy. It does not build a nest, but lays 1-3 red-brown blotched, whitish eggs on bare ground, or in an old building, cave or hollow log. The eggs are incubated by both parents, which takes around 40 days. The young do not leave until around 11 weeks after hatching. The plumage of the adult bird is black-gray, with a naked red face, a long tail and yellow feet. In flight, it has long gray wings with gray along the trailing edge; it glides for hours with its wings held in a shallow V - in the right conditions it rarely has to flap its wings to stay aloft. The juvenile bird has a darker head and bill and paler feet, and could be mistaken for a Black Vulture except for its long tail and different flight pattern.

BLACK VULTURE

Scientific name:	*Coragyps atratus*
Length:	25 inches, wingspan 59 inches
Habitat:	Open country, urban areas
Identification:	Stocky carrion-feeder. Black plumage, white patch near wing tips, large dark gray head, white feet. In flight, has broad wings, takes short glides with wings held flat, punctuated with several rapid flaps
Similar species:	Turkey Vulture has red head, long tail, long black wings edged in gray, small head, soars with wings held in a shallow V

New World vultures are now considered to be related to storks, but they look like birds of prey. The Black Vulture is very common all year round in much of the south, but is rarely seen further north. It soars for hours hunting for food - often in groups - and when one bird spots carrion they all converge on it. It sometimes steals from the Turkey Vulture, which is much more efficient at scenting food. In the tropics, the Black Vulture is often seen around cities and towns, where it performs a useful function by cleaning away carrion and garbage. It does not build a nest, but lays 1-2 blotchy, whitish eggs on bare ground, or sheltered under a rock, on a ledge or in a cave. Incubation takes around 40 days but the young do not leave until 10-11 weeks later. The plumage of the adult bird is black, with a black face and dark feathered cap, a short tail and white feet. In flight, it has broad gray wings with a white patch near the wing tips; it flies in short glides with its wings held flat, punctuated with several rapid flaps.

NORTHERN HARRIER

Scientific name:	*Circus cyaneus*
Length:	18 inches, wingspan 44 inches
Habitat:	Wetlands, marshes, open fields
Identification:	Long-winged, long-tailed hawk. Male light gray above, white rump, white beneath with reddish spots; in flight black wing tips, barred tail. Female brown above, white rump, brown streaks below
Similar species:	Shape and coloring make this species distinctive

A long-winged, long-tailed hawk, the Northern Harrier is common across much of North America, spending summer in the north, then migrating south in winter. It prefers wetlands and open fields, and was previously known as the Marsh Hawk. Its nest is a platform of grass and reeds on the ground in marshes, and holds 4-6 white eggs that are incubated by the female for around 32 days. The chicks stay in the nest for up to 5 weeks; during this time the male bird brings food but they are fed by the female. The Northern Harrier is a slim bird, with an owl-like face. The male is light gray above with a white rump, and white beneath with chestnut-brown spots; in flight it shows black wing tips and a barred tail. The female (*right*) is brown above with a white rump, and whitish below with heavy brown streaks. Juveniles are similar to the female, but are cinnamon-brown below. Harriers are usually seen flying low and gliding with their wings raised in a shallow V, as they hunt for small birds, rodents, frogs and reptiles. They rarely soar, except when migrating or during their acrobatic courtship display.

COOPER'S HAWK

Scientific name:	*Accipiter cooperii*
Length:	14-20 inches, wingspan 28-34 inches
Habitat:	Broken woodlands, groves, telephone poles
Identification:	Short-winged, long-tailed hawk. Rounded, barred tail, blue-gray plumage above, white below with rusty barring. Female is similar, but larger
Similar species:	Coloring similar to Sharp-shinned Hawk, but Cooper's is larger with a longer, rounded tail and thicker legs

Cooper's Hawk is very similar in coloring to the Sharp-shinned, although is quite a bit larger. It shares much the same range, but is usually found in open woods and in streamside groves. Its nest is a platform of sticks and twigs, lined with bark, generally 10-60 feet above ground in a woodland tree. It lays 3-5 bluish-white eggs which are incubated for about 24 days, mainly by the female. The young are fed by the female, but the male hunts for food and brings it to her; the chicks leave the nest around 1 month after hatching. Cooper's Hawk has a long, rounded, barred tail, and a relatively large head. Its plumage is blue-gray above with a strongly contrasting darker cap, and white below with heavy rusty barring. The female is very similar in coloring, but is larger than the male. The juvenile is brown above, and whitish below, either streaked with brown or with reddish-brown spotting. Although it is normally spotted flying low over woods to hunt small birds and mammals, Cooper's Hawk can also be seen perching on telephone poles in open country.

SHARP-SHINNED HAWK

Scientific name:	*Accipiter striatus*
Length:	9-14 inches, wingspan 20-28 inches
Habitat:	Dense woodland
Identification:	Short-winged, long-tailed hawk. Square, barred tail, often notched, blue-gray plumage above, white below with rusty barring. Female is similar, but larger
Similar species:	Coloring similar to Cooper's Hawk, but Sharp-shinned is smaller with a shorter, squarer tail and thin legs

The Sharp-shinned Hawk is the smallest of the North American accipiters - a family of hawks distinguished by short, broad wings that are adapted for fast flight in wooded country. It is fairly common over much of its range, particularly in the east, and is usually found in mixed woods and forests. Its nest is a platform of sticks and twigs, generally 10-60 feet above ground in a dense conifer or other woodland tree. It lays 4-5 bluish, spotted eggs which are incubated for about 35 days by both adult birds; the young leave the nest around 2 months after they have hatched. The Sharp-shinned has a square, barred tail, which often looks notched, a relatively small head and a short neck, and very thin legs. Its plumage is blue-gray above, and white below with heavy rusty barring. The female is very similar in coloring, but is larger than the male. The juvenile is brown above, and whitish below, either streaked with brown or with reddish-brown spotting. Although it normally hunts small birds, rodents and insects in thick woodland, the Sharp-shinned Hawk will also come into the suburbs to take small birds near feeders.

NORTHERN GOSHAWK

Scientific name: *Accipiter gentilis*
Length: 18-26 inches, wingspan 38-46 inches
Habitat: Thick coniferous and mixed forests
Identification: Short-winged, long-tailed hawk. Wedge-shaped tail, blue-gray plumage above, white below with fine gray barring, white eyebrow below dark crown. Female is similar, but has coarser barring and is larger
Similar species: Adults can be mistaken for Gyrfalcon, but lack yellow eye ring and have black crown, juvenile is browner and can resemble Red-shouldered Hawk

The largest of the accipiters, the Northern Goshawk is similar in coloring to both the Sharp-shinned and Cooper's hawks. It is less common than either and has a smaller range, being found in deep woodlands in northern areas and rarely venturing south. Its nest is a bulky mass of sticks and twigs, up to 60 feet above ground in a tree. It lays 2-5 pale blue eggs which are incubated for 36-38 days, by the female. The male hunts for food and brings it to the female, who feeds the young; the chicks leave the nest around 45 days after hatching. Although the typical accipiter shape, the Northern Goshawk has a shorter, wedge-shaped tail, and longer wings than the other two species. Its plumage is blue-gray above, with a bold white eyebrow contrasting against a darker cap, and white beneath with fine gray barring. The female is very similar in coloring, but has coarser barring and is larger than the male. The juvenile is brown above, and buff below, with thick black-brown streaks. The Northern Goshawk hunts birds, ducks and mammals as large as a hare, but tends to lurk in dense cover to ambush its prey.

WHITE-TAILED KITE *(below)*

Scientific name:	*Elanus leucurus*
Length:	16 inches, wingspan 42 inches
Habitat:	Grasslands, farmland
Identification:	Medium-sized long-winged, long-tailed kite. White on head and below, dark gray back and mostly white tail, red eyes
Similar species:	Mississippi Kite is very similar, but is darker gray and lacks white tail

The White-tailed Kite is fairly common within its range in the far south of North America, particularly in California and Texas. Stray birds wander much farther afield, being seen as far north as British Columbia and Wyoming. It prefers grassland and farmland, but is also often seen along open highways. Unlike the Swallow-tailed and Mississippi kites, it does not migrate and may form winter roosts of several hundred birds. Its nest is of twigs lined with grass, well concealed high above the ground in a tree. The 3-5 brown-blotched white eggs are incubated for around 28 days and the young chicks stay in the nest for around 6 weeks. The adult bird has long, pointed wings and a long tail. Its plumage is mainly gray above, with black shoulders, white below, much white in the tail and large red eyes. In flight, the black of the shoulders can be seen on the leading edge of the inner wing; the remainder of the wing is gray above and gray and white below, with a distinctive black patch just behind the bend. The juvenile bird is very similar to the adult, but may be more buff on the chest and upper back. The White-tailed Kite is unusual in that it hovers on rapidly beating wings before dropping to catch its prey, unlike other North American kites. It mainly eats mice, but also takes insects and small reptiles.

MISSISSIPPI KITE

Scientific name:	*Ictinia mississippiensis*
Length:	14½ inches, wingspan 35 inches
Habitat:	Woodlands, swamps
Identification:	Small long-winged, long-tailed kite. Pale gray head and below, dark gray back and black tail, red eyes
Similar species:	White-tailed Kite is very similar, but is lighter gray and has white tail. In flight, the White-tailed Kite hovers when hunting but the Mississippi never does. Can be confused with Peregrine Falcon, but has different wing and tail shape

Unlike the White-tailed Kite, the Mississippi favors woodlands and swamps rather than open grassland. It is fairly common in the southeast, but odd birds can stray as far as the Great Lakes and California. It is mainly seen in spring and summer in North America, often hunting in flocks; in fall it migrates down to South America to spend the winter. Its nest is a large mass of twigs, from 4-100 feet above the ground in a shrub or a tall tree. The 1-3 bluish eggs are incubated for around 32 days by both birds and the young chicks stay in the nest for around 32 days after hatching. The adult birds have long, pointed wings and a long, flared tail. Their plumage is mainly dark gray above, with paler gray below and on the head, a black tail and large red eyes. In flight, whitish patches show on the upper side of the inner wing. The juvenile bird is mainly buff heavily streaked with brown, with pale whitish bars across its tail. The Mississippi Kite catches and eats its prey on the wing - it is totally at home in the air, gliding and diving gracefully like the Swallow-tailed Kite. It mainly eats insects, but will also sometimes take small snakes and frogs.

SWALLOW-TAILED KITE

Scientific name:	*Elanoides forficatus*
Length:	23 inches, wingspan 48 inches
Habitat:	Open woods, wetlands
Identification:	Large long-winged, long-tailed kite. White plumage with black back and deeply forked tail
Similar species:	Forked tail and coloring make it almost unmistakeable in flight - juvenile Magnificent Frigatebirds are much bigger and generally have less white. Black and white coloring is much sharper than coloring of White-tailed and Mississippi kites

Athough the Swallow-tailed Kite is normally limited to Florida and surrounding areas, it does stray further on occasion and has been seen as far north as Ontario and Nova Scotia and as far west as Arizona. Once its range was much larger, but the destruction of its favored habitat by farming has led it to retreat to the swampier areas in the south. It is usually seen during the summer months, since most birds spend the winter in the South American tropics. Its 2-4 red-blotched white eggs are laid in a shallow cup of twigs, built 50-100 feet above the ground in a tree near water and several pairs may nest near each other. The eggs are incubated by both parent birds for about 28 days and the young chicks stay in the nest for around 5-6 weeks. The adult birds have long, pointed wings and a long, deeply forked tail. Their plumage is mainly white, sharply defined against the black back and tail. In flight, the wings are white on the leading edge and black behind. The juvenile bird is very similar to the adult, but may have more white on wings and tail, and the tail is much shorter. The Swallow-tailed Kite is supremely agile and graceful in flight, swooping to catch large insects on the wing and dropping to pick up small snakes, frogs and lizards. It often eats its prey while still flying, and drinks by skimming the surface of the water.

RED-TAILED HAWK

Scientific name:	*Buteo jamaicensis*
Length:	22 inches, wingspan 50 inches
Habitat:	Woods, plains, prairie
Identification:	Large broad-winged, short-tailed hawk. Usually dark brown back with pale mottling, white underneath with belly band of dark streaks, but color varies according to range. Most adults have reddish tail above, whitish beneath, heavy bill
Similar species:	Swainson's Hawk has no pale mottling on back and a smaller bill. Rough-legged Hawk has long white tail

One of the most common American hawks, the Red-tailed is seen across much of North America and in summer up into Canada. It can be spotted soaring over open country, particularly if there are nearby woods offering seclusion for nesting. It builds a large and solid nest, up to 75 feet above ground in a tree or on a cliff, with a small cup in the center lined with fine green shoots. This contains 1-4 whitish eggs, which are incubated for 27-33 days; the chicks stay in the nest for up to 5 weeks after hatching. The coloring of the adult bird varies according to its range, but the differences are not substantial. It usually has a dark brown back with V-shaped lines of pale mottling, and is white underneath with distinctive belly band of dark streaks. The bill is quite heavy and the tail is reddish above and whitish beneath. A variety known as "Harlan's Hawk" is much darker on the body and has a whitish tail with dark marbling. Juvenile birds have a gray-brown tail with dark bars. The Red-tailed Hawk sits for hours on a telegraph pole or fence post, before gliding off to catch its prey; it mainly eats rodents, which makes it very popular with farmers.

FERRUGINOUS HAWK

Scientific name:	*Buteo regalis*
Length:	23 inches, wingspan 53 inches
Habitat:	Dry open country, grasslands
Identification:	Large hawk with broad, pointed wings. Rusty-brown back and leg feathers, whitish underneath, whitish tail with rusty-brown tip. Also dark version, with dark red-brown plumage, whitish under tail and on trailing edge of wings
Similar species:	Dark version can be confused with dark Rough-legged Hawk, but has no dark tail band

The Ferruginous Hawk is the largest of the buteo family and is usually seen across western grasslands and dry open country. It perches in trees, on poles or on the ground in open fields. Its nest is built of sticks, roots, twigs and even old cattle bones, usually at the top of a tree, but failing that on a cliff ledge, bush or hillside. It often returns to the same nest year after year, adding to the construction until it is many feet high. The nest usually contains 3-5 blotched or spotted eggs, which are incubated for around 29 days by both birds; the chicks stay in the nest for up to 7 weeks after hatching. The Ferruginous has a wide head, broad wings tapering towards the ends and feathered legs. It has a pale head, rusty-brown back, shoulders and leg feathers, whitish underneath, and a whitish tail with a rusty-brown tip. In flight, wings are held in a shallow V when soaring and it shows a white crescent-shaped patch on the upper wing. The darker version is quite rare; it has dark red-brown plumage, and is whitish under the tail and on trailing edge of the wings. The juvenile bird is much less rusty-colored and its leg feathers are whitish. The Ferruginous Hawk hovers when hunting; it mainly eats rodents, rabbits and hares.

ROUGH-LEGGED HAWK

Scientific name:	*Buteo lagopus*
Length:	22 inches, wingspan 56 inches
Habitat:	Open country, marshes
Identification:	Large hawk, long white tail with dark tail bands. Pale head, chest and leg feathers with dark streaks, brown back, whitish underneath with dark belly band. Also dark version, with dark brown plumage, whitish under tail with dark bands, white tipped with black on trailing edge of wings
Similar species:	Dark version can be confused with dark Ferruginous Hawk, but has dark tail bands

A bird that prefers the cold, the Rough-legged Hawk spends the summer in the Arctic, moving south to the farmland and prairies of central North America in the winter. It breeds on tundra, building a nest of twigs and moss on a cliff ledge. It lays 2-6 greenish, brown-blotched eggs, which are incubated for around 29 days; the chicks stay in the nest for up to 6 weeks after hatching. The plumage of the adult bird can be quite variable, but it generally has a pale head, chest and leg feathers with dark streaks, a brown back, is whitish underneath with darker belly band, and has a long white tail with dark tail bands. In flight, it shows a square black patch on the underside of the wing and a white patch on the upper side. The darker version is very rare; it has dark brown plumage, the tail is whitish underneath with dark bands, and the underside of the wings is white tipped with black on the trailing edge. The juvenile bird has a stronger dark belly band and a single dark-brown tail band. The Rough-legged Hawk hovers on rapidly beating wings when hunting; it eats lemmings and ptarmigans in the Arctic and rodents and small birds further south.

RED-SHOULDERED HAWK

Scientific name:	*Buteo lineatus*
Length:	17 inches, wingspan 40 inches
Habitat:	Mixed woodland near water
Identification:	Small, long-tailed, long-legged woodland hawk. Rusty-red shoulder patch, body and underwing, black and white bands on tail and wings
Similar species:	Juvenile can be confused with juvenile Broad-winged Hawk, but is larger

A forest bird, the Red-shouldered Hawk is fairly common in Florida and California, and is often seen in the southeast although it is rare elsewhere. Its nest is a large, flat construction of twigs and sticks, built high up in a tall woodland tree near moving water. It comes back to the same nest year after year, freshly decorating the construction with green sprigs after moving back in. It lays 2-5 whitish eggs, which are incubated for around 28 days by both parents; the chicks stay in the nest for 5-6 weeks after hatching. The adult has long wings and tail. Its plumage is quite variable depending on its range, but it generally has a rusty-red shoulder patch, body and underwing, and extensive whitish spotting on the back. In flight, it shows black and white bands on tail and wings and a translucent area near the wing tip. West coast birds tend to be redder, while east coast birds are paler. The juvenile bird is browner with less apparent red. The Red-shouldered Hawk flies with several quick wingbeats followed by a glide and defends its territory at nesting time by soaring in spectacular displays. It eats reptiles, small birds and mammals, frogs and crayfish.

SWAINSON'S HAWK

Scientific name:	*Buteo swainsoni*
Length:	21 inches, wingspan 52 inches
Habitat:	Open plains, prairie
Identification:	Slim hawk with long, narrow, pointed wings. Usually dark brown back, white underneath, dark chest, but color varies. Most adults have white wing lining and dark flight feathers, small head and bill
Similar species:	Red-tailed Hawk has pale mottling on back and a heavier bill. Rough-legged Hawk has long white tail

Swainson's Hawk is only seen in North America in the summer, with most birds migrating to South America for the winter. It can be spotted over western grassland and farmland, or migrating south in large flocks. Its nest is of sticks, built on bare ground, in a tree, bush or cactus, or on a cliff ledge; it is often renovated and reused each year. It contains 2-4 bluish or white eggs, which are incubated for around 28 days by both parent birds; the chicks stay in the nest for up to 4 weeks after hatching. The adult bird is slim-bodied, with a small head and bill, long, narrow, pointed wings and a relatively long tail, but its coloring varies considerably. It typically has a dark brown back, and is white underneath with a darker chest. In flight, white wing linings contrast with dark flight feathers; when soaring the wings are held slightly above horizontal. The wings extend past the tip of the tail when the bird is perched. Darker versions can be uniformly dark brown, some are rusty-red beneath or have strong barring. Juvenile birds have variable streaking and strong markings on the face. Groups of Swainson's Hawk often follow tractors on the ground during harvesting, picking up the rodents and large insects that otherwise would eat the crop - which makes it very popular with farmers.

BROAD-WINGED HAWK

Scientific name: *Buteo platypterus*
Length: 16 inches, wingspan 34 inches
Habitat: Woodland
Identification: Small short-tailed hawk with broad, pointed wings. Dark back, reddish chest, white streaked with red-brown below, broad black and white bands on tail, white underwings with dark borders
Similar species: Juvenile can be confused with juvenile Red-shouldered Hawk, but has a plainer breast and less marking on the back

Another woodland species, the Broad-winged Hawk is seen only during the summer in the eastern half of North America, with most birds migrating to South America early in the fall. It is a social bird, often seen in large flocks. Its nest is a mass of twigs and sticks, built up to 50 feet above the ground in a tall woodland tree. It lays 2-3 brown-and-purple-splashed white eggs, which are incubated for around 28 days by both parents; the chicks stay in the nest for 5-6 weeks after hatching. The adult has broad, pointed wings and a rather short, broad tail. Its plumage is plainer than some other hawks, with a dark back, reddish chest, white barred with red-brown below, and broad black and white bands on the tail. In flight, it shows white underwings with dark borders. The juvenile bird typically has a black streak below the cheeks and less distinct tail bands. The Broad-winged Hawk flies with slower wing beats than many other hawks, soaring with wings held flat. It migrates in very large flocks - often consisting of thousands of birds. When hunting, it sits on a favorite perch near water, watching and waiting, until it suddenly moves swiftly to catch a frog, snake or crayfish.

ZONE-TAILED HAWK

Scientific name:	*Buteo albonotatus*
Length:	20 inches, wingspan 51 inches
Habitat:	Mountains, woodlands, rivers
Identification:	High-soaring hawk. Gray-black plumage, large feathered head, white bands on tail, yellow legs, feet and base of bill. In flight, has barring under wings, soars with wings held in a shallow V
Similar species:	Turkey Vulture is almost identical in flight, but has no white tail bands and a naked red face

Although rather uncommon, the Zone-tailed Hawk spends the summer in the southeast and can be found in wooded canyons, desert mountain country and near forest watercourses. In flight, it closely resembles the Turkey Vulture, which is much more widespread and common. Its nest is a platform of sticks and green branches in a tall tree or on a cliff - often enlarged and used year after year - which holds 2-3 blotched white eggs. The adult bird has a large feathered head, a small bill and quite slim wings. Its plumage is gray-black overall, with white bands on the tail, and yellow legs, feet and base of bill. In flight, it shows barring under the wings, and soars high up with wings held in a shallow V. The juvenile bird often has less obvious tail bands and may have white spots or flecks on its black breast. When hunting, the Zone-tailed Hawk glides slowly and drops to catch small birds, rodents, lizards and fish. Some believe that its resemblance to the Turkey Vulture allows it to approach its prey much closer, since other birds and animals do not fear a carrion-eater.

OSPREY *(above)*

Scientific name:	*Pandion haliaetus*
Length:	23 inches, wingspan 63 inches
Habitat:	Coastal areas
Identification:	Large hawk. Long narrow wings, plumage dark brown above, white below, white head with dark eye stripe
Similar species:	Flying birds may be confused with gulls, but shape and coloring are distinctive

Sometimes known as the "fish hawk" or "fish eagle", the Osprey is fairly common in coastal areas and is sometimes seen along rivers and over inland lakes. It was once threatened by the use of DDT, but since this and other pesticides have been banned, populations have recovered. Its nest is a large construction of sticks in a tall tree, rock pinnacle or any tall structure near water, and is reused year after year. It holds 2-4 buffy eggs, blotched with brown, which are usually incubated by the female for around a month. The young are downy white, and leave the nest around 2 months after hatching. The adult bird has long narrow wings, held above horizontal and slightly arched in flight, with a distinct bend at the wrist. Its plumage is dark brown above and white below, with a white head and a dark eye stripe. The female bird may have some darker streaking on the neck. The juvenile is similar coloring but has white scaling on its back. Unlike other hawks, the Osprey feeds almost exclusively on fish, which it catches by soaring over the water and diving, talons first.

HARRIS'S HAWK *(above)*

Scientific name:	*Parabuteo unicinctus*
Length:	21 inches, wingspan 46 inches
Habitat:	Desert, arid woodland, brushland
Identification:	Medium-size, slim hawk. Black-brown plumage, rust-red shoulders, thighs and wing linings, black tail with white base and tip
Similar species:	No other hawk has the same coloring

Harris's Hawk is a very striking bird, which is seen all year round in America in the desert and brush of southern Texas and Arizona - although its full range extends down through Mexico and into South America. It is often seen in family groups after the breeding season has finished and several birds will hunt in small cooperative flocks during the winter. Its nest is a small platform of sticks and twigs in a low desert tree, or in a yucca or saguaro cactus, which holds 3-5 whitish eggs. Incubation takes around 34 days, by the female bird, but during this time and after the chicks have hatched the male bird keeps the whole family supplied with food - sometimes helped by a second male. The adult bird has mainly dark chocolate black-brown plumage, with rust-red shoulders, thighs and wing linings, and a black tail with white base and tip. Both adults have the same coloring, but the male bird is smaller than the female. The juvenile bird is heavily streaked brown beneath, with much less distinct shoulder patches and narrow tail bands. Harris's Hawk mainly eats small mammals, but will also take birds and reptiles.

GOLDEN EAGLE

Scientific name:	*Aquila chrysaetos*
Length:	30 inches, wingspan 80 inches
Habitat:	Mountains, plains, open country
Identification:	Large bird of prey. Dark brown plumage overall, with golden nape
Similar species:	Adult is unmistakable, juvenile may be mistaken for juvenile Bald Eagle but has smaller head, longer tail and defined white markings under wings and on tail

The majestic Golden Eagle is a solitary bird, sometimes seen in pairs but rarely gathering in groups. It prefers wilderness areas away from humans and is fairly numerous in the west but not so often seen in the east. Its eyrie is a large mass of sticks in a tall tree or on a cliff, and a pair may alternate between several sites in different years. The 2 whitish, brown-blotched eggs are incubated by both parents for up to 44 days, and the chicks leave the nest around 10 weeks after hatching. The adult bird has dark brown plumage overall, with a golden nape, feathered legs and faint bands on the tail. Juveniles are dark brown but have a clearly-defined white wing patch and white tail with a black band at the tip; it takes four years for them to reach full adult plumage. The Golden Eagle soars with long, broad wings held flat or slightly uplifted. Despite rumors of them taking lambs, they rarely do; they normally feed on small mammals such as rabbits, birds, snakes and carrion - although they are quite capable of taking animals the size of a deer.

BALD EAGLE

Scientific name:	*Haliaeetus leucocephalus*
Length:	31 inches, wingspan 80 inches
Habitat:	Rivers, lakes, coastal areas
Identification:	Large bird of prey. White head, neck and tail, brown-black body, yellow bill
Similar species:	Adult is unmistakable, juvenile may be mistaken for juvenile Golden Eagle but has larger head, shorter tail and blotchy, less defined patterning under wings and on tail

The magnificent Bald Eagle has been the national symbol of the United States since 1782. It is seen across much of North America - particularly near water - but is common in Alaska, parts of Florida and during the winter in the midwest. It was endangered in the 1970s, but conservation programs and the banning of pesticides have led to a gradual comeback in many areas. Its eyrie is a large pile of sticks up to 150 feet above the ground, usually in a tall tree near water, and it is renovated and added to every year - increasing in size until either its own weight or a winter storm brings it down. The 1-3 dull, whitish eggs are incubated by both parents for up to 35 days, and the chicks leave the nest around 10 weeks after they have hatched. The adult bird has a pure white head, neck and tail, a brown-black body, and a large yellow bill. Juveniles are mostly dark brown, except for blotchy white underneath and on the wing linings, but achieve a little more white at each molt, taking four to five years to reach the full adult plumage. Although it is a very skilled hunter, the Bald Eagle often eats carrion or will steal fish from the smaller and weaker Osprey. Large numbers of Bald Eagles will often congregate where pickings are easy - particularly at spawning runs.

CRESTED CARACARA

Scientific name:	*Caracara plancus*
Length:	23 inches, wingspan 50 inches
Habitat:	Open savannah, desert
Identification:	Tropical long-necked, long-legged falcon. Black-brown body and crested cap, whitish throat and chest, bare red-orange facial skin, barred underparts, white tail and wing patch with black near tip
Similar species:	Coloring and shape make it unmistakable

Called the "Mexican Eagle" and appearing on the flag of Mexico, the Crested Caracara is a tropical bird that only comes as far north as Texas, parts of Florida and occasionally Louisiana and southern Arizona - although escaped cage birds are sometimes seen in other areas. Its nest is a bulky affair of sticks, built far off the ground in a tree, palmetto or cactus. It holds 2-4 pinky-brown eggs with darker blotches, which are incubated for around 28 days. The adult bird has a large head, long neck, and long legs. Its plumage is mainly black-brown, with a black crested cap, bare red-orange facial skin, a white throat and chest, barred underparts and white tail and wing patches tipped in dark brown. The juvenile has paler facial skin, is much browner overall and has whitish spots and streaks on the wings. The Caracara soars with flat wings and hunts insects and small animals, although it chiefly feeds on carrion and is often seen on the ground with vultures.

AMERICAN KESTREL

Scientific name:	*Falco sparverius*
Length:	10½ inches, wingspan 23 inches
Habitat:	Open country, deserts, urban areas
Identification:	Small long-tailed falcon. Russet crown, back and tail, double black stripes on white face, hooked bill. Male has blue-gray wings, buff breast and white underparts with dark spots
Similar species:	Male is similar to male Merlin, but russet back and tail are distinctive

The smallest and most common American falcon, the American Kestrel is found in open country and in cities across the country - although birds in the far north migrate south for the winter. It was formerly known as the "Sparrow Hawk". It does not build a nest, but lays 3-6 buffy-pink to grayish-white eggs in a tree hole, crevice of a building or an old magpie nest. The eggs are incubated for around 30 days, mainly by the female although the male may also help, and the chicks are ready to leave the nest around one month after hatching. About the size of a jay, the American Kestrel has a hooked bill, a russet crown, back and tail, and double black stripes on a white face. The male has blue-gray wings and on its head, a buff breast and nape and white underparts with dark spots. In flight, both adult birds have pale underwings and the male has a row of circular white spots on the trailing edge of its wings. When hunting, the Kestrel either hovers over the ground or sits on a convenient tree or telephone wire, plunging to catch mice, insects and, in winter, small birds.

MERLIN

Scientific name:	*Falco columbarius*
Length:	12 inches, wingspan 25 inches
Habitat:	Open woods, wooded prairie, towns
Identification:	Small compact falcon. Male blue-gray above, buff with light brown streaks below, black tail bands. Female and juvenile brown above with buff tail bands
Similar species:	Male similar to male American Kestrel, but lacks russet back and tail and has broader wings. Peregrine and Prairie falcons are much larger and lack tail bands

A small, stocky falcon, the Merlin is found in open country across North America, spending summer in the north and migrating south in the winter - although some birds in central areas stay all year round. The Merlin does not build a nest, but lays 3-6 rust-colored, dark spotted eggs in a tree hole, on the ground or in another bird's abandoned nest. The eggs are incubated for around 30 days, by both female and male, and the chicks are ready to leave the nest just under a month after hatching. The male generally has blue-gray plumage above, buff with light brown streaks below, and strong black tail bands. The female (*right*) and juvenile birds are dark brown above with buff tail bands. Adult birds have yellow skin at the base of the bill and round the eyes, juvenile has blue. There are regional variations, ranging from very dark birds in the northwest to pale birds in the north. When hunting, the Merlin does not hover but flies low with a steady wingbeat and catches small birds in midair with a sudden burst of speed. It also eats large insects and small rodents.

GYRFALCON

Scientific name:	*Falco rusticolus*
Length:	22 inches, wingspan 47 inches
Habitat:	Tundra near rocky outcrops, river cliffs
Identification:	Large broad-winged long-tailed falcon. Plumage varies, but adult generally dark gray above, lighter gray beneath, with yellow-orange eye ring and base of bill
Similar species:	Can be confused with Prairie Falcon, but lacks black wing patches, also with the Peregrine Falcon but lacks black helmet. Similar to Northern Goshawk in some color variations, but lacks white flaring eyebrow

The largest of the falcons, the Gyrfalcon was prized by medieval falconers and was reserved for royalty. It is found in the far north, breeding on cliffs along Arctic rivers and only seen further south in winter, along the coast or in open country. Like many other falcons, the Gyrfalcon does not usually build a nest, but lays 3-8 creamy, red-spotted eggs in a scrape on a cliff ledge, or in the abandoned nest of another bird. The eggs are incubated for around a month, mainly by the female bird, and the chicks first fly around 7 weeks after hatching. The adult bird is stocky and powerful, with broad wings and a relatively long, tapered tail that extends far beyond the tip of its wings when it is perched. It has a yellow-orange eye ring, base to the bill and legs; its plumage is generally dark gray above, lighter gray beneath, sometimes with darker barring. There are variations, ranging from very dark birds to almost white. The juvenile is very similar to the adult, but has bluish-gray legs. When hunting, the Gyrfalcon flies fast but with slow wingbeats and catches birds, especially ptarmigan, and small mammals.

PRAIRIE FALCON

Scientific name:	*Falco mexicanus*
Length:	17½ inches, wingspan 40 inches
Habitat:	Dry grassland, desert, prairie
Identification:	Large long-tailed falcon. Adult sandy-brown above with pale barring, white patch behind eye, creamy below with darker spotting. In flight shows long dark patch under wing
Similar species:	Peregrine Falcon can be similar coloring but has distinctive black helmet. Also resembles female and juvenile Merlin, but is larger and lacks strongly marked tail bands

A similar size and shape to the Peregrine Falcon, the Prairie Falcon is much more common and is found over grassland and dry country in the west of America throughout the year. It rarely builds its own nest, laying 3-6 reddish, dark-spotted eggs on a ledge or in the old nest of another bird. The eggs are incubated for around a month and the chicks fly about 6 weeks after hatching. The adult bird is slim and powerful, with quite a long tail; it extends well past the tip of its wings when the bird is perched. The adult is sandy-brown above with pale barring, has a white patch behind the eye, and is creamy below with fine spots. The juvenile is darker, with less contrast, and has heavier streaking underneath. In flight, all birds show a distinctive long dark patch under the wings. When hunting, the Prairie Falcon does not dive from the sky but pursues its prey flying fast and low over the ground, twisting and turning and outmaneuvering ground squirrels, birds and rodents.

PEREGRINE FALCON

Scientific name: *Falco peregrinus*
Length: 17 inches, wingspan 41 inches
Habitat: Open wetlands, cliffs, cities
Identification: Large short-tailed falcon. Male slate-gray above, black on head like helmet, whitish neck, buff beneath, lightly barred breast. Female browner, juvenile dark buff with heavy streaking underneath
Similar species: Prairie Falcon and smaller Merlin can be similar coloring but lack the distinctive black helmet

The Peregrine Falcon was once found across North America, but DDT and other pesticides helped eliminate the eastern population and brought it close to extinction. The banning of such pesticides has led to a slow recovery and captive-breeding programs have reintroduced birds to some areas. The Peregrine does not build a nest, but lays 2-4 reddish, darker flecked eggs in a hollow on a cliff, bare rocky outcrop or on the ledges of tall city buildings. The eggs are incubated for around 28 days, by both female and male, and the chicks are ready to leave 5-6 weeks after hatching. The adult bird is sleek and powerful, with pointed wings and a short tail; the tip of its wings almost reach the end of the tail when it is perched. The male is slate-gray above, with a black crown and nape that extends forward on the head like a helmet, a whitish neck, and is buff beneath with a lightly barred breast. The female is browner and the juvenile dark buff with heavy streaking underneath. There are regional variations, ranging from very dark birds in the northwest to pale birds in the north. When hunting, the Peregrine Falcon flies very fast and makes dramatic swoops to catch small birds in midair, so it is sought after by falconers in the northern continents. It also eats large insects and small mammals.

GRAY PARTRIDGE

Scientific name:	*Perdix perdix*
Length:	12½ inches
Habitat:	Open farmland, grassy fields
Identification:	Ground-dwelling bird. Gray-brown plumage with reddish barring on flanks, red-orange face and throat. Male has chestnut patch on belly
Similar species:	Similar size and shape to Chukar, but different coloring

Brought from the Old World in the 19th century and released in America as a game bird, the Gray Partridge has spread across central North America and is very common in some areas. It prefers open grassy fields, where it tends to walk on the ground in pairs or small groups known as coveys, hidden in the grass. Its nest is a shallow depression in the earth, lined with leaves and grass and hidden under vegetation, in which it lays up to 16 olive-colored eggs. The female incubates them for around 26 days helped by the male, and the chicks leave the nest straight after hatching but cannot fly until around 2-3 weeks later. They stay with the female until the following spring. The adult has mainly gray-brown plumage, with reddish barring on the flanks and a red-orange face and throat, which is paler in the female. The male has a chestnut patch on its belly, but in the female this is much smaller or missing entirely. In flight, orange-red feathers can be seen on the outer edges of the short tail. The Gray Partridge forages for grain and other seeds on the ground and seldom flies far when flushed. It can survive on bare stubble, but huddles with others for warmth when snowy weather arrives.

CHUKAR

Scientific name:	*Alectoris chukar*
Length:	14 inches
Habitat:	Rocky arid mountains
Identification:	Ground-dwelling bird. Gray-brown plumage with black and white barring on flanks, pale buff face and throat outlined in black, gray breast, buff belly, red bill and legs
Similar species:	Similar size and shape to Gray Partridge, but different coloring

The Chukar is native to Asia and the Middle East, but was released in America as a game bird and has successfully established itself in dry rocky canyons in the west. It lives in groups of 5-40 birds known as coveys, and wild birds are very elusive - although game farm birds are released in the east for hunting. Its nest is a shallow depression in the earth, lined with feathers and grass and hidden among rocks, in which it lays 10-15 buffy-white, brown-spotted eggs. The female incubates them for around 25 days helped by the male, and the chicks leave the nest straight after hatching but cannot fly until about 2 weeks later. Families often come together in large groups in late summer. Both adult birds have gray-brown plumage above, black and white barring on the flanks, a pale buff face and throat outlined in black, a gray breast, and a buff belly. The bill and legs are red, and in flight red-orange feathers can be seen on the outer edges of the short tail. The male is larger and has small spurs on the leg. The juvenile lacks the distinctive marking of the adult and is small and mottled. The Chukar mainly eats seeds, grasshoppers and foliage.

SHARP-TAILED GROUSE

Scientific name:	*Tympanuchus phasianellus*
Length:	17 inches
Habitat:	Grasslands, sagebrush, woodland edges
Identification:	Large ground-dwelling bird, sharp pointed tail. Brown mottled plumage above, lighter beneath with darker scaling, mostly white tail, yellow above eye. Male has purple neck sacs to inflate in display
Similar species:	Sage Grouse is much larger with black belly. Female very like female Ring-necked Pheasant, but is smaller, with shorter tail and barring beneath

Although a ground-dwelling bird throughout much of the year, in colder weather the Sharp-tailed Grouse takes to the trees. It is fairly common across much of its range, and in spring large groups of males gather on traditional display grounds or leks to perform a courtship dance, strutting and bobbing and inflating purple neck sacs. The female then lays 10-12 buff eggs speckled with brown, in a shallow depression lined with grass and hidden in vegetation. The female incubates the eggs for around 24 days and the chicks stay with her for 6-8 weeks after hatching. Both adult birds have brown mottled plumage above, lighter beneath with darker brown scaling and spotting, a pointed tail with white outer feathers, and small yellow combs above the eye. Northern birds tend to be darker overall. The purple neck sacs of the male are not generally visible unless they are inflated in display. The Sharp-tailed Grouse sometimes interbreeds with Prairie-Chickens and the Blue Grouse. It eats berries, buds and leaves, but also insects.

SAGE GROUSE

Scientific name:	*Centrocercus urophasianus*
Length:	28 inches
Habitat:	Sagebrush foothills and plains
Identification:	Large ground-dwelling bird, long pointed tail. Gray-streaked plumage above, black belly. Male has black throat, white breast, in courtship fans tail and inflates breast
Similar species:	Sharp-tailed Grouse is much smaller, lacks distinctive black belly, has outer white tail feathers

A very large bird, the Sage Grouse is found across the sagebrush flats of western America but its population is decreasing as its habitat disappears. In spring, large groups of males gather on a traditional display ground, known as a lek, with each male occupying its own small area. They perform a courtship dance (*right*) to attract females, strutting and bobbing with fanned tail and inflated chest, showing two yellow-green air sacs that the bird can rapidly inflate and deflate to produce a loud popping noise. One male can mate with several females, who then lay 7-12 greenish eggs spotted with brown in a shallow depression in the earth under sagebrush. The female incubates the eggs for around 26 days and the chicks stay with her for some time after hatching. Both adult birds have gray-streaked plumage above, a black belly and long pointed tail. The male is slightly larger with a longer spiky tail, and has a black throat and bib and a white collar and breast. The Sage Grouse mainly eats sagebrush buds and leaves, but will also feed on other plants.

SPRUCE GROUSE

Scientific name:	*Dendragapus canadensis*
Length:	16 inches
Habitat:	Coniferous forests with dense undergrowth
Identification:	Medium-size, ground-dwelling bird, short bill, short tail. Male slate-gray above, black beneath, red comb above eye, black tail with chestnut tip. Female mottled light brown, dark barring below
Similar species:	Female very like female Blue Grouse, but is smaller with shorter tail and barring beneath

A common ground-dwelling bird across much of its range, but very hard to spot because it is so tame; it sits still without concern even within a few feet of observers. It is usually seen singly in dense conifer woodland; in spring, the male struts with its tail spread in a fan and drums with its wings. The female lays 6-12 buffy, spotted eggs, in a shallow scrape lined with grass under a plant or log. The female incubates the eggs for around 24 days and the chicks fly 10-12 weeks after hatching. The adult is medium-size and stocky, with a short bill and short tail. The male (*right*) is slate-gray above, has a black throat and chest outlined in white, white spots on the flanks, a red comb above the eye and a black tail with a chestnut tip. In the north, males do not have the chestnut tip but have a row of white spots across the tail instead. The female is mottled light brown, either with a reddish or grayish tinge, with black and white barring below. The Spruce Grouse eats the buds and needles of conifers, but also seeds and insects.

BLUE GROUSE

Scientific name:	*Dendragapus obscurus*
Length:	20 inches
Habitat:	Open coniferous or mixed woodland, brushy lowland, mountain slopes
Identification:	Large, ground-dwelling bird, short bill, long tail. Male blue-gray, orange-yellow comb above eye, dark tail with gray tip, yellow or purplish neck sac only seen inflated in display. Female mottled gray-brown overall
Similar species:	Female very like female Spruce Grouse, but is larger with longer tail and lacks barring beneath

The Blue Grouse is found in open lowland woods in the west, but moves up to higher altitudes in the winter; it is usually seen singly and prefers areas near large clearings. In spring, the male stands high up, often in a tree, spreading its tail in a fan and inflating its yellow or purplish neck sacs, which are surrounded by white-based feathers (*left*). It also flies down to strut with its tail fanned, dragging its wings. The female lays 6-10 creamy, brown-speckled eggs, in a scrape lined with pine needles and grass and sheltered under a tree, rock or log. The female incubates the eggs for around 26 days and the chicks stay with her for around 12 weeks after hatching. The adult is quite large, with a relatively long neck and tail. The male is mostly blue-gray, with an orange-yellow comb above the eye, and a dark tail with gray tip. The female and juvenile birds are fairly even mottled gray-brown all over, with a plainer gray belly and a gray band at the tip of the tail. In the northern Rockies, this species has an all-dark tail. The Blue Grouse eats pine needles in winter, but also seeds, berries and insects in summer.

RUFFED GROUSE

Scientific name:	*Bonasa umbellus*
Length:	17 inches
Habitat:	Deciduous and mixed woodlands
Identification:	Ground-dwelling bird, long neck, long tail. Male brownish with buff streaks above, gray-brown cross-barring on flanks, gray or reddish tail with dark cross-barring and broad black tip, black neck ruff is erected in display. Female mottled gray-brown overall, with smaller ruff and tail
Similar species:	Female Spruce Grouse can look similar, but has barring beneath instead of sides and shorter tail

Fairly common across its range, the Ruffed Grouse is found on the ground in mixed woodland, but also perches high in trees. In spring, the male stands on a fallen log spreading its tail in a fan and puffing up its neck ruff, and drums the air with its wings - often for hours at a time. The female lays 9-12 buffy and sometimes spotted eggs, in a scrape lined with leaves and sheltered under a tree, bush, rock or log. The female incubates the eggs for around 24 days; the chicks fly around a week after hatching but stay with the mother for around 12 weeks. The adult is quite slender, with a long neck, crested head and relatively long rounded tail. The male is brownish with buff streaks above, gray-brown cross-barring on its flanks, a black neck ruff, and a gray or reddish tail with dark cross-barring and broad black tip. In the Pacific northwest, reddish birds predominate, but in the north and west their plumage is grayer. The female is mottled gray-brown overall and has a smaller ruff and tail, with the terminal band of the tail incomplete. The Ruffed Grouse eats buds, catkins and twigs in winter, but will also feed on seeds, berries and fruits in summer.

ROCK PTARMIGAN

Scientific name:	*Lagopus mutus*
Length:	14 inches
Habitat:	High rocky slopes, tundra
Identification:	Ground-dwelling bird with feathered feet. Summer male, dark brown with white wings and belly. Summer female, mottled brown, white wings. Both adults white winter plumage with black tail and bill, distinctive black eye line
Similar species:	In winter plumage, male Willow Ptarmigan lacks black eye line, White-tailed lacks black tail. In summer, male Willow is redder than male Rock. Female Willow and Rock difficult to tell apart

Although its range overlaps with the Willow, the Rock Ptarmigan is found on more barren, rocky tundra and at higher altitudes. It forms small flocks in winter, but is seen singly in summer. The female commonly lays 6-9 buffy eggs - although there can be as many as 16 - in a sheltered scrape on tundra. The female incubates the eggs for around 21 days, while the male defends the territory. The chicks leave the nest immediately after hatching and fly within about 10 days. The adult has feathered feet which act as "snowshoes" to enable it to walk on soft snow, and also to add insulation as white feathers have hollow cells filled with air. In winter, both adults have white plumage with a black tail and small black bill, the male has a distinctive black eye line. In summer the male turns dark brown, sometimes quite grayish, with white wings and belly. The summer female is mottled brown, with white wings; both birds retain the black tail and bill. The Rock Ptarmigan eats buds, fruits, seeds and insects in summer, but relies on twigs and buds in winter; its stomach contains special bacteria enabling it to digest woody material.

WILLOW PTARMIGAN

Scientific name:	*Lagopus lagopus*
Length:	15 inches
Habitat:	Tundra, willow thickets
Identification:	Ground-dwelling bird with feathered feet. Summer male, chestnut with white wings and belly. Summer female, mottled brown, white wings. Both adults white winter plumage with black tail and bill
Similar species:	In winter plumage, male Rock Ptarmigan has black eye line, White-tailed lacks black tail. In summer, male Willow is redder than male Rock. Female Willow and Rock difficult to tell apart

Preferring the cold of the north, the Willow Ptarmigan is the most numerous grouse of the north and is found on open tundra and in willow thickets at the tree line. It gathers in small flocks in winter, but is more likely to be seen singly in summer. The female lays 7-12 pale red-brown spotted eggs, in a depression on tundra sheltered under vegetation, rocks or logs. The female incubates the eggs for around 22 days, while the male defends the territory. The chicks leave the nest immediately after hatching and fly within a week. Several families gather in large flocks to migrate southward when winter begins to set in. The adult has feathered feet to add insulation and enable it to walk on snow, and a distinctive stout black bill. In winter, both adults have white plumage with a black tail and bill. In summer the male turns chestnut, with white wings and belly. The summer female is mottled brown, with white wings; both birds retain the black tail and bill. The Willow Ptarmigan eats buds, fruits, catkins and insects in summer, but relies mainly on the twigs and buds of willows in winter.

WHITE-TAILED PTARMIGAN

Scientific name:	*Lagopus leucurus*
Length:	12½ inches
Habitat:	Rocky mountain slopes, high meadows
Identification:	Ground-dwelling bird with feathered feet. Summer plumage mottled black-brown with white wings and belly, white tail. All white winter plumage with black bill
Similar species:	In both summer and winter plumage, its white tail distinguishes this ptarmigan from the other two

The White-tailed Ptarmigan has a less extensive range than the Willow and the Rock, although it is common on alpine slopes in the northwest. It can be hard to spot as it often sits still when approached, relying on its camouflage. Like other ptarmigan, it gathers in small flocks in winter, but is more likely to be seen singly in summer. The female lays 6-14 buff, faintly spotted eggs, in a scrape lined with grass and hidden in rocks just above the timberline. The female incubates the eggs for around 3 weeks, while the male defends the territory. The chicks leave the nest soon after hatching, but stay with the female until the following spring. The adult is the smallest of the three American ptarmigans; it has feathered feet and a distinctive small black bill. In winter, both adults have entirely white plumage; in summer the plumage becomes mottled black-brown, but with white wings, belly, and tail. The White-tailed Ptarmigan eats flowers, fruits, catkins and insects in summer, but relies mainly on buds in winter.

RING-NECKED PHEASANT

Scientific name:	*Phasianus colchicus*
Length:	21 inches (female), 33 inches (male)
Habitat:	Open country, farmland, woodland edges
Identification:	Large long-tailed game bird. Male iridescent bronze mottled with brown, black and green, glossy green-black head, red eye patches, white collar. Female buffy overall
Similar species:	Male unmistakable. Female very like female Sharp-tailed Grouse, but is larger, with longer tail and lacks barring beneath

A native of Asia, the Ring-necked Pheasant was introduced to America in the late 19th century as a game bird and has established itself in open country, particularly farmland. In many areas it is quite common, although populations are smaller in the east. Each male attracts a number of females, who do not build a nest, but lay 7-14 buff or pale olive eggs in a scrape lined with grass and concealed in grass or weeds - several are often quite close together. The eggs are incubated for around 24 days by the female, with the male playing very little part. The chicks fly around 2 weeks after hatching. The male (*below*) has a very long, pointed tail and short, rounded wings. Its plumage is iridescent bronze with golden brown flanks, blue-black belly and green or rust-colored rump; its bronze tail is barred with black. Its head and neck are glossy green-black, usually with a white collar, and it has red eye patches and iridescent feathered ear tufts. The female is buffy overall and much smaller, with a shorter, barred tail. Other sub-species have also been introduced and have interbred, so there are variations in some areas, such as the white-winged birds found in parts of the west and the Japanese Green Pheasant in Virginia and Delaware. The Ring-necked Pheasant is a fast runner, but rises up noisily when flushed. It eats seeds, nuts, berries and insects.

WILD TURKEY

Scientific name:	*Meleagris gallopavo*
Length:	37 inches (female), 46 inches (male)
Habitat:	Open pine-oak forest, oak woods
Identification:	Very large game bird, huge body, thin neck, small head. Male has bronze iridescent plumage, tip of wings barred with white, bare-skinned blue and red head, long dark breast tuft. Female smaller and duller, sometimes lacks breast tuft
Similar species:	Size and shape make the Wild Turkey unmistakable

The largest North American game bird, the wary Wild Turkey is also the ancestor of the domesticated farmyard bird. It inhabits open forest and, although it feeds on the ground, it is a strong flier and roosts in trees at night. In spring, each male struts in his own small clearing in the forest, with tail feathers spread in a glorious fan, head back and wings dragging, and uttering a gobbling mating call. Around ten or more females will answer, then they depart to lay 8-16 buffy, spotted eggs in a shallow depression in the woods, lined with grass and leaves. The eggs are incubated for around a month by the female only; the fluffy chicks leave the nest soon after hatching and can make short flights within a few weeks, but stay with the mother until the following spring. The adult has a huge body, with long legs, a long thin neck and a small head. The male has bronze iridescent plumage, with the tip of the wings barred with white, a bare-skinned blue and red head, and a long dark breast tuft. In western birds, the tail is tipped with white, in eastern it is tipped with chestnut. The female and juvenile birds are smaller and duller, and sometimes lack the breast tuft. The Wild Turkey was once abundant, but hunting and the destruction of its natural habitat decreased populations - although restocking has led to a comeback and introduced it into new areas. It forages on the ground for seeds, nuts, berries, acorns and insects.

NORTHERN BOBWHITE

Scientific name:	*Colinus virginianus*
Length:	9¾ inches
Habitat:	Brushland, open woodland
Identification:	Small, rounded, ground-dwelling bird. Both adults mottled red-brown, striped flanks, short gray tail. Male has white throat and eye stripe. Female has buffy throat and eye stripe
Similar species:	Is usually the only quail in its range, so size and coloring make it unmistakable

The Northern Bobwhite is usually the only quail to be found in the southeast, although its range does overlap slightly with that of the Scaled Quail. It prefers brushland and open woodland, and is usually seen in flocks or coveys of 25-30 birds, except in the breeding season. Its 10-15 creamy white eggs are laid in a shallow depression lined with grass, concealed in brush or among plants. They are incubated for around 3 weeks, by both female and male, and the chicks stay with both adults until the following spring. The adult is round-bodied, with a very short gray tail, mottled red-brown plumage, and chestnut-striped flanks. The male (*right*) has a white eye stripe and throat, with black between which extends round under the throat. The female has buffy throat and eye stripe. The juvenile is smaller and duller. The Northern Bobwhite prefers berries, insects, seeds and leaves. Coveys often roost huddled in a ring, with heads facing out to give each bird a clear flight path to escape danger.

MONTEZUMA QUAIL

Scientific name:	*Cyrtonyx montezumae*
Length:	8½ inches
Habitat:	Grassy undergrowth of wooded foothills
Identification:	Small, plump, ground-dwelling bird. Male has distinctive black and white facial pattern, brown crest on back of head, back and wings mottled black, brown and tan, sides and flanks dark blue-gray with white spots. Female mottled brown
Similar species:	Male unmistakable. Crest at the back gives female's head a distinctive rounded shape

Secretive and uncommon in the foothills of the southwest, the Montezuma Quail is also easily overlooked as it sits very still when approached, only bursting into flight when it is almost underfoot. It prefers the grassy undergrowth of juniper-oak and pine-oak woodlands, and was previously known as the Harlequin Quail or Mearn's Quail. Its 7-14 white eggs are laid in a shallow depression lined with vegetation, concealed in dense grass. They are incubated for up to 26 days, mainly by the female, but the male helps to brood and rear the chicks. The adult is small and plump, with a short tail and rounded wings. The male (*right*) has a distinctive black and white facial pattern, a rounded brown crest on the back of its head; its back and wings are mottled black, brown and tan, and the sides and flanks are dark blue-gray with white spots. The female is mottled brown, also with a rounded crest to the back of the head. The juvenile is smaller and paler, with darker spotted underparts. The Montezuma Quail is usually found in pairs, although families join together into flocks in fall. It prefers berries and acorns, but also eats insects and scratches up seeds, nuts and bulbs in winter.

SCALED QUAIL

Scientific name:	*Callipepla squamata*
Length:	10 inches
Habitat:	Barren plateau, semidesert scrubland, dry open grassland
Identification:	Stocky ground-dwelling bird. Adults blue-gray with dark tips to body feathers giving a scaled look, fluffy white crest. Female's crest is shorter
Similar species:	No similar birds in its range

Although part of its range overlaps with that of the Northern Bobwhite, the Scaled Quail is distinctive because of its very different coloring. It prefers barren mesas, dry open grassland and semidesert areas, and forms large coveys of 100 or more birds, except in the breeding season. It nests in the rainy season, when moisture produces vegetation and there is water for chicks to drink, and often does not breed in dry summers. It does not build a nest, but lays 9-18 whitish, pear-shaped eggs, speckled with brown, in a shallow depression lined with grass and well concealed in brush or among cactus. The eggs are incubated for about 3 weeks, mainly by the female, and the chicks stay with both parents until the following spring. The adult is stocky and has blue-gray plumage with dark tips to the body feathers, which gives a scaled look, and a fluffy white crest - one of its nicknames is "cottontop". The female's crest is shorter. The juvenile is much like the adult, but is more mottled with less distinct scaling. Some males in southern Texas have a dark chestnut patch on the belly. The Scaled Quail eats insects and seeds; they are often seen near farmsteads, where they can eat left-over grain from animal feed and drink from man-made water holes.

CALIFORNIA QUAIL

Scientific name:	*Callipepla californica*
Length:	10 inches
Habitat:	Open woodland, brushy foothills
Identification:	Small ground-dwelling bird with longish tail. Adults gray-brown above, creamy belly scaled in brown, brown sides streaked white, curved head plume. Male has brown crown and black throat edged with white. Female's plume is smaller
Similar species:	Gambel's Quail almost identical, but has chestnut flanks and no scaling

Common in open woodland, brushy foothills and suburbs near a permanent source of water, the California Quail is restricted to the far west - although it has also been introduced to British Columbia and Utah. It forms large coveys in fall and winter, which break up into breeding pairs in spring. The female lays 12-15 buff, brown-spotted eggs, in a shallow grass-lined scrape under a bush or rock. The eggs are incubated for around 3 weeks by the female and the chicks can fly 10 days after hatching. The adult is rather slender and long-tailed, gray-brown above, with a scaled nape, creamy belly scaled in brown, brown sides streaked with white, and a curved head plume. The male has a pale forehead, and a brown crown and black throat both edged with white. The female's plume is smaller and the juvenile is smaller with less distinct, paler coloring. The California Quail eats insects, fruits, seeds and berries, and roosts in trees at night for safety. In fall and winter, flocks are often seen in city parks, gardens and yards.

GAMBEL'S QUAIL *(above)*

Scientific name:	*Callipepla gambelii*
Length:	11 inches
Habitat:	Desert scrubland, thickets
Identification:	Small ground-dwelling bird with longish tail. Adults grayish above, creamy belly, chestnut sides streaked white, curved head plume. Male has chestnut crown and black throat edged with white, black patch on belly. Female's plume is smaller
Similar species:	California Quail almost identical, but has brown flanks and scaling on underparts

Gambel's Quail is common within its range, which is restricted to the southwest. It inhabits desert scrubland and thickets, preferably near a permanent source of water, and forms large coveys of from 20 to more than 100 birds during fall and winter. In spring, the coveys break up into breeding pairs. The female lays 12-20 buffy-white eggs, with brown markings, in a shallow scrape in the ground lined with grass and well-shaded under a bush or rock or among cactus. The eggs are incubated for around 3 weeks, mainly by the female but the male helps care for the chicks, which stay with both parents until the following spring. The adult is rather slender and long-tailed, and is grayish above, with a creamy belly, chestnut sides streaked with white, and a curved head plume. The male has a dark forehead, a chestnut crown and black throat both edged with white, and a black patch on the belly. The female's plume is rather smaller and the juvenile is smaller with less distinct and paler coloring. Gambel's Quail forages in the desert during the day for insects, fruits, leaves and seeds, but gathers at water sources at nightfall to drink its fill before roosting.

MOUNTAIN QUAIL

Scientific name:	*Oreortyx pictus*
Length:	11 inches
Habitat:	Mountains up to 10,000 feet, brushy foothills, chaparral
Identification:	Ground-dwelling bird with shortish tail. Adults gray-blue head, neck and chest, chestnut throat patch with creamy border, chestnut sides streaked white, brown back, long double head plume. Female's plume is smaller
Similar species:	Longer, straight head plume distinguishes the Mountain Quail from the other two western quails

A common but elusive bird, the Mountain Quail is found in the brushy foothills, chaparral and mountains of the Pacific states. It migrates on foot from higher altitudes to the more protected foothills, where it spends the winter in coveys of 6-12 birds. When disturbed it tends to run through the thick cover, rather than rising into the air. The female lays 8-15 buffy-red eggs, in a shallow scrape lined with grass and leaves and hidden under thick vegetation, logs or rocks. The eggs are incubated for up to 4 weeks by the female and the chicks can fly 14 days after hatching but stay for some time in family groups. The adult is quite short-tailed, with a gray-blue head, neck and chest, a chestnut throat patch with a creamy border, chestnut sides streaked white, a brown back, and a long double head plume. The female's plume is smaller and the juvenile is smaller but with similar coloring to the adult. Coastal birds tend to be browner than those in the interior. The Mountain Quail eats leaves, buds and insects in summer, but also feeds on seeds, nuts and berries in winter.

KING RAIL

Scientific name:	*Rallus elegans*
Length:	15 inches
Habitat:	Freshwater marshes
Identification:	Long-billed, long-necked, wading marsh bird. Tawny edges to black-centered back feathers, tawny wing coverts and breast, barred flanks
Similar species:	Virginia Rail is smaller, Clapper Rail has olive wing coverts, grayish edges to brown-centered back feathers

Unlike the Clapper Rail, the King Rail prefers fresh water and their ranges only overlap in some brackish areas. The largest of the North American rails, it is mainly seen in the freshwater marshes of the Gulf coast, but also sometimes well inland in the east. Like the Clapper, it is rarely seen in the open but is often heard, particularly at dawn and dusk. Its nest is a cup of marsh grass, hidden in the dense vegetation of the shallows. The 5-15 buffy eggs spotted with brown are incubated by both birds for around 3 weeks. The young chicks leave the nest soon after hatching and are independent by the time they are 9 weeks old. The adult has a long neck and body, short tail and a long, slightly decurved bill. The black-centered back feathers have tawny edges, it has tawny wing coverts, a tawny breast, black and white barred flanks and a slate-gray head with gray-brown cheeks. The juvenile is darker above and paler beneath. The King Rail eats crustaceans, grain, berries and insects.

SORA

Scientific name:	*Porzana carolina*
Length:	13¾ inches
Habitat:	Freshwater and brackish marshes, salt marshes
Identification:	Short-billed wading marsh bird. Black face and throat patch, rich brown mottled back, gray head, neck and chest, barred flanks and belly, yellow bill and feet
Similar species:	Short bill and less vivid coloring distinguish the Sora from other rails

Widespread and common across much of North America, the Sora is seen much more often than the other rails. When walking across mud it can often be seen flicking its short tail. During migration and in winter it is usually seen in tidal saltwater marshes, but it prefers large freshwater marshes for breeding. Its nest is a basket woven of marsh plant stalks and fastened above water level, or sometimes just a simple cup of grass. The 7-16 buffy eggs spotted with brown are incubated by both birds for about 3 weeks, and the young, downy chicks leave the nest soon after hatching. The adult is smaller and more chunky than other rails, with a short, thick, yellow or greenish-yellow bill and yellow feet. It has a black face and throat patch, a rich brown mottled back, gray head, neck and chest, barred flanks and belly, and yellow feet. The juvenile is a plainer, buffy-brown color. The Sora rarely flies, except when it is flushed or at night during spring and fall migration. It eats insects, mollusks, seeds and duckweed.

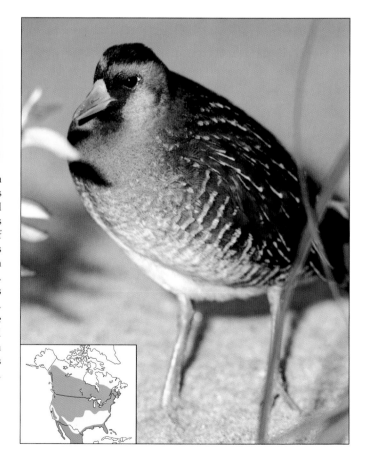

CLAPPER RAIL

Scientific name:	*Rallus longirostris*
Length:	14½ inches
Habitat:	Coastal salt marshes
Identification:	Long-billed, long-necked, wading marsh bird. Grayish edges to brown-centered back feathers, olive wing coverts, tawny breast, barred flanks
Similar species:	Virginia Rail is smaller, King Rail has tawny wing coverts, tawny edges to black-centered back feathers

A common but secretive bird, the Clapper Rail inhabits the salt marshes of the Atlantic and Gulf coasts. It has declined as its habitat vanishes, and is now scarce in the west around California and the Colorado River. Although it is rarely seen in the open it is often heard - its noisy clattering carries far over the reeds. Its nest is made in clumps of marsh grass, a platform of dead plants with surrounding grasses arched over to form a roof. The 5-14 buffy-greenish eggs spotted with brown are incubated by both birds for around 21 days. The young chicks leave the nest soon after hatching and are independent by the time they are 6 weeks old. The adult has a long neck, a long wedge-shaped body and a long, slightly decurved bill. The brown-centered back feathers have grayish edges, it has olive wing coverts, a tawny breast, and barred flanks. The exact color of the plumage does vary - east coast species tend to be duller, west coast birds are brighter below. Unlike most wading birds, the Clapper Rail can swim for short distances and dive under water to escape predators. It eats crabs, mollusks and insects.

VIRGINIA RAIL

Scientific name:	*Rallus limicola*
Length:	9½ inches
Habitat:	Freshwater and brackish marshes, wetlands, coastal salt marshes
Identification:	Long-billed, long-necked, wading marsh bird. Tawny edges to black-centered back feathers, cinnamon-brown wing coverts and breast, barred flanks, gray face, white throat
Similar species:	King Rail is bigger, Clapper Rail has olive wing coverts, grayish edges to brown-centered back feathers

The Virginia Rail has a much wider range than the other two rails and inhabits both fresh and salt water marshes. Like the others, it is also a secretive bird that is heard more often than it is seen, but sometimes comes out into the open at dawn to forage. Its nest is woven of marsh plants, lined with grasses and fastened in dense vegetation above the water level. The 5-12 buff eggs spotted with brown are incubated by both birds for around 3 weeks, and the young, downy black chicks leave the nest soon after hatching. The adult has a long neck and body, short tail and a long, slightly decurved bill. The black-centered back feathers have tawny edges, it has cinnamon-brown wing coverts and breast, strongly black and white barred flanks and a gray face with a white throat. The juvenile is blackish-brown above and mottled gray-black beneath. The Virginia Rail probes down into the mud with its long bill, looking for insects, mollusks and small fish - it also sometimes eats seeds and aquatic plants.

PURPLE GALLINULE

Scientific name:	*Porphyrula martinica*
Length:	13 inches
Habitat:	Freshwater swamps, lagoons, marshes
Identification:	Warm-water marsh bird, long legs, large feet. Bright purplish-blue head, neck and underparts, pale blue forehead shield, red and yellow bill, brown-green back, yellow legs and feet
Similar species:	Coloring is unmistakable

The colorful Purple Gallinule prefers warm-water marshes and is mainly found in the south and around the Gulf, although it often wanders great distances and has been seen much further north in summer. It spends the winter in southern Florida and down into Argentina. Its nest is a shallow cup of grass stems and reeds, lined with leaves and attached to marsh vegetation. It lays 5-10 buff eggs, spotted with brown, and the downy chicks leave the nest soon after hatching. The adult bird has long legs and very large, yellow feet - which allow it to walk across lily pads and floating marsh vegetation. It has a bright purplish-blue head, neck and underparts, white under the tail, a pale blue forehead shield, a red bill tipped with yellow and a brown-green back. The juvenile is much plainer, buffy underneath with an olive back, greenish wings and dull olive legs and feet. The Purple Gallinule can fly, but is reluctant to do so and also rarely swims. It eats seeds, grain, insects, frogs and birds' eggs, as well as vegetation.

AMERICAN COOT

Scientific name:	*Fulica americana*
Length:	15½ inches
Habitat:	Freshwater marshes, wetlands, salt marshes
Identification:	Stocky marsh bird, big lobed feet. Black head and neck, ivory-colored forehead shield with reddish upper edge, whitish bill with dark band near tip, slate body
Similar species:	Common Moorhen has white line and red facial shield

The American Coot is fairly widespread and common on lakes, ponds and marshes across most of North America. It is seen in flocks of hundreds of birds and often becomes quite tame in urban areas, where it lives in parks and on golf courses. Its nest is a platform of reeds and marsh vegetation, usually on the edge of open water, and old nests are used throughout the year for resting and preening. It lays 8-20 buff or pinkish, brown-spotted eggs, which are incubated for around 25 days by both adult birds. The downy chicks have a red and blue frontal shield, which seems to trigger a feeding impulse in the adult; they leave the nest soon after hatching and are independent within 7-8 weeks. The adult is stocky, with big lobed feet that enable it to walk across floating vegetation, and are useful for swimming. It has a black head and neck, ivory-colored forehead shield with a reddish upper edge, a whitish bill with a dark band near the tip, and a slate-gray body. Juveniles are paler, but begin to achieve adult plumage by their first winter. Coots nod their heads as they swim, and in flight the white trailing edge along most of the wing is distinctive. They dive to the bottom to catch fish and mollusks, but also dabble on the surface for insects and pond weed and forage on lawns in urban areas.

COMMON MOORHEN

Scientific name:	*Gallinula chloropus*
Length:	14 inches
Habitat:	Ponds, freshwater marshes, slow-moving rivers
Identification:	Marsh bird, long legs, large feet. Black-gray head and neck, red forehead shield, red bill with yellow tip, brownish-olive back, slate underparts, white streak on flanks, yellow legs and feet
Similar species:	Distinguished from Purple Gallinule and American Coot by white line and red facial shield

Related to the Purple Gallinule, the Common Moorhen was once known in North America as the Common Gallinule. It is fairly widespread and common in freshwater marshes, ponds and slow-moving rivers across much of the country - it is happy with only a small patch of cattails or reeds. Its nest is built of grass stems and reeds, in marsh vegetation a foot or so above the water level, often with a ramp of compressed vegetation leading down to the water. It lays 8-12 buff, dark spotted eggs, which are incubated for around 21 days by both parent birds; the downy chicks are ready to leave the nest quite soon after hatching. Like the Purple Gallinule, the adult has long legs and very large, yellow feet to allow it to walk across lily pads and floating marsh vegetation. It has a black-gray head and neck, a red forehead shield, a red bill with a yellow tip, a brownish-olive back, and slate-gray underparts with a white streak on the flanks. The juvenile is very similar, but is rather duller with a dark bill and no red facial shield. The Common Moorhen has a very wide diet - it eats mosquitoes, spiders, tadpoles, insect larvae, fruits and seeds.

SNOWY PLOVER

Scientific name:	*Charadrius alexandrinus*
Length:	6¼ inches
Habitat:	Dry sandy beaches, salty flats
Identification:	Small, long-legged, short-winged, shore bird. Pale sandy gray-brown above, face and underparts white, dark gray legs and feet, thin black bill. Breeding male black side band
Similar species:	On other similar plovers, the side band extends round as breast band. Wilson's Plover is darker, larger black bill. Piping Plover has shorter, thicker bill, and yellow legs. Semipalmated Plover is much darker, with yellow legs

Many North American plovers are very similar and are quite difficult to tell apart - and parts of their ranges overlap. The Snowy Plover can usually be distinguished by its gray legs and thin, black bill. It is found all year round on the barren sandy beaches of the Pacific, with some also on the Gulf coast, and in summer on salt flats in some areas of the interior. It breeds in coastal areas, but is now an endangered species, threatened by the loss of safe nesting sites. Its nest is a scrape in the sand, in which it lays 3 buffy eggs that are tended by both adults alternately for around 4 weeks. The downy chicks leave the nest soon after hatching and are independent within a month. The adult is small, long-legged and short-winged, with a quite long, thin, black bill. Its plumage is pale sandy gray-brown above, with white face and underparts, and dark gray legs and feet. The breeding male has a black side band and a broken black eye stripe. Its coloring gives the Snowy Plover perfect camouflage on sandy beaches as soon as it stops moving. It mainly eats insects and small crustaceans.

WILSON'S PLOVER

Scientific name:	*Charadrius wilsonia*
Length:	7¾ inches
Habitat:	Sandy beaches, mud flats
Identification:	Small, long-legged, short-winged, shore bird. Dark sandy gray-brown above, face and underparts white, dull pinky-gray legs and feet, long, heavy black bill. Breeding male broad black breast band
Similar species:	Snowy Plover has paler plumage, thin black bill. Piping Plover is paler with shorter thick bill, and yellow legs. Semipalmated Plover is much darker, with more black on face, and yellow legs

Wilson's Plover can usually be distinguished by its pinky-gray legs and long, thick, black bill. It is found all year round on the sandy beaches of Florida and the southern Pacific coast, and in summer round the northern Gulf coast and up along the Atlantic coast. It is seldom seen in large numbers and rarely ventures inland, but casual migrants have been recorded in California and around the Great Lakes. It breeds in coastal areas, making a scrape in the sand in which it lays 2-4 buffy eggs that are tended by both adults alternately for around 3 weeks. The downy chicks leave the nest soon after hatching and are independent within a month. The adult is small, long-legged and short-winged, with a long, thick, black bill. Its plumage is dark sandy gray-brown above, with white face and underparts, and dull pinky-gray legs and feet. The breeding male has a broad black chest band; in the female and winter male, this is dark sandy-brown. The juvenile is similar to the female, but has slight scaling on upperparts. The coloring of Wilson's Plover gives it perfect camouflage on sandy beaches. It mainly eats insects.

BLACK-BELLIED PLOVER

Scientific name:	*Pluvialis squatarola*
Length:	11½ inches
Habitat:	Arctic tundra, coastal areas, Great Lakes
Identification:	Compact, heavy-billed shorebird with white rump and tail, black patch under wing in flight. Summer male has black face, neck, breast and belly, white crown and nape extending to side of breast, black and white mottled back. Summer female less black. Winter adult mottled gray above, pale gray below
Similar species:	American Golden Plover smaller, golden spots above in summer, dark wing, rump and tail, lacks dark patch underwing. Sanderling and Red Knot have similar winter plumage, but are much smaller

Spending the summer on Arctic tundra and mostly wintering in the Southern Hemisphere, the Black-bellied Plover is seen along the coasts of North America and round the Great Lakes as it migrates, although a few winter along southern coasts. It nests on tundra, laying 4 buffy eggs in a shallow scrape lined with lichen and moss. Incubation takes up to 28 days, with both birds taking a turn; the chicks leave the nest soon after hatching and are independent by 7 weeks. Adults have a short, thick dark bill, white rump and tail, and a black wing patch beneath that is only seen in flight. The breeding male has a black face, neck, breast and belly, with the white crown and nape extending to the side of the breast, and a black and white mottled back. The summer female (*left*) is similar, but has less black. In winter, both birds are evenly mottled dark-gray above, and pale gray below. The juvenile bird may be quite gold-speckled. The Black-bellied Plover moves over the ground in short staccato runs, taking marine worms, insects and other invertebrates.

AMERICAN GOLDEN-PLOVER

Scientific name:	*Pluvialis dominica*
Length:	10¼ inches
Habitat:	Arctic tundra, farmland, flooded fields
Identification:	Compact, thin-billed shorebird. Summer male has black face, neck, breast and belly, white crown and nape extending to side of breast, black and white mottled back with pale gold spots. Summer female less black. Winter adult gray-brown upperparts, pale gray-brown underparts, whitish eyebrow
Similar species:	Black-bellied Plover larger, no gold spots above in summer, white rump and tail, dark patch underwing. Winter plumage Mountain Plover has white underwing, black patch on tail

The American Golden-Plover summers on Arctic tundra and mostly winters in South America, passing through the Great Plains as it migrates - sometimes resting on flooded fields. It nests on tundra, laying 4 buff, black-and-brown-spotted eggs in a scrape lined with lichen and moss. Incubation takes up to 27 days, by both birds; the chicks leave the nest soon after hatching. Adults have a small head and bill, and smoky gray beneath the wing in flight. The breeding male has a black face, neck, breast and belly, a white crown and nape extending to the side of the breast, and a black and white mottled back with pale gold spots. The summer female is very similar, but has less black. In winter, both birds are gray-brown above, with pale gray-brown below and a whitish eyebrow (*right*). The American Golden-Plover mainly eats insects and crustaceans.

KILLDEER

Scientific name:	*Charadrius vociferus*
Length:	10½ inches
Habitat:	Grassy fields, lake and river shores
Identification:	Lanky, long-tailed, open-country bird with slender wings. Gray-brown above, underparts white, two black breast bands, pale gray legs and feet, long thin dark bill. Red-orange rump in flight
Similar species:	Double breast band is distinctive

A common bird across much of North America, the Killdeer is found across the south throughout the year and spreads north in summer - although it does not reach the far north. It lives both inland and on the coast, on grassy fields and on lake and river shores. It nests on open ground, usually laying 4 buff eggs spotted with brown in a scrape in gravel or the bare ground, sometimes lined with a few grass stems. Incubation takes around 26 days by both adults. The downy chicks leave the nest soon after hatching and fly within a month; if danger threatens the nest or the chicks, the Killdeer performs a convincing impression of having a broken wing, leading predators away. The adult is a lanky, long-tailed bird with slender wings, pale gray legs and feet and a long thin dark bill. Its plumage is gray-brown above, with white underparts and two distinctive black breast bands. In flight, it has a long red-orange rump, dark tips to the upper wing crossed by a broad white line, white under much of the wing and a dark patch on the tail. The downy chicks have only one breast band, but soon develop a second along with juvenile plumage. The Killdeer feeds in loose flocks, mainly eating earthworms, snails and insects.

MOUNTAIN PLOVER

Scientific name:	*Charadrius montanus*
Length:	9 inches
Habitat:	Short-grass plains, plowed fields, barren flats
Identification:	Long-legged, upland bird. Sandy-brown above, underparts white, pale gray legs and feet, long thin dark bill. Breeding male has black crown, white forehead, black eye line
Similar species:	Inhabits different range to shore plovers. Winter plumage American Golden-Plover has grayish underwing in flight and is grayer below

Unlike most of the other North American plovers, the Mountain Plover is found far away from water, on dry grass plains, plowed fields and barren flats - and this different range can be used to distinguish it from other brown-backed plovers. In winter flocks gather across the south; it breeds in several areas further north, but is uncommon and declining as its breeding range is reduced. It does not build a nest but lays 3 olive, black-spotted eggs in a scrape in the ground, that are tended for about 4 weeks by both adults. The downy chicks leave soon after hatching and fly within a month. The adult is a slim bird with long pale gray legs and a long thin dark bill. Its plumage is sandy-brown above, with white underparts and a buff breast. The breeding male has a small black crown, a white forehead, and an indistinct black eye line. In flight, it has dark tips to the upper wing crossed by a white line, white under much of the wing and a dark patch on the tail. The Mountain Plover feeds in small flocks, mainly eating grasshoppers and other insects.

SEMIPALMATED PLOVER

Scientific name:	*Charadrius semipalmatus*
Length:	7½ inches
Habitat:	Beaches, lake and tidal flats
Identification:	Small, long-legged, long-winged, shore bird. Dark sandy brown above, underparts white, black breast band and eye stripe, white forehead and eyebrow, yellow legs and feet, dark yellow bill with black tip
Similar species:	Piping Plover is paler with shorter thick bill. Snowy Plover has paler plumage, thin black bill, gray legs. Wilson's Plover has pinky-gray legs, bigger bill

The Semipalmated Plover is the most common of the small plovers and can usually be distinguished by its yellow-orange legs and dark yellow bill with black tip. It is found all across America during spring and fall migration and spends the winter on southern beaches along both coasts. It breeds in the far north, making a scrape in the ground or among beach pebbles, in which it lays 4 buff or whitish eggs that are tended by both adults for around 24 days. The downy chicks leave the nest soon after hatching and are independent within a month. The adult is small, long-legged and long-winged, with yellow-orange legs and dark yellow bill with black tip. Its plumage is dark sandy brown above, with white underparts, a single black breast band and a black eye stripe, and a white forehead and eyebrow. The breeding male often lacks the white eyebrow and the juvenile is similar, but with paler plumage and darker legs. The Semipalmated Plover forages by running quickly, stopping suddenly and making a swift jab to catch a crustacean or insect.

PIPING PLOVER

Scientific name:	*Charadrius melodus*
Length:	7¼ inches
Habitat:	Sandy beaches, dunes, lake shores
Identification:	Stocky, long-legged, shore bird. Pale sandy-brown above, underparts white, white forehead and eyebrow, orange legs and feet, short dark bill. Breeding male has orange base to bill, narrow black breast band
Similar species:	Semipalmated Plover is darker with longer bill. Snowy Plover has long thin black bill, gray legs. Wilson's Plover has darker plumage, pinky-gray legs, bigger bill

The Piping Plover can usually be distinguished by its pale plumage, orange-yellow legs and stubby bill. It winters on the sandy beaches and mud flats of the southeast coast, and breeds along the north Atlantic coast and on salt flats round northern prairie lakes and rivers. It is generally uncommon and is now an endangered species, with populations declining in all areas. Its nest is a hollow in the sand, in which it lays 4 buff or gray eggs that are incubated for up to a month by both birds. The downy chicks leave the nest soon after hatching and are independent within a month. The adult is stocky, long-legged and relatively short-winged, with a short bill. Its plumage is sandy-brown above, with a white forehead, eyebrow and underparts, and orange legs and feet. The breeding male has an orange bill with a dark tip, a narrow black breast band - sometimes incomplete - and black stripe between the eyes. Its coloring gives the Snowy Plover perfect camouflage on sandy beaches as soon as it stops moving. It mainly eats insects and small crustaceans.

SANDHILL CRANE

Scientific name:	*Grus canadensis*
Length:	34-42 inches, wingspan 73-90 inches
Habitat:	Tundra, marshes, grasslands
Identification:	Large, long-necked, long-legged wading bird. Gray plumage, sometimes stained rust, bushy tuft of feathers over rump, red patch on head. Flies with neck and head outstretched
Similar species:	Great Blue Heron has longer bill, lacks bushy tuft of feathers over rump, flies with neck folded back

Sandhill Cranes vary in size according to range, with northern birds smallest and southern largest, but they are all tall and stately with very long legs and necks. The species is quite common and is often seen in large flocks of 20-100 birds, spending the winter across the far south and round part of the Gulf coast and the summer in the north. It breeds on Arctic tundra, and also in remote marshes further south, building a large mound of vegetation on which it lays 2 buffy-olive eggs, spotted with reddy-brown. Both parents incubate the eggs, for around one month. The chicks leave the nest soon after hatching and fly at 10 weeks, but remain with the parents until the next spring. The adult has gray plumage, with a bushy tuft of feathers over the rump, and a red patch on the head. Its back and chest feathers are sometimes stained rusty-brown with ferrous mud, transferred there by the bill when preening. The juvenile is grayish with tawny mottling and lacks the red face patch. The Sandhill Crane flies with neck and head outstretched, like other cranes. It eats spilled grain, insects and small animals.

AMERICAN OYSTERCATCHER

Scientific name:	*Haematopus palliatus*
Length:	18½ inches
Habitat:	Coastal beaches, mud flats
Identification:	Stocky, short-tailed, broad-winged coastal bird. Large red-orange bill, black head, dark brown back, white wing and tail patches, white underparts
Similar species:	Bill and plumage distinctive

An exclusively coastal bird, the American Oystercatcher is found on beaches and mud flats along the southern Pacific coast and along most of the Atlantic, where it is still expanding northwards. It can be seen feeding in small, noisy flocks in winter, and in pairs or family groups in the spring and summer. It breeds throughout its range, laying 2-4 greeny-buff spotted eggs in a hollow in the sand that is sometimes lined with bits of plant or odd pebbles. Both parent birds incubate the eggs, for 23-28 days, and the downy young leave the nest soon after hatching and are independent by 5 weeks. The adult bird is stocky, with a short tail and broad wings. Its most distinctive feature is a large red-orange bill, and it has a black head, dark brown back, white wing and tail patches, and white underparts. The juvenile is very similar to the adult, but has some lighter scaling on the back and a dark tip to its bill. When foraging, the large flat bill is used to open oysters and pry limpets off rocks. The American Oystercatcher also eats starfish, crabs and marine worms.

BLACK OYSTERCATCHER

Scientific name:	*Haematopus bachmani*
Length:	17½ inches
Habitat:	Rocky shores
Identification:	Stocky, short-tailed, broad-winged coastal bird. Large red-orange bill, black plumage
Similar species:	Bill and plumage distinctive

The Black and the American Oystercatcher are closely related, but the Black is only found on rocky shores along the Pacific coast. It can be seen in flocks of 40-50 birds in winter, but these break up into pairs at the start of the breeding season. It breeds across its range, laying 2 or 3 large olive-buff eggs blotched with brown among pebbles, or in a shallow rocky depression or a scrape on the beach lined with bits of shell, plant matter or odd pebbles. Both parent birds incubate the eggs, for 24-28 days, and the downy young leave the nest soon after hatching and are independent by around 5 weeks. The adult bird is stocky, with a short tail and broad wings. Its most distinctive feature is a large red-orange bill, and it has entirely black plumage. The juvenile is very similar to the adult, but has some lighter scaling on the back and a dark tip to its bill. The Black Oystercatcher is a very skilled swimmer and is also at home in the air; mating pairs make long courtship flights, twisting and turning, and screeching loudly. It eats oysters, limpets, starfish, crabs and marine worms.

BLACK-NECKED STILT

Scientific name:	*Himantopus mexicanus*
Length:	14 inches
Habitat:	Shallow wetlands
Identification:	Tall, slender, wading bird. Very long spindly reddish legs, black plumage above, white beneath, long thin black bill
Similar species:	Unmistakable

Hunted almost to the point of extinction in the 19th century, the Black-necked Stilt was later protected and has recovered a great deal of ground. It is found in all kinds of wet habitats across much of the south and west, and is often seen in noisy flocks at the water's edge. It needs shallow water for feeding, with adjacent drier ground for breeding. It does not build a nest, but lays around 4 buff eggs spotted with brown in a shallow depression lined with grass and debris on open ground, or in the grass. Intruders near the nesting site are likely to be mobbed by up to 40 noisy, excitable birds. The eggs are incubated for 22-27 days by both parents, and the chicks leave the nest not long after hatching and are independent by around 4-5 weeks. The adult bird is very tall and slender, with very long, thin, reddish legs and a long, thin, black bill. Its plumage is glossy black above and white beneath. The female is somewhat browner, as is the juvenile. The Black-necked Stilt wades through shallows, picking at aquatic insects on the water; it also eats snails.

AMERICAN AVOCET

Scientific name:	*Recurvirostra americana*
Length:	18 inches
Habitat:	Open shallow ponds and lakes, marshes
Identification:	Tall, slender, wading bird. Very long spindly gray legs, black and white back, white beneath, long thin upturned bill, neck cinnamon in summer, gray in winter
Similar species:	Unmistakable

The elegant American Avocet is fairly common in the shallow water of ponds and marshes in the west in summer and along the southern coastline in winter; it is only seen across the east during migration. It nests in small groups on open mud flats or in muddy patches in grass, but each pair has its own separate small area. It does not build a nest, but lays around 4 blotched olive eggs in a shallow depression lined with grass. If predators approach, the parents scream loudly to alarm nearby birds, which mob the intruder. The eggs are incubated for 21-28 days by both parents, and the downy chicks leave the nest not long after hatching and are independent by around 5 weeks. The adult bird is very tall and slender, with very long, thin, gray legs and a long, thin, upturned bill - that of the female is more curved than the male. Its plumage is black and white above and white beneath, with a cinnamon-colored neck and head in winter, light gray in summer. The juvenile is black and white with a pale cinnamon wash on the neck. The American Avocet wades through shallows, sweeping its bill from side to side through the water and mud to catch aquatic insects and shrimp-like crustaceans.

GREATER YELLOWLEGS

Scientific name:	*Tringa melanoleuca*
Length:	14 inches
Habitat:	Shallow waters, swamps
Identification:	Tall, slender, long-necked wading bird. Long, bright yellow legs, gray-brown overall, black and white mottling above, white below, white rump, barred tail, long slightly upturned bill
Similar species:	Almost identical to Lesser Yellowlegs, but larger; size difference only noticeable when birds are together

A large sandpiper, the Greater Yellowlegs is fairly common across its range. It winters in the south and summers in the north, and is seen migrating between the two in spring and fall. It breeds in northern swamps, the taiga and damp boreal forests, laying up to 4 gray-white or buffy eggs splotched with brown in a shallow scrape in woodland - often far from water. The eggs are incubated by the female, for around 3 weeks; the young leave the nest soon after hatching and are independent in around 20 days. The adult is a tall, slender bird with a long, slightly upturned bill. Its plumage is gray-brown overall, with black and white mottling above, white below, a white rump and a barred tail; on dry land it can usually be distinguished by its long, bright yellow legs. In breeding plumage, its throat and breast are heavily streaked, its back is darker and more heavily marked and its flanks are barred with black. In winter, Greater Yellowlegs are found in flocks with other wading birds around the southern coasts and on the muddy shores of inland lakes. It wades into deeper water than some others, sweeping the water with its bill to catch invertebrates or stabbing small fish. It also eats aquatic insects and their larvae, and water snails.

SOLITARY SANDPIPER

Scientific name:	*Tringa solitaria*
Length:	$8\frac{1}{2}$ inches
Habitat:	Shallow backwaters, estuaries, wooded ponds, bogs, boreal forests
Identification:	Slender, short-necked wading bird. Dark gray back with white spotting, white eye ring, long straight bill, white below, greenish legs. In flight has tail with dark center and white cross-barred sides
Similar species:	Spotted Sandpiper is paler, with less obvious eye ring. Yellowlegs are bigger and leg coloring is distinctive

A rather uncommon bird, the Solitary Sandpiper is rarely seen in flocks but usually alone at the edges of creeks, ponds or shallow backwaters. It winters in Central and South America, but migrates across North America to breed in the boggy coniferous forests of the far north. Unlike other sandpipers it does not lay its eggs on the ground, but takes over an old songbird nest high in a tree. It lays 4 pale green or buffy eggs heavily blotched with brown, which are incubated by the female for around 22-24 days; the young leave the nest soon after hatching but stay with the female for some time. The adult is slender, with a short neck, a thin straight bill and greenish legs. Its plumage is mainly dark gray, with white spotting on the back, a distinct white eye ring, and white below. In flight, its upper tail has a dark center and dark-gray and white cross-barred sides. In breeding plumage, its throat and breast are streaked and its back is darker and more strongly marked. The Solitary Sandpiper often shakes one foot rapidly underwater to bring food up out of the mud. It eats insects, spiders, crustaceans and small aquatic animals.

LESSER YELLOWLEGS

Scientific name:	*Tringa flavipes*
Length:	$10\frac{1}{2}$ inches
Habitat:	Tundra, woodland, shallow freshwater ponds, coastal marshes
Identification:	Tall, slender, long-necked wading bird. Long, bright yellow legs, gray-brown overall, black and white mottling above, white below, white rump, barred tail, long straight bill
Similar species:	Amost identical to Greater Yellowlegs, but smaller; size difference only noticeable when birds are together

The Lesser Yellowlegs is common across most of its range, but is seen rather less in the far west. It is found in the same sort of places as the Greater Yellowlegs, but its summer range does not extend as far to the east and its winter range is smaller. It breeds in northern swamps, the taiga and damp boreal forests, laying up to 4 buffy eggs splotched with brown in a shallow depression on bare ground lined with plant material - quite often far from water. The eggs are incubated by the female only for around 3 weeks; the young are ready to leave the nest soon after hatching and are fully independent in around 21 days. The adult is quite a tall, slender bird, with a long neck, a straight bill and long, bright yellow legs. Its plumage is gray-brown overall, with black and white mottling above, white below, a white rump and a barred tail. In breeding plumage, its throat and breast are heavily streaked, its back is darker and more heavily marked and its flanks have short, fine black bars. The Lesser Yellowlegs is often found in small flocks and bobs its head and body when alarmed. It wades in shallow water, picking at the surface to snap up small invertebrates and aquatic insects and their larvae.

WANDERING TATTLER *(above)*

Scientific name:	*Heteroscelus incanus*
Length:	11 inches
Habitat:	Gravel stream banks, rocky coasts
Identification:	Medium-size, bobbing, shore bird. Short yellow legs, dark gray above, gray wash on breast and throat, pale belly, dark eye line with paler patch above, long dark bill. Breeding bird has fine black barring below
Similar species:	Bobs like Spotted Sandpiper but has very different coloring

The Wandering Tattler is found only along the Pacific coast of America - in winter on rocky beaches in the south and in summer along mountain streams further to the north. It is often seen mingling with the other shorebirds that prefer rocky terrain, but may be easier to approach since it does not fear human contact. It breeds on the banks or bars of gravelly streams, laying 4 greenish eggs lightly spotted with brown in a carefully built nest of roots and twigs, lined with leaves. Its nesting habits have only recently been fully studied, as the first nest was only discovered in 1922. The eggs are incubated by both birds, which takes around 3 weeks; the young are ready to leave the nest within a few days after hatching. The adult is of medium size for a sandpiper, with short, dull yellow legs and a dark bill that is somewhat longer than its head. Its plumage is dark gray above, with a pale gray wash on the throat and breast and a pale belly, and it has a dark eye line with a paler eyebrow above. The breeding bird has strong black barring below. Although several Tattlers may spend the winter foraging on the same stretch of beach, each feeds alone, teetering and bobbing as it moves along. It eats insect larvae, mollusks and marine worms.

SPOTTED SANDPIPER

Scientific name:	*Actitis macularia*
Length:	7½ inches
Habitat:	Streams, ponds, lakes, marshes
Identification:	Short-necked, long-tailed wading bird. Olive-brown back and wash on sides of breast, light eye stripe, white eye ring, white below, flesh-colored legs. Breeding bird large round black spots below
Similar species:	Bobbing walk is unmistakable and breeding plumage is distinctive. Winter Solitary Sandpiper is darker, has more distinct eye ring, lacks white upperwing stripe seen in flight

The Spotted Sandpiper is a common bird, widespread across much of North America in summer and spending the winter in the far south and down into South America. It is usually seen singly rather than in flocks, on the edges of coastal mud flats, in marshes and along streams and ponds. When moving across the ground, it has a distinctive bobbing, teetering walk. It lays up to 4 greeny or buffy eggs in a depression in the ground near water. These are incubated for around 21-24 days - often by the male bird only; the young are ready to leave the nest soon after hatching and are fully independent by 3 weeks. The adult is a short-necked bird with a rather long tail and flesh-colored legs. It has an olive-brown back, which extends down as a wash on the sides of the breast, a light eye stripe and white eye ring, and is white below. In breeding plumage, the mature bird has very distinctive large, round, black spots on its underparts. The Spotted Sandpiper flies with stiff, shallow wingbeats and shows a short white stripe on the upper wing. It eats insects, small fish and crustaceans.

WILLET

Scientific name:	*Catoptrophorus semipalmatus*
Length:	15 inches
Habitat:	Wetlands, coastal beaches, marshes
Identification:	Bulky, long-legged, long-billed wading bird. Light sand-gray back, white below, gray legs. Breeding adult heavily mottled. In flight has striking black and white wings
Similar species:	Larger and stockier than most other sandpipers

Found in many habitats, the Willet is a noisy bird that is seen in small flocks or singly on beaches. It winters in the south along both North American coasts, but spends the summer only along the Atlantic and Gulf coasts, and in some areas in the west. It breeds in wetlands, laying 3 or 4 spotted buffy eggs in a cup made of grass or in an unlined scrape in the ground. These are incubated for around 21-30 days by both parent birds; the young are ready to leave the nest soon after hatching, but are looked after by the female until they are ready to fend for themselves. The adult is plump and bulky, with long, thick, gray legs and a rather long, stout, gray bill. It has a plain, light sand-gray back, and is white below, but the breeding adult is heavily mottled. In flight, it has very striking wings, with a black patch and trailing edge, separated by a broad white band. When disturbed, it flashes these wings at predators to startle them. The Willet feeds in small flocks, but the birds are quite widely spaced. It eats insects, small marine animals and seeds.

LONG-BILLED CURLEW

Scientific name:	*Numenius americanus*
Length:	23 inches
Habitat:	Wetlands, coastal mud flats, dry grasslands
Identification:	Large, shore bird with very long downcurved bill. Cinnamon brown with dark mottling above, buff below, in flight has cinnamon underwings
Similar species:	Very long downcurved bill and cinnamon underwings are distinctive

The largest of the North American sandpipers, the Long-billed Curlew is found mainly in the west. It spends the winter on coastal mud flats and farmland and the summer on drier grassland further inland. A social bird, it spends much of its time in flocks, except in the breeding season when it becomes very territorial. It avoids cover and nests in the open, laying up to 4 olive, brown-spotted eggs in a depression lined with grasses. These are incubated for around 26-29 days by both adults; the young leave the nest soon after hatching and are fully independent within 7 weeks. The adult is very large, with an extremely long, very downcurved bill. Its plumage is cinnamon brown with dark mottling above, and buff below. In flight, it has cinnamon underwings. The juvenile has the same coloring but a slightly shorter bill. The Long-billed Curlew walks steadily when it is foraging, reaching ahead with its long bill to pick up food or to probe with the tip for insects and small aquatic animals.

UPLAND SANDPIPER

Scientific name:	*Bartramia longicauda*
Length:	12 inches
Habitat:	Open grassland
Identification:	Long-necked, long-tailed meadowland bird. Mottled brown-black above, whitish below, yellow legs, short bill, large dark eyes
Similar species:	Short bill and long thin neck distinctive

Formerly known as the Upland Plover, the Upland Sandpiper is a meadowland bird that prefers long grass - often only its head can be seen poking up above the stems. It winters in South America, but was once widespread across much of North America in summer, until indiscriminate slaughtering in the late 19th century brought it to the edge of extinction. After protection laws were passed, populations recovered and it is now fairly common within its range. It nests in tall grass at the edge of clearings, laying up to 4 cream or buffy eggs in a hollow lined with grasses. These are incubated for just over 3 weeks by both parent birds; the young leave the nest soon after hatching and are fully independent within 4 weeks. The adult has a small head with large dark eyes set on a long, thin neck, a short bill, dull yellow legs and a very long tail for a sandpiper. Its plumage is heavily mottled brown-black above, and plain whitish below. The Upland Sandpiper often pauses with its wings raised after landing, and can be seen perched on fence posts in its breeding area. It mainly eats insects and grass seeds.

BAR-TAILED GODWIT

Scientific name:	*Limosa lapponica*
Length:	16 inches
Habitat:	Open tundra, beaches, coastal mud flats
Identification:	Medium-size shore bird with long slightly upturned bill. Breeding adult has a dark back with cinnamon patterning, plain chestnut below and on head and neck. Winter birds streaked brown-gray above, whitish below. All plumages, white rump and white cross-barred tail
Similar species:	In winter resembles Marbled Godwit, but lacks warm brown tone, bill and legs are shorter

Only found in Alaska, the Bar-tailed Godwit spends the summer on tundra and migrates to the Old World for the winter, although a few strays find their way along the northwest Pacific coast. It breeds on tundra marshes, laying 4 greeny eggs with brown spots in a scantily-lined hollow. These are incubated by both adults; the young leave the nest soon after hatching and are independent within about a month. The adult has long legs and a long, slightly upturned, pinkish bill with a darker tip. The breeding adult has a dark back with cinnamon and light patterning, and is plain bright chestnut below and on the head and neck. Winter birds are streaked brown-gray above, and whitish below. The female is larger than the male and paler in coloring. In flight, all birds show a white rump, a white cross-barred tail and pointed wings with cross-barred linings. The Bar-tailed Godwit wades in open water, probing with its bill to find crustaceans, mollusks and worms.

MARBLED GODWIT

Scientific name:	*Limosa fedoa*
Length:	18 inches
Habitat:	Tidal flats, grassy marshes, shallow pools
Identification:	Medium-size, long-legged shore bird with long slightly upturned bill. Breeding adult is warm tawny-brown mottled with black above and barred below. Winter birds mottled above, plain buffy-brown below. All plumages, cinnamon wing linings
Similar species:	In winter resembles Bar-tailed Godwit, but is a warmer brown tone, bill and legs are longer

The Marbled Godwit is more widespread than the other North American godwits; it is commonly seen in flocks on the beaches of the Pacific coast in winter and is also found around the Gulf and along the southeast coast. It spends the summer breeding season on the northern prairies, laying 4 greeny-buff eggs in a scrape concealed in grass near water. These are incubated for around 3 weeks; the young leave the nest soon after hatching and are independent within about 21 days. The adult has long legs and a long, slightly upturned, flesh-pink bill with a darker tip. The breeding adult is an even warm tawny-brown all over, mottled with black above and barred below. Winter birds and juveniles are mottled above and plain buffy-brown below. In flight, all birds show cinnamon wing linings and along the trailing edge of upper wings. The Marbled Godwit stands on flooded mud flats and in marshes, probing the mud with its bill to find crustaceans, mollusks and worms.

HUDSONIAN GODWIT

Scientific name:	*Limosa haemastica*
Length:	15½ inches
Habitat:	Grassy marshes, beaches, mud flats, shallow pools
Identification:	Medium-size shore bird with long slightly upturned bill. Breeding adult is mottled brown above, chestnut below finely barred with black. Winter birds gray above and on breast, whitish belly
Similar species:	Dark wing linings and narrow white wing stripe are distinctive in flight

The smallest of the Godwits, the Hudsonian is an uncommon sandpiper that spends the summer in a few scattered areas in the north and migrates in flocks through central North America on its way to wintering grounds in South America. Its nest is a hollow concealed in grass and lined with leaves, in which it lays 4 olive-green, brown-spotted eggs. These are incubated for just over 3 weeks by both adults; the young leave the nest a day or so after hatching and are fully independent within one month. The adult has a typical godwit bill - long, slightly upturned, pinky-yellow with a darker tip. The breeding adult is mottled brown above and rich chestnut below, finely barred with black. The female has the same coloring, but is larger and paler. Winter birds and juveniles are gray above and on the breast, with a whitish belly. In flight, the Hudsonian Godwit has pointed wings with black linings and a white stripe, and a black tail contrasting with its white rump. It probes with its bill to find crustaceans, mollusks, worms and insects.

BLACK TURNSTONE

Scientific name: *Arenaria melanocephala*
Length: 9¼ inches
Habitat: Rocky coasts, mud flats, tundra
Identification: Small, short-legged shore bird with short pointed bill. Breeding adult has black above and on breast, with large white spot before the eye, white line above eye, white spotting on sides of neck and breast, white belly. Winter birds plain black above and on breast, white belly. In flight, wings boldly patterned in black and white
Similar species: In winter, darker than Ruddy Turnstone, Surfbird and Rock Sandpiper

Although it is most never seen inland, the Black Turnstone is seen all along the west coast in winter and spends the summer in northwest Alaska. It breeds on the wet tundra of the Alaskan coast, laying 4 yellow-olive eggs with darker markings in a scrape on pebbly ground or on a gravel bar. These are incubated for around 3 weeks by both adult birds; the young leave the nest quite soon after hatching. The adult is a small, short-legged bird with a relatively short, pointed bill. In its breeding plumage it is black above and on the breast, with a large white spot before the eye, a white line above the eye, white spotting on the sides of neck and breast, and a white belly. Winter birds are black above and on the breast without the white markings, and have a white belly. The juvenile resembles the winter adult. In flight, the wings are boldly patterned in black and white above and clean white below. Like the Ruddy Turnstone, the Black flips over pebbles, rocks and seaweed with its bill to find the crustaceans, mollusks and worms hidden underneath. It is only territorial during the summer breeding season, during the rest of the year it is generally found in small flocks.

SURFBIRD

Scientific name:	*Aphriza virgata*
Length:	10 inches
Habitat:	Rocky beaches, mountain tundra
Identification:	Stocky, short-legged shore bird with stout bill. Breeding adult is gray above and white beneath, with rufous wing patch, all heavily spotted and streaked with brown-black. Winter birds dark gray above and on breast, white belly. In flight, white rump and tail with broad black tip
Similar species:	In winter, lighter than Black Turnstone

The Surfbird is seen on rocky beaches all along the west coast in winter and spends the summer in the mountains of Alaska and northwest Canada. It breeds above the timberline on mountain tundra, laying 4 buffy eggs spotted with other colors among rocks. These are incubated by both adult birds; the young leave the nest soon after hatching. The adult is a stocky bird, with short yellow legs and a stout yellow bill with a dark tip. The breeding adult is gray above and white beneath, with a rufous wing patch, all heavily spotted and streaked with brown-black. Winter birds are plain dark gray above and on the breast, with a white belly. In flight, it shows a white rump and tail with a broad black tip.The juvenile resembles the winter adult, but has some white scaling. In flight, the wings have a white stripe on gray above and are white marked with gray below. The Surfbird uses its stout bill to prise mollusks off rocks; it also eats crustaceans and insects.

RUDDY TURNSTONE

Scientific name:	*Arenaria interpres*
Length:	9½ inches
Habitat:	Rocky coasts, beaches, mud flats, Great Lakes
Identification:	Small, short-legged shore bird with short pointed bill. Breeding adult is white with orange-red back, black patterning on chest and face, bright orange legs and feet, white tail with broad black band. Winter birds dark brown streaked with black above, white below. In flight, wings boldly patterned in black, white and rust
Similar species:	Unmistakable in summer plumage. In winter, wing patterning distinguishes it from similar plovers and sandpipers

Although rarely seen inland, the Ruddy Turnstone is commonly seen along the coast in winter and during migration; it prefers rocks, but is also found on beaches and mud flats. It spends the summer on the coastal shores of Alaska, establishing a territory and laying 4 grayish-green spotted eggs in a scantily-lined scrape on open ground near water. These are incubated for around 3 weeks by both adult birds; the young leave the nest soon after hatching and are independent within about 21 days. The adult is a small, short-legged bird with a short, pointed bill. In its distinctive breeding plumage it is white with an orange-red back marked with black, black and white patterning on the chest and face, bright orange legs and feet, and a white tail with a broad black band. Winter birds are dark brown streaked with black above, and white below. The female is somewhat duller than the male and the juvenile resembles the winter adult, but its back is scaled rather than streaked. In flight, the wings are boldly patterned in black, white and rust. When feeding, the Ruddy Turnstone flips over pebbles, rocks and seaweed with its bill to find crustaceans, mollusks and worms - but it will also eat almost everything else edible it finds.

LEAST SANDPIPER

Scientific name:	*Calidris minutilla*
Length:	6 inches
Habitat:	Rivers, ponds, marshes
Identification:	Small, yellow-legged bird. Breeding adult has mottled warm brown-gray on back, head and upper breast sometimes tinged rufous, white belly. Winter birds gray above, white below
Similar species:	Easily confused with Western and Semipalmated sandpipers, but has yellow legs and is darker above in all plumages

Slightly smaller than the Western and Semipalmated, the Least Sandpiper is more widespread than either. It is the sandpiper seen most often inland in spring and fall across much of North America, as it migrates from its breeding ground in the north to spend the winter in the south or in South America. It spends the summer across Arctic tundra, where it lays 4 pale buff, brown-marked eggs in a depression scantily lined with leaves or grass, or in a scrape in boggy tundra. These are incubated by both birds for around 21 days; the young leave the nest soon after hatching. The adult is small with a short, thin black bill slightly down-curved at the tip and yellow legs and feet. In breeding plumage it is mottled in warm brown-gray on the back, head and upper breast, often with a rusty tint, and has white flanks and belly. Winter birds are gray-brown above and on the chest, and white below. The juveniles are similar to the adult, but more rufous. The Least Sandpiper is often seen foraging for marine animals and aquatic insects with Semipalmated and Baird's sandpipers and it is very difficult to tell them apart at a distance. Sandpipers in general are commonly known as "peeps".

WESTERN SANDPIPER

Scientific name:	*Calidris mauri*
Length:	6½ inches
Habitat:	Coastal flats
Identification:	Small shore bird, black bill decurved at tip. Breeding adult has mottled warm brown-gray above, rusty red on shoulders, crown and ear, white belly with heavy arrow-shaped spotting. Winter birds gray above, white below
Similar species:	In summer plumage, Semipalmated Sandpiper lacks spotting on belly. In winter easily confused with Semipalmated and Least sandpipers

The Western Sandpiper is the west American equivalent of the Semipalmated Sandpiper, and the two birds are very similar. The Western is also seen migrating in large flocks across much of North America, but it breeds on the coastal tundra of Alaska in the northwest and into Siberia and winters along the southwest and southeast coasts. It lays 4 creamy eggs with red-brown markings in a scrape on dry ground, which are incubated by both birds for around 20 days; the young leave the nest soon after hatching and are independent within 2-3 weeks. The adult is small and rather plump, with a longish black bill, slightly curved down at the tip, and black legs and feet. In breeding plumage it is mottled brown-gray above, with rust-red on the shoulders, crown and ear, and a white belly with heavy arrow-shaped spots. Winter birds are gray above and whitish below. The juveniles have a darkish cap, pale face and breast, an indistinct white eye-brow and rufous on the shoulder. The Western Sandpiper wades more than some other sandpipers, foraging for marine animals and aquatic insects.

SANDERLING

Scientific name:	*Calidris alba*
Length:	8 inches
Habitat:	Sandy beaches
Identification:	Small, plump, short-billed shore bird. Breeding adult has mottled gray-white-rust on back, head and upper breast, white belly. Winter birds light gray above, white below. In flight, white wing stripe
Similar species:	In winter plumage, distinguished from pale plovers by longer bill, paler than Western Sandpiper

A small and pale sandpiper, the Sanderling is seen in small flocks in winter along both coasts, running up and down the beach dodging the waves. It spends the short summer breeding period on tundra in the far north and Eurasia. Its nest is a grass-lined hollow, well concealed on dry ground, in which it lays up to 4 olive eggs lightly spotted with brown. These are incubated by both birds for around 25-30 days; the young leave the nest soon after hatching and are independent within only 17 days. The adult is small and plump, with a short black bill and black legs. In breeding plumage it is mottled in gray, white and rust on the back, head and upper breast, and has a white belly. Winter birds are very pale light gray above, sometimes showing a black smudgy patch on the shoulder, and white below. In flight, it shows a distinct white wing stripe. The juvenile has a darker back than the winter adult, with some white scaling. The Sanderling rushes about the beach, keeping just ahead of the waves, picking up mollusks and crustaceans exposed by the surf.

PECTORAL SANDPIPER

Scientific name: *Calidris melanotos*
Length: 8¾ inches
Habitat: Marshes, grassy mudflats, wet fields
Identification: Small, yellow-legged, long-winged bird. Breeding adult mottled warm brown-gray on back, head and upper breast, sharply defined white belly. Winter birds gray above, white below
Similar species: Easily confused with Least Sandpiper, but is larger and has longer wings

Slightly larger than the Least, the Pectoral Sandpiper is very similar in coloring and is also more often seen inland than on the coast. Its breeding grounds are in the far north and it migrates in spring and fall across central North America, on its way to spend the winter in South America. It spends the summer across Arctic tundra in Siberia, and from northwest Alaska to Hudson Bay. There it breeds and lays 4 greenish or buff, brown-marked eggs in a scrape in the grass, which are incubated by the female for around 21 days; the young leave the nest soon after hatching and are independent within 3 weeks. The adult is small with a short, thin black bill slightly down-curved at the tip and yellowish legs and feet. In breeding plumage it is mottled in warm brown-gray on the back, head and breast, the dense streaking of the upper breast finishes abruptly against a white belly. During its breeding display, the male inflates air sacs under its breast feathers and makes a booming call. Winter birds are gray-brown above and on the chest, again with a sharp border against the white belly. The male bird is noticeably bigger than the female; juveniles are similar to the adult. The Pectoral Sandpiper is often seen foraging in small flocks on mud flats and in short grass, looking for insects and small crustaceans.

SEMIPALMATED SANDPIPER *(right)*

Scientific name:	*Calidris pusilla*
Length:	6¼ inches
Habitat:	Mudflats, Arctic tundra
Identification:	Small, short-billed shore bird. Breeding adult has mottled warm brown-gray on back, head and upper breast sometimes tinged rufous, white belly. Winter birds gray above, white below
Similar species:	In winter plumage, easily confused with Western and Least sandpipers. In summer is less rufous than either

The Semipalmated Sandpiper is seen in large flocks in spring and fall across much of North America, as it migrates from its breeding ground in the far north to spend the winter in South America. It spends the summer on Arctic tundra, where it lays 4 buff-olive eggs in a leaf-lined scrape on dry ground. These are incubated by both birds for around 20 days; the young leave the nest soon after hatching and are independent within 2-3 weeks. The adult is small and rather plump, with a short, straight black bill and black legs and feet. In breeding plumage it is mottled in warm brown-gray on the back, head and upper breast - although sometimes with a rusty tint - and has white flanks and belly. Winter birds are gray above fading round onto the chest, and white below. The juveniles have a dark cap, more evenly colored upperparts and a white eyebrow. The Semipalmated Sandpiper is named for the webbing which partly joins its front toes into a "palm" that helps it walk over soft mud to forage for marine animals and aquatic insects.

WHITE-RUMPED SANDPIPER

Scientific name:	*Calidris fuscicollis*
Length:	7½ inches
Habitat:	Marshes, mudflats, flooded fields
Identification:	Small, long-winged shore bird, white rump visible in flight. Breeding adult has warm gray-brown back, black streaks on chest and flanks. Winter birds dark gray above, white below
Similar species:	Baird's Sandpiper similar but is browner overall and lacks white rump

The White-rumped Sandpiper is often seen among other shore birds and so can be easily overlooked. It breeds in the Arctic but is seen inland in spring and fall across east and central North America, as it migrates southwards to spend the winter in South America. It spends the summer on the Arctic tundra of the far north, where it lays 4 buff or greeny-brown eggs in a shallow cup in the ground lined with leaves or grass. These are incubated by both birds for around 3 weeks; the young leave the nest soon after hatching and are independent between 2 and 3 weeks later. The adult is small, with long wings that extend past the tip of the tail in the standing bird, dark gray legs and feet and a reddish patch on the base of the lower bill that may be difficult to see. In breeding plumage it has a warm gray-brown back, and black streaks on white chest and flanks. Winter birds are dark gray above, white below. In all plumages, the white rump is visible in flight. The juveniles are similar to the adult, but more rufous. The White-rumped Sandpiper is often seen looking for marine worms and aquatic insects with other peeps and it is often difficult to tell them apart at a distance. It is perhaps seen foraging in fresh water more often than other small sandpipers.

BAIRD'S SANDPIPER

Scientific name:	*Calidris bairdii*
Length:	7½ inches
Habitat:	Beaches, lakes, wet fields
Identification:	Small, long-winged shore bird. Breeding adult has warm brown-gray back, buff wash on chest, white beneath. Winter birds gray-brown above, white below
Similar species:	White-rumped Sandpiper is grayer overall and has white rump in flight. Least Sandpiper is smaller, shorter bill turns down at tip, has yellow legs

Unlike many other sandpipers, Baird's is often seen foraging on dry mudflats some distance from the water. It breeds in the Arctic but is seen in small flocks in spring and fall across much of North America, as it migrates south to winter high in the Andes of South America. The adult birds tend to move down the center of the country, but juveniles cover a much broader area and may be seen on both the east and west coasts. Baird's Sandpiper spends the summer on Arctic tundra, where it lays 4 buffy, brown-spotted eggs in a shallow, unlined scrape in bare, dry ground. These are incubated by both parent birds for just over 3 weeks; the young leave the nest soon after hatching and are independent around 3 weeks later. The adult is small, with long wings that extend well past the tip of the tail in the standing bird, dark gray legs and feet and a dark bill. In breeding plumage it has a warm brown-gray back, with a buff wash on the neck and chest and white beneath. Winter birds are gray-brown above and white below. The juvenile is very similar to the adult, but pale edges to the brown feathers give its back a scaled look. Baird's Sandpiper mainly eats insects and small crustaceans.

DUNLIN

Scientific name:	*Calidris alpina*
Length:	$8\frac{1}{2}$ inches
Habitat:	Mud flats, Arctic tundra
Identification:	Stocky shore bird, long down-curved bill. Breeding adult gray-brown on head, neck and upper breast, rufous back, belly and flanks whitish with black belly patch. Winter birds brown-gray above, whitish below
Similar species:	Easily confused with Rock Sandpiper, but has a black belly patch rather than dark gray lower breast patch, and darker legs

Large flocks of Dunlins can be seen on mud flats along both North American coasts from fall through to spring. When disturbed, hundreds of birds rise in a tightly-packed swirling mass, flying in perfect formation. The Dunlin spends the summer on Arctic tundra in the far north, where it breeds and lays 4 buff greenish, brown-spotted eggs in a small scrape in the ground lined with grass. These are incubated by both adults for around 3 weeks; the young leave the nest soon after hatching and are looked after by both parents. The adult is stocky with a short neck, a bill that is heavy at the base but slimmer and downcurved at the tip and is longer than the head, and dark legs and feet. In breeding plumage it is gray-brown on the head, neck and upper breast, with a rufous back, and whitish belly and flanks with black belly patch. Winter birds are an even dull brown-gray above, and whitish below. The juvenile is brown above and buff below, with darker streaks on breast and flanks. The Dunlin wades slowly through shallow water, probing with its bill to find mollusks, aquatic insects and small crustaceans.

ROCK SANDPIPER

Scientific name:	*Calidris ptilocnemis*
Length:	9 inches
Habitat:	Rocky shores, tundra
Identification:	Stocky, orange-legged, shore bird, long bill. Breeding adult brown-gray streaked black on head, neck and upper breast, rufous-gray back feathers edged with white or buff, belly and flanks spotted dark gray-brown with dark gray lower breast patch. Winter birds purple-gray above, whitish below
Similar species:	Easily confused with Purple Sandpiper, but has breast patch and a different range. Dunlin also quite similar but has a black belly patch

Like the Purple Sandpiper, the Rock is more a "rockpiper" than a sandpiper. It is the west coast equivalent of the Purple, being seen in winter on coastal rocks along the west coast. It spends the summer on Arctic tundra in the far northwest, where it breeds and lays 4 olive, brown-spotted eggs in a small hollow in the ground. These are incubated by both parents for around 3 weeks; the young leave the nest soon after hatching and are looked after mainly by the male. The adult is stocky with a long, slender, slightly downcurved dark bill, and greeny-yellow legs and feet. In breeding plumage it is brown-gray heavily streaked with black on head, neck and upper breast, the rufous-gray back feathers are edged with white or buff, and breast and flanks are spotted dark gray-brown with a dark gray lower breast patch. Winter birds are gray above with a purple sheen, and whitish below with distinct spotting. In flight, the wings have a bold white stripe. The juvenile is similar to the adult. The Rock Sandpiper forages on coastal rocks for mollusks, insects and small crustaceans.

PURPLE SANDPIPER

Scientific name:	*Calidris maritima*
Length:	9 inches
Habitat:	Rocky east coast shores, Arctic tundra
Identification:	Stocky, orange-legged, shore bird, long bill. Breeding adult brown-gray streaked black on head, neck and upper breast, brown-gray back feathers edged with white or buff, belly and flanks spotted dark gray-brown. Winter birds purple-gray above, whitish below
Similar species:	Easily confused with Rock Sandpiper, but lacks breast patch and has a different range

More a "rockpiper" than a sandpiper, the Purple Sandpiper is mainly seen in winter on coastal rocks and stone breakwaters along the east coast. It spends the summer on Arctic tundra in the far northeast, where it breeds and lays 4 greenish, brown-spotted eggs in a hollow in the ground. These are incubated mainly by the male for around 3 weeks; the young leave the nest soon after hatching and are independent within a further 3 weeks. The adult is stocky with a long, slender, slightly downcurved dark bill that is yellow-orange at the base, and orange legs and feet. In breeding plumage it is brown-gray streaked with black on head, neck and upper breast, the brown-gray back feathers are edged with white or buff, and the belly and flanks are spotted dark gray-brown. Winter birds are gray above with a purple sheen, and whitish below. In flight, the wings have a distinct white stripe. The juvenile is similar to the adult. The Purple Sandpiper forages on coastal rocks for mollusks, algae and small crustaceans.

STILT SANDPIPER

Scientific name:	*Calidris himantopus*
Length:	8½ inches
Habitat:	Shallow muddy pools
Identification:	Slender, long-billed bird with long greenish legs. Breeding bird chestnut ear patch, gray-brown above, white barred with dark brown beneath. Winter birds gray above, whitish beneath
Similar species:	Feeds in the same distinctive way as a dowitcher, but is much smaller. General size and shape more like Lesser Yellowlegs, but lacks bright yellow legs

Since it breeds in the far north and spends the winter in the far south, the Stilt Sandpiper is seen across central North America in migration, traveling in dense flocks. On the coast, it is also often seen in fall as it migrates south, although seldom in large numbers. It prefers muddy fields, shallow pools, mud flats and marshy areas, but spends the brief Arctic summer on tundra, where it breeds and lays 4 olive-greenish eggs, usually spotted with brown, in an unlined hollow in dry ground. The eggs are incubated by both adults for about 3 weeks and the downy young leave the nest soon after hatching and are independent in 2-3 weeks. The adult is a slender bird, with long, thin, greenish legs and a rather heavy, drooping bill. In breeding plumage, it has a chestnut ear patch and is gray-brown above and white barred with dark brown beneath. Winter birds are gray above, and whitish beneath. The juvenile is similar to the winter adult, but more heavily patterned; very young birds have a buff wash on the breast. The Stilt Sandpiper is often seen feeding with dowitchers and both species have the same way of rhythmically bobbing their heads up and down as they hunt for mollusks, worms, aquatic plants and insect larvae.

LONG-BILLED DOWITCHER

Scientific name:	*Limnodromus scolopaceus*
Length:	11½ inches
Habitat:	Mud flats, shallow fresh water
Identification:	Stocky, long-billed, shore bird with greenish legs. Breeding bird has chestnut-orange neck with dark streaks, brown-white-rufous chequered back, orange belly. Winter birds brownish-gray above, white eyebrow stripe, whitish beneath
Similar species:	Short-billed and Long-billed are almost identical, but the Short-billed favors salt water and the Long-billed prefers fresh

The female Long-billed Dowitcher has a much longer bill than the Short-billed, but the bill of the male is the same length. The Long-billed spends the summer in the far northwest Arctic and migrates across central North America to spend the winter in the south. They breed on Arctic tundra marsh, laying 4 greenish eggs, with brown markings, in a scrape in the ground. The eggs are incubated by both adult birds for about 3 weeks and the downy young leave the nest soon after hatching. The adult bird is stocky, with a long, dark bill and greenish legs. The breeding adult has a chestnut-orange neck with dark streaks, a brown-white-rufous chequered back, and an orange belly with dark barring on the flanks. Winter birds (*right*) have brownish-gray plumage above, a white eyebrow stripe, and are whitish beneath. Juveniles are gray-buff below with a whitish belly, and rufous edging to dark back feathers. Long-billed Dowitchers prefer fresh water and are found in muddy fields, shallow pools, mud flats and marshy areas. Like the Short-billed, they feed by rhythmically bobbing their heads up and down as they hunt for snails, crustaceans and insect larvae.

SHORT-BILLED DOWITCHER

Scientific name:	*Limnodromus griseus*
Length:	11 inches
Habitat:	Beaches, mud flats, shallow salt water
Identification:	Stocky, long-billed, shore bird with greenish legs. Breeding bird usually has chestnut-orange neck, brown-white-rufous chequered back, white or orange belly. Winter birds brownish-gray above, white eyebrow stripe, whitish beneath
Similar species:	Short-billed and Long-billed are almost identical, but the Short-billed favors salt water and the Long-billed prefers fresh

The Short-billed Dowitcher is established in three breeding colonies across central Canada, with each having a distinct color variation in plumage. Birds in the west have a white belly with dark barring and a darker, rufous back, birds in the center are orange beneath with no spotting on the neck, and those in the east are similar to western birds but have a less rufous back. In its breeding grounds, it lays 4 buff-greenish eggs, spotted with brown, in a depression in dry ground. The eggs are incubated by both adults for about 3 weeks and the young leave the nest soon after hatching. In winter, the Short-billed Dowitcher is found on beaches, mud flats and marshy areas in southern North America; the plumage of all winter birds is similar (*right*), with brown-gray above, a white eyebrow stripe, and whitish beneath. The adult bird is stocky, with a long, dark bill and greenish legs. Dowitchers feed by rhythmically bobbing their heads up and down as they hunt for snails, crustaceans and insect larvae. The Short-billed Dowitcher prefers salt water which distinguishes it from the Long-billed - the difference in bill length is not readily apparent.

RED KNOT

Scientific name:	*Calidris canutus*
Length:	10½ inches
Habitat:	Sandy beaches, mud flats
Identification:	Medium-size, stout, short-legged shore bird. Breeding bird mottled gray-brown, black and chestnut above, reddish beneath. Winter birds pale gray on back, white beneath
Similar species:	Breeding plumage is distinctive. In winter plumage could be mistaken for a Dowitcher or Willet, but has a much shorter, stout bill

The Red Knot is seen in great numbers in some areas, but hardly at all in others. It frequents open tidal flats and sandy beaches along both coasts in winter, and spends the summer on Arctic tundra; it is only seen infrequently inland during migration. It breeds on dry, open tundra, laying 4 buff, brown-spotted eggs in a scantily lined scrape in gravel. The eggs are incubated by both adult birds for about 22 days and the downy young leave the nest soon after hatching and are independent within 20 days. The adult is one of the larger sandpipers, but is rather stout with a short neck and legs. Its bill is dark-colored, quite short and thick, and it has yellow-olive legs and feet. The breeding plumage (*above*) is mottled gray-brown, black and chestnut above, and reddish beneath. Winter birds are pale gray above and white beneath. The juvenile is similar to the winter adult, but is more spotted below and scaley above. The Red Knot feeds on beaches and mud flats, foraging for mollusks, seeds and insect larvae. Thousands of birds congregate in May each year on Delaware Bay, to feast on the new-laid eggs of horseshoe crabs.

COMMON SNIPE

Scientific name:	*Gallinago gallinago*
Length:	$10\frac{1}{2}$ inches
Habitat:	Marshes, damp fields, muddy pond edges
Identification:	Very stocky, long-billed, short-legged, short-winged marsh bird. Adult bird has striped head, brown mottled back, barred flanks. Rapid, sharp zig-zag flight
Similar species:	Shape, plumage and bill distinctive

A very solitary and secretive bird, the Common Snipe is more often seen in flight after it has been flushed than on the ground. It was previously known as Wilson's Snipe and is found across much of North America - except in the Rockies - in bogs and marshy areas with enough vegetation to provide cover. It spends the summer in the northern half of the continent, breeding in marshes and damp areas where it lays 4 olive-brown eggs in a grass-lined depression in the ground. The eggs are incubated by the female for up to 3 weeks and the downy young leave the nest soon after hatching and are independent within 20 days. In winter it moves further south. The adult bird is very stocky, with a long, straight bill, short neck and legs and short wings. It has lengthwise stripes on the head, a brown mottled back streaked with white, dark barred flanks and a white belly. Its rapid, sharply zig-zagging flight when flushed is distinctive, and during its swooping display flight it vibrates its tail feathers to make a hooting sound. The Common Snipe forages in all kinds of muddy habitats, where it probes with its long bill in a rhythmic, jerky motion, penetrating deeply into the mud to catch crustaceans, insects and other small animals.

WILSON'S PHALAROPE

Scientific name:	*Phalaropus tricolor*
Length:	$9\frac{1}{4}$ inches
Habitat:	Marshes, grassy edges of shallow lakes
Identification:	Slender marsh bird with thin, needle-like bill and long legs. Breeding female has black and chestnut neck stripes, gray and white head, gray back, rusty tint to breast. Male is duller. Winter birds are gray above, white beneath
Similar species:	Breeding bird is distinctive, winter bird similar to Stilt Sandpiper and Lesser Yellowlegs, but Wilson's Phalarope is a more nervous, darting feeder. In flight, is distinguished from other phalaropes by white rump and lack of white wing stripe

Phalaropes are a type of sandpiper, although some experts believe they should be a separate family. Wilson's Phalarope is an inland bird that is never found on open ocean. It spends the summer in western North America, and migrates to winter in the Southern Hemisphere. It nests in marshes, laying up to 4 buff eggs splotched with brown and gray in a grass-lined depression in the ground. The eggs are incubated by the male alone for up to 3 weeks and the downy young leave the nest soon after hatching and are tended by the male until they are ready to fly. The adult bird is slender, with a thin, needle-like bill and long legs that are black in the breeding season and yellow at other times. The breeding female is larger than the male and has black and chestnut neck stripes, a gray and white head, a gray back and a rusty tint to the breast. The male is duller. Winter birds (*right*) are gray above and white beneath. Wilson's Phalarope eats insect larvae, small crustaceans and seeds.

RED-NECKED PHALAROPE

Scientific name:	*Phalaropus lobatus*
Length:	7¾ inches
Habitat:	Tundra ponds, offshore
Identification:	Small sea bird with thin, dark, needle-like bill. Breeding female is gray with bright rusty-red to front and sides of neck, white throat, buff stripes on back. Male is duller. Winter birds are gray above, white beneath with paler streaks on back and black ear and crown markings
Similar species:	Breeding bird is distinctive. In flight, winter bird is distinguished from winter Wilson's Phalarope by bold white wing stripe

The Red-necked Phalarope spends the summer on Arctic tundra, and winters at sea in the Southern Hemisphere. It is often seen off the Pacific coast in migration, and on western lakes in fall, but is rare off the east coast. It nests near ponds on wet ground, laying 2-4 olive-buff, thickly spotted eggs in a grass-lined scrape in the tundra. The larger and more colorful female courts the male and then defends the nest site while the male incubates the eggs for up to 3 weeks. The young leave the nest after hatching and are tended by the male until they are ready to fly at 3 weeks. The adult has a thin, dark needle-like bill and dark legs. The breeding female is dark gray with bright rusty-red to the front and sides of the neck, a white throat, and buff stripes to the back. The male (*right*) is duller, with a buff-colored neck. Winter birds are gray above and white beneath, with paler streaks to the back and black ear and crown markings. In flight, a bold white wing stripe is evident in all plumages. The Red-necked Phalarope prefers to swim rather than wade, and plucks small crustaceans and insects from the surface.

AMERICAN WOODCOCK

Scientific name:	*Scolopax minor*
Length:	11 inches
Habitat:	Damp woodlands and fields
Identification:	Plump, long-billed, short-legged, woodland bird. Adult bird has crosswise black bars on crown, large dark eyes, black-buff-whitish patterned back, orange-buff belly
Similar species:	Shape, plumage and bill distinctive

The American Woodcock is a nocturnal and secretive bird, which hides in brushy woodland during the day but may come out onto damp fields at night. It is found across eastern North America as far north as the Great Lakes in summer, but is seldom seen unless flushed. At the start of the breeding season in early spring, the male performs a nocturnal courtship display, strutting on the ground then taking off, singing and circling round, before swooping down to mate. It nests in damp woodland, laying up to 4 buff-cinnamon eggs in a leaf-lined depression in the ground. The eggs are incubated by the female for up to 3 weeks and the downy young leave the nest soon after hatching and are independent within around 14 days. In winter, birds in the north move further south. The adult bird is round-bodied, with large dark eyes, a very long bill and short legs. Both sexes are similar, with crosswise black bars on the crown, a black-buff-whitish patterned back that blends in with drifts of dead leaves, and an orange-buff belly. The American Woodcock forages in damp habitats, particularly wet fields where it probes with its long bill to find earthworms and insects.

PARASITIC JAEGER

Scientific name:	*Stercorarius parasiticus*
Length:	19 inches, wingspan 42 inches
Habitat:	Offshore, Great Lakes, open tundra
Identification:	Seabird, long pointed wings with white patch below, white flash above near tip. Dark adult uniformly dark brown. Light adult brown above, white below, white neck, yellow tint to cheeks, black cap, gray-brown wash on chest
Similar species:	Long-tailed Jaeger is similar to light variation Parasitic, but lacks gray-brown wash on breast, has long tail streamers. In flight, adult lacks white wing markings. Juvenile Parasitic is warmer colored than grayer juvenile Long-tailed

The name jaeger comes from the German word for hunter; the Parasitic Jaeger preys on young birds and lemmings on its breeding grounds and in winter robs other seabirds. It is the most common jaeger off the southeast and southwest coasts, but is rarely spotted inland. It breeds on Arctic tundra, laying 2 olive, brown-spotted eggs in a depression in the ground, sometimes lined with a few lichens. Both adults incubate the eggs, for up to 4 weeks, and the young birds leave the nest about 5 weeks later. The adult is bulky, with a short, pointed tail and long, pointed wings that in flight show a white patch beneath and usually a white flash above near the tip. The dark variation adult is uniformly dark brown, the light variation is brown above and white below, with a white neck, yellow tint to the cheeks, a black cap, and a gray-brown wash across the chest. The juveniles are uniformly dark. The Parasitic Jaeger flies low over the tundra in summer, snatching eggs, nestlings or lemmings to feed itself and its young. In winter, it harasses other seabirds until they drop their catch, which the jaeger then snatches.

LONG-TAILED JAEGER

Scientific name:	*Stercorarius longicaudus*
Length:	22 inches, wingspan 40 inches
Habitat:	Dry tundra, offshore
Identification:	Predatory seabird, long pointed wings, long tail streamers. Adult brown above, white below, white neck, yellow tint to cheeks, neat black cap
Similar species:	Similar to light variation Parasitic, but lacks gray-brown wash on breast and has long tail streamers. In flight, lacks white wing patch. Juvenile Parasitic is warmer colored than grayer juvenile Long-tailed

The Long-tailed Jaeger is rarely seen from the shore, as it migrates across the open ocean to spend the winter in the Southern Hemisphere. It breeds on dry upland tundra, usually laying 2 olive-brown, spotted eggs in a scrape in the ground or moss. Both adult birds incubate the eggs, for just over 3 weeks, and the young birds are ready to leave the nest a further 3 weeks later. The adult is more slender and delicate than the Parasitic, with long tail streamers - although these may sometimes be broken or missing - and long, pointed wings. Its plumage is brown above and white below, with a white neck, yellow tint to the cheeks, and a neat black cap. The juvenile lacks tail streamers and varies from dark gray to pale gray with a darker back with whitish tips to the feathers; in flight it shows a white patch below the wing, near the tip. The Long-tailed Jaeger also preys on eggs, nestlings and lemmings on its tundra breeding grounds, but robs other birds less frequently in winter.

150

GREAT BLACK-BACKED GULL

Scientific name:	*Larus marinus*
Length:	30 inches, wingspan 65 inches
Habitat:	Great Lakes, coastal areas
Identification:	Large, long-winged seabird with big yellow bill. Mature bird has large white head, black upperparts, white underparts, pink legs
Similar species:	Size is distinctve, but 1st winter juvenile is checkered gray-brown with a black bill and resembles 1st winter Herring Gull, although head and underparts are lighter

A very common gull along the northeast coast, the Great Black-backed Gull is also found some way inland and on the eastern Great Lakes and is expanding further south - although it is still very rare around the Gulf. It nests in colonies, sometimes with other seabirds, building a cup of seaweed, grass and moss to hold 2-3 olive-brown, spotted eggs. These are incubated by both parents for around 28 days; the downy young cannot fly until around 8 weeks, but leave the nest soon after hatching. The Great Black-backed Gull takes 4 years to reach its mature plumage. The 1st winter bird is checkered gray-brown with lighter head and underparts and a large black bill. By the 2nd winter, it has much whiter underparts and head and the back is darker gray. In the 3rd winter the plumage is more like the adult, with a white head and underparts and a mainly yellow bill, although there is still some brown in the wings. The adult has a white head with pale eyes and a yellow bill, black upperparts, white underparts, and pink legs. In flight, its wings are black above, with white along the trailing edge and underneath and it shows a white rump. The Great Black-backed Gull eats fish and the eggs and young of other seabirds; it also scavenges in garbage dumps and eats carrion.

GLAUCOUS GULL *(below)*

Scientific name:	*Larus hyperboreus*
Length:	27 inches, wingspan 60 inches
Habitat:	Arctic coastal areas, offshore
Identification:	Large gull with yellow bill marked in red. Mature bird has white head and neck in summer, head streaked brown in winter, pale gray back, white underparts, wings pale gray with white tips, pink legs and feet
Similar species:	No other gulls are as pale, except the smaller Iceland Gull, which is a rare visitor

An Arctic species, the Glaucous Gull spends the summer all across the far north and winters down both coasts - although it rarely comes down as far as California in the west and Florida in the east. It breeds in colonies on rocks or on Arctic tundra, building a large nest of seaweed or grass on a sheltered ledge or a depression in the ground to hold 2 or 3 buff or olive, brown-blotched eggs. These are incubated by both parents for around 4 weeks. The Glaucous Gull takes 4 years to reach its mature plumage. The 1st winter bird is whitish or pale fawn overall, with a pink bill tipped with black and small dark eyes. Its wings are narrow and pale buff, with white tips. By the 2nd winter its back is very pale gray, and its eyes are pale. The 3rd winter bird is much like the adult, but the yellow bill has a dark smudgy patch and the body still has some buff. The breeding adult generally has a white head and neck, a yellow bill marked with a red spot, pale eyes, a very pale gray back, white underparts, and pink legs and feet. In winter, its head is lightly streaked brown. In flight, its wings are very pale gray, with a narrow band of white along the trailing edge and white wing tips. The Glaucous Gull is a predator which preys on the eggs and young of other sea birds, frequents garbage dumps to scavenge, and forces eiders to drop their catch.

MEW GULL

Scientific name:	*Larus canus*
Length:	16 inches, wingspan 43 inches
Habitat:	Coastal areas, forest lakes
Identification:	Medium-size seabird with thin yellow bill. Mature bird has white head and neck in summer, washed brown in winter, dark-gray back, white underparts, black and white wing tips, yellow legs and feet
Similar species:	Adult Ring-billed Gull has black ring on bill, less white on tips of primary wing feathers, lighter gray back. Black-legged Kittiwake has black legs and lacks white spots on wingtip in flight

The North American Mew Gull is only found in western North America, in summer across Alaska and northwest Canada and in winter down the Pacific coast, but it is very similar to the European Mew Gull, also known as the Common Gull, which is sometimes seen along the east coast in winter. The American Mew Gull is a coastal bird in winter and is rarely seen inland. It breeds in colonies, often with other gulls, building a nest of grass, seaweed or stems on beaches, riverbanks or in a tree to hold 2 or 3 olive-buff, brown-splotched eggs. These are incubated by both parents for around 4 weeks, but the young birds do not fly until about 5 weeks later, although they leave the nest soon after hatching. The juvenile bird takes 3 years to reach mature plumage, but by its 1st winter has a gray mantle and a white-spotted breast, with a pale brown wash on head and neck and a two-tone bill. By the 2nd winter it is gray above and whitish beneath. In summer the adult has a white head and neck, a dark-gray back, white underparts, black and white wing tips, and yellow legs and feet. In winter, its head and neck are washed brown. Its wings are slate-gray above, with white along the trailing edge and beneath, and black wing tips with large white spots. The Mew Gull is not a scavenger, preferring to forage for worms and mollusks.

BLACK-LEGGED KITTIWAKE

Scientific name:	*Rissa tridactyla*
Length:	17 inches, wingspan 36 inches
Habitat:	Coastal cliffs, offshore
Identification:	Medium-size gull with black legs. Mature bird has white head and neck in summer, gray patch on the back of the head in winter, gray back, white underparts, black wing tips, yellow bill
Similar species:	Black legs are distinctive

A true "sea gull", the Black-legged Kittiwake spends much of its life out on the ocean and only comes to land to breed. It spends the summer in the far northwest and northeast and around Baffin Bay and migrates south in winter, sometimes coming as far as Mexico in the west and the Gulf coast in the east. It breeds in large colonies on very narrow ledges, building a neat nest of seaweed to hold 2 buff or pale green, dark-splotched eggs. These are incubated by both parents for about 3-4 weeks. The Black-legged Kittiwake takes 3 years to reach its mature plumage. The juvenile and 1st winter bird is gray above and white beneath, with a black half-collar, black spot behind the eye and with a black bill; in flight it has black stripes forming a W across the back and wings, and a black tail band. By the 2nd winter it is much like the adult, but with more black on the wing tip. In the breeding season the adult has a white head and neck, a yellow bill, dark eyes, a gray back, white underparts, and black legs and feet. In winter, it has a gray patch on the back of the head. In flight, its wings are gray above, paler towards the ends, with white linings and solid black tips. The Black-legged Kittiwake feeds at sea, even during the roughest weather. It follows fishing boats, but only to pick up the small mollusks and crustaceans brought to the surface, and dives underwater to catch small fish.

LAUGHING GULL

Scientific name:	*Larus atricilla*
Length:	$16\frac{1}{2}$ inches, wingspan 40 inches
Habitat:	Offshore, salt marshes, Great Lakes
Identification:	Medium-size, long-winged seabird. Mature bird has black head in summer, gray streaked in winter, white neck and underparts, dark-gray back, black wing tips, reddish bill
Similar species:	Adult Franklin's Gull has very similar summer coloring, but has more white around eye, in flight more white on tips of wing feathers, a white band between black and gray on wings and gray central tail feathers

Common along the southern Atlantic and Gulf coasts, the Laughing Gull ranges north to New England in summer, but is only found inland round Salton Sea. It breeds in colonies on salt marshes, building a nest of reeds and grass to hold 3-4 olive, brown-spotted eggs that are incubated by both adults. The juvenile bird takes 3 years to reach mature plumage, but by its 1st winter has gray sides and back, a whitish head and neck with a gray wash on the nape, brownish wings, a white belly and a black bill. By the 2nd winter, it is gray above and whiter beneath with a gray wash on the nape. In summer the adult has a black hooded head with narrow white crescents round the eyes, white neck and underparts, a dark-gray back, black wing tips and a reddish bill. In winter, the black hood fades to leave gray streaking to the rear of a white head. Its wings are slate-gray above, with white along the trailing edge and black wing tips touched with white, with a white rump and tail. The Laughing Gull eats fish, worms and insects and scavenges garbage from ships.

FRANKLIN'S GULL

Scientific name:	*Larus pipixcan*
Length:	$14\frac{1}{2}$ inches, wingspan 36 inches
Habitat:	Prairie marshes
Identification:	Rather small, long-winged inland gull. Mature bird has black head in summer, half-hooded in dark gray in winter, white neck and underparts, dark-gray back, black and white wing tips, reddish bill
Similar species:	Adult Laughing Gull has very similar summer coloring, but is larger, has less white around eye and on tips of primary wing feathers, all-white tail feathers in flight

In North America, Franklin's Gull is a summer inland bird that is rarely seen on the coast and spends the winter in South America. It breeds in large colonies on prairie marshes, building a nest of reeds and grass to hold 3 olive-buffy-brown eggs that are incubated by both birds for around 3 weeks. The juvenile bird takes 3 years to reach its mature plumage, but by its 1st winter has gray sides and back, a whitish head and neck, brownish wings, a white belly and a black bill. By the 2nd winter, it is gray above and white beneath, with a neat black half-hood. In summer the adult has a black hooded head with broad white crescents round the eyes, a white neck, white underparts tinged pink, a dark-gray back, and a reddish bill. In winter, the black hood becomes a half-hood at the rear of a white head. Its wings are slate-gray above, with white running along the trailing edge and across to form a bar between the gray and black-and-white-striped wing tips; it also has a white rump with gray central tail feathers. Franklin's Gull mainly eats insects - including those that damage crops, so it often follows the plough.

BONAPARTE'S GULL

Scientific name:	*Larus philadelphia*
Length:	13½ inches, wingspan 33 inches
Habitat:	Boreal forests, lakes, coastal areas
Identification:	Small, narrow-winged gull. Mature bird has black head in summer, white in winter with dark ear patch, white neck with gray mantle, white underparts, gray back, white triangle on wings in flight, orange-red legs, black bill
Similar species:	Distinguished from Franklin's Gull by triangle of white on upper wing in flight

The smallest of the common gulls, Bonaparte's spends the summer in boreal forests from Alaska to Hudson Bay and migrates south to winter around the southern coastlines. It does not usually flock with other gulls, and is rarely seen scavenging. It breeds in loose colonies in coniferous forest, building a well-constructed nest up to 20 feet above ground in a tree, in which it lays 2 or 3 olive, brown-blotched eggs. These are incubated by both parents for around 3 weeks. Bonaparte's Gull takes 2 years to reach its mature plumage. Its 1st winter plumage is gray above and white beneath, with diagonal black-brown lines across the wings, and a black tail band. The adult has a white triangle on the upper wings and a white tail in flight, orange-red legs, and a slender, straight black bill. In the breeding season it has a black hooded head, a white neck with gray mantle, white underparts, and a gray back. In winter, its head is white with a dark ear patch. Bonaparte's Gull is dainty and graceful in flight, skimming over the water to snatch fish, or dropping down to pick up insects, crustaceans and marine worms. However, it is often robbed of its catch by marauding jaegers.

HERRING GULL

Scientific name:	*Larus argentatus*
Length:	25 inches, wingspan 57 inches
Habitat:	Coastal areas, large lakes, landfills, fishing docks
Identification:	Large seabird with heavy yellow bill marked in red. Average mature bird has white head and neck in summer, neck extensively streaked brown in winter, gray back, white underparts, black wing tips spotted with white, pink legs and feet
Similar species:	Plumage and size of the Herring Gull is very variable at all ages, so it can be mistaken for several other large gulls

Since the Herring Gull will eat almost anything, its population is expanding in many areas and driving out weaker species. It breeds in large colonies on islets or cliffs, building a nest of seaweed or grass on the ground to hold 2 or 3 bluish or olive, dark-blotched eggs. The juvenile bird takes 4 years to reach mature plumage, but all stages are quite variable so it can be difficult to identify. By its 1st winter it has a pale face and throat, dark patterning on its back, and a black bill with pink at the base. By the 2nd winter its back is pale gray, wings brown, and the bill is pinkish with a black tip. The 3rd winter bird is much like the adult, but the yellow bill has a black patch. The adult has a white head and neck, a heavy yellow bill marked with a red spot, pale eyes with a red orbital ring, a gray back, white underparts, and pink legs and feet. In winter, its neck is streaked brown and the red bill spot turns dusky. Its wings are gray, with a narrow band of white along the trailing edge and black wing tips with white spots. The Herring Gull scavenges on garbage dumps and in harbors, but also catches fish and small crustaceans.

RING-BILLED GULL

Scientific name:	*Larus delawarensis*
Length:	17½ inches, wingspan 48 inches
Habitat:	Beaches, inland water
Identification:	Medium-size gull with heavy yellow bill ringed in black. Mature bird has white head and neck in summer, nape washed brown in winter, pale gray back, white underparts, black wing tips with white spot, yellow legs and feet
Similar species:	Mew Gull lacks black ring on bill. Herring Gull may have pale ring in winter, but has pinkish legs and heavier streaking on neck. California Gull larger, has darker eye, red and black on bill, in flight has much more extensive black on wing tip

An abundant and widespread gull, the Ring-billed breeds in large colonies, often with the California Gull, building a nest of grass and stems on the ground to hold 3 buff, dark-splotched eggs. The juvenile takes 3 years to reach mature plumage, but by its 1st winter has a gray back and is white beneath scaled and spotted in brown, with a brown streaked head and a pink bill with a black tip. Its wings are brown with black-brown tips and pale wing linings. By the 2nd winter it is much like the adult, but its tail is spotted in black across the tip and its bill ring is wider. The adult has a white head and neck, a yellow bill ringed in black, pale eyes with a red orbital ring, a pale gray back, white underparts, and yellow legs and feet. In winter, its nape is washed brown. Its wings are gray above, with white along the trailing edge and beneath, and black wing tips with a small white spot. The Ring-billed Gull eats worms, mollusks, insects and grasshoppers; it also scavenges near urban areas.

CALIFORNIA GULL

Scientific name: *Larus californicus*
Length: 21 inches, wingspan 54 inches
Habitat: Marshes, prairie lakes, coastal areas
Identification: Medium-size gull with heavy yellow bill marked in black and red. Mature bird has white head and neck in summer, nape streaked brown in winter, gray back, white underparts, black wing tips with a touch of white, yellow legs and feet
Similar species: Herring Gull is larger with pinkish legs and extensive streaking on neck. Ringed-bill Gull is smaller, has pale eye, black ring on bill, in flight has white spot on black wing tip

The California Gull is famous for devouring a swarm of locusts and so saving the Mormon settlers' first crop. Its range is more limited than some other gulls, as it spends the summer on western prairie lakes and marshes and winters along the Pacific coast. It breeds in large colonies on lake islands, often with the Ring-billed Gull, building a nest of weeds, grass and sticks on the ground to hold 2 or 3 buff-olive, dark-splotched eggs. These are incubated by both parents for around 3-4 weeks. The California Gull takes 4 years to reach its mature plumage. The juvenile bird is usually pale below with a brown back, pinkish legs and a black bill, but by its 1st winter it has some gray on its back and a pinkish bill with a black tip. Its wings are brown with double dark stripes and pale wing linings; the tail is dark brown. By the 2nd winter its back is mostly gray, its chest and belly are whitish, the legs are grayish. The 3rd winter bird is much like the adult, but the yellowish bill has more black and the wings and tail still have some brown. The breeding adult has a white head and neck, a heavy yellow bill marked with black and red, dark eyes with a red orbital ring, a gray back, white underparts, and yellow legs and feet. In winter, its nape is streaked brown. In flight, its wings are gray above, with a narrow band of white along the trailing edge and whitish underneath, and extensive black wing tips with a small white spot. The California Gull catches fish, but also eats insect larvae, grasshoppers and small rodents - which makes it popular with farmers.

ARCTIC TERN

Scientific name:	*Sterna paradisaea*
Length:	15½ inches, wingspan 31 inches
Habitat:	Offshore, tundra lakes, coastal beaches
Identification:	Medium-size short-legged sea bird, long forked tail. Breeding adult has black cap, red bill, gray body, pale beneath, long wings with dark below on tips of primaries
Similar species:	Arctic, Common and Forster's terns almost identical, but Common Tern has longer legs, shorter tail and red bill tipped black, Forster's has silvery primaries and more orange bill

The Arctic Tern inhabits a different range to the Common, being found in the summer in the far north and northwest, although the two species do overlap in the northeast. The Arctic Tern migrates well offshore to winter near Antarctica. It nests in colonies or single pairs on tundra lakes and beaches, laying 2 or more olive-brown eggs with brown spotting in a scrape in sand or gravel, which may be lined with plant matter. These are incubated by both birds for around 3 weeks, and the young chicks fly around 3-4 weeks later. The Arctic Tern takes 3 years to reach its mature plumage. The juvenile is gray-white with a white breast and forehead, blackish nape and crown and mostly dark bill, but by the 1st winter it is gray above, with a large black patch on the head, a slightly darker shoulder bar and a dark bill. By the 2nd winter it is much like the adult, with a white forehead, and a dark patch on the crown and back of the head. In the breeding season the adult has a black cap, a red bill, the upperparts are gray, and the breast and belly pale. In flight, its long wings are even gray, with a darker gray line along the tips of the primaries on the underwing. The Arctic Tern fiercely attacks and mobs any intruders on its breeding grounds. It eats fish and small crustaceans.

FORSTER'S TERN

Scientific name:	*Sterna forsteri*
Length:	$14\frac{1}{2}$ inches, wingspan 31 inches
Habitat:	Marshes, beaches
Identification:	Medium-size short-legged water bird, long forked tail. Breeding adult has black cap, orange bill with black tip, pale gray body, white beneath, long wings with silvery-white primaries
Similar species:	Forster's, Common and Arctic terns almost identical. Forster's has longer legs, Arctic Tern has longer tail and all-red bill, Common has dark wedge on upper wing and redder bill

The summer range of Forster's Tern overlaps part of that of the Common Tern, but it is also found further south and in the west. It nests in colonies in marshes or on beaches, laying 3-4 buffy, spotted eggs in marsh grasses, in a scrape on sand or on a floating platform of vegetation. These are incubated by both adults for around 24 days, and the young chicks fly about 4 weeks after hatching. The juvenile takes 3 years to reach mature plumage; in its first summer it is gingery-brown with a white breast and forehead and a blackish eye patch, but by the winter it is grayer above, with dark gray on the wing tips. By the 2nd winter it is much like the winter adult, with a white head, black bill, dark eye patch and dark streaks on the nape; the wings are more silvery-white. In the breeding season the adult has a black cap, an orange bill with a black tip, the upperparts are pale gray, and the breast and belly snow-white. In flight, its long wings are pale gray with silvery-white primary feathers, its tail is pale gray with little contrast to the white rump. Forster's Tern plunges into the water to catch fish, and also eats insects.

COMMON TERN

Scientific name:	*Sterna hirundo*
Length:	$14\frac{1}{2}$ inches, wingspan 30 inches
Habitat:	Beaches, islands
Identification:	Medium-size short-legged water bird, long forked tail. Breeding adult has black cap, red bill with black tip, gray body, pale beneath, long wings with dark wedge at tip
Similar species:	Common, Arctic and Forster's terns almost identical. Arctic Tern has shorter legs, longer tail and all-red bill, Forster's has silvery primaries and more orange bill

The most widespread and numerous of the North American terns, the Common Tern breeds across much of Canada and northern America and winters in the Southern Hemisphere. It nests in large colonies on sandbars, beaches or islands, laying 2-3 green to buff eggs with brown markings in a scrape on open ground. These are incubated by both male and female for around 24 days, and the young chicks fly around 4 weeks later. The Common Tern takes 3 years to reach its mature plumage. The juvenile is brownish with a white breast and forehead, blackish nape and orange bill, but by the 1st winter it is gray above, with a black patch on the head, dark bill, dark shoulder bar and brownish wings. By the 2nd winter it has less brown and more gray on the wings. In the breeding season the adult has a black cap, a red bill with a black tip, the upperparts are gray, and the breast and belly pale. In winter, its forehead is white with a dark patch on the crown and back of the head, and a dark shoulder bar. In flight, its long wings are gray with a darker gray wedge towards the tip of the upper wing. The Common Tern flies slowly over water, diving to catch fish or other aquatic prey.

CASPIAN TERN

Scientific name:	*Sterna caspia*
Length:	21 inches, wingspan 50 inches
Habitat:	Coastal areas, wetlands, inland water
Identification:	Large, broad-winged bird, short notched tail. Breeding adult has black cap, large red bill, pale gray body, white beneath
Similar species:	Royal Tern has thinner, more orange bill and a wispy crest, underside of wings much paler at tip

Almost as big as a gull, the Caspian Tern is the largest of the tern family and is seen in small numbers across much of North America - it is the only large tern that is seen inland. It spends the summer in scattered colonies in Canada, western America and along the southern Pacific and much of the Atlantic coasts; northern birds migrate further south in the winter. It nests in wetlands and in some coastal areas, laying 2 to 4 largish, pinky-buff eggs marked with dark brown in a scrape that may be lined with grass. These are incubated by both birds for around 3 weeks, and the young chicks begin to fly about 3-4 weeks after hatching. The adult bird is broad-winged with a short notched tail and a large, thick, red bill. The juvenile is gray-white above, white beneath, with a dark crown streaked with white on the forehead, and dark primaries on the underside of the wing. The winter adult is gray above, white beneath and its dark cap is streaked with white on the forehead and crown; it has some dark gray under the wing tip. In the breeding season the adult has a black cap. The Caspian Tern usually forages alone, flying high and diving into the water to catch fish. It may also rob other birds' nests.

GULL-BILLED TERN

Scientific name:	*Sterna nilotica*
Length:	14 inches, wingspan 34 inches
Habitat:	Salt marshes, beaches, fields
Identification:	Medium-size long-legged sea bird, short forked tail. Breeding adult has black cap, thick black bill, pale gray body, white beneath, long wings
Similar species:	Resembles Forster's Tern but has longer legs, thick black bill

The Gull-billed Tern is fairly common within its North American range. In summer it can be found along much of the Atlantic coast, and the rest of the year around the Gulf and Salton Sea. It breeds in scattered colonies over salt marshes and on beaches, laying 3 to 5 buffy eggs marked with brown in a scrape that may be lined with shells, pebbles or grass. These are incubated by both birds for around 3 weeks, and the young chicks begin to fly about 4-5 weeks after hatching. The juvenile is plain gray with white edging above, white beneath, and a brownish bill. The winter adult has a white head with fine dark streaking, a black bill, dark gray eye patch and whitish wings with darker gray on the primaries. In the breeding season the adult has a black cap, a short, thick black bill, the upper-parts are pale silvery-gray, and the breast and belly white. All ages have black legs and feet. In flight, its long wings are pale gray, and its tail is not as forked as that of Forster's Tern. The Gull-billed Tern catches insects in flight as they swarm over fields and marshland. It also eats frogs, small crustaceans and fish - although it never dives below the surface of the water to catch them.

ROYAL TERN

Scientific name:	*Sterna maxima*
Length:	20 inches, wingspan 41 inches
Habitat:	Coastal marshes, beaches
Identification:	Large, slender sea bird, shallow forked tail. Breeding adult has black cap with wispy crest, large orange-red bill, pale gray body, white beneath
Similar species:	Caspian Tern has thicker, redder bill, underside of wings darker at tip. Elegant Tern is smaller, with a much slimmer bill that appears to droop

The Royal Tern is fairly common around the southern coastlines of North America, but is rare further north and inland. It breeds in huge, dense colonies, sometimes containing tens of thousands of birds, on sandbars and flat islands. It does not build a nest, but lays 1-2 variably colored eggs in a simple scrape in the sand, which are incubated by both birds for around 4 weeks. After hatching, the young chicks are gathered together into large groups until they begin to fly 3-4 weeks later; they may stay with the parent birds for several more weeks. The adult bird is slender and streamlined with a shallow forked tail, a wispy crest on the back of the head, a large, thick, orange-red bill and dark legs. The juvenile is gray-white above, white beneath, with a dark crown, streaked white forehead, and yellow legs; in flight it shows obvious dark bars on the upper wings and darkish primaries underneath. The winter adult (*below*) is gray above, white beneath and has a dark band around the back of the head, beginning behind its dark eyes, and a white face and forehead; it has a small amount of gray under the wings on the primaries. Early in the breeding season the adult has a black cap. The Royal Tern plunges into the sea to catch fish and squid.

ELEGANT TERN

Scientific name:	*Sterna elegans*
Length:	17 inches, wingspan 34 inches
Habitat:	Coastal areas
Identification:	Large, slender sea bird, forked tail. Breeding adult has black cap with longish crest, long thin orange-red bill, pale gray body, white beneath
Similar species:	Royal Tern is larger, with a much thicker bill

Mainly found in southern California, the Elegant Tern sometimes wanders as far north as Washington in late summer, but is a coastal bird that is rarely found inland. Most birds spend the winter in the Southern Hemisphere, but a few do stay in California. It nests in colonies on islands, which sometimes contain hundreds of birds, laying 1-2 variably colored eggs in a simple scrape in the sand. These are incubated by both birds and after hatching the young chicks stay near the nest. The adult bird is slender with a forked tail, a longish drooping crest on the back of the head, a long, slim, orange-red bill that appears to droop and dark legs. The juvenile is gray above, white beneath, with a dark crown extending over the eye and a white forehead; its bill is yellowish as are its legs. The winter adult is gray above, white beneath and has a dark band around the back of the head, extending around its eyes, and a white forehead. In flight, its wings are mostly pale on the underside of the primaries. For a short period early in the breeding season, the adult has a black cap and its white belly may be pinkish. The Elegant Tern dives to catch fish, and the male presents small fish to the female as part of the courtship ritual.

LEAST TERN

Scientific name:	*Sterna antillarum*
Length:	9 inches, wingspan 20 inches
Habitat:	Beaches, river sandbars
Identification:	Small, long-winged sea bird, short forked tail. Breeding adult has black cap and nape with white forehead, long thin yellow bill tipped black, gray body, white beneath, yellow feet
Similar species:	Small size and yellow bill are distinctive

The smallest of the North American terns, the Least Tern is seen only in summer, as it spends the winter in South America and other areas of the Southern Hemisphere. In North America, it is found around the southern Atlantic and Pacific coasts, although its numbers are declining due to loss of habitat. It breeds in colonies on sandbars and beaches, often with other terns, laying 2-3 light-buff eggs, speckled dark brown, in a shallow scrape in the sand. These are incubated by both birds for around 3 weeks, and after hatching, the young chicks stay near the nest until they begin to fly about 2-3 weeks later. The adult bird is small, with a short, forked tail, a long, thin, tapering yellow bill with black on the very tip, and yellow legs. The juvenile is faintly barred gray-white above, white beneath, with a darkish crown and bill, and a dark shoulder bar; in flight it shows dark stripes forming a W across the upper wings and back. The winter adult is gray above, white beneath and has a dark nape and a white crown and forehead. The breeding adult has a black cap and nape, but retains the white forehead. The Least Tern feeds on small fish and crustaceans.

SANDWICH TERN

Scientific name:	*Sterna sandvicensis*
Length:	15 inches, wingspan 34 inches
Habitat:	Coastal beaches and islands
Identification:	Medium-size, slender sea bird, shortish deeply-forked tail. Breeding adult has black cap with wispy crest, long thin black bill, pale gray body, white beneath
Similar species:	Often nests with Royal Tern, which is bigger, with darker gray upperparts and thick, orange-red bill

The Sandwich Tern is found only around the southern Atlantic and Gulf coasts and is often seen with the Royal Tern, although it is much less common. It breeds in large colonies along with the Royal, on sandbars and flat islands. It does not build a nest, but lays 1-2 pinkish-buff eggs, often spotted brown-gray, in a simple scrape in the sand. These are incubated by both birds for around 3-4 weeks, and after hatching, the young chicks are gathered together into large groups with Royal Tern chicks until they begin to fly about 5 weeks later. The adult bird is medium-size and slender, with a shortish, deeply-forked tail, a wispy crest on the back of the head, a long thin black bill with a pale yellowish tip, and dark legs. The juvenile is mottled gray-white above, white beneath, with a dark crown, streaked white forehead, and dark legs; in flight it shows faint bars on the upper wings. The winter adult is pale gray above, white beneath and has a dark band around the back of the head, beginning behind its eyes, a white face and forehead, and a gray tail. Early in the breeding season the adult has a black cap. Like the Royal, the Sandwich Tern plunges into the sea to catch fish and squid; it also eats shrimp.

BROWN NODDY

Scientific name:	*Anous stolidus*
Length:	15½ inches, wingspan 32 inches
Habitat:	Warm ocean water
Identification:	Medium-size, long-billed, long-tailed, water bird. Breeding adult mostly dark gray-brown, with whitish cap, dark legs and feet
Similar species:	Size and plumage distinctive, but rare Black Noddies sometimes appear, a separate species with darker plumage and smaller in size

Noddies are tropical terns, and the Brown Noddy is only found in North America around southern Florida, although stray birds may find their way west as far as Texas and east to North Carolina. It breeds on Dry Tortugas in the Gulf of Mexico off Florida, laying 1 buffy-white or pinkish egg, spotted gray-brown, in a nest of twigs and seaweed on the ground or in a shrub or tree. The eggs are incubated by both birds for around 5-6 weeks, the young chicks begin to fly about 6-7 weeks later. The adult bird is medium-size, with a long, wedge-shaped tail, a long, black bill, and dark legs. Its plumage is mostly dark gray-brown, with a whitish cap, although the juvenile may only have a narrow whitish line on the forehead. The Brown Noddy swoops over the water, dipping to catch small fish and squid.

BLACK TERN

Scientific name:	*Chlidonias niger*
Length:	9¾ inches, wingspan 24 inches
Habitat:	Lake shores, freshwater marshes
Identification:	Small, short-tailed, water bird. Breeding adult mostly black, with dark gray back, wings and tail, white undertail coverts, short black bill, dark legs and feet
Similar species:	Size and plumage distinctive

Only slightly larger than the Least, the Black Tern is also only seen in summer but is more of an inland bird. It is very rarely seen on the west coast, and only on a small part of the east, and spends the winter in the Southern Hemisphere. It breeds in small, dense colonies on lakeshores and in freshwater marshes, laying 2-3 buff eggs, blotched with brown, in a nest constructed of marsh vegetation and usually floating. The eggs are incubated by both birds for around 3 weeks, and after hatching, the young chicks stay in the nest until they begin to fly about 2-3 weeks later. The adult bird is small, with a short, slightly forked tail, a short, black bill, and dark legs. The winter adult and the juvenile are dark gray above, white beneath, with a dark crown and ear patch, and a dark shoulder bar. The breeding adult is mostly black, with dark gray back, wings and tail, and white undertail coverts; in flight it shows a pale gray underwing and darker gray upper wing. The Black Tern circles and hovers buoyantly above water, dipping to catch flying insects, small fish and crustaceans. Populations have declined in many areas, probably due to loss of habitat.

BLACK SKIMMER

Scientific name:	*Rynchops niger*
Length:	18 inches, wingspan 44 inches
Habitat:	Beaches, offshore
Identification:	Large, long-winged, sea bird with lower bill longer than upper. Adult black back and crown, white below, white nape turns black in summer, red legs, red bill tipped black
Similar species:	No other bird has the lower bill longer than the upper

A coastal bird, the Black Skimmer is found around the southern Atlantic and Pacific throughout most of the year, but ranges northwards as far as New Hampshire in summer. It rarely moves inland, except when coastal waters are too rough, but is sometimes seen over quiet, shallow water. A relative of the tern, it breeds on sandy beaches, nesting in colonies and laying up to 5 cream or bluish eggs, often spotted with brown-gray, in a scrape in the sand. The young stay near the nest for some time after hatching. The adult bird has an unusual red bill tipped with black in which the lower mandible is much longer than the upper, long and rather broad wings, and red legs and feet. It is mostly black above, with a black crown, and white beneath; in the breeding season its white nape also turns black. The female bird is much smaller than the male; the juvenile is mottled gray-brown above and white beneath. The Black Skimmer flies gracefully and buoyantly, with long, slow beats, holding its head lower than its tail and showing white wing linings with darker tips. When feeding - usually at night - it flies just above the surface of the water, with its long lower mandible slicing the surface, until it finds a small fish or crustacean, which it catches by snapping shut the upper bill.

RAZORBILL

Scientific name:	*Alca torda*
Length:	17 inches
Habitat:	Cliffs, rocky ground, offshore
Identification:	Large, chunky sea bird, short deep black bill with white band. Breeding adult black above, white beneath, white line from eye to bill
Similar species:	Resembles Thick-billed Murre, but can be distinguished by thicker bill with white band, shorter neck

The Razorbill is an Atlantic sea coast bird, which is found in large numbers around Newfoundland all year round, and ranges as far north as Greenland in summer, and offshore down to North Carolina in winter. It nests in colonies on rocky cliffs and amongst boulders, laying a single greeny-blue, dark-spotted egg on a ledge or on the ground. This is incubated by both adult birds for 5-6 weeks and the young chicks leave the nest around 2 weeks later, but stay with the parents for some time. The adult bird is large and chunky, with a big head, a short, thick neck, and a short, deep black bill with a single white band. It has a longish, pointed tail, which it often carries pointed upwards when swimming. Its plumage is black above and white beneath, and in the summer breeding season it has a thin white line from eye to bill. The juvenile is very similar to the adult, but lacks the white bill band. The Razorbill dives for food, sometimes reaching as far as 60 feet below the surface as it hunts for fish, shrimp and squid.

BLACK GUILLEMOT

Scientific name:	*Cepphus grylle*
Length:	13 inches
Habitat:	Rocky shores, offshore
Identification:	Medium-size, chunky sea bird, with broad rounded wings. Breeding adult all black, except for large white patch on upper wing. Winter adult white, with black mottled back
Similar species:	Pigeon Guillemot almost identical, but in breeding plumage usually has dark bar extending into wing patch. In flight, the Black Guillemot has white underwings edged in black, the Pigeon Guillemot has dark wing linings

A fairly common bird in many areas of the north, northeast and northwest Alaska, the Black Guillemot is a coastal bird which tends to stay near land, particularly in the breeding season. It nests in colonies on rocky shores, laying 1-2 dull white or greenish, dark-spotted eggs in a rocky crevice on the ground. These are incubated by both adult birds for 3-4 weeks and the young chicks leave the nest around 5-6 weeks later, but stay with the parents for some time. The adult bird is a medium-size, chunky bird, with broad, rounded wings and red feet. The breeding adult is all black, except for a large oval white patch on the upper wing. The winter adult is mostly white, with its back heavily mottled with black and a whitish head. The juvenile is similar to the winter adult, but its head is more mottled and its white wing patch is barred with black. In flight, the Black Guillemot has white underwings edged in black, which are distinctive in all plumages. It is often seen sitting on open rocks, and eats fish, shrimp, mollusks and squid.

PIGEON GUILLEMOT

Scientific name:	*Cepphus columba*
Length:	13½ inches
Habitat:	Rocky shores, offshore
Identification:	Medium-size, chunky sea bird, with broad rounded wings. Breeding adult all black, except for large white patch on upper wing with dark bar extending into it. Winter adult white, with black mottled back
Similar species:	Black Guillemot almost identical, but in breeding plumage lacks dark bar extending into wing patch. In flight, the Black Guillemot has white underwings edged in black, the Pigeon Guillemot has dark wing linings

The Pigeon Guillemot inhabits a different range to the Black Guillemot, being found in the west and northwest - the two only overlap in northwest Alaska. Like the Black, the Pigeon Guillemot is a coastal bird that tends to stay near land in the breeding season. It nests in colonies on rocky shores, laying 1-2 greenish or dull white eggs, spotted with brown, in the crevice of a rock. These are incubated by both parent birds for 3-4 weeks and the young birds leave the nest 5-6 weeks later, but swim out to sea with the parents and stay with them for some time. The adult bird is a medium-size, chunky bird, with broad, rounded wings and red feet. In the breeding season (*below*) it is entirely black, except for a large, oval, white patch on the upper wing - usually with a black bar extending into it that may not be very evident on the swimming bird. The winter adult is mostly white, with its back and head heavily mottled with black. The juvenile is whitish but is also heavily mottled in black, and its white wing patch is barred with black. In flight, the Pigeon Guillemot has plain, dark underwings, which are very distinctive in all its plumages. It eats fish, shrimp, mollusks and squid.

RHINOCEROS AUKLET

Scientific name:	*Cerorhinca monocerata*
Length:	15 inches
Habitat:	Offshore
Identification:	Medium-size, stout-billed sea bird. Breeding adult dark gray above, lighter gray throat and breast, white underparts, drooping white whisker each side, white plume above eye, short upright horn at base of bill. Winter adult lacks horn, white whisker and plume less evident
Similar species:	Winter Tufted Puffin can look very similar, but has thicker, more orange-red bill and larger and more rounded head

Despite its name, the Rhinoceros Auklet is more closely related to a puffin than to other auklets. It is quite common and is found along the Pacific coast of North America in great numbers. It breeds in large colonies, laying 1 white egg, often spotted with lilac-gray, at the end of a long burrow in soft earth. Both parent birds take it in turns to incubate the egg for up to 5 weeks; the chick stays in the burrow for about 6 weeks after hatching, then leaves to swim out to sea with the parents. The adult has a big, angular head on a short, thick neck and a stout yellow bill. The breeding adult is dark gray-black above, with a lighter gray throat and breast and white under-parts; it has a drooping white plume on each side like a whisker, a white plume above the eye, and a short upright horn at the base of its bill. The winter adult lacks the horn, and the white whisker and plume are less evident. The Rhinoceros Auklet feeds on fish, which it catches offshore during the day; in the breeding season, it comes ashore at night to feed its chick.

DOVEKIE

Scientific name:	*Alle alle*
Length:	$8\frac{1}{4}$ inches
Habitat:	Offshore, rocky crevices
Identification:	Small, plump sea bird, with short neck and stubby bill. Breeding adult black above, white beneath, breeding adult has black breast
Similar species:	Resembles a murre, but can be distinguished by its much smaller size

The Dovekie is the smallest of the Atlantic auks, and spends much of its life out over the open ocean although it comes ashore to breed on rocky cliffs. It is abundant on its breeding grounds, which are mainly around northern Greenland and Baffin Bay, and it spreads south as far as North Carolina in summer. A few are found all year round in the Bering Sea, off Alaska. The Dovekie nests in huge colonies on rocky cliffs and seacoasts, laying a single white egg in a crevice. This is incubated by both adult birds for around 3 weeks and the young chick leaves the nest around 4 weeks later, but swims with the parents for some time. The adult bird is small and plump, with a very short, thick neck and a stubby bill. It swims tilted forward with its head held low, which makes it appear as if it has no neck. Its plumage is black above and white beneath, with the white curving up behind the eye; in the summer breeding season it has a black upper breast and face. In flight, it has dark wing linings. The juvenile is very similar to the winter adult. The Dovekie fishes for small crustaceans and fish, but other sea birds and Arctic foxes prey on its young to feed their own.

COMMON MURRE

Scientific name:	*Uria aalge*
Length:	17½ inches
Habitat:	Rocky cliffs, offshore
Identification:	Large, slender sea bird, long straight pointed black bill. Breeding adult black, white belly and chest. In winter throat is white with a dark line from eye across cheek
Similar species:	Resembles Thick-billed Murre, but has thinner bill; in winter white of chest is rounded while that of Thick-billed comes up in a point

Murres are the largest surviving North American auks. The Common Murre is numerous off both the east and west coasts, and may be seen in winter in large flocks or small groups. In summer it nests in close-packed colonies on rocky cliffs, laying a single greeny-blue, buffy or white, dark-spotted egg on a ledge; the egg is very pear-shaped, so it rolls in a tight semicircle rather than off the ledge. It is incubated by both adult birds for 4-5 weeks and the young chick leaves the nest around 3-4 weeks later, jumping 30-50 feet into the sea to swim off with its parents. The adult bird is large and slender, with a slender head and thin neck, and a long straight pointed black bill. In summer its plumage is black, with a white belly and chest. In winter the throat, neck and part of the face are white, with a dark line from the eye across the cheek. The juvenile is very similar to the winter adult. In flight, the Common Murre has dark upperwings and whitish wing linings with dusky markings. It dives to catch small fish, shrimp and squid.

THICK-BILLED MURRE

Scientific name:	*Uria lomvia*
Length:	18 inches
Habitat:	Rocky cliffs, offshore
Identification:	Large, stocky sea bird, fairly short arched black bill. Breeding adult black, white belly and chest. In winter throat is white
Similar species:	Resembles Common Murre, but has shorter thicker bill; in winter white of chest comes up in a point while that of Thick-billed is rounded

Slightly larger than the Common Murre, the Thick-billed inhabits much the same range, although it is found across more of the east coast and less of the west. In summer it is abundant in the Arctic, nesting in huge colonies on rocky cliffs and laying a single greenish, dark-spotted egg on a ledge. This is incubated by both adult birds for 4-5 weeks and the young chick leaves the nest around 3 weeks later, often jumping many feet down into the sea to swim off to the open ocean with its parents. The adult bird is large and stocky, with a squarer head and thicker neck, and a fairly short black bill arched at the tip, which often shows a thin white line along the edge of the upper mandible. In summer its plumage is black, with a white belly and chest, rising to a point on the lower neck. In winter the throat is white. The juvenile is very similar to the winter adult. In flight, the Thick-billed Murre has dark upperwings and clean white wing linings. It dives to catch small fish, shrimp and squid.

ATLANTIC PUFFIN

Scientific name:	*Fratercula arctica*
Length:	12½ inches
Habitat:	Offshore
Identification:	Medium-size, massive-billed sea bird. Breeding adult black above, white beneath, white face, brightly-colored parrot-like bill. Winter adult gray face, bill smaller and duller
Similar species:	The only puffin seen on the east coast

The Atlantic Puffin is the only puffin found on the Atlantic coast of North America - although it tends to stay in the north and only comes as far south as Virginia in winter, when it is usually well offshore. In summer it comes to land to nest in large colonies on offshore islands, where it is often seen sitting upright. It lays 1 white egg, sometimes spotted brown, usually at the end of a burrow in soft earth but sometimes in rock crevices. The female incubates the egg alone for 5-6 weeks, and the chicks are ready to leave the nest some 7 weeks later. The adult has a rounded head on a short neck, a stubby body with large, red-orange webbed feet and a thick, parrot-like bill. The breeding adult is black above and white beneath, with a white face and black collar, and a brightly-colored bill. In winter, the face turns gray and the bill is smaller and duller, having shed several brightly-coloured cover plates that will re-grow the following spring. The juvenile resembles the winter adult, but has a darker face and its bill is small and brownish; it takes five years to reach its full adult bill. The Atlantic Puffin dives for fish, "flying" gracefully underwater like the other puffins, and also eats mollusks and crustaceans.

HORNED PUFFIN

Scientific name:	*Fratercula corniculata*
Length:	15 inches
Habitat:	Offshore
Identification:	Medium-size, massive-billed sea bird. Breeding adult black above, white beneath, white face, yellow parrot-like bill, tipped red. Winter adult gray face, bill smaller and duller
Similar species:	Although the Horned Puffin closely resembles the Atlantic Puffin, it is only found on the Pacific coast so the two cannot be confused

The Horned Puffin is found in summer all around the Alaskan coast and rarely ventures much further south - except in winter, when it is well offshore. In summer it nests in large colonies on sea cliffs and rocky offshore islands, often with Tufted Puffins. It lays 1 large, whitish egg, sometimes spotted dark brown, usually in a rocky crevice or in a deep hole amongst boulders, but sometimes at the end of a burrow in soft earth. Both birds incubate the egg for 5-6 weeks, and the chicks are ready to leave the nest some 6 weeks later. The adult has a rounded head on a short neck, a stubby body with large, orange webbed feet and a thick, parrot-like bill. The breeding adult is black above and white beneath, with a white face and black collar, and a bright yellow, red-tipped bill. At close quarters, a small black horn can be seen above the eye. In winter, the face turns gray and the bill is smaller and duller, with a dark gray base. The juvenile resembles the winter adult, but has a darker face and its bill is much smaller and sooty-brown. Like the other members of its family, the Horned Puffin dives for fish, but it will also eat mollusks and small crustaceans.

TUFTED PUFFIN

Scientific name:	*Fratercula cirrhata*
Length:	15 inches
Habitat:	Offshore
Identification:	Medium-size, massive-billed sea bird. Breeding adult black, white face, drooping yellow tuft behind eye, orange-red parrot-like bill. Winter adult face black, less discernible tufts, bill smaller and duller
Similar species:	Juvenile and winter adult can look very similar to Rhinoceros Auklet, but have thicker, more orange-red bill and larger and more rounded head

Widespread and common, the Tufted Puffin is found all along the Pacific coast of North America - although greater numbers are seen in the northern part of its range. It spends the winter out at sea, but in summer nests in large, dense colonies on vertical sea cliffs, where it is often seen sitting upright. It lays 1 whitish-blue egg, frequently spotted, at the end of a burrow in soft earth - which may be up to 7 feet long - or in the crevices of rocks. Little is known about the incubation or nestling period. The adult has a big, rounded head on a short neck, a stubby body with large, red webbed feet and a thick, orange-red parrot-like bill. The breeding adult is overall black, with a white face and a long, drooping yellow tuft behind the eye. In winter, the face is black and the tuft is less discernible, the bill is smaller and duller, having shed several of its brightly-coloured cover plates that will re-grow the following spring. The juvenile resembles the winter adult, but is white underneath and its bill is smaller and duller; it takes several years to reach its full adult plumage. The Tufted Puffin dives for fish, which it catches offshore during the day, and also eats mollusks and crustaceans. It is a sociable bird, often found with other sea birds.

BAND-TAILED PIGEON

Scientific name: *Columba fasciata*
Length: 14½ inches
Habitat: Coniferous forests, oak forests
Identification: Large, long-tailed pigeon. Dark gray above, pale terminal tail band, purple-pink head and chest, narrow white band on nape above iridescent green patch, yellow bill tipped black, yellow legs
Similar species: Can look like Rock Dove, but flocks of Band-tailed Pigeon all have the same plumage

The largest of the native American pigeons, the Band-tailed is common all year round on the Pacific coast and in Mexico, but is only a summer visitor inland to the southwest. It sometimes nests in loose colonies, building a thin platform of sticks and twigs in a tree up to 40 feet above the ground, in which it lays 1 white egg. This is incubated for up to 3 weeks by both parent birds and the chick stays in the nest for around 6-7 weeks; there may be further chicks raised in the same season. The plumage of the adult is dark gray above, with a pale terminal tail band, a purple-pink head and chest, and a narrow white band on the nape above an iridescent green patch. The yellow bill is tipped with black, and the legs are yellow. The juvenile lacks the white band at the nape, but is otherwise similar to the adult. The Band-tailed Pigeon eats nuts, berries and insects, and particularly loves acorns. It is adapting to city life, where it feeds in parks and gardens on ornamental berries, including holly.

EURASIAN COLLARED-DOVE

Scientific name:	*Streptopelia decaocto*
Length:	12½ inches
Habitat:	Urban areas
Identification:	Medium-size, square-tailed dove. Pale gray-buff, black half-collar at nape, white patches on outer tail feathers, dark bill, red legs. In flight, shows gray band across upper wings, dark gray tips
Similar species:	The Ringed Turtle-Dove is very similar, but is a domesticated species which does not thrive in the wild

A native of the Old World, the Eurasian Collared-Dove was introduced to the Bahamas and rapidly spread to Florida from where it began to move west and north across America. It is now found as far as New Mexico and New York and threatens to spread across the entire continent. It mainly lives in urban areas in the suburbs and is very rarely found in wild country. The plumage of the adult is pale gray-buff overall, with a black half-collar at the nape, and white patches on the outer tail feathers. It has a dark bill and red legs. In flight, it shows a gray band across the upper wings, which have dark gray tips. The Eurasian Collared-Dove has adapted well to city life and is often seen perched on roof tops or poles. It eats seeds, grain and berries.

ROCK DOVE

Scientific name:	*Columba livia*
Length:	12½ inches
Habitat:	Urban areas
Identification:	Long-winged domestic pigeon, small round head, short straight bill, variable colors
Similar species:	The feral Rock Doves come in such a wide variety of colors that it can look similar to several of the wild native species

The original habitat of the Rock Dove was on rocky cliffs around the Atlantic and Mediterranean coasts, but they were domesticated worldwide and raised for meat or to carry messages. During centuries of breeding, multicolored birds were developed and descendants of escaped birds now form feral flocks in most areas, except for the taiga and tundra region. The Rock Dove builds a haphazard nest of sticks and grass on the sheltered ledge of a building, bridge, cliff or sometimes in a tree, in which it lays 1-2 white eggs. These are incubated for between 2 and 3 weeks by both birds, and the chicks stay on in the nest for around 7 weeks. The adult nests throughout the year and there may be several broods in a season. The plumage of the adult runs from pure white to black, with cinnamon, piebald and gray birds. The most common is like the wild ancestor - overall blue-gray, with a darker head and iridescent purple-green on the neck, a white rump, a dark terminal band on the tail and two dark bars across the wing. The Rock Dove eats grain and seeds, but will also feed on fruit and scraps of bread.

INCA DOVE

Scientific name:	*Columbina inca*
Length:	8¼ inches
Habitat:	Parks, gardens, urban areas
Identification:	Small, long-tailed dove. Pale gray-brown with darker scaling. In flight shows rust-red wing feathers and white outer tail feathers
Similar species:	Common Ground-Dove has shorter tail and is only scaled on chest and head. Juvenile Mourning Dove also looks scaled, but lacks rufous wings

The sociable Inca Dove is only found in the southwest, where it tends to live in small flocks in urban and semi-urban areas as it prefers to be near humans. It builds a small nest of roots, twigs and weeds in a bush or tree, or sometimes on the ledge of a building, in which it lays 2 white, roundish eggs. These are incubated for around 2 weeks by both parent birds; after hatching the chick stays in the nest for around 12 more days. There may be as many as 5 broods raised in a single season. The adult is a small and slender bird, and has a long, narrow tail with a square tip. Its plumage is pale gray-brown with darker scaling, but in flight it shows rust-red wing feathers and white outer tail feathers. The juvenile is a very similar color to the adult, but has no scaling. The Inca Dove eats seeds and grain.

COMMON GROUND-DOVE

Scientific name:	*Columbina passerina*
Length:	6½ inches
Habitat:	Open ground, dry brushy areas, woodland edges
Identification:	Small, stocky, short-tailed dove. Pale gray-brown with scaling on head and chest, large brown-black spots on wing coverts. In flight shows rust-red wing feathers, black outer tail feathers with white at corners
Similar species:	Inca Dove has longer tail and is scaled on back. Juvenile Mourning Dove also looks scaled, but lacks rufous wings

The tiny Common Ground-Dove is found across much of the south, where it usually walks on the ground in pairs or in small flocks, nodding like a pigeon. It prefers brushy terrain and woodland edges and rarely ventures into urban areas. It builds a rather flimsy nest of roots, twigs and weeds low in a bush or tree, or sometimes just lines a depression in the ground, in which it lays 2 white, roundish eggs. These are incubated for around 2 weeks by both birds, and the chicks stay in the nest for around 10 more days. The adult is a small, stocky bird, and has a short tail and neck. Its plumage is pale gray-brown with scaling on the head and chest, and the wing coverts have large brown-black spots. The adult male has a blue-gray crown and pinkish-gray underparts, but the female is more uniformly gray. In flight, both birds show rust-red wing feathers and black outer tail feathers with white at the corners. Although it has quite short wings, the Common Ground-Dove flies very fast. It pecks seeds and grain from the ground, but will also take berries and insects.

MOURNING DOVE

Scientific name:	*Zenaida macroura*
Length:	12 inches
Habitat:	Open brushland, urban areas
Identification:	Medium-size, slender dove with long pointed tapered tail. Pale gray-brown above with large black spots on wings, buff below. Adult male pinkish on chest and iridescent blue-gray on crown
Similar species:	Juvenile Mourning Dove can be mistaken for Inca Dove or Common Ground-Dove, but lacks rufous wings

Very common across much of America, the Mourning Dove also spreads north into Canada in the summer. It likes a variety of habitats, except for deep woods, and is seen both alone and in flocks, either perched prominently on poles or wires or walking on the ground. At the start of its long breeding season, it builds a rather loose nest of twigs and sticks in a bush or a tree, in which it lays 2 white eggs. These are incubated for around 2 weeks by both birds alternately, and the chicks stay in the nest for around 16 more days; there may be 2-4 broods in one season. The adult is a rather slender dove, with narrow pointed wings and a long, pointed, tapering tail with the side feathers edged with black and tipped with white. It has a light blue ring round the eye, and a large dark spot at the base of the ear. Its plumage is pale gray-brown above, with large black spots on the wings, and buff below. The adult male is pinkish on the chest and iridescent blue-gray on the crown, but the female is plainer and also has a shorter tail. The juvenile is similar to the adult, but is more scaled. The Mourning Dove makes a whistling noise with its wings as it takes flight, but the bird's name comes from the male's mournful cry, which sounds a little like an owl. It mainly eats seeds and grain.

WHITE-WINGED DOVE

Scientific name:	*Zenaida asiatica*
Length:	11½ inches
Habitat:	Desert suburbs, mesquite, open brushy areas
Identification:	Medium-size, broad-winged dove with short rounded tail. Gray-brown above with iridescent purple on crown, neck and shoulder, white wing patch shows as line along flank of perching bird
Similar species:	Mourning Dove lacks white wing patches and has longer, pointed tail

The White-winged Dove is found in the far south in the summer, but most birds go south to the tropics for the winter. It is a similar length to the Mourning Dove, but has a bulkier body and a shorter tail. It often nests in colonies, building a flimsy construction of sticks in a bush, cactus or tree, in which it lays 2 buffy-white eggs. These are incubated for around 2 weeks by both adult birds, and the chicks stay in the nest for around 2 more weeks; there is often more than one brood in a season. The adult has broad wings with a long white wing patch and black ends, and a short, rounded tail with a subterminal band of black and terminal band of white. It is gray-brown above with iridescent purple on the crown, neck and shoulder, and the white wing patch shows as a narrow line along the flank of the perching bird. The White-winged Dove flies fast with heavy wingbeats, and is a game bird. It eats seeds and grain like northern pigeons and doves, but will also feed on fruit like the tropical species - in the desert it eats cactus, but otherwise will take berries.

GREATER ROADRUNNER

Scientific name:	*Geococcyx californianus*
Length:	23 inches
Habitat:	Scrub desert, mesquite groves
Identification:	Large, long-tailed desert bird with crest and heavy bill. Brown with green sheen, streaked black and white above, buff below with brown streaks on breast
Similar species:	Unmistakable

Famous for its odd behavior, the Greater Roadrunner is a member of the cuckoo family that prefers to run smoothly along the ground on its strong feet - although it can fly if it has to. Its range extends across much of southern America, but it is most common in the desert of the southwest, where it darts away to cover at speeds of up to 15 miles per hour if surprised in the open. It builds a small, neat nest in mesquite, a large cactus or shrub in chaparral, in which it lays 3-6 white eggs. These are incubated for up to 3 weeks, with the young chicks hatching at intervals and staying in the nest for a further 2-3 weeks, fed by both parent birds. The adult is a large bird with a long tail edged in white, a bushy crest and heavy dark bill. Its plumage is brown with green sheen above, streaked with black and white, and buff below, with brown streaks on the breast. It sometimes flicks its tail up or raises its shaggy crest, and can adopt a variety of strange postures when resting on a fence post or rock. It runs in fast bursts to catch a wide variety of food, including large insects, scorpions, lizards, snakes, small birds and rodents.

GROOVE-BILLED ANI

Scientific name:	*Crotophaga sulcirostris*
Length:	13½ inches
Habitat:	Woodlands, brushy fields
Identification:	Medium-size, long-tailed cuckoo. Black plumage with iridescent purple and green sheen, large, thick grooved bill
Similar species:	Smooth-billed Ani is similar, but is only found in declining numbers in Florida

The Groove-billed Ani is a tropical cuckoo that is found in summer in southern Texas and sometimes wanders along the Gulf coast as far as Florida in winter. It is fairly common and is often seen in small groups, either clumsily hopping on the ground or perching in the open. A sociable bird, several pairs often share the same nest, a mass of twigs up to 12 feet above the ground in a tree or shrub. Each female lays 3-4 pale blue eggs, which are incubated for around 2 weeks - some may not hatch, so the pair will raise more than one brood in a season. The adult is medium-size, with a long tail and a large, thick grooved bill - although the grooves are not evident at a distance. Its plumage is black, with an iridescent purple and green sheen. The juvenile has a smaller bill and its plumage is more brownish. The Groove-billed Ani tends to fly with a few quick flaps and then goes into a glide; when perching it may dip and wag its tail, or hold it at a strange angle. It eats insects, fruit and lizards.

ORIENTAL CUCKOO

Scientific name:	*Cuculus saturatus*
Length:	12½ inches
Habitat:	Woodland, along streams
Identification:	Medium-size, slender cuckoo with plain underwing coverts, yellow eye ring, two-tone bill. Male gray above, paler beneath and heavily barred, female more brown-gray
Similar species:	Old World Common Cuckoo, also spring and summer visitor to North America, is very similar but is paler gray, with whiter belly and narrower barring, underwing barred not plain

A Eurasian species, the Oriental Cuckoo is a visitor to western North America in both spring and summer, but tends to stay up in Alaska for much of the time. So far, it has not been known to nest in America. The adult is a medium-size, slender bird with a relatively long tail. It has plain underwing coverts, a yellow eye ring, and a bill that is black above and yellowish below. The male is a fairly plain dark gray above, paler gray beneath heavily barred in darker gray. The female (*right*) is generally more brown-gray - although a few are gray - but has barring on both head and back, and on wings and tail, as well as on the belly. The Common Cuckoo, an Old World species, is also a visitor to the same area of North America and looks extremely similar, although its plumage tends to be paler. Like other cuckoos, the Oriental Cuckoo eats caterpillars, insects and berries.

BLACK-BILLED CUCKOO

Scientific name:	*Coccyzus erythropthalmus*
Length:	12 inches
Habitat:	Woodland, along streams
Identification:	Medium-size, slender, long-tailed cuckoo. Gray-brown above, whitish-gray beneath, black bill, red eye ring, undertail gray-brown with narrow white spots
Similar species:	Juvenile Yellow-billed Cuckoo similar but rufous patches on wings in flight are distinctive, white patches on undertail are larger

Fairly common in woodland in summer, the Black-billed Cuckoo is a shy and elusive bird that may be very difficult to spot. Although it sometimes does deposit an egg in the nest of another bird, the female bird usually lays 2-5 greeny-blue eggs in its own, rather flimsy, nest of twigs and grass up to 10 feet above the ground in a tree or dense bush. These are incubated for about 2 weeks by both birds, with the chicks hatched naked and not getting their first feathers until they are around 6 days old; they leave the nest around 2 weeks after hatching. The adult is a slender, medium-size bird with a slim, black bill and a red ring around the eye. Its plumage is gray-brown above and whitish-gray beneath, and it has a gray-brown undertail with narrow white spots. The juvenile has a buff eye ring and the undertail is paler with less contrast. In flight, the Black-billed Cuckoo shows whitish underwings edged with gray-brown, and is relatively plain gray-brown above. It eats caterpillars, insects and berries.

YELLOW-BILLED CUCKOO

Scientific name: *Coccyzus americanus*
Length: 12 inches
Habitat: Open woods, trees along lowland rivers
Identification: Medium-size, slender, long-tailed cuckoo. Gray-brown above, white beneath, mostly yellow curved bill, yellow eye ring, undertail black with large white spots, rufous wing patches in flight
Similar species: Yellow bill and rufous patches on wings in flight are distinctive in adult, but juvenile similar to Black-billed Cuckoo

Although it occupies a somewhat different general area, the ranges of the Black-billed and Yellow-billed cuckoos do overlap. The Yellow-billed is also fairly common in woodland in summer, but hides in dense foliage so can be easily overlooked. It usually builds a frail platform of twigs up to 10 feet above the ground in a small tree or dense bush, in which it lays 2-4 greeny-blue eggs. These are incubated for about 2 weeks by both birds, with the chicks hatched naked and not getting their first feathers until they are around 6 days old; they leave the nest around 2 weeks after hatching. The adult is a slender, medium-size bird with a slim, down-curved bill with a yellow lower mandible, and a yellow ring around the eye. Its plumage is gray-brown above and white beneath, and it has a black undertail with large white spots. The juvenile lacks any yellow on the bill and the undertail is browner with less contrast. In flight, the Yellow-billed Cuckoo shows white underwings edged with bright rufous, and is gray-brown above with rufous patches. It eats insects and berries, and particularly likes hairy caterpillars, which few other birds will touch. Its population is decreasing with the loss of its natural breeding habitat.

NORTHERN PYGMY-OWL

Scientific name:	*Glaucidium gnoma*
Length:	6¾ inches
Habitat:	Dense woodland in foothills and mountains
Identification:	Small, compact owl with long, finely barred tail. Brown or gray-brown with fine buff spotting above, buff with bold brown or gray-brown streaks below, two black spots edged with white on back of neck that look like eyes
Similar species:	Size and coloring distinctive

The Northern Pygmy-Owl is one of the few owls that is often active in daylight hours, but although it is widespread in mountain forests, it is relatively uncommon. Since it is small and prefers to perch high in the trees it is often very difficult to find, although it can sometimes be spotted when other forest birds gather to scold and mob it. It does not build a nest, but lays 2-6 white eggs in an old woodpecker hole. These are usually incubated by the female alone for up to 4 weeks, and the chicks are fed by both adults and are ready to leave about 4 weeks after hatching. The adult is a small, compact bird with yellow eyes and a long, dark tail finely barred with white or buff. Its plumage is either brown or gray-brown, with fine buff spotting above, and buff with bold brown or gray-brown streaks below - grayer birds are found in the Rockies, while browner ones are nearer the Pacific and in the north. All birds also have two black spots edged with white on the back of the neck, which look uncannily like eyes. The Northern Pygmy-Owl is an aggressive predator, which does not hesitate to attack birds even larger than itself. It also eats small mammals and large insects.

ELF OWL

Scientific name:	*Microthene whitneyi*
Length:	5¾ inches
Habitat:	Desert lowlands, foothills, canyons
Identification:	Tiny, short-tailed owl with small head. Gray-brown with fine gray spotting above, faint buff streaks below, yellow eyes, white eyebrows
Similar species:	Size and coloring distinctive

The smallest of the North American owls, the Elf Owl is found in summer in lowland areas, particularly in saguaro desert and mesquite brush, and most birds migrate south in winter. It is only found in a few areas and is quite rare within those, and since it is small and only hunts at night it is often extremely difficult to spot. It does not build a nest, but lays 3 or 4 white eggs in an old, abandoned woodpecker hole in a saguaro cactus or a tree. The eggs are usually incubated by the female alone for about 3 weeks, while the male hunts for food; the chicks are ready to leave about 4-5 weeks after hatching. The adult is a tiny, short-tailed bird with a small head, yellow eyes and white eyebrows. Its plumage is gray-brown with fine gray spotting above, a row of white spots on the shoulder and faint buff streaks below. The Elf Owl population has declined over recent years and it has now almost vanished from California. It eats only large insects, including grasshoppers, beetles and scorpions.

BOREAL OWL

Scientific name:	*Aegolius funereus*
Length:	10 inches
Habitat:	Dense forest
Identification:	Small, chubby, long-winged owl with largish head. Chocolate brown, thickly spotted with white on head, sparsely spotted elsewhere, streaked brown and white below, yellow eyes and bill, large grayish facial discs with dark border
Similar species:	Northern Saw-whet Owl smaller, has dark bill, facial discs buffy and lack dark border

An elusive bird of the north, the Boreal Owl rarely wanders south of its mapped range. It inhabits dense forests and breeds in isolated places high in the Rockies. It does not build a nest, but takes over an old, abandoned woodpecker hole or a tree cavity in which it lays 3-7 white eggs. These are incubated for around 4 weeks by the female and the chicks leave about 4-5 weeks after hatching. The adult is small and chubby, with quite long wings and a largish head with yellow eyes and bill. Its plumage is chocolate brown, thickly spotted with white on the head, sparsely spotted with white elsewhere, streaked brown and white below, and with large grayish facial discs that have a dark border. The Boreal Owl mainly eats large insects and small rodents. It has little contact with humans so it appears very tame, sitting still when approached.

BURROWING OWL *(below)*

Scientific name:	*Speotyto cunicularia*
Length:	9½ inches
Habitat:	Open country
Identification:	Small, long-legged, short-tailed owl with flat head. Brown spotted with white above and on upper breast, barred brown and white below, white throat, yellow eyes
Similar species:	Long legs distinctive

The Burrowing Owl was once well-known and common, but its numbers have declined over recent years. It inhabits open country, including airports and golf courses in urban areas. It does not build a nest, but takes over the abandoned burrow of a ground squirrel or prairie dog - or a gopher tortoise in Florida - in which it lays 5-7 white eggs. These are incubated for around 4 weeks and the chicks appear from the burrow soon after hatching, although little is known about their exact nestling period. The adult is small, with very long legs, a short stubby tail, flat head and yellow eyes. Its plumage is brown spotted with white above and on the upper breast, barred brown and white below, with a white throat and eyebrows. The Burrowing Owl stands upright on the ground or on fence posts and feeds mainly on large insects and small rodents, but will also take small birds. Although it normally hunts in the day, the male hunts both day and night when it is also providing food for the young.

BARN OWL *(opposite)*

Scientific name:	*Tyto alba*
Length:	16 inches
Habitat:	Barns, old buildings, cliffs, trees
Identification:	Medium-size, long-legged owl with heart-shaped face and dark eyes. White face edged with tan, light tan back with fine pale gray streaks, white to cinnamon beneath
Similar species:	Snowy Owl usually whiter, has small head and yellow eyes

Although it is widespread across much of North America, the Barn Owl is quite rare and its population is declining. It hunts over farmland, woodland and suburbs at night and roosts in dark corners of farm and city buildings, or sometimes on cliffs or trees. It does not build a nest, but lays 5-11 white eggs on the bare surface in a cavity such as a cave, or corner of a barn or attic. The eggs are usually incubated by the female alone for up to 5 weeks, and the chicks are ready to leave about 8 weeks after hatching but are not ready to become independent for another month. The adult is a medium-size bird with long, feathered legs, a white heart-shaped face edged with tan and dark eyes. Its plumage is light tan above with fine, pale gray streaks, and white to cinnamon beneath. Darker birds are females, while males are lighter. At night, caught in lights, or seen from below the Barn Owl may look all-white like a Snowy Owl. It hunts during the night, catching mice and rats.

WHISKERED SCREECH-OWL

Scientific name:	*Otus trichopsis*
Length:	$7\frac{1}{4}$ inches
Habitat:	Mountain oak and conifer forests at altitudes between 4000-6000 feet
Identification:	Small, yellow-eyed owl with short ear tufts and yellow-green bill tipped white. Gray plumage, short thick vertical streaks on underparts crossed with bold dark barring
Similar species:	All three Screech-Owls are very similar. The Eastern ranges from gray to rust and has a yellow-green bill tipped white, the Western has a darker bill and prominent bars on its underparts crossed with weak dark barring

A common owl at higher altitudes, the Whiskered Screech-Owl prefers dense pine-oak woods and is quite shy, but will answer whistled imitations of its call. It nests in deep tree cavities, often in an old flicker hole, in which it lays 3-4 round white eggs. The chicks hatch in sequence and vary in age and size within a brood, so if food runs short, the older ones survive at the expense of the smallest. The adult is small with yellow-orange eyes and has short ear tufts, which may be held flat against the head so it appears rounded, and a yellow-green bill tipped with white. It has long bristles at the base of its bill like whiskers, from which it gets its name, and smallish feet. Its plumage is gray with short, thick, vertical streaks on the underparts, crossed with bold dark bars. The Whiskered Screech-Owl hunts at night, mainly for large insects and spiders.

FLAMMULATED OWL

Scientific name:	*Otus flammeolus*
Length:	$6\frac{3}{4}$ inches
Habitat:	Oak and pine woodland
Identification:	Small, dark-eyed owl. Gray-brown above, lighter beneath, streaked and spotted with white and rust, short ear tufts. Females larger than males
Similar species:	Similar to a Screech-Owl, but smaller

A small owl that spends the summer in coniferous and pine-oak woods in the west, the Flammulated Owl migrates south in winter. It is fairly common, but is elusive and its plumage provides good camouflage, making it hard to spot. It sometimes nests in loose colonies, usually taking over an old woodpecker hole or finding a similar tree cavity, in which it lays 3 or 4 white eggs that are mainly incubated by the female while the male hunts for food and protects the nest. The adult is small and has distinctive dark eyes and short ear tufts. Its plumage is gray-brown above and lighter beneath, streaked and spotted with white and rust. Birds in the southeast tend to have more rusty plumage than those in the northwest. Both sexes are similar, but the female is larger than the male. The Flammulated Owl hunts at night for mice, large moths, beetles, spiders and small birds.

LONG-EARED OWL

Scientific name: *Asio otus*
Length: 15 inches
Habitat: Thick woods
Identification: Medium-size, slender owl with long closely-spaced ear tufts. Gray-brown above, whitish with dark vertical streaks beneath, buff or rusty facial discs
Similar species: Great Horned Owl is larger and bulkier and has white throat and horizontal barring

The Long-eared Owl is relatively uncommon, although it may be seen in small flocks during the winter. It is found in forest areas but is strictly nocturnal and often rather quiet, and its excellent camouflage makes it extremely hard to spot. It does not build its own nest, but lays 3-8 white eggs in the nest of a magpie, crow or squirrel, taking over before the original inhabitants are ready to breed and forcing them to build again elsewhere. The eggs are usually incubated by the female alone for about 4 weeks, and the chicks are ready to leave the nest about 5 weeks after hatching. The adult is a medium-size, slender bird with orange-yellow eyes, buff or rusty facial discs with a dark stripe through the eye, and long, closely-spaced ear tufts. Its plumage is gray-brown above, and whitish beneath with dark vertical streaks. The Long-eared Owl is sometimes mobbed by smaller birds, but it very seldom attacks them; it feeds mainly on rodents.

SHORT-EARED OWL

Scientific name:	*Asio flammeus*
Length:	15 inches
Habitat:	Open ground, marshes, fields, tundra
Identification:	Medium-size owl with short ear tufts. Mottled brownish above, buffy with brown vertical streaks beneath, pale facial discs with black round eyes
Similar species:	Long-eared Owl is darker, with much longer ears

It is much easier to spot the Short-eared Owl, as it sometimes hunts in daylight and roosts in the day on the ground or on low, open perches. It is fairly common, and may be seen in small flocks in winter. It is found in open country with short vegetation, such as tundra, marshes and forest clearings. It does not build a nest, but lays 5-9 creamy-white eggs in a shallow, grass-lined depression in the ground - often well hidden in vegetation. The eggs are usually incubated by the female for around 21 days, and the chicks are ready to leave the nest about 6 weeks after hatching. The adult is a medium-size bird with yellow eyes, pale facial discs with black round the eyes, and short ear tufts that may not be visible. Its plumage is mottled brownish above, and buffy with brown vertical streaks beneath. In flight it shows pale wing linings and a dark mark at the wrist, with a buffy patch above. The Short-eared Owl hunts for small rodents at night or on cloudy days, flying low over the ground or watching from a stump - sometimes several birds hunt over the same area.

GREAT HORNED OWL

Scientific name:	*Bubo virginianus*
Length:	22 inches
Habitat:	Forest, open desert, urban areas
Identification:	Large, bulky owl with wide-spaced ear tufts. Mottled gray-brown above, white throat, fine dark gray horizontal barring beneath
Similar species:	Long-eared Owl is smaller and more slender, lacks white throat and has vertical streaking beneath

The most widespread and best known owl in North America, the Great Horned Owl is found in a great variety of habitats and may often be seen perching high up at dusk. It does not build its own nest, but lays 2-4 white eggs in the abandoned nest of a hawk, heron or crow, in a rocky crevice, tree or cliff. The eggs are incubated by the female for about 7 weeks, but the downy whitish chicks are fed by both parents and are ready to leave the nest around 10 weeks after hatching. The adult is a large, bulky bird with yellow eyes and wide-spaced ear tufts that give its head a cat-like look. Its plumage is mottled gray-brown above, with a white throat, and fine dark gray horizontal barring beneath. The Great Horned Owl is a skilled predator with powerful taions, a sharp hooked bill and a big appetite; it is not afraid to tackle quite large prey such as rabbits, squirrels, geese, skunks and snakes. It hunts mainly at night, but is sometimes seen in the day - when it is often mobbed by smaller birds.

EASTERN SCREECH-OWL

(opposite page and right)

Scientific name:	*Otus asio*
Length:	$8\frac{1}{2}$ inches
Habitat:	Large trees, suburban parks
Identification:	Small, yellow-eyed owl with ear tufts and yellow-green bill tipped white. Colour ranges from gray through brown to rust, vertically streaked underparts crossed with dark barring
Similar species:	All three Screech-Owls are very similar. The Western is generally gray and has a dark bill, the Whiskered is slightly smaller than the other two and has bolder barring on its underparts

The Eastern Screech-Owl is very common in most areas across its extensive range, but because of its nocturnal habits, small size and good camouflage it is often not noticed. It likes large mature trees, and lives undetected in many parks and suburban gardens. It nests in tree cavities, often in an old woodpecker hole, or will inhabit a nesting box. It lays 4-6 white eggs that are mainly incubated by the female for up to 4 weeks, while the male hunts for food and protects the nest. The chicks are downy and stay in the nest for around 4 weeks after hatching. The adult is small with yellow eyes and has ear tufts, which are prominent when raised, but may be held flat against the head, which then appears rounded. Its bill is yellow-green at the base, tipped with white, but the plumage is very variable, even within the same population. Some birds are gray (*opposite*), others are brown and some are bright rust (*right*), but in general they have vertically streaked underparts crossed with wide, well-spaced dark bars. Birds in the southeast tend to be rusty, while those on the Great Plains are usually gray. The Eastern Screech-Owl hunts at night for mice and insects and sometimes dives for fish.

WESTERN SCREECH-OWL

Scientific name:	*Otus kennicottii*
Length:	$8\frac{1}{2}$ inches
Habitat:	Open woods, deserts, suburban parks
Identification:	Small, yellow-eyed owl with ear tufts and dark bill. Gray or brown plumage, prominent vertical streaks on underparts crossed with weak dark barring
Similar species:	All three Screech-Owls are very similar. The Eastern ranges from gray to rust and has a yellow-green bill tipped white, the Whiskered is slightly smaller than the other two and has bolder barring on its underparts

The Western and Eastern Screech-Owl were once considered to be one species, and their ranges overlap; they occupy similar habitats, but the Western is also found in desert areas. It is fairly common across much of its range, but again is well-camouflaged and nocturnal and often lives undetected. It nests in tree cavities, often in an old woodpecker hole, in which it lays 4-6 white eggs. These are incubated for up to 4 weeks, mainly by the female, while the male hunts for food. The chicks are downy and stay in the nest for about 27 days after hatching. The adult is small with yellow eyes and has prominent ear tufts, which may be held flat against the head so it appears rounded, and a black bill. Its plumage is gray - or sometimes brown in the northwest - with prominent vertical streaks on the underparts crossed with weak dark barring. The Western Screech-Owl hunts at night for mice, shrews and large insects and sometimes dives for fish.

NORTHERN HAWK OWL

Scientific name:	*Surnia ulula*
Length:	16 inches
Habitat:	Northern forests
Identification:	Medium-size, hawk-like owl with long pointed tail. Dark brown with white blotches and dots above, brown with white horizontal barring below, pale facial discs edged in black
Similar species:	Long tail, facial discs and hawk-like profile are distinctive

Although it is relatively uncommon, the Northern Hawk Owl might be seen flying fast and low between the trees of boreal forests. Since daylight hours are much longer above the Arctic circle in summer, it hunts in daylight and at night but very rarely ventures further south of its mapped range. Since it usually has little contact with humans it may appear very tame, sitting still when approached. It does not build a nest, but lays 3-7 white eggs in the nest of another bird or in a tree cavity or stump. These are mainly incubated by the female for around 3-4 weeks, and the chicks are ready to leave the nest about 4-5 weeks after hatching. The adult is a medium-size, hawk-like bird with yellow eyes and a long pointed tail. Its plumage is dark brown above with white blotches and dots, brown with white horizontal barring below, and it has pale facial discs edged in black and narrow pale bars on the tail. The juvenile lacks most of the cross-barring and is much plainer. The Northern Hawk Owl feeds mainly on rodents, including lemmings, but in winter will also take small birds.

BARRED OWL

Scientific name:	*Strix varia*
Length:	21 inches
Habitat:	Dense conifer or mixed woodland, swamps
Identification:	Large, stocky, broad-winged owl with short tail. Brown with dark barring on upper chest, dark streaking below, dark eyes, yellow bill
Similar species:	The rare Spotted Owl looks similar, but is brown with white spots beneath, has dark bill and is smaller

In southern swamps the Barred Owl is fairly common, but it also inhabits dense forest across a wider range, which is expanding to the northwest. It is more likely than other owls to be heard during the day, hooting, screaming and cackling. Like other owls, it does not build a nest, but lays 3-4 white eggs in the nest of another bird or squirrel or in a tree cavity or stump. These are mainly incubated by the female for around 4 weeks, and the chicks are ready to leave the nest about 6 weeks after hatching. The adult is a large, broad-winged bird with a round head, yellow bill, dark eyes and a short tail. Its plumage is brown-gray, barred with white above and pale with dark barring on the upper chest and dark streaking below. Although it is mainly nocturnal, the Barred Owl may be seen hunting on cloudy days. It feeds mainly on mice, but will also take small mammals, birds, frogs and snakes.

SNOWY OWL

Scientific name:	*Nyctea scandiaca*
Length:	23 inches
Habitat:	Tundra, open country
Identification:	Large, stocky owl with small head and yellow eyes. Mature adult male white, younger birds white with variable black barring
Similar species:	The Barn Owl can be very pale, but has heart-shaped face and dark eyes. Downy young of other owl species also often white

The Snowy Owl is an Arctic bird, but since it depends on the lemming, a small rodent, as its major food it migrates south whenever the lemming population decreases and may be seen perching in the open in the daylight. It does not build a nest, but lays 5-9 white eggs - or even more in a very good season - in a shallow, moss and grass-lined depression in dry ground on tundra. The eggs are usually incubated by the female alone for around 4-5 weeks, and the chicks are ready to leave the nest about 6 weeks after they have hatched. The adult is quite a large, stocky bird with a small head and yellow eyes. The plumage of the mature adult male is almost pure white, but younger birds and females are white with variable amounts of black barring and spotting. The Snowy Owl will hunt by both day and night, since daylight hours are so much longer above the Arctic circle during the summer months. As well as lemmings, it also eats various small mammals and birds - and will also feed on carrion.

NORTHERN SAW-WHET OWL *(above)*

Scientific name:	*Aegolius acadicus*
Length:	8 inches
Habitat:	Dense coniferous or mixed forest, wooded swamps
Identification:	Small, long-winged owl with short tail. Brown above, lightly streaked white on forehead and crown, white beneath streaked red-brown, yellow eyes, dark bill, buffy facial discs
Similar species:	Boreal Owl larger, has yellow bill, facial discs grayish with dark border

The Northern Saw-whet Owl likes dense cover and is strictly nocturnal, roosting during the day in a conifer, or in the breeding season near its nest hole. Although it may be elusive, once spotted in its daytime roost it appears very tame and approachable - it can often even be picked up and held without struggling. It does not build a nest, but takes over an old woodpecker hole or tree cavity in which it lays 4-7 white eggs. These are incubated for around 4 weeks by the female and the chicks leave about 4-5 weeks after hatching. The adult is small, with long wings, a short tail, yellow eyes and a dark bill. Its plumage is warm brown above, lightly streaked with white on the forehead and crown, and white beneath streaked with red-brown; it has buffy facial discs. In their first summer, juveniles are chocolate brown with a plain tawny belly and a white triangular patch on the forehead. The Northern Saw-whet Owl mainly eats small rodents and large beetles.

GREAT GRAY OWL

(opposite)

Scientific name:	*Strix nebulosa*
Length:	27 inches
Habitat:	Boreal forests, wooded bogs, dense coniferous forests
Identification:	Very big, long-tailed owl with large head. Mottled gray-brown above, muted gray vertical streaking below, pale gray facial discs patterned in concentric dark gray circles, yellow eyes and bill
Similar species:	Size and coloring unmistakable

The largest owl in North America, the Great Gray Owl inhabits dense forest and wooded bogs in the north and is relatively uncommon. It is not quite as large as it may appear, since its body is surrounded by a large mass of feathers that provide insulation in the cold climate it lives in. It does not build a nest, but lays 2-5 white eggs in the nest of another bird, usually in a tall tree or on a cliff. These are incubated by the female for around 4-5 weeks, and the chicks are ready to leave the nest about 5 weeks after hatching. The adult has a large head, with big, pale gray facial discs patterned in concentric dark gray circles, yellow eyes and bill and quite a long tail. Its plumage is mottled gray-brown above, with muted gray vertical streaking below; a black chin spot and two white neck marks may be evident. Although it is mainly nocturnal, the Great Gray Owl also hunts at dawn and dusk and sometimes during the day in the far north. It feeds mainly on mice, but will also take small mammals and birds.

COMMON NIGHTHAWK

Scientific name:	*Chordeiles minor*
Length:	9½ inches
Habitat:	Woodland, farmland, city suburbs
Identification:	Slender, very long-winged bird. Mottled brown-black above, paler beneath with bold dusky barring, white bar across wing near base of primaries, male also has white throat and white tail band
Similar species:	Lesser Nighthawk is paler, has more rounded wings, white wing bar is nearer tip of wing

The Common Nighthawk is found all across North America in summer in a variety of habitats including city suburbs, but not in dry desert areas and tundra. It spends the winter in sub-tropical areas of Mexico and South America. On its breeding grounds it does not build a nest, but lays its 2 creamy or greenish-gray eggs, which are often densely speckled, directly on the ground or a flat roof. They are incubated by the female bird for around 20 days, but both parents feed the chicks until they are ready to leave about 3 weeks later. The adult is a slender bird with long, pointed wings and a slightly forked tail. The plumage of the male is a mottled brown-black above and whitish or buffy beneath with bold, dusky barring, and it has a bold white bar across the wing at the base of the primaries, a white throat and a white tail band. Birds in the east tend to be browner, while those in the north are grayer. The female lacks the tail band, and both female and juvenile have a buffy throat and wing bar. The Common Nighthawk flies and glides high above the ground, bounding along with fluttery, rather erratic wingbeats, catching insects on the wing. It is common across much of its range, although numbers are declining.

LESSER NIGHTHAWK

Scientific name:	*Chordeiles acutipennis*
Length:	$8\frac{1}{2}$ inches
Habitat:	Scrubland, desert
Identification:	Slender, long-winged bird of dry country. Mottled sandy brown-gray above, buffy beneath with faint barring, whitish bar across wing close to tip, male also has white throat and white tail band
Similar species:	Common Nighthawk is darker, has longer pointed wings, white wing bar is nearer middle of wing

Despite their name, nighthawks are often seen in daylight. The Lesser Nighthawk prefers dry countryside and is seen in the far south in summer, and sometimes also in southern California and Texas in winter. Its breeding grounds are across the dry, open scrubland and desert of the south; it does not build a nest but lays its 2 buffy-pink or greenish eggs, often lightly spotted with gray-brown, directly on the ground or a flat roof. They are incubated by the female for up to 3 weeks, but both parents feed the chicks until they are ready to leave around 21 days later. The adult is slender with long wings that are fairly rounded at the tip, and a slightly notched tail. The male is an evenly mottled sandy brown-gray above and buffy beneath with faint barring, and has a whitish bar across the wing close to the tip, a white throat and a white tail band. The female lacks the tail band, and both female and juvenile have a buffy throat and wing bar. The Lesser Nighthawk catches insects in its wide mouth while on the wing.

COMMON POORWILL

Scientific name:	*Phalaenoptilus nuttallii*
Length:	7¾ inches
Habitat:	Sagebrush, dry foothills, rocky outcrops
Identification:	Small, short-winged nightjar with large head. Mottled gray-brown, white band above black throat, outer tail feathers tipped white
Similar species:	Smaller and grayer than other nightjars

The Common Poorwill is the smallest of the nightjar family and prefers arid country. It is found across much of western North America in summer but retreats to the south and down into Mexico for the winter, although some birds are known to hibernate in the southwest in cold weather. It is rarely seen during the day, but is often spotted at dawn and dusk sitting on back roads or at the roadside. It does not build a nest, but lays 2 pinky-white eggs directly on bare ground. The eggs are incubated by both adults, but the incubation period and details of the fledglings are not known. The adult is a small bird with a large head and short, rounded wings and a rounded tail. Its plumage is mottled gray to gray-brown with a white band above a black throat. The outer tail feathers tipped with white are more evident on the male. The Common Poorwill sits on the ground, flying up with fluttery wingbeats to catch an insect and then settling back down again.

WHIP-POOR-WILL

Scientific name:	*Caprimulgus vociferus*
Length:	9¾ inches
Habitat:	Open coniferous woods, mixed woods, wooded canyons
Identification:	Medium-size, round-winged nightjar with long rounded tail. Mottled gray-brown-black, black throat with white necklace, outer tail feathers of male mostly white, those of female tipped buff
Similar species:	Chuck-will's-widow is larger and redder, with whitish band above black breast

Found mainly in northeast America, the Whip-poor-will prefers mixed woodland and open conifer woods. Some birds spend the winter in southern Florida, others move down into Mexico and further south. If it is discovered during the day it may well appear tame, sitting still when approached and relying on its camouflage for protection. It does not build a nest, but lays 2 whitish eggs with irregular gray or brown spots directly amongst leaves on the forest floor. The eggs are incubated by the female for about 3 weeks, and the young leave about 2-3 weeks after hatching. The adult has broadly rounded wings, a long rounded tail and large, dark eyes. Its plumage is mottled gray-brown-black, and it has a black throat with a white necklace. The outer tail feathers of the male are mostly white, while those of the female are tipped with buff. The Whip-poor-will glides at night not far above the ground, with mouth gaping widely to catch beetles, moths and other large insects. Nightjars and nighthawks were once known as goatsuckers, because they swarm round animals at night to feed off the insects surrounding them, which led to a belief that they sucked the milk from goats' udders.

PAURAQUE

Scientific name: *Nyctidromus albicollis*
Length: 11 inches
Habitat: Brushland, dense thickets
Identification: Slim, long-winged bird with long rounded tail. Gray-brown above with line of black spots above wings, paler beneath, chestnut ear patch, bold white bar across wing near tip, male also has white tail patches, female has buffy
Similar species: Nighthawks have more pointed wings, nightjars may have white in tail but have no white on wing

A tropical bird, the Pauraque is found in southern Texas and down into Mexico. It is nocturnal, roosting in dense thicket during daylight hours, so it is usually seen at dawn and dusk, or at night when it is caught in headlights as it sits on back roads. On its breeding grounds it does not build a nest, but lays its 2 pinky-buff eggs, which are often spotted red-brown, directly on the ground in a depression lined with leaves. The incubation period and details of the fledglings are not known. The adult is a slim bird with long, rounded wings and a long rounded tail. The plumage of the male is gray-brown above with a line of black spots above the wing, paler beneath, with a gray crown, chestnut ear patch, and a bold white bar across the wing near the tip. The male also has white patches on the tail, the female has buffy. The Pauraque flies low over the ground, with deep wingbeats and quite bouncing flight, catching insects on the wing.

CHUCK-WILL'S-WIDOW

Scientific name: *Caprimulgus carolinensis*
Length: 12 inches
Habitat: Oak and pine woods
Identification: Large, long-winged nightjar with long rounded tail. Mottled reddish buffy-brown, whitish band above black breast, outer tail feathers white centers and tipped buff
Similar species: Whip-poor-will is smaller and grayer, with dark throat and white or buffy necklace

Chuck-will's-widow is the largest of the nightjar family and prefers woodland. It is found across much of southeastern North America in summer and a few birds stay all year in southern Florida. It is rarely seen during the day - its plumage provides excellent camouflage, it lurks in thick woodland and flies away if approached - but it can be spotted at dawn and dusk sitting low in trees along the roadside. It does not build a nest, but lays 2 pinky-buff eggs with lilac or brown spots directly amongst leaves on the ground. The eggs are incubated by the female for about 3 weeks, and the young leave about 2-3 weeks after hatching. The adult has long wings with a rounded point and a longish rounded tail. Its plumage is a mottled reddish buffy-brown, with a whitish band above a black breast. The outer tail feathers of the male have white centers and are tipped with buff. Chuck-will's-widow glides strongly through the air, with mouth gaping widely to catch beetles, moths and other large insects.

CHIMNEY SWIFT

Scientific name:	*Chaetura pelagica*
Length:	5¼ inches
Habitat:	Urban areas, woodland
Identification:	Small, short-tailed bird with slim body and long, narrow, curved wings. Sooty brown overall with paler throat
Similar species:	Vaux's Swift is slightly smaller, usually paler on breast and rump

The Chimney Swift has often been described as looking like a "cigar on wings" and is found all over eastern America in summer, but migrates to the rainforests of South America to spend the winter. It flies fast with quick wingbeats, or sails with wings held stiff. It previously nested in a hole or hollow of a tree, but now builds a half-cup of twigs glued together with saliva inside a chimney or barn, in which it lays 4 or 5 white eggs. These are incubated for up to 3 weeks by both adult birds, and the young leave the nest around 4 weeks after they have hatched. The adult bird is small, with a short, stubby tail, a slim body and long, narrow, curved wings. Its plumage is sooty brown overall, with a paler throat. The Chimney Swift does not perch but clings to a vertical surface when roosting at night. During the day it is always on the wing, sweeping through the air to catch insects.

WHITE-THROATED SWIFT

Scientific name:	*Aeronautes saxatalis*
Length:	6½ inches
Habitat:	Mountains, canyons, cliffs
Identification:	Slender, long-winged bird with long, notched tail. Black overall with white throat and belly, white sides on rump and on trailing edge of wings at base
Similar species:	Only swift with white patches. Violet-green Swallow is similar, but has shorter wings, slower flight and is all white beneath

The White-throated Swift is most often seen near cliffs and canyons, often in large flocks, and is sometimes known as a rock swift. It migrates south in winter, but some birds remain in the southwest all year round. It nests in cliff crevices in colonies, building a half-cup of grass and feathers glued together with saliva, in which it lays 3-6 white eggs. Its incubation habits and nestling periods are uncertain. The adult bird is a slender, long-winged bird with a long, notched tail, which it sometimes holds closed and pointed in flight. Its plumage is black overall with a white throat and belly, and white sides on the rump and the trailing edge of the wings at the base. The White-throated Swift is one of the fastest American birds, with an estimated top speed of 200 miles per hour. It flies with very quick wingbeats followed by a stiff-winged glide, as it sweeps through the air to catch insects.

VAUX'S SWIFT

Scientific name:	*Chaetura vauxi*
Length:	4¾ inches
Habitat:	Woodlands near water
Identification:	Small, short-tailed bird with slim body and long, narrow, curved wings. Sooty brown overall with paler chest and rump
Similar species:	The Chimney Swift is slightly larger and generally darker

The west coast equivalent of the Chimney Swift, Vaux's Swift is found in northwest America in summer, but migrates to Central and South America to spend the winter. It nests inside a hollow tree, or sometimes in a chimney, building a half-cup of twigs glued together with saliva and fixed to the vertical surface, it which it lays 4 or 5 white eggs. These are incubated for up to 3 weeks by both adult birds, and the young leave the nest around 4 weeks after they have hatched. The adult bird is small, with a short, stubby tail, a slim body and long, narrow, curved wings. Its plumage is sooty brown overall, with a paler chest and rump. Like the Chimney Swift, Vaux's Swift does not perch; in both species the tail feathers end with a hard shaft that offers more support to the bird when it is clinging to a vertical surface while roosting at night. Vaux's Swift flies fast with spurts of very quick wingbeats, followed by glides with wings held stiff, as it sweeps through the air to catch insects. Its population is declining, since its mature forest habitat is gradually being destroyed.

BLUE-THROATED HUMMINGBIRD

Scientific name:	*Lampornis clemenciae*
Length:	5 inches
Habitat:	Streams in mountain canyons
Identification:	Large, broad-tailed hummingbird. Male metallic green above, gray below with bright blue gorget, blue-black tail with white corners to outer feathers. Female green above, gray below, white tips to outer tail feathers. Both have white stripe above and below eye
Similar species:	Female Magnificent Hummingbird similar to female Blue-throated, but is more mottled beneath and has smaller white corners to tail

The biggest of the hummers seen in America, the Blue-throated Hummingbird prefers shady, wooded canyons and is fairly common within its range. Its nest is a tiny, beautifully constructed cup of plants with moss woven into the walls, fixed to a plant stalk or vine, or on an electric wire, usually near or over water. It must be sheltered from rain and sun, and once it has found a suitable site the bird returns to the same spot year after year. The nest holds 2 white eggs, which are incubated by the female, with the young birds leaving around 3 weeks after hatching. The adult has a broad tail, which it sometimes holds fanned. The plumage of the male is metallic green above and gray below with a bright blue gorget, and it has a blue-black tail with white corners to the outer feathers. The female is green above and gray below, with white tips to the outer tail feathers. Both have a white stripe above and below the eye. The Blue-throated Hummingbird feeds on nectar and pollen from flowers and also catches small insects.

MAGNIFICENT HUMMINGBIRD

Scientific name:	*Eugenes fulgens*
Length:	5¼ inches
Habitat:	High mountain meadows and canyons, open woods
Identification:	Large, slender, long-billed hummingbird. Male green above with purple crown, breast and upper belly black with metallic green gorget, dark green deeply notched tail. Female duller, lacks purple crown, squarish tail, white-gray tips to outer tail feathers
Similar species:	Female Blue-throated Hummingbird similar to female Magnificent, but has white eye stripes and larger white tips to tail

The second-largest American hummer, the Magnificent Hummingbird is found in high mountain meadows and canyons and is fairly common within its range. Its nest is a small cup of plants with lichens woven into the walls, fixed to a horizontal branch high above the ground. It holds 2 white eggs, but incubation habits and nestling periods are not known. The adult is slender, with a particularly long, thin bill. The plumage of the male is green above with a purple crown and a white spot behind the eye; it has a black breast and upper belly with a metallic green gorget. Its lower belly is dull brown and it has a dark green deeply notched tail. The female is duller with mottled gray-green sides and lacks the purple crown; it has a squarish tail with small white-gray tips to the outer tail feathers. In flight, the Magnificent Hummingbird sometimes skims along rather like a swift. It feeds on nectar and pollen from flowers and also catches small insects.

BUFF-BELLIED
HUMMINGBIRD *(left)*

Scientific name:	*Amazilia yucatanensis*
Length:	$4\frac{1}{4}$ inches
Habitat:	Woodland borders
Identification:	Large, long-bodied hummingbird. Metallic green above, including head and throat, buffy lower breast and belly, rufous tail, red bill with black tip
Similar species:	Berylline Hummingbird is also green with a red tail, but is a Mexican species that rarely comes up into North America

Although it is a Mexican species, the Buff-bellied Hummingbird appeared in Texas at the end of the 1870s and has been fairly common in the far south until a few years ago. It is now only found in a limited area along the Rio Grande during the summer, with most birds returning to Mexico in the winter - although a few are seen around the northern Gulf coast and into Florida. Its nest is a tiny cup of plant down, fibers and lichen, decorated with pieces of bark and lichen and firmly attached to the branch of a tree up to 8 feet above the ground. It usually holds 2 white eggs, but details of the incubation and nestling periods are not currently known. The adult is long-bodied, and has a long, slightly down-curved red-pink bill with a black tip. Its plumage is metallic green above, including the head and throat, and it has a buffy lower breast and belly and a rufous tail. Both male and female have the same coloring and they are easy to distinguish from most other hummingbirds because of their red tails. The Buff-bellied Hummingbird feeds on the nectar and pollen from flowers and also sometimes eats the small insects on the petals.

VIOLET-CROWNED
HUMMINGBIRD *(above)*

Scientific name:	*Amazilia violiceps*
Length:	$4\frac{1}{2}$ inches
Habitat:	Streams, sycamore woods in lower mountain canyons
Identification:	Large, long-bodied hummingbird. Bronze above, white below including throat, violet-blue crown, red bill with dark tip
Similar species:	No other hummingbird with similar coloring

Although the Violet-crowned Hummingbird is only found in a limited area in the south and is fairly uncommon, it is conspicuous when it is seen and is aggressive towards other hummers. It usually breeds outside America, but some birds have nested in Arizona and New Mexico. Its downy and lichen-covered nest is built on the horizontal branch of a tree and holds 2 white eggs, which are incubated by the female for 2-3 weeks, with the young birds leaving around 3 weeks after hatching. The adult is long-bodied, and has a long, slightly down-curved red bill with a dark tip. Its plumage is bronze above and white below - including the throat - and it has a violet-blue crown. Unlike many hummingbirds, both male and female are the same. The Violet-crowned Hummingbird feeds on nectar from flowers and has also been seen at feeders, sometimes coming throughout the winter. The suspended flight of a hummingbird requires around 54 wingbeats per second, while their normal, darting flight requires 75 wingbeats per second - which causes the distinctive humming sound that gives them their name. They have been recorded flying at speeds up to 50 mph.

BLACK-CHINNED HUMMINGBIRD

Scientific name:	*Archilochus alexandri*
Length:	3¾ inches
Habitat:	Woodland in lowlands and foothills
Identification:	Small hummingbird, long, straight, thin bill. Bright green back, white underparts. Male has black face and chin
Similar species:	Male unmistakable in good light because of the purple gorget, but female very similar to other female hummingbirds

The Black-chinned Hummingbird breeds in lowlands and low mountains across western America, where it is quite common in spring and summer. It often builds its nest in vulnerable places, where it can easily be seen by predators, but both mother and nestlings are very quiet - the baby birds do not call for food as those of many other species do. The clutch consists of 2 eggs, which take 13-16 days to incubate. The nestlings take a further 3 weeks to fledge and the female continues to look after the young birds while they are learning to fly, hover and forage. The adult male has a black face, chin and upper throat, a metallic green back and an entirely dark tail. In a very good light, an iridescent purple-violet gorget can be seen at the lower throat. The female (*right*) and immature bird both have a white chin and throat, with variable dark streaking, and a dark tail with white tips to the outer tail feathers. The Black-chinned Hummingbird feeds on nectar and a variety of small insects. It normally winters outside North America, although a few only go as far as the northern Gulf coast or winter in the southeast.

RUBY-THROATED HUMMINGBIRD

Scientific name:	*Archilochus colubris*
Length:	3¾ inches
Habitat:	Gardens, woodland edges
Identification:	Small hummingbird, with long, straight, thin bill. Bright green back, white underparts. Male has black face and chin and iridescent scarlet gorget
Similar species:	Male Broad-tailed Hummingbird is similar to male Ruby-throated, but has rose-red throat rather than ruby. Female very similar to other female humming birds

The Ruby-throated is the only hummingbird regularly seen in the east. They are anti-social birds, so they only pair to mate; the female builds a tiny nest of spiders' webs and plant down, often near water, where she incubates 2 white eggs for 11-14 days. The young take 14-28 days to fledge and she rears 2-3 clutches alone. The male defends the breeding area and nectar resources with stylized displays; the female defends the nest in the breeding season, but also defends the nectar resources at other times. The adult male has a black face and chin, an iridescent ruby or scarlet gorget at the throat, a metallic green back and an entirely dark, forked tail. The female (*right*) and immature bird both have a white chin and throat, with variable thin dark streaking and a dark, shallow-forked tail with white tips to the outer tail feathers. Despite its tiny size, the Ruby-throated Hummingbird migrates across the Gulf of Mexico to winter in Central America. Red tubular flowers are a particularly favorite source of food, but it also eats tiny flying insects and small spiders.

LUCIFER HUMMINGBIRD

Scientific name:	*Calothorax lucifer*
Length:	3½ inches
Habitat:	Desert, lower mountain canyons
Identification:	Small, large-headed hummingbird with long decurved bill and deeply-notched tail. Male iridescent green above with green crown and purple gorget, white below, buff on flanks. Female similar but buff below and lacks forked tail
Similar species:	Several other hummingbirds have a slightly decurved bill. Costa's Hummingbird has similar gorget, but also purple on forehead, rounded tail and lacks decurved bill

The tiny Lucifer Hummingbird is a Mexican hummer that is rather uncommon in America, found only in the desert areas of southeast Arizona, southwest New Mexico and western Texas. Its nest is a small cup of downy plant fibers with cobwebs and lichens woven into the walls, situated near the ground in vegetation. It holds 2 white eggs, but incubation habits and nestling periods are not known. The adult is tiny, with a relatively large head and a long, distinctly decurved bill. The plumage of the male (*above*) is iridescent green on its upperparts, with a green crown and purple gorget, and white below with buff on the flanks, and it has a black, deeply-notched tail. The female is similar but warm buff below, with a whitish belly, and a rounded tail with the outer feathers rufous at the base and tipped with white. The outer tail feathers of the male are narrow and stiff and create a loud hum when it is displaying in the air. The Lucifer Hummingbird feeds on nectar and pollen from flowers and also catches small insects. The metabolism of hummers is very rapid, so birds must feed every 10-15 minutes on nectar and flying insects.

RUFOUS HUMMINGBIRD

Scientific name:	*Selasphorus rufus*
Length:	3¾ inches
Habitat:	Woodlands
Identification:	Small, compact hummingbird, with rather short wings. Male rufous above and on sides, with bright orange-red gorget and white breast. Female green above, with rufous on sides, white beneath with orange-red spotted throat patch, outer tail feathers rufous at base, black in middle and white at tip
Similar species:	Male distinctive. Juvenile similar to juvenile male Allen's Hummingbird. Female is similar to female Broad-tailed, but has shorter tail and reddish throat patch, and also to female Allen's but has less rufous in tail

Although it is mainly found along the north Pacific coast in summer, the Rufous Hummingbird is also sometimes seen over much of the east in fall, as it migrates south. Some birds stay along the Gulf coast in winter, but most fly on to southern Mexico. Its nest is a carefully woven cup of plant down, decorated with moss and lichen, fastened to a horizontal branch, in which the female incubates 2 white eggs. The young leave the nest around 3 weeks after hatching. The adult is a small, compact hummer, with rather short wings. The male is rufous above and on the sides, with a bright orange-red gorget and a white breast. The female (*above*) has a green back with rufous on the sides, white beneath with a small orange-red spotted throat patch, and has outer tail feathers that are heavily rufous at the base, black in the middle and white at the tip. The juvenile is similar to the female. In flight, the male may produce a whistling buzz with its wings. Both male and female defend their territory and nectar sources; they also eat tiny flying insects and running tree sap.

ALLEN'S HUMMINGBIRD

Scientific name: *Selasphorus sasin*
Length: 3¾ inches
Habitat: Open woods, suburbs
Identification: Small hummingbird, with short wings and a long bill. Male iridescent green crown and back, rufous rump and below, bright copper-red gorget and white breast. Female green above, with rufous sides, white beneath with small orange-red spotted throat patch, outer tail feathers rufous base, black middle and white tip
Similar species: Male distinguished from male Rufous by green on back. Juvenile similar to juvenile male Allen's. Female similar to female Broad-tailed, but has shorter tail, reddish throat patch, also to female Allen's but has more rufous in tail

Common in North America within its rather limited summer range, Allen's Hummingbird is also seen in the southwest during winter and fall as it migrates; some birds stay all year round on the islands off the California coast. Its nest is a tightly woven cup of plant down and stems, decorated with lichen and fastened to a sheltered branch, in which the female incubates 2 white eggs for 2-3 weeks. The adult is small, with rather short wings and relatively long bill. The male has an iridescent green crown and back, rufous on the rump and below, a bright copper-red gorget and a white breast. The female is green above, with rufous on the sides, white beneath with a small orange-red spotted throat patch, and outer tail feathers heavily rufous at the base, black in the middle and white at the tip. Like the Rufous, the male Allen's produces a whistling buzz with its wings in flight.

BROAD-TAILED HUMMINGBIRD *(below)*

Scientific name: *Selasphorus platycercus*
Length: 4 inches
Habitat: Mountain meadows
Identification: Medium-size hummingbird, with long body and long broad tail. Metallic green above, white underparts. Male has rose-red gorget. Female is buffy beneath with spotted cheeks, outer tail feathers rufous at base, black in middle and white at tip
Similar species: Male could be confused with male Ruby-throated, but lacks black face and chin, little overlap in range. Also similar to juvenile male Anna's Hummingbird. Female similar to female Rufous and Allen's hummingbirds, but has longer, broader tail with less rufous, lacks reddish throat patch

In summer, the Broad-tailed Hummingbird is fairly common across western America, but it winters in South America. It is often heard before it is seen, its wings making a loud metallic hum as it flies. Its nest is a woven cup of plant down, lichen and spider web, fastened to a horizontal branch, in which the female incubates 2 white eggs for about 15-17 days. The young take around 3 weeks to fledge. The adult has a long body and a long, broad tail, metallic green plumage above and white beneath; the male *(below)* has a rose-red gorget and greenish sides. The female is buffy beneath with spotted cheeks, the outer tail feathers are rufous at the base, black in the middle and white at the tip. Red flowers are a favourite source of nectar for the Broad-tailed Hummingbird; it also eats spiders and flying insects.

CALLIOPE HUMMINGBIRD

Scientific name:	*Stellula calliope*
Length:	3¼ inches
Habitat:	Mountain meadows
Identification:	Tiny, short-tailed hummingbird, with short thin bill. Male metallic green above, white gorget with purple-violet streaks, whitish breast. Female green above, white beneath with dark streaks on throat, buff on flanks, outer tail feathers white at tip
Similar species:	Streaked throat of male distinctive. Juvenile similar to juvenile Allen's and Broad-tailed hummingbirds. Female is similar to female Rufous and Broad-tailed, but is smaller with less rufous in tail

The smallest North American bird, the Calliope Hummingbird is common in mountain meadows across the northwest in summer and migrates across the southwest to winter in Mexico. Its nest is a small cup of moss and lichen, decorated with spider web, fastened to a sheltered branch on a bush or small tree. The female lays 2 white eggs, which are incubated for just over 2 weeks. The young leave the nest around 3 weeks after hatching. The adult is a tiny, short-tailed hummer, with a short, thin bill. The male is metallic green above, with a white gorget with purple-violet streaks, and a whitish breast. The female is green above, white beneath with dark streaks on the throat, and has buff on its flanks and outer tail feathers tipped with white. The juvenile is similar to the female, but has some red on the throat by the end of the summer. The Calliope Hummingbird feeds on nectar, small insects and spiders.

ANNA'S HUMMINGBIRD

Scientific name:	*Calypte anna*
Length:	4 inches
Habitat:	Coastal lowlands, mountains, deserts
Identification:	Medium-size, stocky hummingbird with tubular body and short straight bill. Adult birds metallic green above. Male rose-red crown and gorget, grayish-green chest. Female spotted throat with red central patch, whitish gray-green underparts, white-tipped outer tail feathers
Similar species:	Juvenile lacks red on throat and could be confused with female of several other hummers. Female very similar to other female hummingbirds

Found all year round along the Pacific coast, Anna's Hummingbird is common in woodlands, along streams and also in suburban gardens. Its nest is a tiny cup of woven twigs and lichens, fixed to a sheltered horizontal branch. It holds 2 white eggs, which are incubated by the female for 2-3 weeks; the young birds leave the nest about 26 days after hatching. The adult is a medium-size, sturdy hummer, with a rather tubular body and short straight bill. Both adults are metallic green above; the male has a distinctive rose-red crown and gorget, and a grayish-green chest. The female has a spotted throat, with red spots in the center forming a patch of color, whitish gray-green underparts, and white-tipped outer tail feathers. The juvenile is similar to the female adult, but usually has an unmarked throat. Anna's Hummingbird tends to hold its tail still and in line with its body when hovering. It feeds on nectar and small insects, and frequently comes to feeders in suburban gardens. Like other hummingbirds, it defends its feeding territory against interlopers.

COSTA'S HUMMINGBIRD

Scientific name:	*Calypte costae*
Length:	3½ inches
Habitat:	Desert, dry country
Identification:	Small, short-tailed hummingbird with round head and short thick neck. Adult birds metallic green above. Male violet-purple crown and gorget extending down sides of neck, whitish-green chest. Female white throat and breast, greeny-buff on sides, white-tipped outer tail feathers
Similar species:	Female very similar to other female hummingbirds. Costa's Hummingbird prefers arid country, which is a useful indicator

Costa's Hummingbird is found in arid, desert areas, and is fairly common in southern California, Arizona and Nevada. Its nest is a woven cup decorated with leaves and lichens, fixed low down on a branch or yucca stalk. It holds 2 white eggs, which are incubated by the female for 14-17 days; the young birds leave the nest about 3 weeks after hatching. The adult is a small, short-tailed hummer, with a round head, a short thick neck and a metallic green back; the male (*above*) has a whitish-green chest and a rich violet-purple crown and gorget, extending down each side of the neck, which may appear black in some lights. The female has a white throat and breast, greeny-buff on sides, and white-tipped outer tail feathers. Costa's Hummingbird feeds on nectar and small insects, and is particularly fond of red beardtongue. Unlike other hummers, it tends to soar as it moves from one cluster of flowers to the next.

BROAD-BILLED HUMMINGBIRD

Scientific name: *Cynanthus latirostris*
Length: 4 inches
Habitat: Desert canyons, low mountain woodlands
Identification: Medium-size, stocky hummingbird, with broad tail. Male dark green above and below, with bright metallic-blue gorget, mostly red bill, white undertail coverts, blue-black notched tail. Female duller green above, gray beneath, white eye stripe, red bill, square tail with white at tip of outer feathers
Similar species: Forked tail and lack of white ear stripe distinguish male from male White-eared. Plain gray underparts distinguish female from female White-eared, and red bill from other female hummers

The Broad-billed Hummingbird is a Mexican species that is mainly seen in North America in southern Arizona, where it is often quite common during the summer. Its nest is a rather loosely-woven, rough cup of plant stems, fastened to a branch of a tree near a stream, in which the female incubates 2 white eggs. The adult is a medium-size, stocky hummer, with a broad tail and a long, red-orange, slightly decurved bill. The male (*above*) is dark green both above and below, with a bright metallic-blue gorget, a blue-black notched tail and white undertail coverts. The female is duller green above and gray beneath, with a white eye stripe, and a square-ended tail with white at the tip of the outer feathers. The Broad-billed Hummingbird is less active than many other hummers - it will often sit on a perch for quite long periods of time. It flies in a rather irregular, jerky way and flicks its tail while hovering. Like other hummingbirds, its favorite food is the nectar sucked from flowers with its long bill, but it will also eat tiny flying insects and small spiders.

WHITE-EARED HUMMINGBIRD

Scientific name:	*Hylocharis leucotis*
Length:	3¾ inches
Habitat:	Mountain coniferous forest, canyons
Identification:	Small, stocky hummingbird, with broad square tail, broad white ear stripe and red bill tipped black. Male dark green above and below, with bright purple-blue crown and chin, emerald-green gorget, white undertail coverts. Female green above, whitish beneath with green spotting and barring on throat and sides, white at tip of outer tail feathers
Similar species:	Male Broad-billed has forked tail and no white ear stripe and longer bill. Female Broad-billed has plain gray underparts. Red bill distinguishes female White-eared from other female hummers

A Mexican and South American species that is mainly seen in North America in southeastern Arizona during the summer, the White-eared Hummingbird is fairly rare. Although their ranges overlap, the White-eared prefers to live at rather higher elevations than the Broad-billed. As the breeding season arrives, several males gather in one area and the female visits to choose a mate to take back to her nest. The nest is made of moss interwoven with lichens and twigs or conifer needles and fastened to a branch, in which the female incubates 2 white eggs. The adult is a small, stocky hummer, with a broad square tail, a broad white ear stripe and a long, straight, red bill tipped with black. The male (*below*) is dark green above and below, with a purple-blue crown and chin, an emerald-green gorget, and white undertail coverts. The female is green above, whitish beneath with green spotting and barring on the throat and sides, and has white at the tip of the outer tail feathers. The White-eared Hummingbird lives mainly on the nectar from flowers but will also eat small flying insects and tiny spiders.

GREEN VIOLET-EAR *(above)*

Scientific name:	*Colibri thalassinus*
Length:	$4\frac{3}{4}$ inches
Habitat:	Mountain woodlands
Identification:	Small tropical hummingbird, curved bill, metallic green overall, blue-green tail with darker band, blue-green wing linings. Male has blue-violet ear patch and breast
Similar species:	Coloring distinctive

The Green Violet-ear is very common in the tropics but is usually only seen in North America in the hilly regions of Texas and in some areas of the east - although it has been recorded as far north as Canada. It has not so far been known to nest in North America, although this may be just because a nest has not yet been discovered. The adult is a small, brightly-colored bird, with a curved dark bill, and both male and female have similar plumage: vivid metallic green overall, with a broad, rounded, blue-green tail crossed by a darker band just above the tip, buffy undertail coverts and blue-green wing linings. The male has a blue-violet ear patch and breast. The juvenile bird is very similar, but tends to be slightly duller, with more gray on the belly. Like other hummingbirds, the Green Violet-ear eats the nectar and pollen from flowers and small insects - it has also been known to visit hummingbird feeders.

ELEGANT TROGON *(right)*

Scientific name:	*Trogon elegans*
Length:	$12\frac{1}{2}$ inches
Habitat:	Mountain woodlands near streams
Identification:	Medium-size tropical bird, with short broad yellow bill. White breast band, barred tail, red belly running down under tail. Male bright green above, female much duller
Similar species:	Elegant Trogon is unmistakable - Eared Trogon is similar, but lacks white breast band, has mainly white undersurface to the tail and is only rarely seen in North America

In North America, these brightly colored tropical birds are mainly restricted to southeastern Arizona, although a few have been seen in southern Texas. They prefer to live in woods at high altitudes near streams, and they remain in roughly the same area all year round. Their nests are built in cavities and they raise a clutch of 3-4 eggs. The adult male is bright green above, with a bright red belly, white breast band and a short, broad, yellow bill. The tail feathers are green above and white beneath with delicate barring and are tipped with black. The female and the immature bird are both similar to the male in coloring, but are browner and duller. Their diet mainly consists of fruit and small insects. The song of both male and female is a series of croaking *co-ah* notes.

RINGED KINGFISHER

Scientific name:	*Ceryle torquata*
Length:	16 inches
Habitat:	Large rivers, lakes
Identification:	Large kingfisher with ragged crest and stout dark-tipped bill. Blue-gray above and on head, white collar. Male is rust-red beneath with white undertail coverts. Female has blue-gray breast, white band, rust-red belly and undertail coverts, rust-red on underwing
Similar species:	Male unmistakable. Female Belted Kingfisher similar general coloring but smaller and only has rust belly band, white under wing

The largest kingfisher in North America, the Ringed Kingfisher has extended its range north from Mexico and now inhabits the lower Rio Grande Valley, although it is also sometimes seen elsewhere in Texas. It is usually found near large areas of water. It does not build a nest, but digs a long tunnel in the side of a steep river bank, and lays its 4-5 white eggs on bare soil at the end. Details of its incubation habits and nestling periods are not currently known. The adult is much larger than the Belted Kingfisher, with a ragged crest and a stout dark-tipped bill. Its plumage is blue-gray above and on the head, with a white collar. The male is rust-red beneath with white undertail coverts, and the female has a white band between the blue-gray breast and rust-red belly and undertail coverts. In flight, the female shows rust-red under the wing, with blue-gray along the trailing edge - the male has white underwing coverts. The Ringed Kingfisher perches high up above lakes and rivers and dives for fish and frogs.

GREEN KINGFISHER

Scientific name:	*Chloroceryle americana*
Length:	$8\frac{3}{4}$ inches
Habitat:	Narrow streams
Identification:	Small kingfisher with small crest and large bill. Dark metallic-green above and on head, white collar, white belly, flanks spotted green, wings speckled white. Male has broad red breast band. Female has green spotting across breast forming a band
Similar species:	Both male and female are unmistakable

A mainly tropical bird, the Green Kingfisher is only found in North America in southern Texas, with a few birds resident in Arizona and New Mexico. It is a fairly uncommon bird and not easy to see, lurking in the shaded edges of woodland pools and narrow streams. It does not build a nest, but digs a tunnel around 3 feet long in the side of a steep bank and lays its 4-6 white eggs on bare soil at the end. The eggs are incubated for around 3 weeks and the young birds leave the burrow after about 4 weeks when they are fully fledged. The adult is small, with an insignificant crest and a long, pointed bill. Its plumage is dark metallic-green above and on the head, with a white collar and white belly; its flanks are spotted green and wings speckled white. The male has a broad red breast band, while the female has green spotting across the breast forming a band. In flight, both male and female show mainly white under the wing and white outer tail feathers. The Green Kingfisher sits low down near the water, wagging its tail up and down, until it swiftly plunges into the depths to catch a small fish.

BELTED KINGFISHER

Scientific name:	*Ceryle alcyon*
Length:	13 inches
Habitat:	Rivers, streams, ponds and lakes, estuaries
Identification:	Medium-size kingfisher with shaggy crest and heavy bill. Blue-gray above and on head, white collar. Male has blue-gray breast band and white belly. Female has blue-gray breast band, and rust-red belly band across white belly
Similar species:	Male unmistakable. Female Ringed Kingfisher similar general coloring but larger and has all-rust belly, and rust-red under wing

The only kingfisher found across most of North America, the Belted Kingfisher is common and single birds are easily spotted near woodland water. It is a solitary bird, defending its fishing territory and only associating with others of its kind in the breeding season. It does not build a nest, but digs a tunnel up to 7 feet long in the side of a steep river bank, and lays its 5-8 white eggs on the bare soil at the end. The eggs are incubated for around 3-4 weeks and the young birds leave the burrow after about 7 weeks when they are fully fledged. The adult is medium size, with a shaggy crest and a heavy bill. Its plumage is blue-gray above and on the head, with a white collar. The male has a blue-gray breast band and white belly, and the female has a has a blue-gray breast band and a white belly with a rust-red belly band. In flight, both male and female have white under the wing, with blue-gray along the trailing edge. When flying between perches, it often gives a loud, harsh, rattling call. The Belted Kingfisher perches on a branch over a lake or river until it spots a fish, then hovers over the water before diving for its catch. It also eats frogs, tadpoles and insects.

ACORN WOODPECKER

Scientific name:	*Melanerpes formicivorus*
Length:	9 inches
Habitat:	Oak woods
Identification:	Medium-size woodpecker. Red crown, black nape, back, wings and tail, yellow-white forehead and throat, white belly with heavy dark streaking on breast and flanks, white rump and wing patches, dark eyes with white eye ring. Female has black bar between crown and forehead
Similar species:	At a distance, sometimes mistaken for male White-headed Woodpecker, which has more white on head and large white wing patch in flight

The Acorn Woodpecker does not have a wide range, but is locally quite common. It prefers woods where oak trees are abundant, where it is found in small, noisy colonies. It does not build a nest but excavates a suitable cavity in a dead tree, up to 80 feet above the ground, in which it lays 4-5 white eggs. These are incubated by both adults for around 14 days - often helped by other members of the colony - and the fledglings leave around 4 weeks after they have hatched, leaving the parents free to raise a second brood. The adult bird is medium size, with a red crown, dark eyes with white eye ring, a black nape, back, wings and tail, a yellow-white forehead and throat, and a white belly with heavy dark streaking on breast and flanks. In flight, it shows a white rump and wing patches. The female has a black bar between the crown and forehead. The Acorn Woodpecker collects acorns, and sometimes almonds and walnuts, which it stores in holes drilled in trees, fence posts or utility poles, packing the nuts in very tightly so squirrels cannot take them. The same holes are often reused by the colony year after year. In mild weather, this species also flies out to catch insects in midair.

LEWIS'S WOODPECKER

Scientific name:	*Melanerpes lewis*
Length:	$10\frac{3}{4}$ inches
Habitat:	Open woodlands
Identification:	Large, long-winged, long-tailed woodpecker. Metallic-green black above, collar and breast gray, dark red face, pink-red belly
Similar species:	Size and coloring make it unmistakable, although from a distance its slow flight, broad wings and dark color mean it might be mistaken for a crow

Lewis's Woodpecker is fairly common locally within its range, which is limited to groves of tall trees in open country in areas of western North America. It is a gregarious bird, so several birds form breeding colonies and are often seen together. Its 5-8 eggs are laid in a cavity excavated in a dead stump or tree branch, often very high above the ground. The eggs are incubated by both parent birds for around 12 days and the young leave the nest around 4-5 weeks after hatching. The adult bird is large, with long wings and a long tail. Its plumage is metallic-green black above, with a gray collar and breast, a dark red face, and a pink-red belly. The juvenile is duller, with no collar or red face and usually only a faint reddish belly. Lewis's Woodpecker flies slowly, with smooth, steady wingbeats. It does not peck at bark like other woodpeckers to find insects and beetles, but sits on a prominent perch and flies out to catch insects in midair. It also eats fruit, berries and nuts and stores acorns to eat in winter.

RED-HEADED WOODPECKER

Scientific name:	*Melanerpes erythrocephalus*
Length:	$9\frac{1}{4}$ inches
Habitat:	Open and dense woods
Identification:	Medium-size, broad-winged woodpecker. Bright red head, neck and throat, blue-black back, pure white underparts
Similar species:	Adult unmistakable

Although still common across its extensive range, the Red-headed Woodpecker population is declining in many areas - partly due to loss of its breeding habitat and partly because of competition from starlings and other birds for nesting holes. Like other woodpeckers it favors dead wood in which to excavate its hole, but dead and dying trees are now routinely removed. In a suitable cavity, it lays 4-6 white eggs, which are incubated by both parent birds for around 14 days; the young leave the nest around 4 weeks after hatching, and there is often a second brood. The adult bird is medium size, with a bright red head, neck and throat, a blue-black back, and pure white underparts. In flight it has large white wing patches and a white rump. The juvenile is duller, with a brownish head and dark bars across the wing patch. The Red-headed Woodpecker pecks at bark to find insects and beetles, but also sometimes flies out to catch insects in midair and eats nuts and acorns.

GOLDEN-FRONTED WOODPECKER

Scientific name:	*Melanerpes aurifrons*
Length:	9¾ inches
Habitat:	Dry woodlands, brushland
Identification:	Medium-size, heavy-bodied woodpecker. Head and underparts pale buff with a yellow tint to the belly, golden-orange nape, black and white barred back, black tail feathers. White wing patches and white rump in flight. Male has small red cap
Similar species:	Female and juvenile Gila Woodpecker similar to female Golden-fronted, but have barred central tail feathers and lack golden-orange nape. Red-bellied Woodpecker has a red nape

The Golden-fronted Woodpecker is found in the southeast, across Texas into Oklahoma and down into Mexico, and is closely related to both the Gila and Red-bellied woodpeckers. It excavates a nesting hole in a dead tree or mesquite, up to 25 feet above the ground, which is often used for several years. Its 4-6 white eggs are incubated by both adults for around 2 weeks and the chicks leave the nest about 4 weeks later, but remain with the parents for some time. The adult bird is a medium-size, heavy-bodied bird, with a fairly long bill and short wings. The adult has a pale buff head and underparts with a yellow tint to the belly, a golden-orange nape and gold feathering above the bill, a black and white barred back and black tail feathers. In flight, it shows white wing patches and a white rump. The juvenile is similar to the female; the male (*right*) has a small red cap. The Golden-fronted Woodpecker eats insects, fruit and acorns.

RED-BELLIED WOODPECKER

Scientific name:	*Melanerpes carolinus*
Length:	9¼ inches
Habitat:	Open woodland, swamps, suburbs, city parks
Identification:	Medium-size, heavy-bodied woodpecker. Head and underparts pale buff with a reddish tint to the belly, red nape, black and white barred back and central tail feathers. White wing patches and white rump in flight. Male has red crown
Similar species:	Very similar to Gila and Golden-fronted woodpeckers, but red nape is distinctive

Found across much of eastern North America, the Red-bellied Woodpecker is common and is extending its range northwards. The southernmost part of its range overlaps with that of the Golden-fronted Woodpecker, and the two species have interbred. The Red-bellied excavates a nesting hole in a dead tree, fence post or utility pole, which can be up to 70 feet above the ground. Its 4-6 white eggs are incubated by both adults for around 2 weeks and the chicks leave the nest about 3-4 weeks later, but remain with the parents for some time. The adult bird is a medium-size, heavy-bodied bird, with a fairly long bill and short wings. The adult has a pale buff head and underparts with a reddish tint to the belly, a red nape, a black and white barred back and a black tail with barred central feathers. In flight, it shows white wing patches and a white rump. In the male (*right*), the red nape extends up and over the head. The Red-bellied Woodpecker eats insects, fruit and seeds, and in Florida spears oranges with its bill to suck the juice.

GILA WOODPECKER

Scientific name:	*Melanerpes uropygialis*
Length:	$9\frac{1}{4}$ inches
Habitat:	Scrub desert, cactus country, town suburbs
Identification:	Medium-size, heavy-bodied woodpecker. Head and underparts gray-brown, black and white barred back and rump, central tail feathers barred. Prominent white wing patches in flight. Male has small red cap
Similar species:	Female Golden-fronted Woodpecker similar to female and juvenile Gila, but has black tail and golden-orange nape. Female Red-bellied Woodpecker has a red nape

Found in the low desert scrub of southwest North America and down into central Mexico, the Gila Woodpecker is a very noisy bird.

It prefers giant saguaro cactus and mesquite for nesting, although it will also use trees, excavating a cavity up to 25 feet above the ground in which it lays 3-5 white eggs. These are incubated by both adults for around 2 weeks and the parents often go on to raise a second brood in the same season. The adult bird is a medium-size, heavy-bodied bird, with a fairly long bill and short wings. The adult has a gray-brown head and underparts, a black and white barred back and rump; its outer tail feathers are black and the central ones are barred. In flight, it shows prominent white wing patches. The juvenile is similar to the female; the male (*above*) has a small red cap. The Gila Woodpecker digs into cactus and bark, hunting for insects and their larvae; it often performs a service to the plant by removing larvae that are damaging its tissues. The Gila will also eat cactus fruit and berries, and may visit garden feeders - particularly for suet and corn.

LADDER-BACKED WOODPECKER

Scientific name:	*Picoides scalaris*
Length:	7¼ inches
Habitat:	Dry brushland, cactus country, town suburbs
Identification:	Small woodpecker. Distinct black and white bars on back, face buff with black markings, underparts buffy-gray with spotted flanks, white barred outer tail feathers. Male has red crown, female black
Similar species:	Nuttall's Woodpecker almost identical, but has more black on face, less red on crown, white rather than buff underparts

The Ladder-backed Woodpecker is common in dry and desert areas across the south. Part of its range overlaps with that of the very similar Nuttall's Woodpecker, and the two species have interbred. The Ladder-backed often nests in the tall, dry stalk of the agave plant, or excavates a hole high above the ground in a yucca, cottonwood tree or fence post. It lays 4 or 5 white eggs, that are incubated by both parents. The adult bird is one of the smaller woodpeckers, with distinct black and white bars across the back, a buff face with black markings, buffy-gray underparts with spotted flanks, and white barred outer tail feathers. The male (*right*) has a red crown, that of the female is black. The Ladder-backed Woodpecker eats the larvae of the agave beetle, so controlling its infestation of the plant. It also eats wood-boring insects, caterpillars and cactus fruit.

WHITE-HEADED WOODPECKER

Scientific name:	*Picoides albolarvatus*
Length:	9¾ inches
Habitat:	Coniferous mountain forests
Identification:	Medium-size woodpecker. White head and throat, small white wing patch, otherwise all black. Male has red patch on back of head
Similar species:	Black body and white head are distinctive. In flight the male could be confused with the male Acorn Woodpecker, which has a red crown, more black on face and a white rump

Despite its distinctive coloring the White-headed Woodpecker is inconspicuous and hard to spot, since the black and white plumage provides very good camouflage when the bird is still. Unlike most woodpeckers, it rarely taps or drums. Within its limited range it is fairly common, although it is rare further north and at lower altitudes. It breeds in mountain pine forests, excavating a hole up to 50 feet above the ground in a dead conifer in which it lays 3-5 white eggs. These are incubated by both parents, for around 10 days. The adult is a medium-size woodpecker with a white head and throat, a white wing patch, and an all-black body - although the male (*right*) has a small red patch on the back of the head. The White-headed Woodpecker mainly eats pine cone seeds, but also flakes off tree bark to find the insects and larvae underneath.

BLACK-BACKED WOODPECKER

Scientific name:	*Picoides arcticus*
Length:	$9\frac{1}{2}$ inches
Habitat:	Coniferous forests, burned-over pines
Identification:	Large, strong woodpecker with fairly short tail. Black head with thin white line behind eye, white face stripe, black above, white underparts, barred flanks. Male has yellow cap
Similar species:	Male Three-toed also has yellow cap, but has black and white barred back

The Black-backed Woodpecker inhabits a very similar range in the north of America to the Three-toed Woodpecker and is fairly uncommon, although it is sometimes seen some way south of its mapped area. It also prefers dead and dying trees, flaking off the bark rather than drilling to find the insects underneath - although it does drum frequently like other woodpeckers to mark its territory. In the breeding season it excavates a hole up to 15 feet above the ground in a dead or dying conifer in which it lays 4-5 white eggs. These are incubated by both parent birds, for around 2 weeks. The adult is a big, strong woodpecker with a largish head and a fairly short tail. Like the Three-toed, the Black-backed has only 3 toes, which all point forward. It has a black head with a thin white line behind the eye, a wide white facial stripe like a mustache, and is black above with white underparts and heavily barred flanks. The male (*above*) has a yellow cap. The Black-backed Woodpecker eats wood-boring insects, as well as other insects, spiders and berries.

HAIRY WOODPECKER (above)

Scientific name:	*Picoides villosus*
Length:	$9\frac{1}{4}$ inches
Habitat:	Open and dense forests
Identification:	Medium-size woodpecker with long, sturdy bill. White back, black forehead and crown, broad black eye stripe, white face and underparts, wings black with white spots. Male has red patch on nape
Similar species:	Downy Woodpecker almost identical, but is much smaller with a shorter bill

Fairly common across the whole continent, except in the southwest and the far north, the Hairy Woodpecker is seen in mature woodland with large trees. When breeding it excavates a hole high above the ground in a dead tree limb, and often uses the same cavity year after year. It lays 4-7 white eggs, which are incubated by the male at night and the female during the day, for around 2 weeks. The young birds leave the nest around 4-5 weeks after hatching. The adult bird is fairly large and strong, with a long, sturdy bill. It has a white back, black forehead and crown, a broad black eye stripe, a white face and underparts, and black wings with white spots. The male (*above*) has a red patch on the nape. In the Pacific northwest, birds tend to have a gray-brown back and underparts, but are otherwise the same. In flight, the outer tail feathers are white and usually lack any barring - although this may be difficult to see. The Hairy Woodpecker drills into trees to find the wood-boring insects under the bark and also eats berries and seeds. Like many other woodpeckers, it also drums on trees and posts to proclaim its territory.

THREE-TOED WOODPECKER

Scientific name:	*Picoides tridactylus*
Length:	$8\frac{3}{4}$ inches
Habitat:	Coniferous forests, burned-over pines
Identification:	Medium-size, stocky woodpecker with short bill. Black head with white face stripes, black and white barred back, white underparts, black wings, rump and tail, barred flanks. Male has yellow cap
Similar species:	Male Black-backed also has yellow cap, but has plain black back

Although they cover a wide range in the north, the Three-toed Woodpecker is uncommon to rare and is hard to spot because it is fairly quiet for a woodpecker, only hammering on trees to mark its territory. It prefers dead and dying trees, and instead of drilling into the wood to find food it flakes off the bark to find the insects underneath. It does not build a nest but excavates a hole high above the ground in a dead tree - usually a conifer - in which it lays 4 white eggs. These are incubated by both parents, for around 2 weeks. The adult is a medium-size, stocky woodpecker, with a short bill. Most woodpeckers have 4 toes, 2 pointing forwards and 2 back, but the Three-toed has only 3, which all point forward. It has a black head with white face stripes, black and white barring down the center of the back, white underparts, black wings, rump and tail, and barred flanks. The male has a yellow cap. The Three-toed Woodpecker eats wood-boring insects, as well as other insects, spiders and berries.

RED-COCKADED WOODPECKER

Scientific name:	*Picoides borealis*
Length:	8½ inches
Habitat:	Open mature pine forests
Identification:	Slender, long-tailed woodpecker with small bill. Black and white barred back, black forehead and crown, white cheeks and underparts with spotting on flanks. Male has tiny red cockade behind eye
Similar species:	White cheek patch is distinctive

An endangered species, the Red-cockaded Woodpecker is found only in mature pine woods in the southeast and populations are still declining due to destruction of its preferred nesting habitat. Unlike other woodpeckers it does not excavate a cavity in a dead tree, but chooses a large, living pine tree infected with fungal heartwood disease - and such trees are now usually felled before they are big enough. The nest hole is dug into the decayed heart of the tree and the opening is surrounded by small holes that ooze pitch, apparently to deter predators. Nests are situated in small colonies, and may be used for several years. The female lays 2-5 white eggs, which are incubated by the male at night and the female during the day. The adult bird is slender, with a long tail and a small bill. It has a black and white barred back, a black forehead and crown, a large white cheek patch and white underparts with spotting on the flanks. The male has a tiny red cockade behind the eye, which is difficult to spot; the juvenile is similar to the female but may show some red on the crown. The Red-cockaded Woodpecker drills into trees to find the wood-boring insects under the bark.

DOWNY WOODPECKER

Scientific name:	*Picoides pubescens*
Length:	6¾ inches
Habitat:	Woodland, suburbs, parkland
Identification:	Small woodpecker with very short bill. White back, black forehead and crown, broad black eye stripe, white face and underparts, wings black with white spots. Male has red patch on nape
Similar species:	Hairy Woodpecker almost identical, but is larger, has longer bill

The Downy Woodpecker is the smallest North American woodpecker and is common across the whole continent, except in drier regions in the southwest and the cold far north. It is often seen in suburbs, parks and orchards as well as woodland. As a nest it excavates a hole up to 50 feet above the ground in a dead tree trunk or branch, in which it lays 4-7 white eggs, which are incubated by both parents for around 2 weeks. The young birds leave the nest just over 3 weeks after hatching, and there is often a second brood. The adult bird has a very short bill - although that of the male is slightly longer. Both birds have a white back, black forehead and crown, a broad black eye stripe, white face and underparts, and black wings with white spots. The male (*right*) is slightly larger and has a small red patch on the nape. In the Pacific northwest, birds tend to have a gray-brown back and underparts, but are otherwise the same. In flight, the outer tail feathers are white, barred with black - although this may be difficult to see. The Downy Woodpecker will often come to bird tables for suet, but also eats wood-boring insects, berries and seeds.

WILLIAMSON'S SAPSUCKER

Scientific name:	*Sphyrapicus thyroideus*
Length:	9 inches
Habitat:	Dry coniferous forests
Identification:	Long-winged, delicate woodpecker. Male has black head, breast and back, white facial stripes, bright red throat, large white wing and rump patches, lemon yellow belly with black and white barred flanks. Female has brown head, dark brown and white barring above and on flanks, large dark bib and yellow patch on belly
Similar species:	Coloring is distinctive

The largest sapsucker, Williamson's is fairly common in dry conifer forests in summer, moving south or to lower elevations in winter. In its breeding grounds, it excavates a cavity high above the ground in a dead tree, usually a pine. It may reuse the same tree the following year, but will dig a new hole, leaving the old one for other species. It lays 3-7 white eggs, which are incubated by both parent birds. The adult has long wings, and male and female have very different plumage. The male has a black head, breast and back, white facial stripes, a bright red throat, large white wing and rump patches, and a bright lemon-yellow belly with black and white barred flanks. The female (*right*) has a brown head, dark brown and white barring above and on the flanks, a large dark bib and small, dull yellow belly patch. The juvenile resembles the adult, but acquires its adult plumage by the beginning of winter. Williamson's Sapsucker eats ants, insects and berries, and drinks the sap from trees.

YELLOW-BELLIED SAPSUCKER

Scientific name:	*Sphyrapicus varius*
Length:	8½ inches
Habitat:	Deciduous forests
Identification:	Long-winged, delicate woodpecker. Black and white striped head, red forehead, black back spotted with white, white rump, long white wing patch, yellowish underparts with black breast band. Male has red chin and throat, female has white
Similar species:	Red-naped Sapsucker has red on back of head

Like woodpeckers, sapsuckers drill holes in trees but as well as insects they are after the oozing sap, which they return to drink. The Yellow-bellied Sapsucker is common in the forests of the north in summer, and migrates south to spend the winter in the southeast. In its breeding grounds, it excavates a cavity up to 45 feet above the ground in a dead tree, in which it lays 4-6 white eggs. These are incubated for just under 2 weeks, by both parent birds and the young leave the nest about 4 weeks after hatching. The adult is a delicate woodpecker with long wings. It has a black and white striped head, a red forehead, black back spotted with white, a white rump, a long white wing patch, and yellowish underparts with a black breast band. The male has a red chin and throat, that of the female (*right*) is white. The juvenile bird is mainly brown until late in its first winter. The Yellow-bellied Sapsucker eats insects and berries, and drinks the sap from trees.

RED-BREASTED SAPSUCKER

Scientific name: *Sphyrapicus ruber*
Length: 8½ inches
Habitat: Coniferous and mixed humid forests
Identification: Long-winged, delicate woodpecker. Red head and breast, black back lightly spotted with white, white rump, long white wing patch, yellowish belly
Similar species: Red head and breast are distinctive

The Red-breasted and the Red-naped sapsucker were both once considered to be a subspecies of the Yellow-bellied, but they are now thought to be different - although all three species are known to interbreed. The Red-breasted is common in the deciduous and mixed forests of the Pacific coast, most birds spending the summer in the north and migrating south in the winter, or moving to lower elevations. A few stay in the same area all year round. In its breeding grounds, it excavates a cavity up to 45 feet above the ground in a dead tree, in which it lays 4-6 white eggs. These are incubated for just under 2 weeks, by both parent birds and the young leave the nest about 4 weeks after hatching. The adult is a delicate woodpecker with long wings. It has a red head and breast, a black back lightly spotted with white, a white rump, a long white wing patch, and a yellowish belly. Northern birds tend to have more yellow spots on the back and a yellower belly, southern birds are more white. The juvenile bird is mainly brown but quickly acquires its adult plumage. The Red-breasted Sapsucker eats insects and berries, and drinks the sap from trees.

RED-NAPED SAPSUCKER

Scientific name: *Sphyrapicus nuchalis*
Length: 8½ inches
Habitat: Deciduous forests
Identification: Long-winged, delicate woodpecker. Black and white striped head, red forehead and nape, black back spotted with white, white rump, long white wing patch, yellowish underparts with black breast band. Male has extensive red on chin and throat, female has white chin and red throat
Similar species: Yellow-bellied Sapsucker almost identical, but lacks red on back of head and female has white throat

The Red-naped and the Red-breasted sapsuckers were both once considered to be a subspecies of the Yellow-bellied, but they are now thought to be different. The Red-naped is common in the deciduous forests of the northwest in summer, and migrates south to spend the winter in the southwest. In its breeding grounds, it excavates a cavity up to 45 feet above the ground in a dead tree, in which it lays 4-6 white eggs. These are incubated for just under 2 weeks, by both parent birds and the young leave the nest about 4 weeks after hatching. The adult is a delicate woodpecker with long wings. It has a black and white striped head, a red forehead and nape, black back spotted with white, a white rump, a long white wing patch, and yellowish underparts with a black breast band. The male has an extensive red chin and throat, the female has a white chin and variable amounts of red on the throat. The juvenile bird is mainly brown until late in its first winter. The Red-naped Sapsucker eats insects and berries, and also drinks the sap from trees.

PILEATED WOODPECKER

Scientific name:	*Dryocopus pileatus*
Length:	16½ inches
Habitat:	Dense mature forests, large trees in city parks
Identification:	Large, long-necked, broad-winged, long-tailed woodpecker with prominent crest. Mostly black, red crest and mustache, white chin, white stripe running across face and down neck, white under wings seen in flight
Similar species:	Large size and coloring distinctive

The largest North American woodpecker - after the Ivory-billed, which is now believed to be extinct - the Pileated Woodpecker lives in dense, mature forest. It is locally common in some areas, and stays in the same area all year round. At breeding time, it excavates a cavity up to 70 feet above the ground in the dead limb of a large, mature tree, or in the trunk of a dead tree, in which it lays 3-5 white eggs. These are incubated for about 2-3 weeks, by both parents; the young leave the nest about 3-4 weeks after hatching. The male is a large, long-necked, broad-winged woodpecker with a long tail and a prominent bright red crest. Its plumage is mostly black, with a bright red mustache, a white chin, and a white stripe running across the face and down the neck. In flight, it shows white under the wings and white flanks. The female (*below*) is very similar, but has less red on the head and lacks the red mustache. The staple diet of the Pileated Woodpecker is carpenter ants, which live in dead wood. It also eats other wood-boring insects, and berries in winter.

NORTHERN FLICKER

Scientific name:	*Colaptes auratus*
Length:	12½ inches
Habitat:	Open woodlands, suburbs
Identification:	Large, broad-winged, long-tailed woodpecker. Brown barred back, spotted underparts, black crescent bib, white rump in flight. Either yellow wing lining and undertail, gray crown, tan face, black mustache, red crescent on nape, or reddish wing lining and undertail, brown crown, gray face, red mustache, with no red on nape
Similar species:	Gilded Flicker has yellow wing linings, but cinnamon-brown crown

The distinctive coloring of flickers means they are easy to identify, although the two species are similar. The Northern Flicker is common in woodland, ranging north in summer but retreating south in winter. In spring it excavates a cavity high above the ground in a tree, fence post or cactus, in which it lays 5-10 white eggs. The adult is broad-winged and long-tailed and has two distinct color variations. Both have a brown barred back, spotted underparts, a black crescent bib, and a white rump in flight. The "yellow-shafted" male (*right*) in the west and north has yellow wing linings and undertail, a gray crown, tan face with a black mustache, and a red crescent on the nape. The "red-shafted" male in the east has red wing linings and undertail, a brown crown, gray face with a red mustache, and no red on the nape. The female is similar in each case, but lacks the mustache. Where the two overlap they interbreed, producing many variations. The Northern Flicker forages on the ground for ants and insects; it also eats berries in winter.

GILDED FLICKER

Scientific name:	*Colaptes chrysoides*
Length:	11½ inches
Habitat:	Desert woodlands, cactus country
Identification:	Large, broad-winged, long-tailed woodpecker. Buff-brown barred back, spotted underparts, large black crescent bib, white rump in flight. Yellow wing lining and undertail, cinnamon-brown crown, gray face. Male has red mustache
Similar species:	"Yellow-shafted" Northern Flicker has yellow wing linings, "red-shafted" Northern Flicker has brown crown

The Gilded Flicker was once considered to be a subspecies of the Northern Flicker, but has now been accorded full species status. However, it is known to interbreed with the "red-shafted" Northern Flicker where their ranges overlap. Although the range of the Gilded Flicker is quite small, it is common in desert woodland and saguaro and stays in the same general area all year round. In its breeding season, it excavates a cavity in a giant saguaro cactus or in a riverside tree, in which it lays 5-10 white eggs. These are incubated for about 1-2 weeks, by both parent birds; the young leave the nest about 3-4 weeks after hatching. The adult is a large, broad-winged, long-tailed woodpecker with a buff-brown barred back, spotted underparts, a large black crescent bib, and a white rump in flight. It has yellow wing linings and undertail, a cinnamon-brown crown, and a gray face with a red mustache. The female is very similar, but lacks the mustache mark. The Gilded Flicker eats ants and other ground insects and also berries in winter.

ALDER FLYCATCHER

Scientific name:	*Empidonax alnorum*
Length:	5¾ inches
Habitat:	Swamps, birch and alder thickets, brush near bogs
Identification:	Small, long-winged flycatcher with large bill, flat forehead and small peak at rear of crown. Olive-gray above, white throat, olive-gray wash across upper breast, whitish lower breast, belly and undertail coverts, pale eye ring, longish primaries on wings, two whitish wing bars
Similar species:	All the *empidonax* flycatchers are very alike and mainly told apart by habitat and song

The Alder and the Willow flycatchers are so similar that they were once thought to be one species. The Alder is found in summer in birch and alder thickets near bogs across northern America, but migrates to the Southern Hemisphere for the winter. In the breeding season it builds an untidy nest of roots and fibers up to 20 feet above the ground in an upright fork of a tree or bush, in which it lays 3 or 4 white eggs with fine brown spotting. These are incubated for around 2 weeks and the young leave the nest about 14 days after hatching. The adult is a small bird with long wings and tail; its head has a flat forehead with a peak on the rear crown and it has a large bill. It is olive-gray above, with a white throat, olive-gray wash across the upper breast, a whitish lower breast, belly and undertail coverts, and a pale eye ring. The wings have longish primaries and it has two whitish wing bars. Its song is a monotonous *fee-BEE-oh* and its call a short, sharp *kep*. The Alder Flycatcher hunts below the spreading branches of tall alders, sitting on a twig and darting out to catch flying insects.

YELLOW-BELLIED FLYCATCHER

Scientific name:	*Empidonax flaviventris*
Length:	5½ inches
Habitat:	Bogs, swamps, wet conifer forests
Identification:	Small, compact flycatcher with round head, long wings and short tail. Olive above, yellow belly and throat, olive breast, broad yellow eye ring, lower bill pale orange, two white wing bars
Similar species:	All the *empidonax* flycatchers are very alike and mainly told apart by habitat and song

The Yellow-bellied Flycatcher is common in summer in the wet coniferous woodland and bogs of northern America; it migrates to the Southern Hemisphere for the winter. In the breeding season it builds a bulky nest of grass and twigs on a branch, in which it lays 3-5 white, lightly brown-spotted eggs. These are incubated for up to 2 weeks and the young leave the nest around 14 days after hatching. The adult is a small, compact bird with a round head, relatively long wings and a short tail. It is olive above, with a yellow belly and throat, olive across the breast, a broad yellow eye ring, pale orange lower bill and two white wing bars. Its song is a soft, liquid *chebunk* and its call a plaintive *perwee*. The Yellow-bellied Flycatcher tends to stay fairly near the ground in very dense cover and mainly eats flying insects.

ACADIAN FLYCATCHER (above)

Scientific name:	*Empidonax virescens*
Length:	5¾ inches
Habitat:	Woodland, swamps
Identification:	Small, long-winged flycatcher with long, broad bill, flat forehead, peak on rear crown. Olive above, grayish throat, olive wash across upper breast, white lower breast, yellow belly and undertail coverts, pale yellow eye ring, lower bill yellowish, long primaries on wings, two buffy-white wing bars
Similar species:	All the *empidonax* flycatchers are very alike and mainly told apart by habitat and song

Fairly common in swamps and woods near streams, the Acadian Flycatcher is found in summer across southeastern North America, but it migrates down to the Southern Hemisphere for the winter. In the summer breeding season it builds a nest of grass and twigs up to 25 feet above the ground, in which it lays 3-5 white, brown-spotted eggs. These are incubated for up to 2 weeks and the young chicks leave the nest around 14 days after they have hatched. The adult is a small bird with long wings; its head has a flat forehead and a distinct peak on the rear crown and it has a long, broad bill that is dark above and pale yellow beneath. It is olive above, with a grayish throat, an olive wash across the upper breast, a white lower breast, yellow belly and undertail coverts, and a pale yellow eye ring. The wings have long primaries and it has two buffy-white wing bars. The juvenile is brownish-olive above, edged with buffy. The song of the adult is a sharp *PEE-tsah* and its call is a loud, flat *peek*. On the breeding ground it will also give a *ti ti ti ti* call. The Acadian Flycatcher eats flying insects and berries.

"WESTERN" FLYCATCHER

Scientific name:	*Empidonax difficilis/Empidonax occidentalis*
Length:	5½ inches
Habitat:	Wet coniferous forest, shaded canyons
Identification:	Small flycatcher, round head with small ragged crest, longish tail. Olive-brown above, yellow throat and belly, dusky-olive breast, white eye ring, lower bill bright yellow-orange, two whitish wing bars
Similar species:	All the *empidonax* flycatchers are very alike and mainly told apart by habitat and song

The Pacific-slope Flycatcher (*Empidonax difficilis*) and the Cordilleran Flycatcher (*Empidonax occidentalis*) are almost identical so they are sometimes considered together as the "Western" Flycatcher. They are very difficult to tell apart in the field, differing only in their summer range and in details of their call. They both prefer wet coniferous or mixed woodland and migrate to Mexico and Central America for the winter. In the breeding season they build a cup-shaped nest of twigs and roots lined with moss, on a branch against the tree trunk, among the roots of an upturned tree, in a bank, or in the eaves of a forest cabin. It holds 3 or 4 white, brown-spotted eggs, which are incubated for up to 2 weeks. The adult is a small bird and has a round head with a small ragged crest, and a longish tail. It is olive-brown above, with a yellow belly and throat, dusky-olive across the breast, a white eye ring, bright yellow-orange lower bill and two white wing bars. Its song is a series of notes, including a sharp *tsip*, a slurred *tsuweeat*, and quick *ptik*. The female's call is a sharp *seet*. The Pacific-slope male's call is *psee-yeet*, the Cordilleran male's a two-note *pit peet*. Both the Pacific-slope Flycatcher and the Cordilleran Flycatcher mainly eat flying insects.

WILLOW FLYCATCHER *(above)*

Scientific name:	*Empidonax traillii*
Length:	$5\frac{3}{4}$ inches
Habitat:	Wet brushy areas, mountain pastures, willow thickets
Identification:	Small, long-winged flycatcher with large, broad bill, flat forehead and distinct peak at rear of crown. Either olive-gray or olive-brown above, white throat, olive-gray-brown wash across upper breast, whitish lower breast, belly and undertail coverts, indistinct pale eye ring, longish primaries on wings, two whitish wing bars
Similar species:	All the *empidonax* flycatchers are very alike and mainly told apart by habitat and song

Almost identical to the Alder, the Willow Flycatcher is found in summer in brushy thickets near bogs, but also in pasture and mountain meadows. Its range extends across northern America, but spreads further south than that of the Alder. In the breeding season the Willow builds a neat but loose-woven nest of grass and bark not far above the ground in an upright fork of a low bush, in which it lays 3 or 4 white eggs, which are often spotted with brown. These are incubated for around 2 weeks and the young leave the nest about 14 days after hatching. The adult is a small bird with long wings and tail; its head has a flat forehead with a distinct peak on the rear crown and it has a large, broad bill. It has two color variations: eastern birds are olive-gray above, with a white throat, olive-gray wash across the upper breast, a whitish lower breast, belly and undertail coverts, and an indistinct pale eye ring; birds in the northwest have darker heads and are browner. The wings of both have longish primaries and two whitish wing bars. Its song is an explosive *fitz-bew* and its call a sharp *phwit*. The Willow Flycatcher eats flying insects.

HAMMOND'S FLYCATCHER

Scientific name:	*Empidonax hammondii*
Length:	$5\frac{1}{2}$ inches
Habitat:	Mountainous coniferous forest
Identification:	Small, compact, short-tailed flycatcher with small dark bill, long primaries on wings. Olive-gray above, whitish-gray throat, olive-gray wash across breast, pale yellow belly and undertail coverts, thin white eye ring, two narrow white wing bars
Similar species:	All the *empidonax* flycatchers are very alike and mainly told apart by habitat and song

Common during the summer in the west, in mature coniferous forests at high altitudes, Hammond's Flycatcher migrates south to northern Mexico and Central America to spend the winter. In the breeding season it arrives at its nesting site early in the year and builds a very carefully constructed nest of bark, roots and plant fibers, situated up to 60 feet above the ground on the horizontal branch of a conifer. The female lays 3-5 white eggs, which are incubated for around 2 weeks; the young chicks leave the nest around 18 days after hatching. The adult is a small, compact bird with a relatively short tail, a small dark bill and long primary feathers on the wing. It is olive-gray above, with a whitish-gray throat, an olive-gray wash across the breast, a pale yellow belly and undertail coverts, a thin white eye ring, and two narrow white wing bars. In fall, it tends to be more olive above and its belly is a somewhat brighter yellow. Its song is a low-pitched *sweep-tsurp-pweet*, rising on the last syllable and its call a high *peep*. Hammond's Flycatcher often sits in the highest branches of a conifer tree, flicking its wings and tail vigorously, before darting out quickly to snap up a passing bug or insect. It then returns to its perch to wait for another meal to pass by.

LEAST FLYCATCHER *(below)*

Scientific name:	*Empidonax minimus*
Length:	$5\frac{1}{4}$ inches
Habitat:	Deciduous woods, parks
Identification:	Small, compact, short-winged flycatcher with short triangular bill, large head, short narrow tail. Olive above, whitish throat, gray wash across breast, pale yellow belly and undertail coverts, bold white eye ring, lower bill pale, two buffy-white wing bars
Similar species:	All the *empidonax* flycatchers are very alike and mainly told apart by habitat and song

Fairly common in the east but less so in the west, the Least Flycatcher is found in summer across northern America in deciduous woods, orchards and parks - in fall it migrates to the Southern Hemisphere for the winter. In the summer breeding season it builds a nest of stems and plant fibers up to 60 feet above the ground on a horizontal branch, in which it lays 3-5 white eggs. These are incubated for up to 2 weeks and the young birds are ready to leave the nest around 14 days after they have hatched. The adult is a small, compact bird with fairly short wings; it has a large head and a short triangular bill that is dark above and mostly pale beneath. It is olive above, with a whitish throat, a gray wash across the breast, a very pale yellow belly and undertail coverts, a bold white eye ring and two buffy-white wing bars. The wing bars of the juvenile are rather more buffy, but it is otherwise like the adult. The song of the adult is a snappy *CHE-bek* and its call a dry *whit*. The Least Flycatcher eats flying insects and berries.

DUSKY FLYCATCHER

Scientific name:	*Empidonax oberholseri*
Length:	$5\frac{3}{4}$ inches
Habitat:	Open woodland, mountain brush, aspen groves
Identification:	Small, short-winged flycatcher, dark bill with orange beneath at base, longish tail. Gray-olive above, whitish throat, pale olive-gray wash across upper breast, pale yellowish beneath, narrow white eye ring, two narrow white wing bars
Similar species:	All the *empidonax* flycatchers are very alike and mainly told apart by habitat and song

The Dusky Flycatcher is common in open mature woodland with brushy undergrowth across much of the west during the summer, and migrates south to Mexico for the winter. In the breeding season it builds a neat nest of twigs and plant fibers only around 7 feet above the ground in the crotch of a shrub or small tree, in which it lays 3-5 white eggs. These are incubated for up to 2 weeks and the young leave the nest around 18 days after hatching. The adult is a small, relatively short-winged bird with a longish tail, and a dark bill with the lower mandible orange at the base and becoming dark at the tip. It is gray-olive above, pale yellowish beneath, with a whitish throat, a pale olive-gray wash across the upper breast and has a narrow white eye ring and two narrow white wing bars. Its song is a staccato *se-lip churp treep* and its call a soft, high *wit*. The Dusky Flycatcher is almost identical to Hammond's Flycatcher, but generally prefers lower altitudes. It eats flying insects.

OLIVE-SIDED FLYCATCHER

Scientific name:	*Contopus borealis*
Length:	$7\frac{1}{2}$ inches
Habitat:	Coniferous forests, bogs
Identification:	Large, sturdy flycatcher with pointed wings and short tail. Dark brown-gray above, olive-gray flanks almost meeting across breast, throat and belly dusky white, white downy tufts on lower back
Similar species:	Coloring is distinctive

In the coniferous forests and bogs of the north and northwest, the Olive-sided Flycatcher is fairly common in summer, and it is also seen across much of America as it migrates south to spend the winter in the Southern Hemisphere. In its nesting area it builds a shallow cup of twigs, stalks and roots high above the ground in a tree - usually a conifer. It lays 3 or 4 creamy-white to buff eggs, blotched brown-gray at the larger end, which are incubated for about 1-2 weeks. The adult is a large, sturdy bird with pointed wings and short tail. It is dark brown-gray above, with olive-gray flanks almost meeting across the breast, and a dusky white throat and belly. Its distinctive white downy tufts on the lower back behind the wing are not always visible. The Olive-sided Flycatcher establishes a hunting perch high above the ground in a tall conifer and flies out to catch passing insects; it does not eat anything without wings.

WESTERN WOOD-PEWEE

Scientific name:	*Contopus sordidulus*
Length:	$6\frac{1}{4}$ inches
Habitat:	Open woodlands, wooded canyons, rivers
Identification:	Medium-size, slender flycatcher with long pointed wings and long tail. Dark olive-gray above, lighter breast and sides, pale yellowish chin and belly, two pale buff wing bars
Similar species:	Eastern Wood-Pewee is almost identical, only identified by range. All the *empidonax* flycatchers also look very similar, but generally have pale eye ring

A rather plain bird, the Western Wood-Pewee is common in summer in wooded canyons and riversides throughout western North America; it migrates further south for the winter. In the nesting season it builds a tight cup of stems and plant matter on a horizontal branch up to 20 feet above the ground in a tree. It lays 3 or 4 creamy-white, spotted eggs, which are incubated for about 1-2 weeks by the female; the young leave the nest around 15-19 days after hatching. The adult is a medium-size, slender bird with long pointed wings and long tail. It is dark olive-gray above, with a lighter breast and sides, a pale yellowish chin and belly, and two pale buff wing bars. The Western Wood-Pewee establishes a hunting perch high above the ground on the exposed edge branches of a tree and flies out to catch passing insects. About half its diet consists of flies, but it also eats berries.

EASTERN WOOD-PEWEE

Scientific name: *Contopus virens*
Length: 6¼ inches
Habitat: Woodlands
Identification: Medium-size, slender flycatcher with long pointed wings and long tail. Dark olive-gray above, lighter breast and sides, pale yellowish chin and belly, two whitish wing bars
Similar species: Western Wood-Pewee is almost identical, only identified by range. All the *empidonax* flycatchers also look very similar, but generally have pale eye ring

Almost identical to the Western, the Eastern Wood-Pewee can be safely identified by range. It is common in summer in woodland throughout eastern North America; it migrates further south for the winter. In the breeding season it builds a tight nest of stems and plant matter on a horizontal branch up to 20 feet above the ground in a tree. It lays 3 or 4 creamy-white, spotted eggs, which are incubated for about 1-2 weeks by the female; the young leave the nest around 15-19 days after hatching. The adult is a medium-size, slender bird with long pointed wings and long tail. It is dark olive-gray above, with a lighter breast and sides, a pale yellowish chin and belly, and two whitish wing bars. The Eastern Wood-Pewee perches high above the ground on the exposed branches of a tree near a clear area for foraging, and flies out to catch passing insects. About half its diet consists of flies, but it also eats berries.

EASTERN PHOEBE

Scientific name:	*Sayornis phoebe*
Length:	7 inches
Habitat:	Along streams, suburbs near water
Identification:	Slender, long-winged, long-tailed flycatcher, with rounded head. Brownish-gray above, darker on head, wings and tail, white beneath, pale olive wash on sides and breast. In early fall has pale yellow wash on belly
Similar species:	Distinguished from pewees by all-dark bill, lack of distinct wing bars, habit of wagging tail up and down

The Eastern Phoebe spends the summer in the woodlands and open suburbs of east and central North America, and the winter in the far south and down into Mexico. Its nest is a cup of mud and moss, lined with soft down and firmly attached on a cliff ledge over water, under a bridge, or on a building. The female lays 3-8 white eggs, sometimes faintly spotted with brown, which are incubated for 2-3 weeks. The young leave the nest after about 16 days to make way for a second brood - there is sometimes even a third. The adult bird is slender, with long wings, a long tail and a rounded head. Its plumage is brownish-gray above - darker on the head, wings and tail - and white beneath, with a pale olive wash on the sides and breast. Early fall birds have a pale yellow wash on the belly and faint wing bars. The juvenile is browner with a dark cinnamon rump and two buff wing bars, but soon gains its adult plumage. The Eastern Phoebe often perches on low branches over streams, wagging and fanning its tail. It eats insects and spiders, which it captures in flight.

SAY'S PHOEBE

Scientific name:	*Sayornis saya*
Length:	$7\frac{1}{2}$ inches
Habitat:	Dry open areas, canyons, cliffs
Identification:	Slender, long-winged, long-tailed flycatcher, with smallish head. Gray-brown above, darker on wings, black tail, pale gray-brown breast and throat, pale tawny-rust belly and undertail coverts
Similar species:	Coloring is distinctive

Fairly common in dry, open areas, Say's Phoebe spends the summer on the tundra, prairie and desert of western North America, and the winter in the southwest and down into Mexico. Its nest is a platform of grass, stems and wool, on a high, sheltered ledge on a cliff or building, in which it lays 4 or 5 white eggs that are incubated by the female for about 2 weeks; the young leave the nest after about 15 days. The adult bird is slender, with long wings, a long tail and a relatively small head. Its plumage is gray-brown above - darker on the wings - with a black tail, a pale gray-brown breast and throat, and a pale tawny-rust belly and undertail coverts. The juvenile is browner with two cinnamon wing bars, but soon gains its adult plumage. Say's Phoebe perches on bushes, boulders and fences, wagging its tail. It mainly eats insects, which it captures in flight, but will turn to berries in cold weather when insects are scarce.

BLACK PHOEBE

Scientific name:	*Sayornis nigricans*
Length:	6¾ inches
Habitat:	Near water in woodland, parks and suburbs
Identification:	Slender, long-winged, long-tailed flycatcher, with peaked head. Slate-black except for white belly and undertail coverts
Similar species:	Coloring and habits distinctive

Rarely found far from water, the Black Phoebe is solitary and territorial and often remains all year round in its established area - although a few juvenile, non-breeding birds do wander further afield. Its nest is a cup of mud, moss and grass, lined with soft down and very firmly attached on a ledge, under a bridge, in the crevice of a building or among roots at the top of a bank. The female lays 3-6 white eggs, sometimes faintly spotted with brown, which are incubated for 2-3 weeks. The young are fed by both parents, but leave the nest after about 3 weeks to make way for a second brood. The adult bird is slender, with long wings, a long tail and a slightly peaked head. Its plumage is slate-black, except for a white belly and white undertail coverts. The juvenile is browner with a dark cinnamon rump and wing bars, but soon gains its adult plumage. The Black Phoebe sits very erect on low branches, wagging and fanning its tail. It eats insects, which it captures in flight.

GREAT CRESTED FLYCATCHER

Scientific name:	*Myiarchus crinitus*
Length:	8 inches
Habitat:	Open woods
Identification:	Large, long-tailed flycatcher with bushy head. Dark olive gray-brown above, dark gray throat and upper breast, bright lemon-yellow lower breast, belly and undertail coverts, cinnamon-rust primaries and tail feathers, two white wing bars
Similar species:	The other *myiarchus* flycatchers are almost identical and it is difficult to tell them apart in the field. The Brown-crested Flycatcher has darker underparts, bigger bill; the Ash-throated Flycatcher is generally paler

Common in a variety of deciduous open woodland, the Great Crested Flycatcher is seen across the east in summer, but winters further south. In the breeding season it takes over a tree cavity, or old woodpecker hole, in which it builds a nest of twigs and grass up to 70 feet above the ground. The female lays 3-7 buff purple-brown-blotched eggs. These are incubated for around 2 weeks and the young leave the nest about 16 days after they have hatched. The adult is a large, long-tailed bird with a bushy head. It is dark olive-gray-brown above, with a dark gray throat and upper breast, a bright lemon-yellow lower breast and belly, and cinnamon-rust primaries. The cinnamon tail feathers are dark-tipped and it has two white wing bars. The Great Crested Flycatcher perches in the dense canopy of mature trees, catching large insects in flight - but it also eats on berries when insects are scarce.

BROWN-CRESTED FLYCATCHER

Scientific name:	*Myiarchus tyrannulus*
Length:	8¾ inches
Habitat:	Cactus country, wooded rivers, foothill canyons
Identification:	Large, long-tailed flycatcher with bushy head and heavy black bill. Brownish-olive above, white-gray throat and breast, light yellow belly, cinnamon-rust primaries and tail feathers, two white wing bars
Similar species:	The other *myiarchus* flycatchers are almost identical and it is difficult to tell them apart in the field. The Ash-throated Flycatcher has paler underparts, smaller bill; the Great Crested Flycatcher is generally darker and has all-yellow underparts

The Brown-crested Flycatcher prefers dry, arid areas and spends the summer in the saguaro desert and lower mountain woodlands of the southwest and southeast, migrating south for the winter; a few birds stay all year in western Mexico. In the breeding season it takes over an old woodpecker hole or a natural cavity in a saguaro cactus or tree, in which it builds a nest lined with hair and feathers. Its 3-5 creamy, brown-blotched eggs are incubated for around 3 weeks and the chicks leave the nest around 16 days after hatching. The adult is a large, long-tailed bird with a bushy head and a heavy black bill. It is brownish-olive above, with a white-gray throat and breast, a light yellow belly, and cinnamon-rust primaries. The cinnamon tail feathers are dark-tipped and it has two white wing bars. The Brown-crested Flycatcher feeds on large insects caught in flight, but also eats berries in colder weather when insects are hard to find.

ASH-THROATED FLYCATCHER *(right)*

Scientific name:	*Myiarchus cinerascens*
Length:	$8\frac{1}{2}$ inches
Habitat:	Dry open areas
Identification:	Large, long-tailed flycatcher with bushy head. Olive gray-brown above, white-gray throat and upper breast, white lower breast, light yellow belly, cinnamon-rust primaries and tail feathers, two white wing bars
Similar species:	The other *myiarchus* flycatchers are almost identical and it is difficult to tell them apart in the field. The Brown-crested Flycatcher has darker underparts, bigger bill; the Great Crested Flycatcher is generally darker and has all-yellow underparts

The Ash-throated Flycatcher prefers dry and arid areas and spends the summer in the open woodland of the west, where it is quite common, migrating south for the winter; a few birds stay all year round in western Mexico. In the breeding season it takes over an old woodpecker hole or natural tree cavity, in which it builds a loose nest of grass, roots and stems to hold 3-5 creamy eggs finely streaked with brown. These are incubated for around 2 weeks and the young leave the nest about 16 days after they have hatched. The adult is a large, long-tailed bird with a bushy head. It is olive gray-brown above, with a white-gray throat and upper breast, white lower breast, a light yellow belly, and cinnamon-rust primaries. The cinnamon tail feathers are dark-tipped and it has two white wing bars. The Ash-throated Flycatcher perches in the upper branches of mature trees at the edge of woodland, where it can spot and catch large insects flying in open areas nearby.

DUSKY-CAPPED FLYCATCHER

Scientific name:	*Myiarchus tuberculifer*
Length:	$7\frac{1}{4}$ inches
Habitat:	Wooded mountains, canyons
Identification:	Large, long-tailed flycatcher with rounded head. Olive-brown above, white-gray throat and upper breast, yellow belly and undertail coverts, rufous edges to secondaries, two white wing bars
Similar species:	The other *myiarchus* flycatchers are almost identical and it is difficult to tell them apart in the field. The Ash-throated Flycatcher has a more rufous tail and paler belly; the Great Crested Flycatcher is generally darker and has all-yellow underparts

Unlike the Ash-throated, the Dusky-capped Flycatcher prefers shady oak mountain woodland, and is found in Southern Arizona and Mexico in summer, with some birds straying into western Texas. It migrates south for the winter - although a few birds stay all year round in Mexico. In the breeding season it builds a loose nest of grass, roots, stems and strips of bark in a natural tree cavity or an abandoned woodpecker hole, in which it lays 4-5 creamy eggs finely streaked with brown and purple. The adult is a large, long-tailed bird with a rounded head. It is olive-brown above, with a white-gray throat and upper breast, a yellow belly and undertail coverts, two white wing bars and a dark tail. Unlike the other *myiarchus* flycatchers, its secondary feathers have reddish edges. When foraging, the Dusky-capped Flycatcher hovers in midair over dense bushes and tree foliage and plucks insects from amongst the leaves or conifer needles.

VERMILION FLYCATCHER

Scientific name: *Pyrocephalus rubinus*
Length: 6 inches
Habitat: Streams, wooded ponds
Identification: Medium-size, short-tailed flycatcher with small bill. Male has bright vermilion-red head and underparts, brown-black narrow mask, back, wings and tail. Female is gray-brown above, with whitish forehead and eyebrow, black tail, white breast lightly streaked with dusky brown, pink-peach wash on belly and undertail coverts
Similar species: *Coloring and pattern unmistakable*

Most flycatchers are rather drab in color, but the Vermilion Flycatcher is an exception and is very striking. It is also fairly common within its rather limited North American range, and it commonly perches in the open, low down on a shrub or bush near water, so it can be quite easy to spot. In the summer breeding season it builds a flat nest of twigs, stems and roots lined with hair, to hold 2 or 3 whitish eggs heavily blotched with lilac-brown. These are incubated for around 2 weeks by the female bird and the young are ready to leave the nest and fend for themselves about 15 days after they have hatched. The adult is a medium-size, short-tailed bird with a small bill. The male has a bright vermilion-red head and underparts, and a brown-black narrow mask, back, wings and tail. The female is gray-brown above, with a whitish forehead and eyebrow, a black tail, a white breast lightly streaked with dusky brown, and a pink-peach wash on the belly and undertail coverts. The juvenile is similar to the female, but more spotted than streaked and it may have a pinky-yellowish belly. When the Vermilion Flycatcher is perched, it often dips its tail like a phoebe. It eats large insects, which it catches in flight.

SCISSOR-TAILED FLYCATCHER *(below)*

Scientific name:	*Tyrannus forficatus*
Length:	13 inches
Habitat:	Open country
Identification:	Large flycatcher with very long, deeply-forked tail. Pearl gray head and back, lighter breast with salmon-pink on flanks, belly and undertail coverts, blackish wings with salmon-pink lining and reddish patch at the shoulder, black and white tail
Similar species:	Coloring and tail make adult unmistakable

Closely related to kingbirds, the Scissor-tailed Flycatcher is an exotic and elegant bird. It is common in open country in the south in summer, but spends the winter in Mexico and Central America - although a few birds winter in Florida. In the breeding season it builds a shallow saucer-shape nest of twigs and grass in a tree, bush or on a utility pole up to 30 feet above the ground, to hold 4-6 creamy-white eggs spotted with brown. These are incubated for around 2 weeks by the female bird and the young leave the nest about 14 days after they have hatched. The adult is a fairly large bird with very long, deeply-forked tail, which is often twice as long as the body. It has a pearl gray head and back, a lighter breast with salmon-pink on the flanks, belly and undertail coverts, blackish wings with a salmon-pink lining and a reddish patch at the shoulder, and a black and white tail. The female has a shorter tail, as does the juvenile, which is also paler and grayer overall. The Scissor-tailed Flycatcher catches insects in flight, but also eats grasshoppers, berries and seeds.

COUCH'S KINGBIRD

Scientific name:	*Tyrannus couchii*
Length:	9¼ inches
Habitat:	Shrubs and groves of trees near water
Identification:	Long-winged, short-tailed flycatcher with thick bill and slightly notched tail. Olive-gray above, yellow beneath, white throat, gray head and breast, yellow belly, dusky brown tail
Similar species:	Almost identical to the Tropical Kingbird, which is mainly found further west

Couch's Kingbird is common in the Rio Grande valley and the southern coast in summer, but is much less numerous in winter since most birds move south during the fall to Mexico and South America. It is so similar to the Tropical Kingbird, which is mainly found further west in southern Arizona and western Mexico, that until recently they were regarded as one species. Couch's Kingbird likes native woodland trees, particularly if they are near ponds or rivers. In its breeding area, it builds a shallow cup-shaped nest of twigs, roots and grass, lined with soft fibers, up to 20 feet above the ground on the branch of a tree, in which the female lays 3-5 buffy-pink eggs, spotted with brown and lilac. The parent bird is very protective of the nesting site and will often chase away much bigger birds. The adult is a relatively long-winged, short-tailed bird with a short, heavy bill and a slightly notched tail. Its plumage is olive-gray above, with a gray head and breast, a white throat, bright yellow belly and undertail, and a dusky brown tail. The juvenile is very similar to the adult. Couch's Kingbird sits silently very high in a tree, darting out to catch passing winged insects. In colder weather, it will also eat berries.

WESTERN KINGBIRD

Scientific name:	*Tyrannus verticalis*
Length:	8¾ inches
Habitat:	Dry open country
Identification:	Long-winged, short-tailed flycatcher with heavy bill and square tail. Olive-gray above, gray head, light gray throat and breast, bright yellow belly and undertail, black tail with outer feathers edged white
Similar species:	Cassin's Kingbird lacks white edges to outer tail feathers, tail is tipped white, head and breast are darker gray

The Western Kingbird is fairly common in dry, open country in the west in summer, moving south in fall to spend the winter in South America - although a few birds winter in southern Florida. In its breeding area, it builds a bulky but carefully constructed nest of twigs, roots, plant fibers and grass, lined with animal hair, up to 40 feet above the ground on a horizontal tree limb, or the crossarm of a utility pole. The female lays 3-6 pinky-white eggs, spotted with brown, which are incubated for up to 2 weeks; the young leave the nest about 2 weeks after they have hatched. The adult is a long-winged, short-tailed bird with a heavy bill and a square tail. Its plumage is olive-gray above, with a gray head, a light gray throat and breast, bright yellow belly and undertail, and a black tail with the outer feathers edged white. The juvenile is more olive on the back and has a brownish tint on the breast and a paler belly. The Western Kingbird perches on trees, fences and utility poles, darting out to catch passing winged insects. It is common on ranches, where flying insects flock round the livestock.

EASTERN KINGBIRD

Scientific name:	*Tyrannus tyrannus*
Length:	8½ inches
Habitat:	Woodland clearings, forest edges
Identification:	Medium-size flycatcher with narrow pointed wings. Black head, slate-gray back, white underparts with pale gray wash on breast, black tail with white across tip, narrow strip of red feathers on crown usually not visible
Similar species:	Coloring and habits distinctive

A conspicuous and common bird, the Eastern Kingbird is seen perching on treetops, fences and utility poles in summer across much of eastern and central North America, migrating south in fall. In its breeding area, it builds a large and bulky nest of twigs, roots, straw and grass, lined with hair, up to 60 feet above the ground on the horizontal limb of a tree. The female lays 3-5 white eggs, spotted with brown, which are incubated for up to 2 weeks; the young leave the nest about 2 weeks after they have hatched. The adult is a medium-size bird with narrow pointed wings. It has a black head, with a slate-gray back, white underparts with a pale gray wash on the breast, and a black tail with a white terminal band. It also has a narrow strip of red feathers on the crown, but this is not usually visible. The juvenile is brownish-gray above, with a darker breast. The Eastern Kingbird is an aggressive bird that perches out in the open and defends its territory vigorously even against much larger birds. It darts out to catch passing winged insects, but also sometimes eats berries and seeds.

CASSIN'S KINGBIRD

Scientific name:	*Tyrannus vociferans*
Length:	9 inches
Habitat:	Dense woods, riversides, canyons
Identification:	Long-winged, short-tailed flycatcher with heavy bill and square tail. Dark olive-gray above, white throat, dark gray head and breast, yellow belly and undertail, black tail lightly tipped white
Similar species:	Western Kingbird has white edges to outer tail feathers, paler gray on head and breast

Although it is found in a wide variety of habitats, Cassin's Kingbird prefers open areas with scattered trees. It is fairly common in hilly country in the southwest in summer, moving south in fall to winter in Mexico and South America. In its breeding area, it builds a well-hidden, bulky nest of twigs, roots and bark, lined with grass or animal hair, up to 40 feet above the ground on a horizontal tree limb. The female lays 3-5 white eggs, spotted with brown, gray and lilac, which are incubated for up to 2 weeks; the young leave the nest about 2 weeks after they have hatched. The adult is a long-winged, short-tailed bird with a heavy bill and a square tail. Its plumage is dark olive-gray above, with a dark gray head and breast, a white throat, yellow belly and undertail, and a black tail lightly tipped with white. The juvenile is duller and browner. Cassin's Kingbird sits quietly high in a tree, darting out to catch passing winged insects. In colder weather, it will also eat berries.

NORTHERN SHRIKE

Scientific name:	*Lanius excubitor*
Length:	10 inches
Habitat:	Spruce and thicket at tundra edge, farmland, open country
Identification:	Medium-size, long-winged, long-tailed predatory songbird with heavy hooked bill, smallish head. Pale blue-gray above, white with fine barring beneath, black mask, wings and tail, white throat, rump and outer tail feathers, large white wing patches
Similar species:	Loggerhead Shrike is slightly smaller, less heavy bill, face mask meets above bill. Mockingbird lacks white side patches and undertail coverts

The Northern Shrike is a fairly uncommon bird that spends the summer on northern tundra and winters across much of central North America - although its exact range is unpredictable from year to year. In its breeding grounds, it builds a bulky nest of twigs, lined with feathers, up to 20 feet above the ground in a conifer or bush, in which it lays 3-9 greenish-white eggs, blotched with brown. These are incubated by the female bird for just over 2 weeks; the young leave the nest about 3 weeks after they have hatched. The adult is a medium-size bird with long wings and a long tail, and has a smallish head and a heavy, hooked bill. Its plumage is pale blue-gray above, white with fine barring beneath, with a black mask, wings and tail, a white throat, rump and outer tail feathers, and large white wing patches. The juvenile is brownish above, and has heavier barring. Although it is a songbird, the Northern Shrike behaves more like a bird of prey, sitting high in a tree and swooping down to catch mice, snakes, frogs and other birds. It kills more than it can eat, storing excess food on a thorn or in a forked twig to feed from on days when prey is scarce.

LOGGERHEAD SHRIKE

Scientific name:	*Lanius ludovicianus*
Length:	9 inches
Habitat:	Open country
Identification:	Medium-size, long-winged, long-tailed predatory songbird with dark hooked bill, smallish head. Blue-gray above, white with very faint barring beneath, black mask, wings and tail, white throat, rump and outer tail feathers, large white wing patches
Similar species:	Northern Shrike is slightly larger, has heavier bill, face mask does not meet above bill. Mockingbird lacks white side patches and undertail coverts

Fairly common over much of its range, the Loggerhead Shrike is seen all year round across southern North America, with many birds moving further north in the summer - although its exact range does vary from year to year. In its breeding grounds, it builds a nest of twigs, well-lined with feathers, up to 20 feet above the ground in a tree or thorny bush, in which it lays 3-8 greenish-white eggs, speckled with brown. These are incubated by the female bird for just over 2 weeks; the young leave the nest about 3 weeks after they have hatched. The adult is a medium-size bird with long wings and a long tail, and has a smallish head and a dark hooked bill. Its plumage is blue-gray above, white with very faint barring beneath, with a black mask that meets above the bill, black wings and tail, a white throat, rump and outer tail feathers, and large white wing patches. The juvenile is paler with a brownish tint above and has heavier barring. The Loggerhead Shrike feeds mainly on large insects, but will hunt mice and other birds when other food is scarce. Like the Northern Shrike it stores excess food on a thorn or barbed wire, for days when prey is scarce.

WHITE-EYED VIREO

Scientific name:	*Vireo griseus*
Length:	5 inches
Habitat:	Thickets, dense undergrowth
Identification:	Stocky, short-tailed songbird with short sturdy bill. Gray-olive above, white beneath, pale yellow sides and flanks, yellow "spectacles" round eyes, two whitish wing bars
Similar species:	Yellow "spectacles" are distinctive

The White-eyed Vireo is found across much of southeast America in summer, and stays all year round along the southern Atlantic Coast,

in Florida and around the Gulf Coast. Despite its fairly extensive range it can be difficult to spot, as it tends to stay in dense foliage. It builds a small nest of bark, plant material and spider web, which is suspended from the twigs of a small sapling or bush up to 9 feet above the ground. It lays 3-5 white eggs, speckled with brown-black and these are incubated by both adult birds for just over 2 weeks. The adult is a stocky, short-tailed bird with a short neck and a sturdy bill with a slightly hooked tip; at very close range it has a distinctive white iris. Its plumage is gray-olive above and white beneath, with pale yellow sides and flanks, yellow "spectacles" round the eyes, and two whitish wing bars. The juvenile is duller with gray-brown eyes. The White-eyed Vireo feeds mainly on large insects, spiders and berries.

BLUE-HEADED VIREO *(below)*

Scientific name: *Vireo solitarius*
Length: 5 inches
Habitat: Mixed woodlands
Identification: Stocky, short-tailed songbird with stout bill. Bright olive above, white beneath, yellow sides and flanks, white "spectacles" round eyes, two yellowish wing bars. Male has blue-gray hood, female and juvenile have partly gray hood
Similar species: Cassin's Vireo is slightly smaller and duller, Plumbeous Vireo is entirely gray and white

The Blue-headed, Cassin's and Plumbeous vireos were once considered one species, the Solitary Vireo. The Blue-headed is common across the far north in summer, and migrates south in fall, with some birds spending the winter along the southern Atlantic Coast, in Florida and around the Gulf Coast. For a nest, it builds a woven basket of grasses and fibers, which is suspended within a fork near the end of a branch up to 9 feet above the ground. The exterior is decorated with bark, lichens and leaves and the inside lined with soft down. The female lays 3-5 creamy-white, spotted eggs, and these are incubated by both adult birds for around 12 days. The adult is a small, stocky, short-tailed bird with a stout bill. Its plumage is bright olive above and white beneath, with yellow sides and flanks, white "spectacles" round the eyes, and two yellowish wing bars. The male has a blue-gray hood, the female and juvenile have partly gray hoods. The Blue-headed Vireo forages in the mid and upper levels of trees, and feeds mainly on insects, spiders and berries.

PLUMBEOUS VIREO

Scientific name: *Vireo plumbeus*
Length: $5\frac{1}{4}$ inches
Habitat: Wooded mountain canyons
Identification: Stocky, short-tailed songbird with big, stout bill. Gray above, white beneath, white "spectacles" round eyes, two white wing bars
Similar species: Both Cassin's and Blue-headed vireos have more olive backs and yellow on sides

The Plumbeous, Blue-headed and Cassin's vireos were once considered to be one species, known as the Solitary Vireo. The Plumbeous is common inland in western North America in the summer months, living in the pine and oak woods of mountain canyons. It migrates south in the fall, with some birds spending the winter in southern Arizona. Like the Blue-headed and Cassin's, it builds a woven basket of grasses and fibers suspended within a fork near the end of a branch, which can be up to 9 feet above the ground. The exterior is camouflaged with bark, lichens and leaves and the inside is lined with soft downy material. The female lays 3-5 creamy-white, spotted eggs, and these are incubated by both adult birds for around 12 days. The adult is a small, stocky, short-tailed bird with a big, stout bill. Its plumage is gray above and white beneath, with white "spectacles" round the eyes, and two white wing bars. At the end of the summer, when its plumage is very worn, it can look very similar to the Gray Vireo - although the Gray has rather shorter wings. The Plumbeous Vireo feeds mainly on insects, spiders and berries.

WARBLING VIREO

Scientific name:	*Vireo gilvus*
Length:	$5\frac{1}{2}$ inches
Habitat:	Deciduous woods
Identification:	Stocky songbird with short bill. Gray-olive above, whitish beneath, pale yellow on flanks, white eyebrow, no wing bars
Similar species:	Red-eyed Vireo is larger and darker, has gray crown and white eyebrow with dark borders, red eyes. Tennessee Warbler has smaller bill, more olive back

Found across much of North America in summer, the Warbling Vireo spends the winter in Mexico and Central America. It is very common and is often heard in parks and wooded gardens, as well as in deciduous woodland. In the breeding season, it builds a woven cup of plant fibers and spider web suspended from a forked branch up to 60 feet above the ground. The interior is lined with soft material and holds 3-5 white, brown-spotted eggs. These are incubated by both adult birds for around 2 weeks and the young birds leave the nest about 14 days after they have hatched. The adult is a small, stocky bird with a short bill. Its plumage is gray-olive above and whitish beneath, with pale yellow on the flanks, a white eyebrow above the eye and no wing bars. The Warbling Vireo sings very sweetly from high in a tree, but hides in leaves and is hard to see. It feeds mainly on insects, spiders and berries.

BELL'S VIREO

Scientific name:	*Vireo bellii*
Length:	$4\frac{3}{4}$ inches
Habitat:	Wet woods, mesquite, thickets, stream edges
Identification:	Small, long-tailed songbird with stout bill. Gray-olive above, white beneath, buffy-yellow sides, indistinct white eye ring, two narrow white wing bars
Similar species:	Plumage can be variable, so could be confused with several other vireos, but indistinct eye ring and longish tail are distinctive

Although it is an endangered species in California, Bell's Vireo is locally common in other areas of its North American summer range; it spends the winter in Mexico and further south. It is a plain and shy bird, so can be difficult to spot - although when nesting it is fearless and can be approached quite closely. Its nest is a small hanging cup woven from bark, plant material and spider web, which is suspended from a small sapling or bush up to 10 feet above the ground. It lays 3-5 white eggs, spotted with brown-black and these are incubated by both adult birds for just over 2 weeks. The young birds leave the nest after around 12-13 days, making way for a second brood. The adult is a small, relatively long-tailed bird and has a stout, curved bill with a hook at the end. Its plumage is gray-olive above and white beneath, with buffy-yellow sides, an indistinct white eye ring, and two narrow white wing bars. Although it is quite small, Bell's Vireo will take larger prey than some other vireos; it feeds on caterpillars, aphids, larvae and spiders

YELLOW-THROATED VIREO

Scientific name:	*Vireo flavifrons*
Length:	5½ inches
Habitat:	Oak and mixed woods
Identification:	Stocky, very short-tailed songbird with large head. Olive above, gray rump, bright yellow breast and throat, white belly, bright yellow "spectacles" round eyes, two white wing bars
Similar species:	Pine Warbler has greeny-yellow rump, streaked sides, thinner bill, less defined "spectacles", Yellow-breasted Chat is larger, with brown upperparts

Although it is fairly common in woods across the east of America during the summer months, the Yellow-throated Vireo is very hard to spot because it stays high up in the dense foliage of the canopy. It migrates south in fall, to spend the winter in the Southern Hemisphere. In its summer breeding area, it builds a small basket-shaped nest of bark, plant material and grass, bound with spider web, which is suspended from the forked branch of a small sapling or a bush up to 60 feet above the ground. It lays 3-5 white eggs, blotched with brown-lilac, which are incubated by both adult birds for just over 2 weeks; the young fledglings leave the nest to begin fending for themselves around 14 days after they have hatched. The adult is a stocky, very short-tailed bird with a relatively large head and a thick bill. Its plumage is olive above, with a gray rump, a bright yellow breast and throat, white belly, bright yellow "spectacles" round the eyes, and two white wing bars. The juvenile is similar but is rather duller and has gray-brown eyes. The Yellow-throated Vireo forages high up in the trees, feeding mainly on insects and berries.

RED-EYED VIREO *(right)*

Scientific name:	*Vireo olivaceus*
Length:	6 inches
Habitat:	Woodland
Identification:	Small, stocky, long-winged songbird with long bill. Gray-olive back, blue-gray crown, white eyebrow with dark borders, white beneath, darker wings and tail, no wing bars, red eyes
Similar species:	Warbling Vireo is smaller and paler

The Red-eyed Vireo is common in summer in the woodland of the east and its range spreads across North America to the northwest. In the breeding season, it builds a small, beautifully woven cup of plant fibers and spider web suspended from a forked branch up to 60 feet above the ground in a deciduous tree. The interior is lined with soft material and holds 3 or 4 whitish eggs, lightly spotted with brown. These are incubated by the female for around 2 weeks and the young birds leave the nest about 12 days after they have hatched. The adult is a small, stocky bird with long wings and a longish, heavy bill. It has a gray-olive back and is white beneath, with a blue-gray crown, a white eyebrow with dark borders, darker wings and tail, and no wing bars. Its red eyes may be difficult to see, except at close range. The juvenile has brown eyes and fall adults may have some yellow on the flanks and undertail coverts. The Red-eyed Vireo forages high in trees, and may sing for many hours during the day. It feeds mainly on insects and berries.

HUTTON'S VIREO

Scientific name:	*Vireo huttoni*
Length:	5 inches
Habitat:	Oak woodland
Identification:	Stocky songbird with thick, hooked bill. Gray-olive above, paler drab olive beneath, yellow on flanks, broken white eye ring, two white wing bars
Similar species:	Ruby-crowned Kinglet is smaller, has slimmer bill and dark area behind wing bar

Hutton's Vireo is fairly common within its limited North American range, but it moves high up in the forest canopy so may be difficult to spot. It is often mistaken for the Ruby-crowned Kinglet, which is seen across a much wider range; the two birds are strikingly similar - particularly as the male kinglet's small red crown is often not apparent. Hutton's Vireo builds a woven cup of lichens, plant fibers and spider web suspended from a forked twig, which can be up to 35 feet above the ground. The interior is lined with soft feathers and moss and holds 3 or 4 white, brown-spotted eggs. These are incubated by both adult birds for just over 2 weeks and the young birds leave the nest about 14 days after they have hatched. The adult is a small, stocky bird with a thick, hooked bill. Its plumage is gray-olive above, with paler drab olive beneath, yellow on the flanks, a white eye ring broken above the eye, and two white wing bars. Hutton's Vireo flicks its wings like a kinglet when perched. It feeds mainly on insects, spiders and berries.

CASSIN'S VIREO

Scientific name:	*Vireo cassinii*
Length:	5 inches
Habitat:	Oak and conifer woods
Identification:	Stocky, short-tailed songbird with stout bill. Olive above, pale gray head, white beneath, pale yellow sides and flanks, white "spectacles" round eyes, two yellowish wing bars
Similar species:	Blue-headed Vireo is slightly bigger and brighter, Plumbeous Vireo is entirely gray and white

Once called the Solitary Vireo, and considered one species along with the Blue-headed and Plumbeous vireos, Cassin's Vireo is common along the north Pacific Coast in summer. In fall it migrates south, with some birds spending the winter in southern Arizona and down into Mexico. In the breeding season, it builds a woven basket nest of grasses and fibers, which is suspended in a fork near the end of a branch up to 9 feet above the ground. The exterior is covered with bark, lichens and leaves and the inside lined with soft material. The female lays 3-5 creamy-white, spotted eggs, and these are incubated by both adult birds for around 12 days. The adult is a small, stocky, short-tailed bird with a stout bill. Its plumage is olive above and white beneath, with a pale gray head, pale yellow sides and flanks, white "spectacles" round the eyes, and two yellowish wing bars. Cassin's Vireo prefers oak and conifer woods and often flicks its wings when perched. It feeds mainly on insects, spiders and berries.

BLUE JAY

Scientific name:	*Cyanocitta cristata*
Length:	11 inches
Habitat:	Suburbs, parks, woodland
Identification:	Crested, broad-winged, rather short-tailed woodland bird. Blue above, gray-white underneath with black necklace, black barring on wings and tail, white patches on wings, outer feathers of tail white
Similar species:	Coloring distinctive, but often mimics the calls of other birds

Common in suburbs, woodlands and parks, the Blue Jay is found across most of eastern North America and is occasionally seen in the northwest and west. Some birds migrate south in the fall, moving in large flocks. Like other jays, it has a harsh, strident voice and often mimics other birds - particularly the Red-shouldered Hawk. The Blue Jay builds a bulky nest of twigs, moss and leaves on a branch or in the crotch of a tree up to 50 feet above the ground, in which it lays 3-5 olive, blue or buffy eggs spotted with brown. These are incubated by the female for about 17 days and the young birds leave to fend for themselves around 3 weeks after hatching. The adult has a crest at the back of the head, broad, rounded wings and rather a short, broad tail. It is blue above, gray-white underneath with a black necklace, and has black barring on wings and tail, white patches on the wings, and white across the corners of the tail. The Blue Jay eats nuts, seeds, fruit and insects.

STELLER'S JAY

Scientific name:	*Cyanocitta stelleri*
Length:	$11\frac{1}{2}$ inches
Habitat:	Pine-oak woods, coniferous forests
Identification:	Crested, broad-winged, rather short-tailed woodland bird. Head, throat, chest and upper back all black, with deep blue wings, rump, tail and belly
Similar species:	The only crested jay that is all dark

Steller's Jay is North America's largest jay and lives in dense forests - conifers in the northwest, pine and oak in the south and mixed oak and redwood in northern California. It often travels in small groups and is bright-colored and conspicuous. It prefers conifers for nesting, building a neat and sturdy bowl of twigs lined with mud on a high branch, in which it lays 3-5 greeny-blue spotted eggs that are incubated by the female alone for about 16 days. The adult has a long crest at the back of the head, broad, rounded wings and rather a short, broad tail. Its head, throat, chest and upper back are all black - although it may have paler spots and streaks on the forehead and near the eye - with deep blue wings, rump, tail and belly. Like other jays, Steller's Jay is an accomplished mimic. It is bold and aggressive and often visits bird feeders and picnic grounds, but otherwise likes to eat nuts, seeds, fruit and insects.

GRAY JAY

Scientific name:	*Perisoreus canadensis*
Length:	$11\frac{1}{2}$ inches
Habitat:	Mountain forests
Identification:	Long-tailed, short-billed woodland bird with fluffy plumage. Dark gray above, white or pale gray beneath, white forehead and face. Far north birds, brownish crown and nape; Rocky Mountain birds mostly white head, northwest coast birds, large dark crown
Similar species:	Looks rather like a very big chickadee, but much larger size is distinctive

Previously known as the Canada Jay, the Gray Jay is a familiar visitor to mountain camp sites and cabins, where it will help itself to as much food as possible - earning itself the nickname "camp-robber". It breeds very early - often when there is still snow on the ground - building a bowl-shaped nest of twigs lined with feathers or moss up to 30 feet above the ground in a tree. It lays 3-5 greeny-gray spotted eggs, which are incubated by the female alone for about 17-18 days; the young birds stay in the nest for around 2 weeks before leaving to fend for themselves. The adult is a long-tailed bird with a short bill and distinctive fluffy plumage. It is dark gray above, white or pale gray beneath, and has a white forehead and face. There are three distinct color variations; birds in the far north on the taiga have a brownish crown and nape; those in the Rocky Mountains have a mostly white head, and northwest coast birds have a large dark crown. The juvenile of all types is dark slate-gray overall, with a faint white streak like a mustache. The Gray Jay stores scraps of frozen meat and other morsels in trees, to eat when its other staples of insects, fruit, mice and birds' eggs are not available.

PINYON JAY *(above)*

Scientific name:	*Gymnorhinus cyanocephalus*
Length:	$10\frac{1}{2}$ inches
Habitat:	Mountain pine woods
Identification:	Small, plain, short-tailed woodland bird with long, slender bill. Entirely gray-blue, slightly darker head, some white streaking on throat
Similar species:	The only all-blue jay

The Pinyon Jay is a very sociable bird that is usually seen in large flocks, often consisting of hundreds of birds, and inhabits the pine woods of the west. It is unusual in that its courting and breeding cycle begins much earlier than many American birds - the male and female pair up in winter and the nest is built at the end of January - often while there is still snow around. It nests in loose colonies, building a cup of twigs up to 20 feet above the ground in a small tree. The female lays 3 or 4 greeny-white, speckled eggs, which are incubated for about 16 days; the chicks are ready to leave the nest around 3 weeks after hatching. The adult is a small, short-tailed bird with a long, slender bill. It is entirely gray-blue, slightly darker on the head and with some white streaking on the throat. Juveniles are gray. The Pinyon Jay mainly eats pine nuts, which it buries in fall for use in the following winter and spring. This enables the female to sit on the nest and keep the eggs warm even though the external temperature is still so low, while the male feeds her from their stored supply. The Pinyon also eats seeds, berries, insects and the eggs and young of other birds.

WESTERN SCRUB-JAY

Scientific name:	*Aphelocoma californica*
Length:	11 inches
Habitat:	Urban areas, parks, brushland, oak and juniper woods
Identification:	Slender, long-tailed woodland bird. Gray back, blue head with white eyebrow, blue wings and tail, white throat and underparts, blue breast band
Similar species:	Florida and Island scrub-jays are similar but are restricted to specific areas - the Florida only in a small part of that state and the Island to Santa Cruz Island. The three were formerly considered one species. Mexican Jay lacks white throat and eyebrow, shape stouter

Common in the suburbs, woodlands and parks of the west, particularly coastal California, the Western Scrub-Jay is quite tame. It prefers scrub oaks and pinyon-juniper woods and is sometimes seen in small groups. It builds a nest of twigs up to 12 feet above the ground, well hidden in a small tree or dense bush, in which it lays 3-6 greenish eggs spotted with red and brown. These are incubated by the female for about 17 days and the young birds leave to fend for themselves around 2-3 weeks after hatching. The adult is a slender, long-tailed bird with a large strong bill. It has a gray back, a blue head with a white eyebrow, blue wings and tail, white throat and underparts, and a blue breast band. Inland birds tend to be duller in color than those on the coast. The Western Scrub-Jay mainly eats insects in summer - but also likes acorns, as well as nuts, seeds and fruit.

GREEN JAY

Scientific name:	*Cyanocorax yncas*
Length:	10½ inches
Habitat:	Riverside woods, dry brushland, parks, oak groves
Identification:	Long-tailed, rather small woodland bird. Bright olive-green above, pale green beneath, black breast, crown and back of head blue, face blue and black, outer tail feathers bright yellow
Similar species:	Coloring unmistakable

A tropical species, the Green Jay is only found in North America in southern Texas, where it is common in brushy areas and woods near streams. It is a noisy and gregarious bird that often travels in small groups and like other jays it is inquisitive - so will usually allow close approach. It builds a nest of sticks on a branch up to 15 feet above the ground in a small tree or bush, in which it lays 3-5 buffy, blue or white eggs spotted with brown. These are incubated by the female for about 16 days and the young birds leave the nest around 3-4 weeks after hatching. The adult is rather a small bird with a long tail. Its plumage is bright olive-green above, pale green beneath, with a black breast, blue on the crown and back of the head, blue and black markings on the face, and bright yellow outer tail feathers. The Green Jay eats seeds, fruit and insects.

MEXICAN JAY

Scientific name:	*Aphelocoma ultramarina*
Length:	11½ inches
Habitat:	Pine-oak woods, mountain canyons
Identification:	Stoutish, long-tailed woodland bird. Gray back, blue-gray head, rump, wings and tail, pale gray underparts
Similar species:	Scrub-jays are similar but have white throat and eyebrow, blue breast band, more slender shape

Although in America it is restricted to mountain canyons and oak woods near the Mexican border, the Mexican Jay is quite common within these areas. It was previously known as the Gray-breasted Jay. It lives in clans of 10-15 birds that are all closely related, and in the breeding season it builds a nest of twigs lined with horsehair up to 6 feet above the ground, hidden in a small tree or dense bush. The female lays 4 or 5 green eggs, which are incubated for about 17 days, but other members of the clan help to feed and rear the chicks until they are ready to leave the nest around 2-3 weeks after hatching. The adult is a heavily-built, long-tailed bird with a dark, strong bill. It has a gray back, blue-gray head, rump, wings and tail, and pale gray underparts. Juveniles have pale bills, which darken as they mature. The Mexican Jay has a diet mainly of acorns, but it also eats insects and takes eggs and chicks from the nests of other birds.

CLARK'S NUTCRACKER

Scientific name:	*Nucifraga columbiana*
Length:	12 inches
Habitat:	Mountain coniferous forests
Identification:	Long-winged, short-tailed woodland bird with long, pointed bill. Mostly light gray, black wing with large white wing patch on trailing edge, black tail with white outer feathers, white face and belly
Similar species:	Gray Jay has much smaller bill and lacks white on wings and tail

A mountain bird, Clark's Nutcracker is a familiar visitor to camp sites, picnic spots and cabins where it comes to seek handouts or to steal scraps. Although it normally lives far inland, it sometimes ranges much further afield and can reach the Pacific coast in lean years when pine nuts - its staple food - are scarce. It breeds quite early in the year, building a bulky bowl of twigs lined with grass in a conifer. The female lays 2-6 green, brown-spotted eggs, which are incubated for about 17 days by both parent birds; the chicks leave the nest to fend for themselves around 4 weeks after they have hatched. The adult has long wings, a short tail, and a long, pointed bill. It is mostly light gray, with black wings that have a large white wing patch on the trailing edge, a black tail with white outer feathers, and a white face and belly. Clark's Nutcracker flies with slow, deep wingbeats, rather like a crow. It mainly eats pine nuts, which it stores in fall for the following winter and spring. It also eats juniper berries, and insects in summer.

BLACK-BILLED MAGPIE

Scientific name:	*Pica pica*
Length:	19 inches
Habitat:	Open woodlands, thickets, suburbs, trees along streams
Identification:	Large, long-tailed open-country bird with stout black bill and broad wings. Black head, back and breast, iridescent green-blue on wings and tail, white shoulders and belly, white wing patches in flight
Similar species:	Very similar Yellow-billed Magpie is slightly smaller and has yellow bill, but is only seen in a tiny part of California

Often seen in pairs or small flocks walking on the ground in the open, the Black-billed Magpie is very common across most of western North America. It generally nests in pairs - but also sometimes in loose colonies - building a very large, bulky nest of sticks in a tree, which is covered with a thorny dome of twigs to protect the eggs and chicks. The female lays 7-9 greenish-buff, brown-splotched eggs, which are incubated for about 17 days; details of the nestling period are not known. The adult is a large bird with a very long tail, a stout black bill and broad wings. It has a black head, back and breast, iridescent green-blue on the wings and tail, white shoulders and belly, and shows white wing patches in flight. The Black-billed Magpie eats insects and carrion, but is also known to steal the eggs and chicks of other birds.

FISH CROW

Scientific name:	*Corvus ossifragus*
Length:	15$\frac{1}{2}$ inches
Habitat:	Tidal marshes, rivers, swamps
Identification:	Large, short-tailed crow with powerful bill and broad wings. All black
Similar species:	American Crow is slightly larger, but can only be distinguished by its call. Fan-shaped tail and heavier bill distinguish Common and Chihuahuan ravens from crows. Blackbirds are much smaller

Slightly smaller than the American Crow, the Fish Crow is only found in the southeast, spreading along the Atlantic coast to the north and the Gulf coast to the west. It is also seen inland, but only along rivers since it prefers to be near water. In winter it is sometimes seen in flocks with the American Crow. The Fish Crow generally breeds in loose colonies, building a nest of sticks and twigs in a tree near a river or marsh. The female lays 4 or 5 greenish, brown-spotted eggs, which are incubated for about 17 days; the young are ready to leave the nest and fend for themselves within about 3 weeks after hatching. The adult is a large bird with a short tail, a powerful bill and broad wings. Its plumage is entirely black and its call is a nasal, high-pitched *ca-hah*, with the second syllable lower. The Fish Crow forages in the shallows for fish, crabs, shrimp and crayfish, but will also eat carrion.

AMERICAN CROW (above)

Scientific name:	*Corvus brachyrhynchos*
Length:	$17\frac{1}{2}$ inches
Habitat:	Open country, cities
Identification:	Large, short-tailed crow with powerful bill and broad wings. All black
Similar species:	Fish Crow is slightly smaller, but can only be distinguished by its call. Fan shaped tail and heavier bill distinguish Common and Chihuahuan ravens from crows. Blackbirds are much smaller

The largest of the crows, the American Crow is very common across most of America, also ranging further north and up into Canada during the summer months. Once a mainly woodland bird, it has adapted to changing circumstances over the years and now also lives on farmland and in urban areas. It generally breeds in rather loose colonies - which can consist of hundreds of birds - building a well-constructed nest of sticks lined with plant fibers, in a tree. The female lays 3-6 greenish, brown-splotched eggs, which are incubated for about 17 days; the young are ready to leave the nest and start fending for themselves in about 5 weeks. The adult is a very large bird with a short tail, a powerful bill and broad wings. Its plumage is black and its call is a harsh *caw*. The American Crow is both resourceful and intelligent and has developed a communication system to alert others in the colony of approaching danger and to pass on the position of new food supplies. It is a predator that will eat almost anything - including the eggs and chicks of other birds.

CHIHUAHUAN RAVEN

Scientific name:	*Corvus cryptoleucus*
Length:	$19\frac{1}{2}$ inches
Habitat:	Desert, scrub grassland
Identification:	Medium-size, long-winged raven with heavy bill and deep voice. All black
Similar species:	Common Raven is slightly larger, and has longer bill and different call. Fan-shaped tail and heavier bill distinguish Common and Chihuahuan ravens from crows. Blackbirds are much smaller

The Chihuahuan Raven is only found in southern grasslands and desert areas, with its range just extending into southwest Kansas and southeast Colorado. It is very gregarious, gathering in flocks of hundreds of birds after the breeding season and soaring high in the sky in group displays of swooping, diving and tumbling. It builds a large platform nest of sticks, sometimes incorporating barbed wire, which is lined with animal fur and placed up to 40 feet above the ground in a tree or mesquite or on a utility pole. The female lays 4-8 greenish eggs, sometimes blotched with brown, which are incubated for about 3 weeks by both parents. The adult is medium-size between the American Crow and the Common Raven, with long wings and a heavy bill. Its plumage is entirely black, but the neck feathers are white at the base - although usually obscured - so it was once known as the White-necked Raven. Its call is a flat, drawn out *craaaaak*, higher pitched than that of the Common Raven. The Chihuahuan Raven will eat a wide variety of food, including carrion, rodents, insects and the eggs and chicks of other birds

COMMON RAVEN

Scientific name:	*Corvus corax*
Length:	24 inches
Habitat:	Mountains, desert, forest
Identification:	Large, long-winged raven with long heavy bill and low, resonant voice. All black
Similar species:	Chihuahuan Raven is slightly smaller, and has shorter bill and different call. Fan shaped tail and heavier bill distinguish Common and Chihuahuan ravens from crows. Blackbirds are much smaller

The most widespread raven in North America, the Common Raven is numerous in the north and west and spreading in the east - and is moving into cities in some areas. Pairs of birds mate for life and are often seen soaring high in the sky. It builds a large, loose nest of sticks and branches, which is lined with soft animal fur or wool, and placed high in a tree or on a cliff face. The female lays 4-7 green eggs, spotted with brown, which are incubated for up to 3 weeks by the female; the chicks are ready to leave the nest about 5-6 weeks after hatching. The adult is a large bird, with long wings and tail and a long heavy bill. Its plumage is entirely black, with a thick, heavy neck ruff. Its call is a low, resonant *craaak*, deeper than that of the Chihuahuan Raven, but it also makes a variety of other noises including screams, whistles and a melodious *kloo-klok*. The Common Raven is a resourceful and intelligent bird, which learns new behaviour in different situations. It eats carrion, rodents, insects and the eggs and chicks of other birds, and often feeds at garbage dumps.

HORNED LARK

Scientific name:	Eremophila alpestris
Length:	$6\frac{3}{4}$ to $7\frac{3}{4}$ inches
Habitat:	Barren ground
Identification:	Slender, long-winged open-country songbird with short, stout bill and square tail. Pale brown above, white below, yellow wash on face and throat, black bib and mustache marks, small black horns, black tail feathers with white outer edges
Similar species:	Juvenile lacks horns and strong face markings and is streaked below, so can be confused with Sprague's Pipit

The only native North American lark, the Horned Lark is widespread from coast to coast, and spreads right up to the far north in summer. It prefers open ground with low vegetation - dirt fields or short grass, gravel ridges, dunes, airports - and in winter it becomes much more conspicuous as it gathers in large flocks of thousands of birds. In the breeding season it does not build a nest, but lays its 3-5 whitish, dark-spotted eggs in a sheltered depression in the ground lined with grass. These are incubated by the female for only around 11 days, and the young birds leave the nest a further 11 days after hatching. The adult is a slender, long-winged bird with a short, stout bill and a square tail. Its plumage is pale brown above, white below, with a yellow wash on the face and throat, a black bib and mustache marks, small black horns, and a black tail with a paler center and white edges. The female is duller than the male and the juvenile lacks the horns, has indistinct whitish face markings, and is streaked below. The Horned Lark walks or runs on the ground, moving in an erratic way as it forages for grain, seeds, insects and spiders.

TREE SWALLOW

Scientific name:	*Tachycineta bicolor*
Length:	$5\frac{3}{4}$ inches
Habitat:	Woodland near water
Identification:	Stocky, broad-winged swallow with shallow forked tail. Metallic blue-black above, white beneath. Juvenile gray-brown above, often with indistinct dusky breast band
Similar species:	Violet-green Swallow has white on cheek and sides of rump, differing iridescent color in a good light. Juvenile Tree Swallow could be confused with Bank Swallow, which is similar coloring but has darker and more sharply defined breast band

The Tree Swallow is common and widespread in much of North America in summer, and spends the winter in the southern states and down into Central America. It is seen in a variety of habitats, often in huge flocks as it prepares to migrate in fall, but is never found far from water. It builds a cup nest of grass lined with soft feathers in a tree hollow, abandoned woodpecker hole or nesting box, in which it lays 4-6 white eggs. These are incubated for around 2 weeks and the young are ready to leave the nest about 2-3 weeks after hatching. The adult is a stocky, broad-winged bird with a shallow forked tail. Its plumage is sharply-defined metallic blue-black above against white beneath. The juvenile is gray-brown above, often with an indistinct dusky breast band. The Tree Swallow often perches in long rows on wires and branches. It eats insects and spiders caught on the wing, but turns to berries in winter when other food is scarce.

PURPLE MARTIN

Scientific name:	*Progne subis*
Length:	8 inches
Habitat:	Streams, ponds, woods, urban areas
Identification:	Large, long-winged, large-billed swallow with forked tail. Male glossy blue-black, wings and tail duller black. Female and juvenile dusky black above, light beneath, smoke-gray throat and breast
Similar species:	The European Starling looks alike and will nest in martin houses, but has longer bill, browner wings, lacks forked tail and typical swallow flight

Although populations are declining in North America, particularly in the west, the Purple Martin is still locally common in other areas. It is only seen in summer, as it migrates south in fall, to winter in South America, returning in early spring. It prefers the open countryside, but is also seen in suburban areas where there are suitable nest sites. It builds a loose nest of grass, leaves, feathers and other materials in a tree hollow, abandoned woodpecker hole or in the eaves of a building; birds in the east will use a purpose-built martin house. The 3-6 dull white eggs are incubated by the female for around 15-17 days and the young are ready to leave the nest about 4 weeks after hatching. The adult is the largest North American swallow, with long, angular, pointed wings, a large bill and a forked tail. The male is glossy blue-black, with duller black wings and tail. The female and juvenile are dusky black above, light beneath, with a smoke-gray throat and breast. The Purple Martin typically flies low with rapid wingbeats, alternating with short glides. It eats insects and airborne spiders, caught on the wing.

NORTHERN ROUGH-WINGED SWALLOW

Scientific name:	*Stelgidopteryx serripennis*
Length:	5 inches
Habitat:	Riverbanks, cliffs
Identification:	Stocky, broad-winged swallow with short, square tail. Brown above, white beneath with dull gray-brown wash on throat and upper breast
Similar species:	Bank Swallow is smaller and has white throat and brown breast band

The Northern Rough-winged Swallow rarely comes together in flocks and is usually seen singly or in pairs - although it may migrate in small groups. It is common across most of North America in summer, spending the winter in Central and South America. It nests in pairs in riverbanks, cliffs or under bridges, building a shallow saucer of grass and leaves at the end of a burrow or in a ready-made cavity in stonework. It lays 4-8 white eggs that are incubated for around 2 weeks; the young birds are ready to leave the nest about 3 weeks after hatching. The adult is a stocky bird with long, broad wings and a short, square tail. Its plumage is brown above, white beneath with a dull gray-brown wash on the throat and upper breast. It gets its name from a row of small hooks on the edge of the outer feather of each wing; their function is unknown. The juvenile is similar to the adult, but has two bright cinnamon bars on each wing. The Northern Rough-winged Swallow eats flying insects caught on the wing.

VIOLET-GREEN SWALLOW

Scientific name:	*Tachycineta thalassina*
Length:	5¼ inches
Habitat:	Evergreen forest, rocky cliffs, riversides
Identification:	Medium-size, narrow-winged swallow with short, forked tail. Metallic bronze-green above, iridescent violet rump and tail, white beneath coming up onto rump and almost meeting above tail, white on cheek. Juvenile gray-brown above, dusky on face
Similar species:	Tree Swallow lacks white on cheek and sides of rump, differing iridescent color in a good light. Juveniles of both species are very alike

Only seen in the west, the Violet-green Swallow is very common in North America in summer, spending the winter in Central America. It is seen in a variety of woodland habitats, and breeds in loose colonies. It builds a nest of grass and feathers in a tree hollow, abandoned woodpecker hole, under the eaves of a building or in a nesting box, in which it lays 4 or 5 white eggs. These are incubated for around 2 weeks and the young are ready to leave the nest about 11 days after hatching. The adult is a narrow-winged bird with a short forked tail. Its plumage is sharply-defined metallic bronze-green above, with an iridescent violet rump and tail, white beneath coming up onto rump and almost meeting above tail, and white on the cheek. The juvenile is gray-brown above, dusky on the face. The Violet-green Swallow either flies very high or skims low over the water, searching for airborne insects to catch on the wing.

CLIFF SWALLOW

Scientific name:	*Hirundo pyrrhonota*
Length:	5½ inches
Habitat:	Cliffs, rural buildings
Identification:	Medium-size swallow with broad rounded wings and short square tail. Blue-black crown and back, pale rust rump, dark wings and tail, chestnut throat and cheek, buffy collar, white forehead, whitish belly
Similar species:	Cave Swallow is very alike, but has cinnamon forehead, buffy throat and cheek and is only found in America in small areas of Texas and Florida

Although it is found across most of North America in summer, the Cliff Swallow is common in the west and much less numerous in the east. It migrates in fall in large flocks to spend the winter in South America, returning in early spring, after which it can be spotted near cliffs in open country, or round bridges and rural buildings. It breeds in very large colonies of hundreds of birds, building a gourd-shaped nest of mud lined with grass and feathers on a natural cliff face, under the eaves of a building or on a bridge. It lays 4-6 creamy, lightly spotted eggs that are incubated for around 2 weeks by both parent birds; the young chicks are ready to leave the nest about 3 weeks after hatching. The adult is a medium-size swallow with broad rounded wings and a short square tail. It has a blue-black crown and back with a pale rust rump, dark wings and tail, a chestnut throat and cheek, a buffy collar and a white forehead and whitish belly. Some southwest birds have a dark forehead, like the Cave Swallow. The juvenile is grayer than the adult, with a paler throat and darker forehead. The Cliff Swallow feeds on small insects caught in flight, but sometimes takes berries or other fruit when insects are scarce.

BARN SWALLOW

Scientific name:	*Hirundo rustica*
Length:	6¾ inches
Habitat:	Rural buildings, culverts, bridges
Identification:	Largish swallow with long, slender, pointed wings and long, deeply-forked tail. Blue-black above, pale cinnamon or buffy-white below, chestnut-red throat and forehead, white spots under tail
Similar species:	Shape and plumage are unmistakable

A graceful and elegant bird, the Barn Swallow is found across most of North America in summer, gathering in large flocks in fall to migrate south to winter in South America. It breeds in small colonies, building a cup-shaped nest of mud and straw lined with feathers attached to a wall or on a vertical surface of a bridge - it now very rarely nests away from man-made structures. It lays 3-6 white, red-brown-spotted eggs that are incubated for around 14-18 days; the young birds leave the nest to fend for themselves about 3 weeks after hatching. The adult is a largish swallow with long, slender, pointed wings and a long, deeply-forked tail. It is blue-black above, pale cinnamon or buffy-white below, with a chestnut-red throat and forehead and white spots under the tail that may be hard to distinguish. The juvenile has paler underparts than the adult, and a shorter tail. The Barn Swallow feeds on insects caught in flight, and hunts communally. In flight, it may fold its forked tail into one long point.

BANK SWALLOW

Scientific name:	*Riparia riparia*
Length:	4¾ inches
Habitat:	Riverbanks, gravel pits
Identification:	Small, slender, narrow-winged swallow with long, notched tail. Brown above, white beneath with brown band across upper breast
Similar species:	The Northern Rough-winged Swallow is larger, and has a brown wash on the throat instead of the breast band

The smallest swallow in North America, the Bank Swallow is common across most of North America in summer, migrating south in large flocks to spend the winter in South America. It breeds in very large colonies - sometimes containing hundreds of birds - digging a deep tunnel in a soft earth bank, with a chamber at the end which is lined with grass and feathers. Tunnels are often renovated and reused the following year, due to a shortage of sufficient suitable sites. It lays 4-6 white eggs that are incubated for around 2 weeks by both parent birds; the young chicks are ready to leave the nest about 3 weeks after hatching. The adult is a small, slender, narrow-winged swallow with a long, notched tail. Its plumage is brown above, white beneath with a brown band across the upper breast. The juvenile is similar to the adult, but has two narrow buffy bars on each wing. The Bank Swallow flies with very fast, shallow wingbeats and eats insects caught in flight.

CAROLINA CHICKADEE

Scientific name:	*Parus carolinensis*
Length:	$4\frac{3}{4}$ inches
Habitat:	Open deciduous woods, forest edges, suburbs
Identification:	Small, long-tailed woodland songbird, with large head. Gray above, creamy beneath with buff flanks, black throat patch and cap, white face
Similar species:	Almost identical to Black-capped Chickadee, which is slightly larger, mainly told apart by range, although this overlaps in places. In fresh plumage, the Black-capped has white edges on secondary wing feathers. Mountain Chickadee is like both, but has distinguishing white eyebrow

The Carolina Chickadee is found in the woods of the southeast, replacing the Black-capped abruptly south of a line that runs halfway across central North America. It is very common within its range, and like other chickadees often comes to feeders. It nests in a tree cavity, often excavating a hole in a rotten stump and lining it with plant fibers and feathers to hold 4-8 white eggs lightly spotted with rust-brown. These are incubated for 10-12 days and the young are ready to leave the nest just over 2 weeks after hatching. The adult is a small, long-tailed bird, with a largish head. It is gray above, creamy beneath with buff flanks, and has a black throat patch and cap, and a white face. The lower edge of the throat patch is usually neater than that of the Black-capped, which can look a bit ragged. The Carolina Chickadee eats insects, seeds and berries.

BLACK-CAPPED CHICKADEE

Scientific name: *Parus atricapillus*
Length: 5¼ inches
Habitat: Open woodland, suburbs
Identification: Bold, long-tailed woodland songbird, with large head and fluffy plumage. Gray above, creamy beneath with buff flanks, black throat patch and cap, white face
Similar species: Almost identical to Carolina Chickadee, which is slightly smaller, mainly told apart by range, although this overlaps in places. In fresh plumage, the Black-capped has white edges on secondary wing feathers. Mountain Chickadee is like both, but has distinguishing white eyebrow

A small and constantly active bird, the Black-capped Chickadee is found right across central North America in open woodland - but also often visits suburban bird feeders, where it is particularly fond of sunflower seeds and suet. It nests in a tree hole, often in a rotten stump, making a loose cup of plant material and feathers to hold 4-8 white eggs lightly spotted with rust-brown. These are incubated for 10-12 days and the young are ready to leave the nest just over 2 weeks after hatching. The adult is a bold, long-tailed bird, with a large head and rather fluffy plumage. It is gray above, creamy beneath with buff flanks, and has a black throat patch and cap, and a white face. The secondary wing feathers are boldly edged in white, but this may only be apparent in fresh plumage. After the breeding season is over, the Black-capped Chickadee forms small flocks to roost and forage together. It eats insects, seeds and berries.

MOUNTAIN CHICKADEE (*below*)

Scientific name:	*Parus gambeli*
Length:	$5\frac{1}{4}$ inches
Habitat:	Mountain coniferous and mixed forests
Identification:	Long-winged woodland songbird with longish bill. Gray above, creamy beneath with pale gray flanks, black throat patch and cap, white eyebrow and white face
Similar species:	Very similar to both Black-capped Chickadee, which is slightly larger, and Carolina Chickadee, which is slightly smaller; both lack distinguishing white eyebrow. Bridled Titmouse has crested head

At higher elevations the Mountain Chickadee is common in coniferous and mixed woods, although some birds come down to the lowlands in winter. It nests in a tree cavity, either taking over an old woodpecker hole or excavating its own in a rotten stump, lining it with hair, fur or feathers to hold 6-8 white eggs, sometimes spotted with brown. These are incubated for about 2 weeks and the young are ready to leave the nest around 3 weeks after hatching. The adult is a long-winged bird, with a relatively long bill. It is gray above, creamy beneath with pale gray flanks, and has a black throat patch and cap, with a white eyebrow and a white face. Like other chickadees, the Mountain Chickadee flits among the trees, clambering among the branches like a tiny acrobat. It forages in small flocks, often with other small birds, and eats insects, seeds and berries.

BOREAL CHICKADEE

Scientific name:	*Parus hudsonicus*
Length:	$5\frac{1}{2}$ inches
Habitat:	Dense coniferous forests
Identification:	Long-tailed woodland bird with large head. Gray-brown above, whitish beneath with pale rust flanks, dark brown cap, black throat patch, white cheeks
Similar species:	Similar to Black-capped Chickadee, but browner

Although it is fairly common within its range, the Boreal Chickadee is shy and quiet and normally inhabits such dense coniferous forest that it may be difficult to spot. In Europe, the same species also occurs but there they are known as tits rather than chickadees. It nests in a tree cavity, sometimes natural or sometimes excavating its own in a rotten stump, lining it with animal fur or feathers to hold 6-9 white eggs, faintly speckled with brown. These are incubated for about 2 weeks by the female; the young birds are ready to leave the nest around 2-3 weeks after hatching. The adult is a long-winged bird, with a fairly long tail. It is gray-brown above, whitish beneath with pale rust flanks, and has a black throat patch and a dark brown cap and white cheeks. The Boreal Chickadee eats insects, seeds and caterpillars; in late summer and early fall, when there is an abundance of food, it stores supplies for winter among the needles or under the bark of tree branches. Since it spends most of its life in the northern forest and has not learned to fear man, the Boreal Chickadee may appear very tame.

CHESTNUT-BACKED CHICKADEE

Scientific name:	*Parus rufescens*
Length:	$4\frac{3}{4}$ inches
Habitat:	Dense wet coniferous forest, pine-oak woodland
Identification:	Small, shortish-tailed woodland bird with large head. Chestnut-brown flanks and back, whitish beneath, black throat patch and sooty-brown cap, white cheeks
Similar species:	Chestnut coloring distinctive

The smallest and most colorful North American chickadee, the Chestnut-backed inhabits damp coniferous forests along the west coast, although in California it also lives in pine-oak woods and willows next to streams. Outside the summer breeding season it tends to travel in small flocks, often with other insect-eating birds such as warblers, kinglets or juncos. It nests in a tree cavity - either a natural hole, an abandoned woodpecker nest or excavating its own in a rotten stump - lining it inside with animal fur and moss to hold 5-9 white eggs, lightly spotted with red-brown. Exact details of the incubation period and nestling habits are not known. The adult is a small, shortish-tailed bird with a relatively large head. It has chestnut-brown flanks and back and is whitish beneath, with a small black throat patch and sooty-brown cap, and white cheeks. On the central Californian coast, some birds have grayer flanks with almost no chestnut. The Chestnut-backed Chickadee forages high up in the top of conifer or deciduous trees and eats insects, seeds and berries.

TUFTED TITMOUSE *(above)*

Scientific name:	*Parus bicolor*
Length:	6½ inches
Habitat:	Deciduous woodland, mature city parks
Identification:	Stocky woodland songbird with broad tail and distinct crest. Gray above, whitish beneath with pale orange-buffy flanks, gray crest, black forehead. Some birds have black crest and pale forehead
Similar species:	Coloring is distinctive

The Tufted Titmouse is fairly common across eastern North America and often visits feeders - particularly in winter. It is usually seen in pairs or in small flocks, but will also join other small birds in winter to form mixed flocks. In the breeding season it nests in a natural tree cavity, similar hole or a nesting box, building a loose cup of moss, bark and hair at the bottom to hold its 5-8 white, brown-speckled eggs. These are incubated for about 2 weeks by the female bird and the young are ready to leave the nest and fend for themselves about 17-19 days after hatching. The adult is a stocky bird with a distinct crest, a relatively short, broad tail and a small bill. It is gray above and whitish beneath, with pale orange-buffy flanks, a gray crest and a black forehead. In parts of Texas, birds have a black crest and a pale forehead and were formerly considered a separate species, the Black-crested Titmouse. The Tufted Titmouse is an active and sociable bird. It mainly eats insects, fruit and seeds and is particularly fond of sunflower seeds.

JUNIPER TITMOUSE

Scientific name:	*Baeolophus griseus*
Length:	5¼ inches
Habitat:	Dry juniper and pinyon pine woods
Identification:	Small woodland songbird with a small crest. Gray or gray-brown, underparts lighter
Similar species:	Oak Titmouse is slightly smaller, darker and browner

When it was considered to be one species along with the Oak Titmouse, the Juniper Titmouse was known as the Plain Titmouse. Although they are extremely similar in looks, they inhabit a somewhat different range and prefer rather different habitats - as their new name suggests, the Juniper prefers juniper and pinyon pine and the Oak prefers oak woods. In the summer breeding season, both will nest in a natural tree cavity, fence post hole or a crevice in a building - although they will also accept a nesting box - building a loose cup of grass, fur and feathers at the bottom to hold 4-8 white, brown-speckled eggs. The adult is a small, plain songbird with a small crest. Its plumage is gray or gray-brown, with lighter underparts. The Juniper Titmouse is slightly larger, and its plumage is paler and grayer than the Oak. Both the Oak and Juniper titmouse are usually found singly or in pairs - they very rarely gather into flocks. They eat insects, seeds and berries.

BRIDLED TITMOUSE *(above)*

Scientific name:	*Parus wollweberi*
Length:	$5\frac{1}{4}$ inches
Habitat:	Foothill and canyon oak woods at elevations between 5000 and 7000 feet
Identification:	Small woodland songbird with a distinct crest. Gray above, whitish beneath with black and gray crest, black throat and black "bridle" on white face
Similar species:	Mountain Chickadee has similar black and white facial pattern, but lacks crest

Although its American range is limited, the Bridled Titmouse is locally common - although it is elusive and may be hard to spot. Despite its small size, it will attack much larger birds in self-defence and will also join other small birds to mob predators. In the breeding season it nests in a natural tree cavity or takes over an abandoned woodpecker hole - although it will accept a nesting box - building a loose cup of cottonwood down, plant fibers and grass at the bottom to hold its 5-8 white eggs. The adult is a small bird with a distinct crest, a relatively long tail and a short bill. It is gray above and whitish beneath, with black and gray crest, a black throat and black "bridle" on a white face. The Bridled Titmouse is an acrobatic bird, often hanging upside down from a twig to reach a tasty morsel. It mainly eats insects and small spiders.

OAK TITMOUSE

Scientific name:	*Baeolophus inornatus*
Length:	5 inches
Habitat:	Dry oak woods, wooded suburbs
Identification:	Small woodland songbird with a small crest. Gray or gray-brown, underparts lighter
Similar species:	Juniper Titmouse is slightly larger, paler and grayer

The Oak Titmouse and the Juniper Titmouse were once considered to be one species, known as the Plain Titmouse. They are very similar in looks, but inhabit a slightly different range and prefer different habitats - the Oak prefers oak woods, and the Juniper prefers juniper and pinyon pine. In the breeding season, both nest in a natural tree cavity, fence post hole or building crevice - although they will accept a nesting box - building a loose cup of grass, fur and feathers at the bottom to hold 4-8 white, brown-speckled eggs. The adult is a small, plain songbird with a small crest. Its plumage is gray or gray-brown, with lighter underparts. The Juniper Titmouse is slightly larger, and its plumage is paler and grayer. Both the Oak and Juniper titmouse are usually found singly or in pairs - they rarely gather into flocks. They eat insects, seeds and berries.

267

Bushtit

Scientific name:	*Psaltriparus minimus*
Length:	$4\frac{1}{2}$ inches
Habitat:	Deciduous woods, parks, gardens
Identification:	Small, long-tailed songbird with short stubby bill. Gray above, lighter beneath. Pacific coast birds have brown crown, some in west Texas may have black ear patch
Similar species:	Juvenile Verdin may be mistaken for Bushtit, but has shorter tail and is never seen in flocks

The Bushtit spends most of the year in flocks of up to 30 birds, flitting through the trees of deciduous woods and constantly twittering. The flocks only break up in the breeding season, when birds pair up to build a hanging, gourd-shaped nest of tightly-woven plant fiber with its entrance near the top, to hold 5-14 white eggs. These are incubated for about 11-13 days by both birds, and the young leave the nest about 2 weeks after hatching but join the parents to form a family group. The adult is a small, long-tailed bird with a short, stubby bill. It is mainly gray above and lighter beneath, but Pacific coast birds have a brown crown, and some in west Texas may have a black ear patch - they were once considered to be a separate species, the Black-eared Bushtit. The Bushtit forages in flocks, moving from one feeding spot to another in a unit. It eats insects, spiders and berries.

VERDIN *(above and right)*

Scientific name: *Auriparus flaviceps*
Length: 4½ inches
Habitat: Desert, dense thorny scrub
Identification: Small, short-tailed songbird with short sharp-pointed bill. Gray above, white beneath, bright yellow head and throat, small chestnut-red patch on shoulder often not visible
Similar species: Coloring of adult is distinctive. Juveniles lack yellow and chestnut, distinguished from similar Bushtit by shorter tail

A slender and active bird, the Verdin prefers arid country and is common in the desert areas of North America. It is usually seen alone or in pairs and sometimes visits hummingbird feeders. In the breeding season it builds a ball-shaped nest of thorny twigs in a cactus or mesquite, with its entrance at the side, to hold its 3-5 greenish, brown-spotted eggs. These are incubated for about 9-11 days and the young are ready to leave the nest and make way for a second brood about 3 weeks after hatching. The adult is a small, short-tailed bird with a short, sharp-pointed bill. It is gray above and white beneath, with a bright yellow head and throat, and a small chestnut-red patch on the shoulder, which is often not visible. The juvenile is plain gray. The Verdin feeds on insects, seeds and berries, but also takes nectar from flowers.

RED-BREASTED NUTHATCH

Scientific name:	*Sitta canadensis*
Length:	4½ inches
Habitat:	Conifer and mixed forests
Identification:	Small, short-tailed woodland bird. Blue-gray above, black cap over white eyebrow, broad black eye stripe, rusty-red breast, belly, undertail coverts. Female and juvenile slate-gray cap, paler beneath
Similar species:	Coloring is distinctive

Nuthatches climb up, down and around tree trunks and branches, using their strong legs and feet. Since they do not use the tail as a brace, they can also move head downward. The Red-breasted Nuthatch is fairly common across North America, spreading through most of the south in winter. In the summer, it prefers the conifer forests and mixed woodland of the north, nesting in an excavated tree cavity up to 100 feet above the ground, or in a nesting box. It lines the nest cavity with feathers, moss, grass and bark and lays 5-8 white, red-brown-speckled eggs. These are incubated for about 11-13 days by both adults and the young are ready to leave the nest and fend for themselves about 19-22 days after hatching. The adult is a small, short-tailed bird with a fairly long, pointed bill. It is blue-gray above, with a black cap over a white eyebrow, a broad black eye stripe, and rusty-red breast, belly and undertail coverts. The female and juvenile have a more slate-gray cap, and are paler beneath. The Red-breasted Nuthatch eats conifer seeds and insects. It stores excess food in larders and in lean years will migrate further south.

BROWN-HEADED NUTHATCH

Scientific name:	*Sitta pusilla*
Length:	4½ inches
Habitat:	Pine woodlands
Identification:	Tiny, short-tailed woodland bird with long bill. Blue-gray above, brown cap, blackish eyeline, creamy-buff beneath, white spot on nape
Similar species:	Almost identical to Pygmy Nuthatch, but ranges are different

The Brown-headed Nuthatch is usually seen in pairs or small groups, and is common in the pine woods of the southeast. It nests at the bottom of a cavity in a dead tree stump, up to 20 feet above the ground, or in a nesting box, lining the hole with plant fibers, bark strips and wood chips. It lays 4-9 white eggs, speckled and blotched with red-brown, which are incubated for about 2 weeks by both adult birds; the young are ready to leave and fend for themselves about 17 days after hatching. The adult is a tiny, short-tailed bird with a long bill. It is blue-gray above, with a brown cap, a blackish eyeline, creamy-buff underparts and a white spot on the nape that is visible at close range. The Brown-headed Nuthatch eats nuts, seeds, larvae, spiders and insects. In winter it often joins other birds to form a mixed flock that forages together.

WHITE-BREASTED NUTHATCH *(above)*

Scientific name:	*Sitta carolinensis*
Length:	5¾ inches
Habitat:	Oaks, conifers, leafy forests, mature parks
Identification:	Medium-size, short-tailed woodland bird with long, upturned bill. Blue-gray above, black crown and nape, white face, white beneath
Similar species:	The only nuthatch with a white face

The White-breasted Nuthatch prefers mature trees and is found across most of central North America, preferring leafy trees in the east and oaks and conifers in the west. It nests in an excavated or a natural tree hole up to 50 feet above the ground, or in a nesting box, lining the cavity with fur and bark chips. It lays 5-9 white eggs, with red, brown and gray spots. These are incubated for about 11-13 days by both adults and the young are ready to leave the nest and fend for themselves about 2 weeks after hatching. The adult is a medium-size, short-tailed bird with a long, slightly upturned bill. It is blue-gray above, with a black crown and nape, white face and white underparts. The White-breasted Nuthatch is inquisitive and acrobatic; like other nuthatches, when creeping down a tree it often pauses to look round with its head held upwards. It eats nuts, seeds, fruit and insects.

PYGMY NUTHATCH

Scientific name:	*Sitta pygmaea*
Length:	4¼ inches
Habitat:	Pine forest
Identification:	Tiny, short-tailed woodland bird with long bill. Blue-gray above, gray-brown cap, indistinct black eyeline, creamy-buff beneath, white spot on nape
Similar species:	Almost identical to Brown-headed Nuthatch, but ranges are different

Usually seen in small flocks, the Pygmy Nuthatch is common in the coniferous forest of the western mountains. It nests at the bottom of a cavity in a dead tree stump, up to 15 feet above the ground, or in a nesting box, lining the hole with plant down, feathers and pine cone scales. It lays 5-9 white eggs, speckled with red-brown, which are incubated for about 17 days, usually by the female; the young are ready to leave and fend for themselves about 3 weeks after hatching. The adult is a tiny, short-tailed bird with a long bill. It is blue-gray above, with a gray-brown cap, an indistinct black eyeline, creamy-buff underparts and a white spot on the nape that is only visible at close range. Like other nuthatches, the Pygmy Nuthatch eats nuts, seeds, larvae and insects and stores excess food for the following winter. Although they forage independently during the day, at night many birds will often gather to roost together in one tree cavity.

BROWN CREEPER

Scientific name:	*Certhia americana*
Length:	$5\frac{1}{4}$ inches
Habitat:	Coniferous and mixed forests, wooded swamps
Identification:	Small, slender woodland bird with long, thin, stiff tail and thin down-curved bill. Mottled brown above, whitish eyebrow, white underparts
Similar species:	Behavior makes it unmistakable

Unlike the nuthatch, the Brown Creeper uses its tail as a brace so it can only climb trees upwards, circling the trunk in a spiral from the base until it reaches the top, then flying to the base of the next. It is quite common, but easy to overlook, and although it is usually a solitary bird, it sometimes joins flocks of other birds in winter. It builds a nest of bark, moss and twigs held together with spider web, up to 15 feet above the ground and concealed behind a loose piece of bark on a conifer. It lays 4-8 white eggs, speckled with red-brown, which are incubated for about 2 weeks; the young are ready to leave and fend for themselves a further 2 weeks after hatching. The adult is a small, slender bird with a long, thin, stiff tail and thin down-curved bill. It is mottled brown above, with a whitish eyebrow and white underparts. The Brown Creeper eats spiders and insects, as well as insect eggs and larvae, which it digs out of the cracks and crevices of tree bark.

BEWICK'S WREN

Scientific name:	*Thryomanes bewickii*
Length:	$5\frac{1}{4}$ inches
Habitat:	Brushland, hedgerows, open woods, river edges
Identification:	Slender songbird with long tail. Warm brown above, white or grayish underparts, long bold white eyebrow, white outer tips to tail visible when it is fanned, unique slow sideways flicking of tail
Similar species:	Carolina Wren is richer in color, lacks white corners on tail

Common in many areas of the west, Bewick's Wren is vanishing in the east - probably because of the destruction of its preferred nesting habitat. It lives in pairs throughout the year, favouring open areas with lots of undergrowth for cover. It builds a nest of moss and leaves lined with down in a tree hole, building crevice or a nesting box, in which it lays 4-9 pinky-white eggs, speckled with brown and lilac. These are incubated for about 2 weeks by the female bird; the young are ready to leave and fend for themselves a further 2 weeks after hatching; there may be a second brood in the season. The adult is a slender bird with a long tail, which it flicks slowly sideways and up and down in a unique way. It is warm brown above with white or grayish underparts, a long, bold, white eyebrow and white tips to the outer tail feathers, visible when it is fanned. Birds in the east are richer in color. Bewick's Wren eats insects and spiders, which it extracts from crevices with its long bill.

CAROLINA WREN

Scientific name:	*Thryothorus ludovicianus*
Length:	$5\frac{1}{2}$ inches
Habitat:	Wet woodland, swamps
Identification:	Stocky, large-headed songbird with slightly down-curved bill. Rich rusty-brown above, warm buff underparts, white throat, bold white eyebrow
Similar species:	Bewick's Wren is less rich in color, has white corners on tail

The Carolina Wren is found all over southeast America and spreads north during mild weather, although populations decrease sharply after a hard winter. It lives in pairs throughout the year and is common, although usually concealed in the underbrush of wet woodland and swamps. It builds a nest of bark, grass and stems up to 10 feet above the ground in a tree hole or a nesting box, in which it lays 4-8 pinky-white eggs, speckled with brown. These are incubated for about 2 weeks by the female bird; the young are ready to leave and fend for themselves a further 2 weeks after hatching, and there may be further broods in the season. The adult is a stocky bird with a large head and a slightly down-curved bill. It is rich rusty-brown above and warm buff underneath, with a white throat and a bold white eyebrow. The Carolina Wren eats insects and spiders, and sometimes seeds or berries.

ROCK WREN

Scientific name:	*Salpinctes obsoletus*
Length:	6 inches
Habitat:	Rocky desert, arid scrubland, dry washes
Identification:	Medium-size songbird with a long bill. Finely mottled gray-brown above, cinnamon rump, pale breast with fine streaking, pale eyebrow, buffy tips to outer tail feathers
Similar species:	Distinctive within range

The Rock Wren is often seen on the ground or on a rock in arid areas, bobbing its body up and down - particularly if it is alarmed. It is fairly common in its range, and is sometimes seen further east in fall and winter. It builds a nest of weeds, grass, bark and roots, lined with hair, feathers or wool, hidden among rocks or in a crevice of a hillside or adobe building. It often builds a pathway of stones leading to the entrance, the purpose of which is not fully understood. It lays 4-7 white eggs, speckled with purple-brown, which are incubated by the female, although details are unknown.The adult is a medium-size bird with a long bill. It is finely mottled gray-brown above, with a cinnamon rump, pale breast with fine streaking, a pale eyebrow, and buffy tips to the outer tail feathers. The Rock Wren eats insects, spiders and earthworms.

CANYON WREN

Scientific name:	*Catherpes mexicanus*
Length:	$5\frac{3}{4}$ inches
Habitat:	Canyons, cliffs
Identification:	Medium-size songbird with very long bill and short, broad tail. Finely mottled brown above, chestnut rump and tail with black bars on tail, white throat and breast, finely streaked dark chestnut belly
Similar species:	Coloring distinctive

Although its range covers much of the west and it is fairly common, the Canyon Wren is elusive and hard to spot as it moves about among boulders and in cracks on canyon walls. It builds a cup-shaped nest of twigs, leaves, grass and moss, lined with hair or fur, on a ledge or hidden in a crevice of a rock, cliff or building. It lays 4-6 white eggs, finely speckled with brown, but details of the incubation and nestling periods are unknown.The adult is a medium-size bird with a very long bill and a short, broad tail. It is finely mottled brown above, with a chestnut rump and chestnut tail with black bars, a white throat and breast, and a finely streaked dark chestnut belly. The Canyon Wren eats insects and spiders, which it extracts from deep crevices in the rock with its long bill.

CACTUS WREN

Scientific name:	*Campylorhynchus brunneicapillus*
Length:	8½ inches
Habitat:	Cactus country, arid hillsides
Identification:	Large, bulky songbird with long heavy bill and rounded tail. Brown head, dark brown above streaked white, cross barring on wings and tail with white spotting on outer tail feathers, white eyebrow, dark spotting on underparts concentrated on white breast, pale rust belly
Similar species:	Sage Thrasher is grayer, lacks white eyebrow

The largest of the North American wrens, the Cactus Wren is conspicuous in the desert and other arid ground in noisy family groups. It builds a bulky ball-shaped nest of grass and twigs with an entrance at the side, placed about 10 feet above the ground in a prickly cholla cactus or spiky-leaved yucca; the nest is also used for roosting and for shelter in bad weather. It lays 4-7 pinkish eggs, heavily spotted with brown, which are incubated for about 15-17 days by the female bird; the young are ready to leave and fend for themselves about 3 weeks after hatching. The adult is a large, bulky bird with a long, heavy bill and a rounded tail. It has a brown head, a white eyebrow, is dark brown above streaked with white, with cross barring on wings and tail, white spotting on the outer tail feathers, and dark spotting on the underparts concentrated on the white breast and sparser on the pale rust belly. When foraging, the Cactus Wren searches under leaves and pebbles very carefully for insects; it also eats berries and seeds.

275

MARSH WREN

Scientific name:	*Cistothorus palustris*
Length:	5 inches
Habitat:	Dense marshland
Identification:	Small, stocky songbird with quite long bill. Brown overall, plain brown cap, black back with white stripes, lightly barred wings and tail, white eyebrow, whitish-buff underparts
Similar species:	Sedge Wren has indistinct eyebrow, streaked crown and back, heavier barred wings

Found across most of North America at different times of the year, the Marsh Wren lives in the dense reeds and cattails of marshes and swamps. It is common, but quite hard to spot as it remains well hidden in the vegetation even when it is singing. Its nest is a ball-shaped mass of cattail leaves and sedges, fastened to reed stems just above the water level in a marsh, in which it lays 5-9 brown, spotted eggs. These are incubated by the female alone for 13-17 days; the young birds leave the nest about 11-15 days after hatching. The adult is a small, stocky bird with a relatively long bill and a short, round tail. It is brown overall, with a plain brown cap, a black back with white stripes, lightly barred wings and tail, a white eyebrow, and whitish-buff underparts. Eastern birds are richer in color, western are duller. The Marsh Wren eats insects and spiders, which it takes from plants or the surface of the water.

SEDGE WREN

Scientific name:	*Cistothorus platensis*
Length:	4½ inches
Habitat:	Wet meadows, sedge marshes
Identification:	Small short-tailed songbird with short bill. Buffy-brown overall, narrow streaks on crown and back, barred wings, indistinct whitish eyebrow, buff underparts
Similar species:	Marsh Wren has bold eyebrow, plain crown, white stripes on back, plainer wings

A small, secretive bird, the Sedge Wren hides in dense grass in marshes and sedge meadows. It is locally common across the northeast in summer, spending the winter in the southeast, but is quite hard to spot. Its nest is a ball-shaped mass of grass and sedges, with an entrance at the side, built just above the water level in a marsh. It lays 3-8 white eggs, which are incubated by the female alone for around 2 weeks; the young birds leave the nest about 2 weeks after hatching. The adult is a small bird with a short bill and a short, round tail - when it is alarmed it bobs and flicks the tail upwards. It is buffy-brown overall, with bold narrow streaks on the crown and back, barred wings, an indistinct whitish eyebrow, and buff underparts. Populations of Sedge Wren may be declining, due to destruction of its preferred habitat. It eats insects and spiders.

HOUSE WREN

Scientific name:	*Troglodytes aedon*
Length:	4¾ inches
Habitat:	Scrubs, farmland, gardens, parks
Identification:	Small, slender songbird with long, slightly curved bill and short tail. Gray-brown above, cross barring on back and tail, faint eyebrow, buffy gray-brown beneath
Similar species:	Winter Wren has more prominent barring on belly and is smaller

Familiar and common across America, the House Wren is found in a variety of habitats and often visits suburban gardens. Its loud, fast, bubbling song is very musical and is heard throughout the summer. It builds a simple nest of twigs and sticks, lined with feathers, in a natural or man-made hole, or in a nesting box. It competes with other birds for a suitable nest site, sometimes throwing out the nest, eggs or chicks of its rival. It lays 5-7 white eggs, finely speckled with brown, which are incubated by the female alone for around 2 weeks; the young birds leave the nest about 2-3 weeks after hatching.The adult is a small, slender bird with a long, slightly curved bill and a short tail, which it may hold upright. It is gray-brown above, with cross barring on the back and tail, a faint eyebrow, and buffy gray-brown underparts - although some birds in the west are more rufous overall. The House Wren eats insects and spiders.

WINTER WREN

Scientific name:	*Troglodytes troglodytes*
Length:	4 inches
Habitat:	Dense brush, stream edges, wet conifer woods
Identification:	Small, slender songbird with long, thin bill and short tail. Reddish-brown overall, strong cross barring on back, tail and underparts, faint eyebrow
Similar species:	House Wren has less prominent barring on belly and is larger

The Winter Wren is found in the damp, evergreen forests of the north in summer and spreads down the west coast and into southeastern America in winter. It is hard to spot, as it creeps around in thick cover - under fallen logs, in dense underbrush and along streamside thickets. It nests in a tree cavity or among the roots of a fallen tree, lining the hole with soft moss and laying 4-7 white eggs, finely speckled with red-brown. These are incubated by the female alone for around 15-17 days; the young birds leave the nest about 2-3 weeks after hatching.The adult is a small, slender bird with a long, thin bill and a short tail, which it usually holds upright. It is reddish-brown overall with cross barring on the back, tail and underparts. Birds in the northwest are slightly larger and paler. The Winter Wren eats insects.

RUBY-CROWNED KINGLET

Scientific name: *Regulus calendula*
Length: $4\frac{1}{4}$ inches
Habitat: Woodlands, thickets
Identification: Small songbird with short, slender bill and short, slightly notched tail. Olive-green above, buffy-whitish beneath, white wing bars, incomplete white eye ring. Male has red crown, visible only when raised
Similar species: *Empidonax* flycatchers have longer tails, Hutton's Vireo is larger, has thicker bill and lacks dark area behind wing bar

The Ruby-crowned Kinglet is common in the south in winter, but may be difficult to spot in the north in summer, since it spends most of its time high in conifers. In its breeding area it builds a delicate, woven nest with high walls, made of lichens and moss and thickly lined with moss and feathers, with a small entrance at the top and suspended from the tip of a conifer branch up to 100 feet above the ground. It lays 5-11 creamy-white eggs, speckled with brown and gray, which are incubated for around 2 weeks. The adult is a small bird with a small, slender bill and a short, slightly notched tail. It is olive-green above, buffy-whitish beneath, with white wing bars and an incomplete white eye ring. The male has a red crown, which is visible only when raised. The Ruby-crowned Kinglet is less sociable than the Golden-crowned and is more often seen foraging alone, but like the other kinglet, it often flicks its wings. It eats caterpillars, spiders, insects and their larvae.

AMERICAN DIPPER

Scientific name: *Cinclus mexicanus*
Length: $7\frac{1}{2}$ inches
Habitat: Fast-flowing mountain streams
Identification: Large, stocky aquatic songbird with dark bill and quite long legs. Slate-gray overall, white eyelids seen when blinking
Similar species: The only songbird that swims

The American Dipper is only found along clear, fast-flowing, rocky streams in the west. It is solitary most of the year, and never seen in flocks or away from water. Its nest is bulky, made of grass and moss with an entrance at the side, and built among roots, in a rock crevice, under a bridge or on rocks above the water. It lays 3-6 white eggs, which are incubated by the female alone for 14-17 days; the young birds leave the nest about 21-25 days after hatching. The adult is a relatively large bird with a dark bill, short tail and quite long legs. It is slate-gray overall, with white eyelids that flash when the bird blinks. Juveniles are paler mottled beneath, and have pale edgings to the wings and a pale bill. The American Dipper flies low over the water, or jumps in to swim, dive or walk along the bottom. It eats aquatic insects and water snails.

GOLDEN-CROWNED KINGLET

Scientific name:	*Regulus satrapa*
Length:	4 inches
Habitat:	Dense coniferous woods
Identification:	Small songbird with short, slender bill and short, slightly notched tail. Olive-green above, whitish beneath, yellow crown bordered with black, white eyebrow, black eyeline, white wing bars
Similar species:	Head coloring distinctive

Although in general it much prefers conifers, the Golden-crowned Kinglet is also found in mixed woodland in winter, foraging in flocks with other small birds. It has been helped by the advent of conifer plantations - when the mature trees are harvested, the birds can move on to a new plantation home. In its breeding area it builds a delicate nest with high walls, made of lichens and moss and thickly lined with moss and feathers, with a small entrance at the top and suspended from twigs up to 100 feet above the ground in a conifer. It lays 5-11 gray-white eggs, heavily spotted with brown and lilac, which are incubated for around 2 weeks. The adult is a small bird with a short, slender bill and a short, slightly notched tail. It is olive-green above, whitish beneath, with a yellow crown bordered with black, a white eyebrow, black eyeline, and white wing bars. The male has a central orange area to the yellow crown. The Golden-crowned Kinglet is an acrobatic bird that often hangs upside down to feed, hopping among the branches and flicking its wings while foraging; it eats insects and their larvae.

ARCTIC WARBLER

Scientific name:	*Phylloscopus borealis*
Length:	5 inches
Habitat:	Grassy tundra, birch woods and willow thickets
Identification:	Medium-size Arctic bird with square tail. Olive-green above, dark eye line, greenish-yellow eyebrow, whitish throat and belly, olive-gray sides, indistinct single wing bar
Similar species:	Closely resembles Tennessee Warbler but their ranges do not overlap

The Arctic Warbler is not related to American warblers; it comes from a large family of very similar colored Old World warblers. Its ancestors came from the Asian mainland after the last glacial age and it is now very common in western Alaska during the summer months, also ranging across Siberia and as far as Norway, but returning to southern Asia in the winter. It prefers birch woods and dense willow thickets along rivers, but nests on grassy Arctic tundra, building a domed, cup nest on the ground to hold its 5-7 white, pink-speckled eggs. The adult is a medium-size bird with a square tail and pale, straw-colored legs and feet. It is olive-green above, with a broad, dark eye line, a pale greenish-yellow eyebrow, a whitish throat and belly, olive-gray sides and a single indistinct wing bar. Both male and female have the same coloring. Like other warblers, the Arctic Warbler mostly eats insects.

BLACK-TAILED GNATCATCHER

Scientific name:	*Polioptila melanura*
Length:	4 inches
Habitat:	Desert, mesquite brush, open flats
Identification:	Small gnatcatcher with short, thin bill and rounded wings. Gray above, white beneath, long black tail with white tips to outer feathers so tail looks black with white spots from beneath, narrow white eye ring, thin white edging to secondary wing feathers. Male has black crown in summer
Similar species:	In winter the species of gnatcatcher can look very similar, but the Blue-gray has a tail that is mostly white when seen from beneath

The Black-tailed Gnatcatcher is a desert bird, which prefers dense mesquite brush, dry washes and open flats. It is fairly common within its limited North American range. It builds a small, cup-shaped nest of grass, bark and plant fibers in mesquite, a desert bush or a low tree. It lays 4-6 pale blue eggs, spotted with brown, which are incubated for about 2 weeks by both adult birds; the young are independent around 9-12 days after hatching. The adult is a small bird with a short, thin bill and rounded wings. It is gray above and white beneath, with a narrow white eye ring, thin white edging to the secondary wing feathers and a long black tail that has white tips to the outer feathers so it looks black with white spots from beneath. The male has a black crown in the breeding period. The female is slightly less gray and more brownish. The Black-tailed Gnatcatcher eats spiders and insects.

Blue-gray Gnatcatcher

Scientific name:	*Polioptila caerulea*
Length:	4¼ inches
Habitat:	Leafy woodlands, thickets
Identification:	Small long-tailed gnatcatcher with long, pale bill and rather pointed wings. Blue-gray above, white beneath, long black tail with white outer feathers so tail looks white from beneath, narrow white eye ring, white edging to secondary wing feathers. Male has black eyebrow in summer
Similar species:	In winter the species of gnatcatcher can look very similar, but the Black-tailed has a tail that is mostly black when seen from beneath

In the east, the Blue-gray Gnatcatcher lives high in leafy trees in summer, but in the west it tends to be found lower in oaks and junipers. It is quite common in both areas, but is perhaps easier to spot at lower levels. It builds a tiny, woven nest of grass, bark and plant fibers, camouflaged on the outside with pieces of lichen, on the branch of a tree up to 70 feet above the ground. It lays 4 or 5 pale blue eggs, sometimes spotted with brown, which are incubated for about 2 weeks by both adult birds; the young are ready to be independent around 9-12 days after hatching. The adult is a small bird with a long tail, a long, pale bill and rather pointed wings. It is blue-gray above and white beneath, with a narrow white eye ring, white edging to the secondary wing feathers and a long black tail that has white outer feathers so it looks white from beneath. The male has a black eyebrow in the breeding period. The female is slightly less blue and more gray. The Blue-gray Gnatcatcher is a very lively bird that constantly flicks its tail upward as it forages for spiders and insects.

281

VARIED THRUSH

Scientific name:	*Ixoreus naevius*
Length:	$9\frac{1}{2}$ inches
Habitat:	Dense wet woods, conifer forest
Identification:	Large, long-necked songbird with short tail. Slate-gray above, rust-orange eyebrow, throat and breast, broad slate-black breast band, whitish belly. Buff wingstripe seen in flight
Similar species:	Plumage distinctive

Within its limited North American range, the Varied Thrush is common. It prefers dense, wet woodland - particularly coniferous forests - but is a fairly shy and elusive bird. It nests in trees, building a large, sturdy cup of stems, twigs, leaves and mud, lined with moss, to hold its 3-5 pale blue, brown-spotted eggs. These are incubated by the female bird for about 2 weeks. The adult is a large, long-necked bird with a short tail. It is slate-gray above, with a rust-orange eyebrow, throat and breast, a broad slate-black breast band and a whitish belly. The female is paler and juveniles lack the breast band and are speckled beneath with a whitish belly. In flight, all birds show a distinctive buff wingstripe. The Varied Thrush mostly stays hidden in trees and undergrowth, although it does forage in open areas for earthworms. It also eats insects, spiders, nuts, seeds and fruit.

WOOD THRUSH

Scientific name:	*Hylocichla mustelina*
Length:	$7\frac{3}{4}$ inches
Habitat:	Wet woodland, shady suburbs
Identification:	Stocky, short-tailed songbird. Red-brown above, rump and tail browner, whitish beneath with large dark spots, large dark eye, white eye ring, streaked face
Similar species:	Brown Thrasher has striped, rather than spotted breast, yellow eyes, longer tail

The largest of the spotted thrushes, the Wood Thrush is found in leafy and mixed woodland across the east in summer; migrating south in fall. Although it is still fairly common, numbers have been decreasing. It nests up to 50 feet above the ground in a tree, building a sturdy and compact cup of grass, twigs and mud, lined with moss, in which it lays 2-5 bluish-green eggs. These are incubated by the female for around 2 weeks; the young are ready to leave the nest about 12-14 days after hatching. The adult is a stocky, short-tailed bird with a rather rounded belly and a relatively large bill. Its plumage is red-brown above, browner towards the rump and tail, whitish beneath with large, round, dark spots, and it has a large dark eye, a white eye ring, and a streaked face. The Wood Thrush forages on the ground in thick undergrowth, looking for berries, insects, spiders and earthworms. It is popular with gardeners as it eats a range of garden pests.

AMERICAN ROBIN

Scientific name: *Turdus migratorius*
Length: 10 inches
Habitat: Woodland, swamps, urban parks and gardens
Identification: Large, sturdy songbird with long legs and tail. Gray-brown above, white throat, red-orange breast, blackish head and tail, yellow bill
Similar species: Plumage distinctive

Common and widespread, the American Robin is one of the best-known American birds and is often seen in suburban gardens. In

summer it spreads right up into Canada and the far north, but it is found all year round across most of America. It nests in shrubs, trees or on buildings, building a sturdy cup of roots, twigs and mud, lined with soft material, to hold its 3 or 4 blue eggs. These are incubated by the female bird, with the young leaving the nest around 2-3 weeks after hatching. The adult is a large, sturdy bird with long legs and tail. It is gray-brown above, with a white throat, red-orange breast, yellow bill and a blackish head and tail. The female is duller and juveniles lack the red breast and are spotted beneath. The American Robin often forages on lawns with its head held cocked, looking for earthworms; it also eats insects and berries.

SWAINSON'S THRUSH

Scientific name:	*Catharus ustulatus*
Length:	7 inches
Habitat:	Wet cool woodland, swamps
Identification:	Slender plain songbird. Olive-brown above, white belly, pale olive-brown flanks, dark spotting on buff breast, buff eye ring
Similar species:	All the *catharus* thrushes are very similar, mainly told apart by range and song

Fairly common across the north and west in summer, Swainson's Thrush is found in dense, moist woodland and swamps. It migrates south in fall, flying at night and feeding and resting in the day, to spend the winter in South America. In its breeding area it nests low down in a coniferous tree, building a tight cup of leaves, twigs and roots, lined with moss. It lays 3-5 blue eggs, spotted with buff-brown, which are incubated for around 10-14 days; the young are ready to leave the nest about 2 weeks after hatching. The adult is a slender, plain bird; its song is clear and fluty, rising up the scale in a series of notes, and its call a soft *whit*. Its plumage is olive-brown above, with a white belly, pale olive-brown flanks, dark spotting on a buff breast and a buff eye ring. Western birds are much more reddish-brown, with fainter spotting on the breast. Swainson's Thrush forages in shady undergrowth for berries, insects, spiders and earthworms.

GRAY-CHEEKED THRUSH
(above)

Scientific name:	*Catharus minimus*
Length:	$7\frac{1}{4}$ inches
Habitat:	Coniferous and mixed woodland
Identification:	Large, long-winged songbird. Olive-brown above, white beneath, olive-gray flanks, paler round eye, pale gray face and throat, heavy spotting on breast
Similar species:	All the *catharus* thrushes are very similar, mainly told apart by range and song

The Gray-cheeked Thrush is found in the mixed and coniferous forests of the far north in summer, and migrates across east and central America to spend the winter in Central and South America. It may be hard to spot, as it is a shy bird that keeps mostly under cover. In its breeding area, it nests near the ground in a bush or low in a tree, building a neat cup of grass, leaves, bark and mud. It lays 3-5 pale greeny-blue eggs, lightly dotted with brown, which are incubated for about 2 weeks by the female; the young are ready to leave the nest about 10-14 days after hatching. The adult is a long-winged bird; its song is a nasal *vee-oh vee vee vee-oh* and its call *veeyah*. Its plumage is olive-brown above and white beneath, with olive-gray flanks, a paler area round the eye, a pale gray face and throat, and heavy spotting on the breast. The Grey-cheeked Thrush searches for berries, insects, spiders and earthworms on the ground.

HERMIT THRUSH

Scientific name:	*Catharus guttatus*
Length:	$6\frac{3}{4}$ inches
Habitat:	Coniferous and mixed woodland
Identification:	Stocky, short-winged songbird. Olive-brown above, reddish tail, whitish belly, pale olive-gray flanks, black-brown spotting on buff breast, white eye ring
Similar species:	All the *catharus* thrushes are very similar, mainly told apart by range and song

In summer, the Hermit Thrush is found in coniferous and mixed woodland across the north; it spends the winter in the south and down into Mexico. It is widespread and common, but spends much of its time in dense undergrowth. In its breeding area it nests on or just above the ground, building a neat cup of grass, leaves and rootlets, lined with moss, in which it lays 3-5 bluish-green eggs. These are incubated by the female for around 12-14 days; the young are ready to leave the nest about 10-12 days after hatching. The adult is a stocky, short-winged bird; its song is loud and slow, with similar phrases repeated moving up and down the scale, and its call a soft *chup*. Its plumage is olive-brown above, with a reddish tail, whitish belly, pale olive-gray flanks, black-brown spotting on a buff breast and a white eye ring. The Hermit Thrush forages on the ground in dense cover for berries, insects, spiders and earthworms.

TOWNSEND'S SOLITAIRE

Scientific name:	*Myadestes townsendi*
Length:	8½ inches
Habitat:	Mountain coniferous forests, valleys, juniper woods
Identification:	Large, slender, long-tailed songbird with short bill and small head. Gray overall, slightly darker above, bold white eye ring, white outer tail feathers, pale rusty-buff wing patch
Similar species:	Mockingbird lacks eye ring and buffy wing patch, perches less upright

As its name implies, Townsend's Solitaire is never found in flocks. It is actually a member of the thrush family that prefers to live in mountainous woodland - although there are other mountain-forest thrushes in the New World, this is the only one found in North America. It may move to lower elevations during the winter and is sometimes even seen in desert oases. It nests on the ground, either among tree roots, in a shallow hole in a bank or in a crevice of a rock, building a large, loose cup of weeds, grass and rootlets. It lays 3 or 4 gray-white eggs, with brown speckles concentrated at the larger rounded end and tailing off towards the point. The adult is a large, slender, long-tailed bird with a short bill and a small head. Its plumage is gray overall, slightly darker above, and it has a bold white eye ring, white outer tail feathers, and a pale rusty-buff wing patch. The juvenile is mottled gray and white. Townsend's Solitaire forages on the ground for berries and insects, but will also eat spiders and pine nuts.

VEERY

Scientific name:	*Catharus fuscescens*
Length:	7 inches
Habitat:	Dense wet woods, streamside thickets
Identification:	Slender plain songbird. Tawny-brown above, white belly, pale gray flanks, pale buff face and throat, pale spotting on breast
Similar species:	All the *catharus* thrushes are very similar, they are mainly told apart by their range and differences in their song

A rather secretive bird that lives in dense shade, the Veery is common in moist, leafy woods in the northeast in summer, but is somewhat rarer in the west. It is usually very hard to spot, as it slips away through the undergrowth upon any close approach. It migrates at night across much of the east to spend the winter in South America. In its breeding area, it nests on or very near the ground, either at the base of a bush or among weeds, building a tight cup of leaves, stems and grass. It lays 3-5 pale blue eggs, which are incubated for around 9-12 days, and the young are ready to leave the nest about 9-10 days after hatching. The adult is a slender, plain bird; its song is a descending whistled *veer* and its call a soft *veeyew*. Its plumage is tawny-brown above, with a white belly, pale gray flanks, a pale buff face and throat, and pale spotting on the breast. Western birds are duller, with more spotting on the breast. The Veery mainly forages on the ground, for berries, insects, spiders and earthworms.

MOUNTAIN BLUEBIRD

Scientific name:	*Sialia currucoides*
Length:	7¼ inches
Habitat:	High open country, mountain meadows
Identification:	Medium-size songbird with long tail and wings. Male sky blue, lighter blue breast, white belly. Female gray with brown tint, blue wash on wings, rump and tail, white belly
Similar species:	Pale blue of male is distinctive, Indigo Bunting is darker blue with thicker bill. Female has longer wings and tail than other bluebirds

The Mountain Bluebird prefers open areas at higher altitude in summer, as long as there are stands of trees nearby for cover. In the winter it will come lower down, and also migrates further south. It nests in a natural cavity, woodpecker hole or will even use a nesting box, lining the bottom of its chosen site with grass, bark chips and feathers. It lays 4-6 pale blue-green eggs, which are incubated for around 2 weeks. The adult is slightly more slender than other bluebirds, with a longer tail and wings. The male is sky blue with a lighter blue breast and a white belly. The female is gray with a brown tint, and has a blue wash on wings, rump and tail and a white belly; some have a rufous wash on the throat and breast. The juvenile is similar to the female, but is spotted beneath. The Mountain Bluebird often hovers low over the ground, or darts out from a branch to catch insects and spiders. In fall and winter it also eats berries.

WESTERN BLUEBIRD

Scientific name:	*Sialia mexicana*
Length:	7 inches
Habitat:	Woodlands, farmland, open country
Identification:	Stocky, short-tailed songbird with stout bill and short wings. Male deep blue above, blue throat, chestnut breast and flanks, blue-grayish belly and undertail coverts. Female brownish-gray above, throat gray, breast and flanks washed chestnut
Similar species:	Eastern Bluebird has chestnut throat and white belly, Lazuli Bunting has two white wing bars and thicker bill

Widespread and quite common across much of the west, the Western Bluebird often gathers in large flocks in winter. It nests in a natural cavity or woodpecker hole up to 40 feet above the ground, lining the bottom with a loose cup of grass. It lays 4-6 pale blue eggs, which are incubated by the female for around 2 weeks; the young are independent about 3 weeks after hatching. The adult is a stocky, short-tailed bird with a stout bill and short wings. The male is deep blue above, with a blue throat, chestnut breast and flanks, and a blue-grayish belly and undertail coverts. The female is brownish-gray above, with a plain gray throat and breast and flanks washed chestnut. The juvenile is very similar to the female, but is grayer with speckling beneath. The Western Bluebird eats insects and spiders in summer, but in fall and winter turns to berries.

EASTERN BLUEBIRD

Scientific name:	*Sialia sialis*
Length:	7 inches
Habitat:	Open woodland, farmland, parks, forest edge
Identification:	Stocky, short-tailed songbird with stout bill and short wings. Deep blue above, chestnut throat, sides of neck, breast and flanks, white belly and undertail coverts. Female is grayer
Similar species:	Western Bluebird has blue throat and blue-gray belly

Found in small groups in open country, often perched on wires or fence posts, the Eastern Bluebird was once in decline due to competition with other birds for suitable nesting sites. Specially-designed nesting boxes have reversed this trend and it will use these, or a natural cavity or woodpecker hole, lining the bottom with a loose cup-shape made of grass and plant stems. It lays 2-7 pale blue-white eggs, which are incubated by the female for around 2 weeks; the young are independent about 3 weeks after hatching. The adult is a stocky, short-tailed bird with a stout bill and short wings. It is deep blue above, with a chestnut throat, sides of neck, breast and flanks, and a white belly and undertail coverts. The female is grayer, the juvenile brownish and heavily spotted, but with a trace of blue above. The Eastern Bluebird eats insects, spiders and berries and will also visit bird feeders.

WRENTIT

Scientific name:	*Chamaea fasciata*
Length:	6½ inches
Habitat:	Coniferous brushland, dense thickets, chaparral
Identification:	Small, long-tailed songbird with large head and stout bill. Overall brown, streaked breast, white eyes
Similar species:	Only bird of its kind

The Wrentit is part of an Old World family, and is the only bird of its kind in North America. It is only found along the west coast, where it is common in chaparral and coniferous brushland, but as it hides in the undergrowth it may be difficult to spot. It nests in dense shrubs, building a neat and compact cup of plant fiber and bark, held together with spider web, to hold its 3-5 pale greenish-blue eggs. These are incubated by the female bird for about 1 week; the young birds are ready to leave the nest around 15-17 days after they have hatched. The adult is a small bird with a large head, stout bill and a long tail that it usually holds upright. It is brown overall, with a dark streaked breast and distinctive white eyes. Birds in the north are redder, while those in the south are a more gray-brown. The Wrentit mates for life and stays very much in the same area, being reluctant to cross open spaces. It eats insects, spiders and berries.

GRAY CATBIRD

Scientific name:	*Dumetella carolinensis*
Length:	8½ inches
Habitat:	Woodland thickets, dense garden shrubs
Identification:	Slender, long-tailed songbird. Overall slate-gray, black cap, chestnut-red under tail
Similar species:	Coloring is distinctive

Very common in the east in summer, the Gray Catbird is rarely found west of the Rockies. Its call sounds like the mewing of a cat, hence its name, and it is often found in suburban gardens as well as in dense woodland thickets. It nests fairly low down in a tree or dense shrub, building a rough cup of twigs and stems, lined with rootlets, to hold its 3-5 bluish-green eggs. These are incubated by the female bird for about 12-14 days; the young birds are ready to leave the nest around 9-15 days later. The adult is a slender bird with a long tail that it often holds upright, and is slate-gray overall, with a black cap and chestnut-red under the tail. The Gray Catbird is an excellent mimic, copying all the birdsongs in the area and adding its own shrieks and whistles. It forages on the ground for insects, either in dense cover or out in the open, and also eats berries in late summer and fall.

NORTHERN MOCKINGBIRD

Scientific name: *Mimus polyglottos*
Length: 10 inches
Habitat: Woodland, urban gardens, desert, farmland
Identification: Slender, long-tailed songbird with long legs and short
                       bill. Gray above, white beneath, two white wing bars.
                       In flight, tail is black with white outer feathers, large
                       white wing patch
Similar species: Coloring and shape are distinctive

A bird that prefers warmer climates, the Northern Mockingbird is found across the south - its name comes because there are other mockingbirds in the Southern Hemisphere. It nests low down in a

tree or shrub, building a cup of twigs lined with soft plant fibers, to hold its 3-5 blue-green eggs. These are incubated by the female bird for about 12-13 days; the young birds are ready to leave the nest around 9-12 days later. The adult is a slender bird with a long tail that it often flicks sideways. It is gray above and white beneath, with two white wing bars. In flight, its tail is black with white outer feathers, and it flashes large white wing patches. It is an excellent mimic, not only copying birdsongs but also the sound of cars, machinery and sirens. The Northern Mockingbird is very territorial and defends its ground aggressively. It likes open grassy areas for feeding, with nearby foliage to hide its nest, and perches for the male to sing and warn off intruders - so suburban gardens are an ideal habitat. It eats insects, spiders and berries; often flashing its wings while foraging on the ground - possibly to scare insects out of hiding.

BENDIRE'S THRASHER

Scientific name:	*Toxostoma bendirei*
Length:	9¾ inches
Habitat:	Open farmland, grassland, brushy desert
Identification:	Medium-size, plain, long-tailed songbird. Light gray-brown overall, lighter beneath, arrow-shaped spots on breast, yellow eyes, white corners to tail
Similar species:	Curve-billed Thrasher has longer, darker, more down-curved bill, orange-yellow eyes, but juvenile can look almost identical

Numerous in some areas, uncommon in others, Bendire's Thrasher is found in North America only in the desert scrub of the southwest. In winter it moves slightly south, but in summer it spreads right up to southern Utah and Colorado. It nests just above the ground in a desert bush, small tree or cactus, building a cup of sticks, lined with soft material, to hold its 3 or 4 pale greenish eggs, spotted with buff. The adult is a medium-size bird with a longish, slightly down-curved bill and a long tail. It is light gray-brown above, paler beneath, with arrow-shaped spots on the breast, yellow eyes and white corners to the tail. Unlike other thrashers, which rarely fly, Bendire's flies from bush to bush. However, it still forages on the ground for caterpillars, beetles and insects.

LONG-BILLED THRASHER

Scientific name:	*Toxostoma longirostre*
Length:	11½ inches
Habitat:	Dense thickets, woodland edges
Identification:	Large, long-billed songbird with long wings. Gray-brown above, whitish beneath with thin, dark streaks, two white wing bars, white outer corners to tail, orange eyes
Similar species:	Brown Thrasher has shorter bill, yellow eyes, is redder above

The Long-billed Thrasher is a Mexican bird that is only found in North America in southern Texas, where it lives in dense thickets. It is most likely to be seen in the breeding season, when it sings from a high, open perch. It nests just above the ground in a dense thicket or cactus, building a tight cup of thorny twigs, lined with soft material, to hold its 2-5 bluish-green, red-brown-speckled eggs. The adult is a rather large bird with a long, down-curved bill and long wings. It is gray-brown above, whitish beneath with thin, dark streaks, and has two white wing bars, white outer corners to the tail, and orange eyes. The Long-billed Thrasher forages on the ground, turning over leaves and other debris with its bill to find insects, spiders and berries.

BROWN THRASHER

Scientific name:	*Toxostoma rufum*
Length:	11½ inches
Habitat:	Hedgerows, brush, woodland, thickets
Identification:	Large, short-billed songbird with long, pointed wings. Bright red-brown above, buffy beneath with thin, dark streaks, two white wing bars, white outer corners to tail, yellow eyes
Similar species:	Long-billed Thrasher has longer bill, orange eyes, is grayer above. Wood Thrush has spotted rather than striped breast, dark eyes, shorter tail

Spreading across most of the east in summer, the Brown Thrasher lives in hedgerows, brush and thickets - often near humans. Although it is declining it is still quite common within its range, and some birds are seen all year round in the southeast - it is often noticed singing from treetops in the breeding season. It nests on the ground or in a dense brush pile or thicket, building a well-hidden, bulky cup of twigs, leaves and grass to hold its 2-4 bluish-white, brown-speckled eggs. These are incubated by both birds for up to 2 weeks, and the young are ready to leave the nest some 2 weeks later. The adult is a large bird with a short bill and long, pointed wings. It is bright red-brown above, buffy beneath with thin, dark streaks, and has two white wing bars, white outer corners to the tail, and yellow eyes. The Brown Thrasher forages on the ground, scattering leaves by moving its bill from side to side as it searches for insects, spiders and berries.

SAGE THRASHER

Scientific name:	*Oreoscoptes montanus*
Length:	8½ inches
Habitat:	Sagebrush flats, juniper woods
Identification:	Small, short-billed songbird with long wings. Gray-brown above, whitish beneath with heavy brown streaking, two white wing bars, white outer feathers to tail, yellow eyes
Similar species:	Faded summer plumage resembles Bendire's Thrasher, which is less streaked beneath

Found on sagebrush flats in the west in summer, the Sage Thrasher spends the winter in juniper woods in the south. It nests on the ground or well-hidden in dense brush, building a bulky cup of twigs, stems and sage leaves to hold its 4 or 5 glossy blue, boldly brown-spotted eggs. These are incubated by both birds, but details are unknown. The adult is a small bird with a short bill and long wings. It is gray-brown above, whitish beneath with heavy brown streaking, and has two white wing bars, white outer feathers to the tail, and yellow eyes. The Sage Thrasher sometimes mimics other birds, but also warbles its own sweet song. It usually flies low above the ground, but will also run from bush to bush instead. It sometimes eats fruit in gardens, but also takes spiders and forages on the ground for the insects that damage crops.

CALIFORNIA THRASHER *(above)*

Scientific name:	*Toxostoma redivivum*
Length:	12 inches
Habitat:	Chaparral, brushy foothills
Identification:	Large, long-tailed songbird with long, black, deeply down-curved bill. Dark brown above, pale throat, light gray-brown breast, buffy-cinnamon belly and undertail coverts, dark brown eyes, pale eyebrow, dark cheek, buffy corners to tail
Similar species:	Crissal Thrasher is lighter overall

The California Thrasher is only found in chaparral and brushy foothills along the west coast, but is fairly common within its limited range. It can be difficult to spot as it tends to stay under cover in dense thickets, but it comes out in the open to sing - often for long periods. It nests in a low shrub or a tree, building a bowl of sticks and roots, lined with softer material, to hold its 2-4 pale blue-green, speckled eggs. These are incubated by both birds for 2 weeks, with the young leaving the nest a further 2 weeks after hatching. The adult is a large bird with a long tail and a long, black, deeply down-curved bill. It is dark brown above, with a pale throat, light gray-brown breast, buffy-cinnamon belly and undertail coverts, buffy corners to the tail and has dark brown eyes with a pale eyebrow and a dark cheek. The California Thrasher is an excellent mimic. It forages on the ground under bushes, using its strong bill to turn the soil and toss aside debris as it searches for insects, spiders, seeds and berries. If spotted, it scurries under cover rather than flying away.

CRISSAL THRASHER

Scientific name:	*Toxostoma crissale*
Length:	11½ inches
Habitat:	Dense mesquite, streamside willows, desert washes
Identification:	Large, long-tailed songbird with long, black, deeply down-curved bill. Brown above, light gray-brown underneath, chestnut-brown undertail coverts, yellow-brown eyes, pale throat, dark mustache mark, buffy corners to tail
Similar species:	California Thrasher is darker overall

Although the Crissal Thrasher strongly resembles the California, their ranges do not overlap. The Crissal is found in southeast California, spreading further east through Utah to west Texas and south down into Mexico. It is fairly common but secretive and elusive, staying hidden in mesquite thickets and other dense growth and rarely coming into the open. It nests in dense mesquite or other thick shrubs, building a large bowl of twigs, lined with softer material, to hold its 2-4 pale blue-green eggs. These are incubated by both birds for about 2 weeks, with the young leaving the nest 11-13 days after hatching. The adult is a large bird with a long tail and a long, black, deeply down-curved bill. It is brown above and light gray-brown beneath, with a pale throat, chestnut-brown undertail coverts, buffy corners to the tail, yellow-brown eyes and a dark mustache mark. The Crissal Thrasher very rarely flies but forages on the ground under cover, using its strong bill to turn the soil and toss aside leaves as it searches for insects, spiders and berries.

CURVE-BILLED THRASHER

Scientific name:	*Toxostoma curvirostre*
Length:	11 inches
Habitat:	Canyons, arid brush, desert
Identification:	Large, plain, long-tailed songbird with long, black, down-curved bill. Light gray-brown overall, lighter beneath, round spots on breast, orange-yellow eyes, white corners to tail, narrow white wing bars
Similar species:	Bendire's Thrasher has shorter, paler, less down-curved bill, yellow eyes. Juvenile Curve-billed has shorter bill and can look almost identical to Bendire's

Common in the cactus deserts of the south and down into Mexico, the Curve-billed Thrasher can often be seen out in the open and is a permanent resident within its range. It nests up to 12 feet above the ground in a cholla cactus - or sometimes a tree - building a woven cup of thorny twigs, lined with soft material, to hold its 2-4 pale blue-green, spotted eggs. The adult is a large, rather plain bird with a long tail and a long, black, down-curved bill. It is light gray-brown above, paler beneath, with round spots on the breast, orange-yellow eyes, white corners to the tail and two narrow white wing bars. The juvenile has a shorter, straighter bill and more obvious spots on the upper breast. The Curve-billed Thrasher forages on the ground, tossing aside debris as it searches for insects, seeds and berries.

AMERICAN PIPIT

Scientific name:	*Anthus rubescens*
Length:	$6\frac{1}{2}$ inches
Habitat:	Tundra, mountains, open fields, mudflats
Identification:	Slender, long-tailed, long-legged songbird. Breeding plumage gray-brown above, buffy with faint streaking below, browner in winter, with heavier streaking. Dark bill and legs, white outer tail feathers
Similar species:	Slender bill, long legs and bobbing tail distinguish it from similar-colored birds

The American Pipit is common and widespread, spending the summer on tundra in the north and the winter on open fields and beaches in the south. It nests on the ground, lining a cavity with a soft cup of grass and hair to hold its 3-7 whitish, brown-blotched eggs. These are incubated for about 2 weeks by the female, and the young are ready to leave the nest around 2 weeks after hatching. The adult is a slender bird with long legs and a relatively long tail, which it wags up and down. In the breeding season it is gray-brown above and buffy with faint streaking below, in winter it is browner with heavier streaking. In all plumages it has a dark bill, dark legs sometimes tinged pink, and white outer tail feathers. The American Pipit lives in flocks for most of the year and walks, rather than hopping. It eats insects, spiders and small snails.

EUROPEAN STARLING

Scientific name:	*Sturnus vulgaris*
Length:	$8\frac{1}{2}$ inches
Habitat:	Urban areas, farmland, orchards
Identification:	Chunky, short-tailed bird with straight, pointed bill. Breeding plumage black with iridescent green-purple gloss, yellow bill, duller and speckled white in winter with darker bill
Similar species:	Size, coloring and habits distinctive

Perhaps the most abundant bird in North America, the European Starling is not a native bird but was introduced from the Old World in 1890. It nests in holes in trees or buildings, often displacing other birds, lining the cavity with a soft cup of grass and other soft material to hold its 5 or 6 pale blue eggs. These are incubated by both birds for about 11-14 days, with the young leaving the nest 3 weeks after hatching. The adult is a chunky bird with a short, square tail and a thin, straight, pointed bill. In the breeding season it is black with an iridescent green-purple gloss and has a yellow bill, in winter it is duller and speckled white, with a darker bill. The juvenile is gray-brown, with paler underparts. The European Starling competes with native birds, steals grain and fruit and fouls city streets. However, it also eats many of the insect pests that would otherwise damage crops.

CEDAR WAXWING

Scientific name:	*Bombycilla cedrorum*
Length:	$7\frac{1}{4}$ inches
Habitat:	Trees with wild berries
Identification:	Round-bodied, short-tailed songbird with crested head. Brown-gray above, yellow beneath, white undertail coverts, yellow and white wing markings, red spot on wing, yellow tip to tail, black face mask edged white, black chin
Similar species:	Bohemian Waxwing is grayer, has chestnut under tail, gray belly

Like the Bohemian, the Cedar Waxwing is a very sociable bird and is almost always seen in quite large flocks, except when the birds pair up to breed. It is found across most of North America during various times of the year, but flocks will move around a great deal in winter in search of berries. In its breeding area it builds a loose nest of twigs, grass and lichens, lined with moss and woven onto a horizontal branch up to 50 feet above the ground. It lays 3-6 blue-gray eggs, which are incubated for 12-14 days; the young birds are ready to start fending for themselves about 17-19 days later. The adult is a rather round-bodied bird, with a short tail and a crested head. Its plumage is brown-gray above and yellow beneath, with a black face mask edged with white, a black chin, white undertail coverts, yellow and white wing markings with a red spot on each wing, and a yellow tip to the tail. Juvenile birds are similar in general coloring but are streaky beneath. The Cedar Waxwing is particularly fond of berries, but it will also eat flying insects and flower petals.

PHAINOPEPLA

Scientific name:	*Phainopepla nitens*
Length:	7¾ inches
Habitat:	Desert, mesquite brushland
Identification:	Slender, long-tailed songbird with rounded wings and ragged crest. Male glossy black, white wing patch only seen in flight. Female gray, with pale edges to wing feathers, pale wing patch. Both birds have red eyes
Similar species:	Shape and coloring distinctive

Only found in North America in the southwest, the Phainopepla is a tropical bird that prefers a hot climate and open country so it tends to inhabit desert scrub areas. It builds a shallow nest of plant fibers up to 50 feet above the ground in a tree, in which it lays 2-4 whitish-green eggs, speckled with brown and black. These are incubated for around 2 weeks by both adults and the young birds are ready to start fending for themselves about 17-19 days later. The adult is a slender bird, with a long tail, rounded wings and a ragged crest. The male is glossy black, but has a white wing patch that is only seen in flight. The female is gray, with pale edges to the wing feathers and a pale wing patch. Both birds have red eyes. Juvenile birds are similar to the female, but have browner eyes. The Phainopepla lives mostly on mistletoe berries, so can be found wherever the desert mistletoe grows. Since they are seasonal, it also eats flying insects.

BOHEMIAN WAXWING

Scientific name:	*Bombycilla garrulus*
Length:	8¼ inches
Habitat:	Open coniferous and mixed woods, spruce forest, bogs
Identification:	Round-bodied, short-tailed songbird with crested head. Cinnamon-gray above, gray beneath, chestnut undertail coverts, yellow and white wing markings, red spot on wing, yellow tip to tail, black face mask edged white, black chin
Similar species:	Cedar Waxwing is browner, lacks chestnut under tail, yellow belly

A bird of the far northwest, the Bohemian Waxwing is very sociable and is almost always seen in flocks. Although it usually spends the summer in boreal forests and the edge of the taiga and winters in the prairie provinces, it is sometimes seen in large numbers much further afield - possibly due to food shortages in its normal range. In its breeding area it builds a twiggy nest, lined with moss, high in a conifer to hold its 4-6 bluish eggs. These are incubated for 12-14 days and the young birds are ready to start fending for themselves about 2 weeks later. The adult is a rather round-bodied bird, with a short tail and a crested head. Its plumage is cinnamon-gray above and plain gray beneath, with a black face mask edged with white, a black chin, chestnut undertail coverts, yellow and white wing markings with a red spot on each wing, and a yellow tip to the tail. Juvenile birds are similar in general coloring but are streaky beneath. The Bohemian Waxwing mainly eats insects and berries.

GOLDEN-WINGED WARBLER

Scientific name: *Vermivora chrysoptera*
Length: 4¾ inches
Habitat: Woodland edges, overgrown pasture, swamps, second-growth woods
Identification: Small, short-tailed woodland bird with slender bill. Male blue-gray above, bright yellow crown, black throat, whitish-gray underparts, black ear patch edged white, blue-gray wings, yellow wing patch. Female duller
Similar species: Interbreeds with Blue-winged Warbler, so many intermediate color variations

Much less common than the Blue-winged, the Golden-winged Warbler is found in the northeast in summer, but migrates across much of the east to spend the winter in Central America. Its numbers are declining as the Blue-winged spreads into its area and the two species interbreed. It nests on the ground, building a cup of bark, grass and plant fibers, hidden at the base of a shrub or among weeds, in which it lays 4-7 creamy-white eggs, speckled with brown-gray. These are incubated by the female for 9-12 days - although the male helps to feed the nestlings - and the young birds are ready to leave the nest around 10 days after hatching. The adult is a small, short-tailed bird with a slender bill. The male is blue-gray above, with a bright yellow crown, a black throat, whitish-gray underparts, a black ear patch edged white, and blue-gray wings with a yellow wing patch. The female is similar, but duller. The Golden-winged Warbler forages high in foliage, hunting for insects, spiders and caterpillars.

BLUE-WINGED WARBLER

Scientific name:	*Vermivora pinus*
Length:	4¾ inches
Habitat:	Woodland edges, thickets, second-growth woods
Identification:	Small, short-tailed woodland bird with slender bill. Male has bright yellow crown and underparts, black eyeline, yellowish-white undertail coverts, blue-gray wings, two white wing bars. Female duller
Similar species:	Interbreeds with Golden-winged Warbler, so many intermediate color variations

The Blue-winged Warbler is locally common in North America in summer and its range is spreading to the north and west. Since it prefers more open woodland and has such bright coloring, it may be easier to spot than many other warblers. It nests on the ground, building a cup of bark, grass and animal hair, hidden at the base of a shrub or among weeds. It lays 3-7 white eggs, speckled with brown-gray, which are incubated by the female for 9-12 days; the young birds are ready to leave the nest around 9-11 days after hatching. The adult is a small, short-tailed bird with a slender bill. The male has a bright yellow crown and underparts, a black eyeline, yellowish-white undertail coverts, and blue-gray wings with two white wing bars. The female is similar, but duller. The Blue-winged Warbler often forages on the ground, but also high in foliage. It eats insects and spiders.

WORM-EATING WARBLER

Scientific name:	*Helmitheros vermivorus*
Length:	5¼ inches
Habitat:	Dense undergrowth in woodland
Identification:	Stocky, short-tailed woodland bird with long, spike-like bill. Brownish-olive above, buffy beneath, bold black stripes on buffy head
Similar species:	Coloring distinctive

A fairly common bird, the Worm-eating Warbler is not easy to spot as it stays in dense undergrowth in woodland - and when it stays still, its coloring provides excellent camouflage. It nests on the ground, building a cup of dead leaves and other plant matter, hidden at the base of a shrub or tree. It lays 3-5 white eggs, speckled with brown, which are incubated by the female for just under 2 weeks; the young birds are ready to start fending for themselves around 9-11 days after they have hatched. The adult is a stocky, short-tailed bird with a long, spike-like bill. Its plumage is brownish-olive above and buffy beneath, with bold black stripes on a buffy head. Despite its name, the Worm-eating Warbler does not live on earthworms - although it does eat caterpillars as well as insects and spiders.

TENNESSEE WARBLER

Scientific name:	*Vermivora peregrina*
Length:	4¾ inches
Habitat:	Coniferous and mixed woodland, clearings, bogs
Identification:	Small, short-tailed woodland bird with sharp bill and long wings. Breeding male has gray crown and nape, olive-green above, whitish underparts, black eyeline, white eyebrow. Female has less evident crown, yellow breast and eyebrow. Winter adults plain olive-green above, yellow below, white undertail coverts
Similar species:	Orange-crowned Warbler similar to fall birds but lacks white undertail coverts. Warbling and Red-eyed vireos have thicker bill, grayer back

Despite its name, the Tennessee Warbler is found in the bogs and clearings of northern boreal forests in summer, only visiting Tennessee during migration as it heads to Central America and the Caribbean for the winter. It nests on or near the ground, building a solid cup of grass and plant fibers, lined with animal hair and sheltered under a clump of tall grass or a low bush. It lays 4-7 white eggs, lightly spotted with red-brown, which are incubated for around 11-14 days. The adult is a small, plump, short-tailed bird with a sharp bill and long wings. The breeding male has a gray crown and nape and is olive-green above with whitish underparts, a black eyeline and a white eyebrow. The female has a less evident crown, and a yellow breast and eyebrow. Winter adults and juveniles are plain olive-green above and yellow below, with white undertail coverts. The Tennessee Warbler forages fairly high in trees, snatching flying insects and eating spiders, berries and seeds.

ORANGE-CROWNED WARBLER

Scientific name:	*Vermivora celata*
Length:	5 inches
Habitat:	Open brushy woodland, forest edges, leafy thickets
Identification:	Small woodland bird with sharply pointed, slightly down-curved bill. Olive-green above, olive-yellow below with very faint streaking on breast, orange crown usually not visible except in display
Similar species:	Tennessee Warbler in fall plumage has white undertail coverts

The rather plain Orange-crowned Warbler is one of the most common warblers in western North America, although it is rarer in the east. It nests on or near the ground, building a large bowl of grass and plant fibers, lined with feathers or animal fur and sheltered under a low bush or in a shrub. It lays 4-6 white eggs with red or lavender spotting, often more thickly concentrated at the rounded end. The adult is a small bird with a fairly long tail and a sharply pointed, slightly down-curved bill. Its plumage is olive-green above and olive-yellow below, with very faint streaking on the breast. The orange crown is usually not visible, except in courtship display or when the bird is alarmed. The Orange-crowned Warbler forages both fairly low in thick growth and high in trees, snatching flying insects and eating berries.

NASHVILLE WARBLER

Scientific name:	*Vermivora ruficapilla*
Length:	$4\frac{3}{4}$ inches
Habitat:	Second-growth woods, spruce bogs
Identification:	Small, stubby, short-tailed woodland bird with sharp bill. Male has blue-gray head, white eye ring, olive-green upperparts, bright yellow chin and throat, yellow beneath with whitish belly. Chestnut crown usually not visible except in display. Female duller
Similar species:	Size, coloring and active habits distinctive

Although it is common in the northeast and the west in summer, the Nashville Warbler is only seen near Nashville during migration, as it moves to its wintering grounds in Mexico. It nests on the ground, building a cup of grass, rootlets and plant fibers sheltered in vegetation or in a depression on a steep slope. It lays 3-5 reddish-brown spotted eggs, which are incubated for about 11-14 days by the female; the young are ready to begin fending for themselves about 10 days after they have hatched. The adult is a small, stubby bird with a short tail and a sharp bill. The breeding male has a blue-gray head with a white eye ring, olive-green upperparts, a bright yellow chin and throat, and is yellow beneath with a whitish belly patch. The chestnut crown is usually not visible, except in courtship display or when the bird is alarmed. The female, juvenile and winter male are duller, but still have the distinctive eye ring. The Nashville Warbler often bobs its tail up and down. It forages high in the canopy, catching insects and caterpillars.

LUCY'S WARBLER

Scientific name:	*Vermivora luciae*
Length:	$4\frac{1}{4}$ inches
Habitat:	Desert, mesquite, cottonwoods
Identification:	Small, short-tailed desert bird with slender bill. Gray above, creamy-white underparts, bright chestnut rump, white eye ring, chestnut crown usually not visible
Similar species:	Only desert warbler

The smallest American warbler - and the only one adapted to live in the desert - Lucy's Warbler is found in the southwest in summer, but spends the winter in Mexico. It prefers mesquite and brushy woods, arriving in early spring and leaving again in late summer. It nests in holes in mesquite branches or under bark, lining the cavity thickly with bark strips, plant fibers, hair and fur, and laying 4 or 5 white eggs, lightly speckled with brown. The adult is a slender, short-tailed bird with a small bill. Its plumage is gray above, with creamy-white underparts, a bright chestnut rump and a white eye ring. It also has a chestnut crown, which is usually not visible except in display. Juveniles are similar to the adult, but have a buff rump. Lucy's Warbler often flicks its tail up and down and moves about rapidly as it hunts for insects.

NORTHERN PARULA

Scientific name:	*Parula americana*
Length:	$4\frac{1}{2}$ inches
Habitat:	Coniferous and mixed woods near water
Identification:	Small, plump, short-tailed woodland bird with sharp pointed bill. Blue-gray above with greenish upper back, broken white eye ring, bright yellow throat and breast, white belly, two white wing bars. Male has distinct black and rufous breast bands, breast bands of female and juvenile are faint or lacking
Similar species:	Tropical Parula, rare in south Texas, lacks eye ring and black breast band

A small warbler, the Northern Parula is common across the east in summer, in coniferous and mixed woodlands; in fall it migrates south to spend the winter in the tropics. Its nest is a loosely woven ball of plant fibers hidden in Spanish moss, usnea lichen or similar hanging plant matter, up to 60 feet above the ground. It lays 3-6 creamy-white eggs, spotted with brown, which are incubated for around 2 weeks by the female. The adult is a small, plump bird with a short tail and a sharp bill. Its plumage is blue-gray above with a greenish upper back, a broken white eye ring, a bright yellow throat and breast, a white belly and two bold white wing bars. The male has distinct black and rufous breast bands; the breast bands of the female and juvenile birds are faint or lacking. The Northern Parula stays high in the tops of trees, hunting for insects and spiders.

PROTHONOTARY WARBLER

Scientific name:	*Protonotaria citrea*
Length:	$5\frac{1}{2}$ inches
Habitat:	Swampy woods
Identification:	Plump, short-tailed woodland swamp bird with long bill. Golden yellow head and underparts, white undertail coverts, blue-gray wings and tail, white tail patches, large dark eyes. Female duller
Similar species:	Several other warblers have similar coloring. Female orioles have white wing bars and thicker bill

The Prothonotary Warbler is fairly common across the southeast in summer, preferring swampy woods and rarely found far from water. It is the only warbler apart from Lucy's to nest in a tree hole, using a natural cavity, abandoned woodpecker hole or any similar site, if possible right next to the water. It lines the hole with plant fiber and moss, and lays 3-7 pinky-white eggs, spotted with gray-brown, which are incubated for around 2 weeks by the female; the young leave the nest around 10-12 days after hatching and are sometimes followed by a second brood. The adult is a plump bird with a short tail and a long bill. It has a golden yellow head and underparts, white undertail coverts, plain blue-gray wings, a blue-gray tail with large white patches, and large dark eyes. The female is duller. The Prothonotary Warbler sings high in trees, and uses its thin, sharp bill to pull insects and spiders from their hiding places.

YELLOW WARBLER

Scientific name:	*Dendroica petechia*
Length:	5 inches
Habitat:	Willows, alders, wet open woodland
Identification:	Stout, short-tailed woodland bird with thick bill. Yellow overall, dark eye, wings and tail yellow-olive with yellow markings and spots. Male has chestnut stripes on breast and flanks, female and juvenile duller and may have faint streaking
Similar species:	Male Wilson's Warbler has black cap, females difficult to tell apart

A very common and widespread bird across most of North America, the Yellow Warbler inhabits open woods, often preferring those along streams, and winters in the tropics - although every year a few birds only move as far as Mexico. It nests in the crotch of a small tree or shrub, building a deep cup of plant material lined with down. The Cowbird will often deposit its egg in a Yellow Warbler nest, usually leading the bird to build another floor over the alien egg and begin all over again - nests have even been found with several floors. The female lays 4 or 5 whitish eggs, spotted with brown, and incubates them for around 9-10 days; the young leave the nest around 10-12 days after hatching. The adult is a stout bird with a short tail and a thick bill. It is yellow overall, with dark eyes, and yellow-olive wings and tail with yellow markings and spots. The male has chestnut stripes on breast and flanks, the female and juvenile are duller and may have faint streaking. The Yellow Warbler usually forages around the mid-level in the foliage of trees, where it will hunt for insects and spiders.

CHESTNUT-SIDED WARBLER

Scientific name:	*Dendroica pensylvanica*
Length:	5 inches
Habitat:	Second-growth deciduous woods
Identification:	Long-tailed woodland bird with stout bill. Breeding male has yellow crown, black eyeline and mustache, white cheeks, white underparts, chestnut stripe on flanks. Female has greenish crown. Fall adults lime green above, white eye ring on pale gray face, two yellow wing bars
Similar species:	Breeding plumage distinctive

A bird that prefers open woodland, the Chestnut-sided Warbler is fairly common in the northeast in summer, although it is rarely seen in the west. It nests a few feet above the ground in the fork of a small tree or a shrub, building a cup of bark, plant fiber and down, in which it lays 3-5 creamy-white eggs, spotted with purple-brown. These are incubated for around 2 weeks by the female; the young leave the nest around 10-12 days after hatching. The adult is an active bird with a stout bill and a short tail, which it sometimes holds up above the wingtips. The breeding male (*below*) has a yellow crown, a black eyeline and mustache, white cheeks, white underparts, and a chestnut stripe on each flank. The female is duller with a greenish crown. In fall, both adults are lime green above, with a white eye ring on a pale gray face and two yellow wing bars. The Chestnut-sided Warbler stays low in trees, and sometimes darts out to catch a flying insect. It also eats berries and seeds.

BLACKBURNIAN WARBLER
(above)

Scientific name:	*Dendroica fusca*
Length:	5 inches
Habitat:	Coniferous and mixed forests, spruce woods
Identification:	Slim, long-tailed woodland bird with pointed wings. Breeding male has bright orange throat, black triangular ear patch, white wing patch, black back with white stripes. Female similar but has orange-yellow throat, two white wing bars on black wings
Similar species:	Unmistakable

The brilliantly colored Blackburnian Warbler is fairly common in conifer woods in the northeast in summer, although it is very rare in the west. It can also be spotted as it migrates through the eastern states to winter in South America. It nests up to 80 feet above the ground on a horizontal branch, building a large, firm cup of twigs, rootlets, lichens and down, in which it lays 4 or 5 greenish-white eggs, spotted with brown. These are incubated for around 10-12 days by the female bird. The adult is a slim, streamlined bird with a long tail and pointed wings. The breeding male has a bright orange throat, a black triangular ear patch, a white wing patch, and a black back with white stripes. The female is similar, but has an orange-yellow throat, and two white wing bars on black wings. The Blackburnian Warbler stays high in the upper branches of trees, and mainly eats insects and berries. Several species of warbler often share the same territory, but because they tend to forage at different levels in the trees they do not compete with each other for the available food.

YELLOW-THROATED WARBLER

Scientific name:	*Dendroica dominica*
Length:	5½ inches
Habitat:	Open pine-oak woodland, tall sycamore
Identification:	Long-bodied woodland bird with long bill. Bright yellow throat and upper breast, white neck spot, black crown and face, white eyebrow, gray above, white beneath, black stripes on flanks, white wing bars
Similar species:	Grace's Warbler, only seen in southwestern mountains, is almost identical but lacks white neck spot

In the southeast, the Yellow-throated Warbler begins to arrive at its summer breeding grounds very early in the spring. It prefers open pine forest and sycamore woods along rivers, but when it moves south for the winter some birds stay in Florida palm trees. It nests as much as 120 feet above the ground, weaving a loose cup of plant fibers and down, often concealed in hanging Spanish moss. It lays 4 or 5 greenish-gray eggs, spotted with red or mauve. These are incubated by the female bird, and there is sometimes a second brood in the season. The adult is long-bodied with a long bill. It has a bright yellow throat and upper breast, a distinctive white neck spot, a black crown and face and a white eyebrow, and is gray above and white beneath, with black stripes on the flanks and two white wing bars. The Yellow-throated Warbler forages high in trees, often probing the bark with its long bill to find insects and spiders.

CAPE MAY WARBLER

Scientific name:	*Dendroica tigrina*
Length:	5 inches
Habitat:	Spruce forest
Identification:	Short-tailed woodland bird with sharp, dark, slightly down-curved bill. Breeding male is streaked yellow-green above, black crown, chestnut-red ear patch, yellow spot on side of neck, white wing patch, yellow-green patch on rump, yellow underparts with heavy black streaks on breast. Female duller and grayer with two narrow white wing bars
Similar species:	Breeding plumage distinctive. Juveniles variable and can be difficult to identify

A small but distinctive bird, the Cape May Warbler spends the summer in northern conifer forests and the winter in the Caribbean, but is seen across much of the east in spring and fall as it migrates between the two. It nests near the top of a conifer, building a large cup of grass, twigs and stems on a horizontal branch, in which it lays 6-8 creamy eggs, spotted with brown and gray. The adult is a short-tailed bird with a sharp, dark, slightly down-curved bill. The breeding male is streaked yellow-green above, with a black crown, a chestnut-red ear patch, a yellow spot on the side of the neck, a large white wing patch and yellow underparts with heavy black streaks on the breast. A yellow-green patch on the rump may not be evident. The female is duller and grayer with two narrow white wing bars. Juveniles are very variable and can be difficult to place. The Cape May Warbler eats insects and spiders, and also punctures fruit to drink the juice.

YELLOW-RUMPED WARBLER

Scientific name:	*Dendroica coronata*
Length:	5½ inches
Habitat:	Coniferous and mixed woodland, parks
Identification:	Long-tailed woodland bird with stout black bill. Dark gray above with black streaks, white belly. Breeding male has yellow rump, yellow patch on flanks, yellow crown patch, white tail spots. Either yellow throat, white wing patch or white eyebrow, throat and sides of neck, black cheek, two white wing bars. Female and fall males similar but duller
Similar species:	Yellow-rumped Warbler is two former species combined, so there are many color variations

The Myrtle Warbler in the east and Audubon's Warbler in the west combined and interbred where their ranges overlapped and are now considered one species, the Yellow-rumped Warbler. It is found across the north in summer and spends the winter in the south and Central America, but is seen in migration across most of the continent. It nests fairly high in a conifer, building a cup of twigs and stems lined with feathers on a horizontal branch, in which it lays 4 or 5 white eggs, spotted with brown and gray. The adult is a long-tailed bird with a stout black bill and is dark gray above with black streaks and a white belly. The breeding male has a yellow rump, a yellow patch on each flank, a yellow crown patch, and white tail spots. Audubon's has a yellow throat and a white wing patch, the Myrtle a white eyebrow, a white throat extending up the side of the neck, a black cheek and two white wing bars. Female and fall males are similar but duller. The Yellow-rumped Warbler eats insects and spiders, berries and seeds.

MAGNOLIA WARBLER *(above)*

Scientific name:	*Dendroica magnolia*
Length:	5 inches
Habitat:	Damp and open conifer forests
Identification:	Long-tailed woodland bird with round head and small bill. Breeding male is gray above, black mask and back, white eyebrow, large white patch on wing, tail white underneath with black terminal band, yellow rump and underparts, heavy black streaks on breast. Fall adults and juveniles gray-olive above, white eye ring, yellowish beneath with faint gray breast band
Similar species:	Juvenile Prairie Warbler similar to juvenile Magnolia, but lacks eye ring and breast band

Common in damp coniferous forest, the Magnolia Warbler spends the summer in the north but is seen across much of the east in spring and fall as it migrates. It was discovered in a magnolia tree, hence its name, but otherwise there is no special connection. It nests fairly low down in a conifer, building a loose, shallow cup of grass and rootlets on a horizontal branch, in which it lays 3-5 creamy-white eggs, spotted with brown mainly at the rounded end. These are incubated for up to 2 weeks by the female bird, with the young leaving the nest some 9 days later. The adult is a long-tailed bird with a round head and a small bill. The breeding male is gray above, with a black mask and back, a white eyebrow, a large white patch on the wing, and a yellow rump and underparts with heavy black streaks on the breast. In flight, the tail is white underneath, with a black terminal band. Fall adults and juveniles are gray-olive above with a white eye ring, and yellowish beneath with a faint gray breast band. The Magnolia Warbler eats insects and spiders.

BLACK-THROATED GRAY WARBLER

Scientific name:	*Dendroica nigrescens*
Length:	5 inches
Habitat:	Oak and juniper woodland, dry foothills, chaparral
Identification:	Long-tailed woodland bird with stout bill. Breeding male has black and white striped head, yellow spot between bill and eye, blue-gray back with black stripes, black bib, white below with black stripes on flanks, two white wing bars, white outer tail feathers. Female, juvenile and fall male lack black bib
Similar species:	Blackpoll Warbler has white cheeks, Black-and-white Warbler has striped crown

Fairly common in the dry foothills and oak-juniper woods of the west during the summer months, the Black-throated Gray Warbler spends the winter mainly in central Mexico. In the breeding season it nests quite low down in a bush or a tree, building a tightly-woven cup of plant fibers lined with feathers and animal hair, in which it lays 3-5 creamy-white eggs, splashed with brown. The adult has a long, straight tail and a rather stout bill. The breeding male has a black and white striped head, a yellow spot between bill and eye, a blue-gray back with black stripes, a black bib, and is white below with black stripes on each flank, two white wing bars and white outer tail feathers. The female, juvenile and fall male are similar but lack the black bib. The plumage of the Black-throated Gray Warbler provides ideal camouflage in the gray-green of juniper woods, so it can be very hard to see. It eats insects, spiders, and small caterpillars.

BLACK-THROATED GREEN WARBLER

Scientific name:	*Dendroica virens*
Length:	5 inches
Habitat:	Coniferous and mixed forests, cypress swamps
Identification:	Long-tailed woodland bird with stout bill, bright olive-green back and crown. Male has greenish ear spot, black throat and upper breast, bright yellow face, white underparts tinted yellow across vent and often on breast, sides streaked black, dark gray wings and tail, two white wing bars, white outer tail feathers. Female and juvenile have partly white throat
Similar species:	All black-throated warblers very similar, but Black-throated Green can usually be distinguished by bright olive-green upperparts

In North America a mainly northeastern bird, the Black-throated Green Warbler lives in coniferous forest in the summer - although some birds prefer to breed in cypress swamps along the east coast. It nests up to 80 feet above the ground in a crotch of a tall tree, building a neat cup of plant fibers, moss and bark, in which it lays 4 or 5 creamy-white eggs, marked with brown and purple. The adult has a long, straight tail, a rather stout bill and a bright olive-green back and crown. The male has a greenish ear spot, black throat and upper breast, a bright yellow face and lower breast, white underparts tinted yellow across the vent and often on the breast, black-streaked sides, and dark gray wings and tail with two white wing bars and white outer tail feathers. The female and juvenile have a partly white throat. The Black-throated Green Warbler forages high up and eats insects and berries.

BLACK-THROATED BLUE WARBLER

Scientific name:	*Dendroica caerulescens*
Length:	$5\frac{1}{4}$ inches
Habitat:	Deciduous forests
Identification:	Stocky, short-tailed woodland bird. Male blue above, white beneath with black throat, cheeks and flanks, bold white patch on wing. Female brownish-olive above, buffy underparts, pale eyebrow, pale wing patch
Similar species:	Coloring of both adults is distinctive

The Black-throated Blue Warbler prefers the dark, shady understory of deciduous woods and spends the summer in the northeast, migrating south in fall to winter in the Caribbean - although a few birds stay in southern Florida. It builds its nest near the ground in a dense shrub, creating a firm cup of bark, twigs and plant fiber lined with fine rootlets, in which it lays 3-5 creamy-white eggs, spotted with brown and gray. These are incubated for about 10-12 days by the female and the young are ready to leave the nest some 10 days later. The adult is a stocky bird with a short tail. The male is blue above and white beneath with a black throat, cheeks and flanks and a bold white patch on the wing. The female is brownish-olive above with buffy underparts and a pale eyebrow and pale wing patch. Juveniles are similar to the relevant adult. The Black-throated Blue Warbler stays low and forages in woodland bushes and shrubs, hunting for insects, seeds and berries.

BLACK-AND-WHITE WARBLER

Scientific name:	*Mniotilta varia*
Length:	5¼ inches
Habitat:	Mixed woodland
Identification:	Short-tailed woodland bird with long, down-curved bill. Mainly striped black and white, white crown stripe. Male has black throat and cheeks in breeding season, white chin in winter. Female and juvenile, whitish throat and cheeks, buffy flanks with gray streaks
Similar species:	Breeding male Blackpoll Warbler has black cap, Black-throated Gray Warbler has black crown

Like a nuthatch, the Black-and-white Warbler creeps around the trunks and large branches of trees - the only warbler that behaves in this way. It is common in summer in the mixed woodlands of the eastern states, but also occasionally strays into the west; a few birds spend the winter in Florida, but most head much further south. It builds its nest on the ground, sheltered among the roots of a tree or tucked under a log or rock, creating a thickly-woven cup of bark, moss, twigs and plant fiber, in which it lays 4 or 5 whitish-cream, brown-speckled eggs. These are incubated for 9-12 days and the young leave the nest 1-2 weeks later. The adult is a rather short-tailed bird with a long, slightly down-curved bill. Its plumage is mainly striped black and white, with a white crown stripe. The male has a black throat and cheeks in the breeding season, but in winter has a white chin. The female and juvenile have a whitish throat and cheeks and buffy flanks with gray streaks. The Black-and-white Warbler probes tree bark with its long bill, hunting for insects and spiders.

CERULEAN WARBLER

Scientific name:	*Dendroica cerulea*
Length:	4¾ inches
Habitat:	Tall trees in swamps, riverside trees
Identification:	Small, short-tailed woodland bird with stout bill and pointed wings. Male sky blue above, white beneath with black necklace and black streaking on flanks, two white wing bars. Female blue-green above, yellowish throat and breast, whitish underparts with pale streaking on flanks, pale eyebrow, two white wing bars
Similar species:	Coloring of both adults is distinctive

A rather uncommon bird, the Cerulean Warbler is also difficult to spot because it lives high in the foliage of tall trees. Its summer range is expanding to the northeast, but declining elsewhere; it migrates south in late summer to spend the winter in South America. It builds its nest up to 100 feet above the ground in a fork near the end of a branch, weaving a neat cup of bark, moss and plant fiber, in which it lays 4 or 5 greenish-cream, brown-spotted eggs that are incubated for up to 2 weeks by the female. The adult is a small bird with a short tail, stout bill and very pointed wings. The male is sky blue above and white beneath with a black necklace, black streaking on the flanks and two white wing bars. The female is blue-green above with a yellowish throat and breast, whitish underparts with pale streaking on the flanks, a pale eyebrow and darker wings with two bold white wing bars. Juveniles are similar to the female. The Cerulean Warbler forages high in the canopy, hunting for insects.

PRAIRIE WARBLER

Scientific name: *Dendroica discolor*
Length: 4¾ inches
Habitat: Dense second-growth woods, scrubland, mangrove swamps
Identification: Small, round-headed woodland bird with long, narrow tail. Olive above, faint chestnut streaks on back, bright yellow eyebrow, yellow patch beneath eye outlined in black, bright yellow beneath with black streaks on sides and flanks, two dull wing bars. Female and juvenile duller
Similar species: Juvenile Magnolia Warbler similar to juvenile Prairie, but has eye ring and gray breast band

Despite its name, the Prairie Warbler is a woodland bird. It is common in summer in the second-growth woods, scrubland and mangrove swamps of the eastern states, occasionally wandering further west; a few birds spend the winter in Florida, but most head much further south. It builds its nest a few feet above ground level in a bush or mangrove, creating a small cup of bark and grass lined with plant down, in which it lays 3-5 whitish-green eggs, spotted with brown. These are incubated by the female for up to 2 weeks and the young are ready to start fending for themselves some 9-11 days later. The adult is a small, round-headed bird with a long, narrow tail. It is olive above with faint chestnut streaks on the back, and has a bright yellow eyebrow, a yellow patch beneath the eye outlined in black, bright yellow underparts with black streaks on the sides and flanks and two dull wing bars. The female and juvenile are similar but duller. The Prairie Warbler bobs its tail up and down as it forages in underbrush and low branches for insects and spiders.

PALM WARBLER *(above)*

Scientific name:	*Dendroica palmarum*
Length:	$5\frac{1}{2}$ inches
Habitat:	Brush near spruce bogs, open ground
Identification:	Long-tailed, round-winged woodland bird. Olive above. Eastern breeding adult has chestnut cap, yellow eyebrow, yellow underparts with chestnut streaks on sides. Fall adults and juveniles lack cap and streaking, yellow duller. Western breeding adult similar, but has whitish underparts with darker streaks on sides. Fall adults and juveniles dull brown, no cap, whitish eyebrow, yellow only on undertail coverts
Similar species:	Constant tail bobbing is distinctive

The Palm Warbler was discovered on a Caribbean island but is rarely found on palms in North America, preferring the brush and spruce bogs of the north in summer, and open areas and marshes in the southeast in winter. It nests low in a bush or on a mossy mound, building a smallish cup of bark and grass, in which it lays 4 or 5 white eggs, spotted and splotched with brown. The adult is long-tailed with rounded wings, and is olive above. The less common eastern breeding adult has a chestnut cap, a yellow eyebrow and yellow underparts with chestnut streaks on the sides. Fall adults and juveniles lack the cap and streaking, and the yellow is duller. The western breeding adult is similar, but has whitish underparts with darker streaks on the sides. Fall adults and juveniles are dull brown, with no cap, a whitish eyebrow, and yellow only on undertail coverts. The Palm Warbler forages in the open in winter, bobbing its tail up and down as it hunts for insects and berries.

PINE WARBLER

Scientific name:	*Dendroica pinus*
Length:	$5\frac{1}{2}$ inches
Habitat:	Pine trees, mixed woodland
Identification:	Stocky, long-tailed, round-headed woodland bird with stout bill. Greenish-olive above, yellow throat and breast with darker streaks on sides, two white wing bars, white belly and undertail coverts. Female plainer and duller, juvenile very variable
Similar species:	Yellow-throated Vireo has gray rump, plain sides, thicker bill, well-defined yellow "spectacles"

Common in pine forests in the northeast in summer and in mixed woods in the southeast during the winter, the Pine Warbler is not a long-distance migrant - some birds stay all year round in the south-eastern states. In the breeding season it nests up to 80 feet above the ground in a tree - usually a conifer - building a tight cup of stems, bark and pine needles hidden in a tuft of needles near the end of a horizontal branch. It usually lays 4 or 5 greenish-white eggs, which are spotted with brown. The adult is a stocky, long-tailed bird with a rounded head and a rather stout bill. It is greenish-olive above, and has a yellow throat and breast with darker streaks on the sides, two white wing bars on darker wings, and a white belly and undertail coverts. The female is plainer with no streaking and is a duller color. The coloring of the juvenile can be very variable, ranging from plain yellowish to gray-white. The Pine Warbler creeps along branches pressed close to the surface, probing the bark to find insects and spiders; in fall and winter it will also eat seeds and berries.

NORTHERN WATERTHRUSH *(below)*

Scientific name:	*Seiurus noveboracensis*
Length:	$5\frac{3}{4}$ inches
Habitat:	Woodland bogs, swamps, thickets
Identification:	Large, short-tailed woodland bird with narrow head and long legs. Olive-brown above, creamy-white below with dense brown streaks, creamy eyebrow, dull pink legs
Similar species:	Louisiana Waterthrush has pink-buff tinge on flanks, large bill, bright pink legs

Rarely found far from water, the Northern Waterthrush spends the summer in the bogs and along wooded streams and ponds across the north. It nests in a cavity on the ground or among roots on the bank of a stream, building a cup of plant material lined with moss, in which it lays 4 or 5 white eggs, spotted with gray-brown. The adult is a large, short-tailed bird with a narrow head and long legs. It is olive-brown above and creamy-white below with dense brown streaks, and has a creamy eyebrow and dull pink legs. The Northern Waterthrush walks on the ground with a bobbing motion, wagging its tail up and down rhythmically and rapidly. It forages along the edges of the water, lifting leaves and other debris to find the insects and small aquatic animals hiding beneath.

LOUISIANA WATERTHRUSH

Scientific name:	*Seiurus motacilla*
Length:	6 inches
Habitat:	Mountain streams in dense woodland
Identification:	Large, short-tailed woodland bird with narrow head and long legs. Olive-brown above, creamy-white below with brown streaks, pink-buff tinge on flanks, creamy eyebrow, bright pink legs
Similar species:	Northern Waterthrush lacks pink-buff tinge on flanks, has smaller bill, dull pink legs

Almost identical to the Northern, the Louisiana Waterthrush is less common and has a different range; it also prefers swift mountain streams in dense woods and is rarely found in swamps. It nests in a cavity on the ground or among tree roots near water, building a cup of plant material lined with moss, in which it lays 4-6 white eggs, spotted with gray-brown. The adult is a large, short-tailed bird with a narrow head and long legs. It is olive-brown above and creamy-white below with brown streaks, a pink-buff tinge on each flank, and has a creamy eyebrow and bright pink legs. The Louisiana Waterthrush walks on the ground with a bobbing motion, wagging its tail up and down constantly but slowly. It forages along the edges of the water, lifting leaves and other debris to find the insects and small aquatic animals hiding beneath.

OVENBIRD

Scientific name:	*Seiurus aurocapillus*
Length:	6 inches
Habitat:	Mature forest
Identification:	Large, short-tailed woodland bird with large dark eye. Olive above, white below with dark streaky spots, rust-orange crown edged with blackish stripes, white eye ring, pinkish legs
Similar species:	Similar brown thrushes lack crown stripes

Although it may easily be overlooked, the Ovenbird is actually very common in the woods of the east in summer. It lives close to the ground, walking with its tail held upright, rather than hopping around like most of the other warblers. It nests on the ground, building a dome-shaped structure of leaves, grass and stems that looks rather like an old-fashioned oven - hence its name - in which it lays 4-6 white eggs, spotted with gray-brown. These are incubated for up to 2 weeks by the female and the young are ready to start fending for themselves some 9-11 days after hatching. The adult is a large, short-tailed bird with a relatively large, dark eye. It is olive above and white below with dark streaky spots, and has a rust-orange crown edged with blackish stripes, a bold white eye ring, and pinkish legs. The Ovenbird picks its way across the forest floor, moving delicately with precise footsteps, as it hunting for insects, earthworms, snails and spiders.

KENTUCKY WARBLER
(above)

Scientific name:	*Oporornis formosus*
Length:	5¼ inches
Habitat:	Wet woodland with dense undergrowth
Identification:	Heavy, short-tailed woodland bird with long legs. Black crown, black below eye down sides of neck, bold yellow "spectacles", bright olive above, yellow below
Similar species:	Common Yellowthroat lacks "spectacles"

A shy and rather secretive bird, the Kentucky Warbler spends the summer in the southeast and is common in areas of rich, damp woodland with very thick undergrowth - although it might be quite hard to spot. It sometimes strays as far west as California and other areas in the southwest. In its breeding area it nests on the bare ground under a bush or among a large clump of weeds, building a fairly large bowl of leaves, grass and stems, in which it lays 3-6 creamy-white eggs, liberally spotted with brown. The adult is a heavy, short-tailed bird with quite long legs. The adult has a black crown and is black below the eye and down the sides of the neck with bold yellow "spectacles", and is bright olive above and yellow below. The female is rather duller, with the black areas less vivid and even seeming much more olive-colored on the juvenile female. The Kentucky Warbler hops and runs on the ground, hidden away for most of the time underneath the dense undergrowth, feeding mainly by plucking the insects and spiders hiding on the undersides of leaves.

MACGILLIVRAY'S WARBLER

Scientific name:	*Oporornis tolmiei*
Length:	5¼ inches
Habitat:	Dense undergrowth
Identification:	Sturdy, short-winged woodland bird with long body. Gray hood, distinct broken white eye ring, olive above, yellow below. Male has darker face and black across lower breast. Female and juvenile have paler throat
Similar species:	Mourning Warbler lacks distinct broken eye ring but females and juveniles of both species difficult to distinguish

A common western bird, MacGillivray's Warbler is found in the northwest and all down the Pacific coast in summer, spreading eastwards only as far as the Rockies, and spends the winter in Mexico and South America. It nests on or close to the ground among weeds or in a low bush, building a cup of leaves, grass and stems, in which it lays 3-5 white, brown-spotted eggs. These are incubated for around 11-13 days by the female, and the young are ready to leave the nest just over a week after hatching. The adult is a sturdy, rather short-winged bird with a long body. It has a gray hood, a distinct broken white eye ring, and is olive above and yellow below. The male has a darker face and is black across the lower breast; the female and juvenile have a paler throat. MacGillivray's Warbler hops, rather than walking. It eats insects and spiders.

MOURNING WARBLER

Scientific name:	*Oporornis philadelphia*
Length:	5¼ inches
Habitat:	Dense undergrowth, wet woodland, thickets
Identification:	Sturdy, short-tailed woodland bird with long body. Gray hood, olive above, yellow below. Male has darker face and black flecks across breast. Female and juvenile have thin incomplete white eye ring, juvenile often has yellow throat
Similar species:	MacGillivray's Warbler has distinct broken white eye ring but females and juveniles of both species difficult to distinguish. Juveniles have more yellow belly than female Common Yellowthroat

The Mourning Warbler spends the summer in dense woodland undergrowth in the northeast, migrating west of the Appalachians to spend the winter in Central and South America. It nests on the ground among weeds, ferns or grasses, building a cup of leaves, grass and stems, in which it lays 3-6 creamy-white eggs, spotted with brown. These are incubated for around 11-12 days by the female, and the young are ready to leave the nest just over a week after hatching. The adult is a sturdy, short-tailed bird with a long body. The adult has a gray hood, and is olive above and yellow below. The male has a darker face and black flecks across the breast. The female and juvenile have a thin, incomplete white eye ring; the juvenile often has a yellow throat. Although the Mourning Warbler usually hides near the ground under dense undergrowth, the male comes out into the open to sing in the breeding season. It eats insects and spiders.

HOODED WARBLER

Scientific name:	*Wilsonia citrina*
Length:	5¼ inches
Habitat:	Swamps, damp woodland, dense undergrowth
Identification:	Long-tailed woodland bird. Olive above, yellow below, tail has white outer feathers and white beneath. Male has black hood framing yellow face. Female usually lacks hood but may have some black round face
Similar species:	Female Wilson's Warbler may resemble female Hooded, but tail is dark beneath

Found across most of the southeast during the summer, the Hooded Warbler prefers leafy and damp deciduous forests where it hides in the dense and shady undergrowth. In spring and fall it migrates in flocks of hundreds of birds - often along with other small species. In its breeding area it nests very close to the ground in a tree or low bush, building a neat and tidy cup of leaves, bark and plant fibers, in which it lays 3-5 creamy, brown-spotted eggs. These are incubated for around 11-13 days, and the young are ready to leave the nest around 8-10 days after hatching. The adult has a long tail, which it flicks continuously while foraging. It is olive above and yellow below, and the tail has white outer feathers and is white beneath. The male has a black hood framing a yellow face, the female usually lacks the full hood but may have some black around the face. The juvenile female has no black around the head. The Hooded Warbler forages for insects and small spiders - the female tends to hunt close to the ground but the male sometimes catches insects in flight.

WILSON'S WARBLER

Scientific name:	*Wilsonia pusilla*
Length:	4¾ inches
Habitat:	Dense wet woodland, bogs, willow thickets
Identification:	Long-tailed woodland bird with small bill and rounded wings. Olive above, yellow below, tail dark above and beneath. Male has black cap
Similar species:	Female Hooded Warbler may resemble female Wilson's, but has white under tail

Although it is common in the west, Wilson's Warbler is much less numerous in the east. It spends the summer in dense, wet woodland, bogs and willow thickets, preferring to be near water, and migrates south to winter in Mexico and Central America. It nests on or near the ground in dense vegetation, building a large cup of leaves and rootlets, in which it lays 3-6 white, brown-spotted eggs. These are incubated for around 9-11 days, and the young are ready to leave the nest around 9-10 days after hatching. The adult has a long, thin tail, a small bill and rather rounded wings. It is olive above and yellow below, and the tail is dark above and beneath. The male has a black cap; the female may have some black on the crown. Wilson's Warbler is easy to spot, as it flits actively around the ends of leafy branches. It eats insects and spiders, which it often catches in flight.

CANADA WARBLER

Scientific name:	*Wilsonia canadensis*
Length:	5¼ inches
Habitat:	Dense woodland, brush
Identification:	Long-tailed woodland bird with rounded head. Blue-gray above, yellow below, bold yellow eye ring, white undertail coverts. Male has black streaky necklace, female is duller, necklace indistinct
Similar species:	Plumage distinctive

The Canada Warbler is not only found in Canada, but ranges as far south as Georgia in summer and winters in South America. It prefers dense, leafy woods, preferably near water, where it lives in the undergrowth and up to around mid-level. It nests on or near the ground in dense vegetation, among rocks or in a cavity on a bank, building a large cup of leaves, bark and grass, in which it lays 3-6 cream or white, brown-spotted eggs. The adult has a rather rounded head and a long, thin tail, which it flips constantly when foraging. It is blue-gray above and yellow below, with a bold yellow eye ring and white undertail coverts. The male has a necklace of black streaks, the female is generally duller and may have a rather indistinct necklace. The Canada Warbler lurks in the undergrowth or on low branches, hunting for insects which it sometimes catches in flight.

AMERICAN REDSTART

Scientific name:	*Setophaga ruticilla*
Length:	5¼ inches
Habitat:	Second-growth woods
Identification:	Long-tailed woodland bird with short broad bill, rounded wings. Male black, white belly, orange patches on sides, wings and outer tail feathers. Female gray above, white beneath, with yellow patches on sides, wings and outer tail feathers
Similar species:	Coloring distinctive

A very distinctive warbler, the American Redstart is common in North America across much of the north and southeast in summer, where it prefers open deciduous woods. It is rare in the southwest and spends the winter in Mexico and northern South America. It nests up to 70 feet above the ground in an upright crotch of a tree, building a firm cup of twigs lined with finer material, in which it lays 3-5 creamy-white or bluish eggs, spotted with brown. These are incubated for around 11-12 days by the female, and the young are ready to leave the nest just under 3 weeks after hatching. The adult is a long-tailed bird with a short broad bill and rounded wings. The male is black, with a white belly and orange patches on the sides, wings and outer tail feathers. The female is gray above and white beneath, with yellow patches on the sides, wings and outer tail feathers. The American Redstart fans its tail and spreads its wings frequently to flash its bright patches, so it is fairly easy to spot. It eats insects and spiders, frequently caught in midair.

YELLOW-BREASTED CHAT
(above)

Scientific name:	*Icteria virens*
Length:	$7\frac{1}{2}$ inches
Habitat:	Dense thicket, brush
Identification:	Long-tailed woodland bird with thick black bill, rounded wings. Olive-brown above, gray head with white "spectacles", black eye patch, bright yellow throat and breast, white belly
Similar species:	Common Yellowthroat smaller, with different face markings

The largest warbler seen in North America, the distinctive Yellow-breasted Chat is rather shy and prefers dense thickets, so may be difficult to spot. It nests low in a bush or tangle of vegetation, building a cup mainly of grass, in which it lays 3-5 white eggs, spotted with brown and lilac. These are incubated for around 11-12 days by the female, and the young are ready to leave the nest 1-2 weeks after hatching. The adult is a long-tailed bird with a thick, black bill and rounded wings. It is olive-brown above, and has a gray head with white "spectacles", a black eye patch, a bright yellow throat and breast and a white belly. The male and female look alike, the juvenile is paler and lacks the eye patch. The Yellow-breasted Chat often mimics other birds and the male displays by hovering with slow-flapping wings and its legs dangling, while it sings. It eats insects and berries.

COMMON YELLOWTHROAT

Scientific name:	*Geothlypis trichas*
Length:	5 inches
Habitat:	Grassy fields, open marshes
Identification:	Stumpy grassland bird with short neck, small bill, round tail and wings. Male olive-green above, bright yellow below fading to dull white belly, black mask edged with white across crown. Female brownish olive above, buffy beneath with yellow on throat
Similar species:	Juvenile Mourning Warbler like female Common Yellowthroat but has yellow belly

One of the most widespread warblers in North America, the Common Yellowthroat is found in summer across most of the continent and some birds also spend the winter across the south. It prefers grassland, marshes and other open habitats with low vegetation, rather than woods. It nests on or near the ground among weeds or grasses or in a low shrub, building a bulky, woven cup of plant material lined with fine grass, in which it lays 3-6 white eggs, marked with brown. These are incubated for around 11-12 days by the female, and the young are ready to leave the nest just over a week after hatching. The adult is a rather stumpy bird with a short neck, small bill, and a rounded tail and wings. The male is olive-green above and bright yellow below, fading to a dull white on the belly, and has a black mask edged with white across the crown. The female is brownish olive above and buffy beneath, with yellow on the throat. The Common Yellowthroat spends much of its time hidden in dense undergrowth, but the male climbs a tall stalk to sing in the breeding season. It eats insects and spiders.

SUMMER TANAGER

Scientific name:	*Piranga rubra*
Length:	7¾ inches
Habitat:	Pine-oak woods, cottonwood groves
Identification:	Large woodland bird with stout pale yellow bill and small crest. Male rosy-red, female olive-yellow above, orange-yellow beneath, greenish under tail. Juvenile has variable amounts of yellow and red
Similar species:	Hepatic Tanager has gray cheeks and dark bill. Female similar to female Scarlet Tanager, but tail is greenish beneath instead of gray

Found across the south in summer, the Summer Tanager lives in pine-oak forest in the southeast and streamside cottonwoods in the southwest and rarely spreads any further north than its mapped range. It nests up to 35 feet above the ground in a tree, building a rather frail and shallow cup of grass and leaves on a horizontal branch, in which it lays 3 or 4 blue-green eggs with brown blotches. The adult is a large bird with a stout pale yellow bill. The male is overall rosy-red, the female is olive-yellow above, orange-yellow beneath; its tail is greenish underneath. The juvenile has variable amounts of yellow and red. Birds in the west tend to be larger and paler than those in the east, and the female may have more gray above. The Summer Tanager forages high in the canopy and eats insects, larvae, spiders and berries - it also eats fruit.

HEPATIC TANAGER

Scientific name: *Piranga flava*
Length: 8 inches
Habitat: Mixed mountain forest
Identification: Large woodland bird with stout dark gray bill. Male red-orange, gray cheek patch, gray wash on flanks. Female olive-green above, gray cheek patch, deep yellow beneath
Similar species: Summer Tanager lacks gray cheeks, has pale bill

A tropical bird, the Hepatic Tanager is only found in North America in the northwest in summer, where it lives in mountainous pine-oak forest. It nests up to 30 feet above the ground in a tree, building a rather shallow cup of rootlets, grass and weeds on a horizontal branch, in which it lays 3-5 bluish eggs with heavy brown and lilac blotches. The adult is a large bird with a stout dark gray bill. The male is red-orange, with a gray cheek patch and a gray wash on the flanks. The female is olive-green above with a gray cheek patch, and is deep yellow beneath. The juvenile resembles the female, but is streaked overall. The Hepatic Tanager eats insects, larvae, spiders and berries - it is particularly fond of bee and wasp larvae. In its winter grounds it also eats fruit.

SCARLET TANAGER

Scientific name:	*Piranga olivacea*
Length:	7 inches
Habitat:	Leafy forest
Identification:	Medium-size woodland bird with thick gray bill. Male has black wings and tail, white wing linings, in breeding season is brilliant red overall, in winter greenish-yellow. Female is greenish-yellow with darker wings and tail, white wing linings
Similar species:	Male distinctive. Female similar to female Summer Tanager, but tail is gray beneath instead of greenish

The Scarlet Tanager lives in the leafy deciduous forests of the northeast in summer, but is also seen across the southeastern states as it migrates to the tropics in fall for the winter, and when it returns in spring. It nests up to 75 feet above the ground in a tree, building a shallow cup of grass and leaves at the tip of a horizontal branch, in which it lays 3-5 blue-green eggs finely spotted with brown. These are incubated by the female for around 2 weeks, with the young leaving the nest about 10-12 days after hatching. The adult is a medium-size bird with a thick gray bill. The male has black wings and tail, with white wing linings, and is brilliant red overall in the breeding season and greenish-yellow in winter. The female is greenish-yellow, with darker wings and tail and white wing linings. The Scarlet Tanager usually forages high in the canopy, but may come down lower to hunt for food as it migrates. It eats insects, caterpillars, spiders and berries - as is very popular with gardeners because of its voracious appetite for garden pests.

WESTERN TANAGER

Scientific name:	*Piranga ludoviciana*
Length:	$7\frac{1}{2}$ inches
Habitat:	Coniferous forest, mountain pine woods
Identification:	Medium-size woodland bird with long pointed wings. Male has brilliant red head, bright yellow body, black wings and tail, upper wing bar yellow, lower wing bar white. Female is yellow-green above, yellow below, wing bars as male.
Similar species:	Male distinctive. Female similar to female orioles, but has thicker bill

In cool conifer forests and mountain pine woods across the west the Western Tanager is fairly common in summer, but it is also seen in many different habitats during its migration across the western states. It nests up to 65 feet above the ground in a fork on the horizontal branch near the top of a tall conifer, building a shallow saucer of moss, stalks and bark. It lays 3-5 bluish-green eggs finely spotted with brown, which are incubated by the female for around 2 weeks. The adult is a medium-size bird with a fairly small, thick bill and long, pointed wings. The male has a brilliant red head, a bright yellow body and black wings and tail, with two wing bars - the upper yellow and the lower white. The female is yellow-green above and yellow below, with the same wing bars as the male. The Western Tanager usually forages high in the canopy, but may come down lower to hunt for food as it travels in migration. It generally eats insects - which it will often catch on the wing - berries and other small fruit. Although it looks wonderful, like other tanagers it does not have a notable song.

EASTERN TOWHEE

Scientific name:	*Pipilo erythrophthalmus*
Length:	7½ inches
Habitat:	Second-growth woods with dense undergrowth
Identification:	Stocky ground-dwelling bird with long tail and rounded wings. Blackish upperparts and hood, white wing patch and corners to tail, red flanks, white belly
Similar species:	Spotted Towhee has white spotting on wings, back and corners of tail, American Robin has red breast

Once known as the Rufous-sided Towhee - along with what is now known as the Spotted Towhee - the Eastern Towhee is currently accepted as a separate species - although the two will interbreed wherever their ranges overlap. The Eastern Towhee is common across most of the southeast, with some birds spreading north in summer and west in winter. In its breeding area it nests on the ground, building a cup of grass, twigs and rootlets, in which it lays 2-6 cream or greenish eggs spotted with brown. These are incubated by the female for just under 2 weeks and the young are ready to leave the nest around 10-12 days after hatching. The adult is a stocky bird with a long tail and rounded wings. It has a blackish hood and upperparts with a white wing patch and corners to the tail, red flanks and a white belly. The female is chocolate-brown above but otherwise similar, the juvenile is brownish and streaked. The Eastern Towhee forages on the ground for insects, spiders, seeds and berries.

GREEN-TAILED TOWHEE

(below)

Scientific name: *Pipilo chlorurus*
Length: 7¼ inches
Habitat: Dense brush, chaparral, high plateaus
Identification: Medium-size ground-dwelling bird with long tail and rounded wings. Rusty-red cap, olive-green above, white throat with dark mustache mark, gray breast, white belly
Similar species: Coloring distinctive

Common in dense brush and chaparral in the west in summer the Green-tailed Towhee spends the winter across the far south and down into Mexico. In its breeding area it nests on the ground or low down in a dense bush or cactus, building a loose, deep cup of plant fibers, in which it lays 4 white eggs heavily spotted with brown. The adult is a medium-size bird with a fairly long tail and rounded wings. It has a rusty-red cap and is olive-green above, with a white throat crossed by a dark mustache mark, a gray breast, and a white belly. The juvenile is heavily streaked and lacks the reddish crown. The Green-tailed Towhee often raises its head feathers in a small crest and also runs with its tail held high to distract intruders near the nest site. It hunts for food under cover, scratching at the ground to find seeds, berries and insects.

SPOTTED TOWHEE

Scientific name: *Pipilo maculatus*
Length: 7½ inches
Habitat: Chaparral, open woods, brushy hillsides
Identification: Stocky ground-dwelling bird with long tail and rounded wings. Blackish upperparts and hood with bold white spots on wings, back and corners of tail, red flanks, white belly
Similar species: Eastern Towhee lacks white spotting

The Spotted and the Eastern Towhee were once considered to be one species, known as the Rufous-sided Towhee. The Spotted is common across most of the west, with some birds spreading northeast in summer and southeast in winter. In its breeding area it nests on the ground, building a cup of grass, twigs and rootlets, in which it lays 2-6 cream or greenish eggs spotted with brown. These are incubated by the female for just under 2 weeks and the young are ready to start fending for themselves some 10-12 days later. The adult is a stocky bird with a long tail and rounded wings. It has a blackish hood and upperparts with bold white spots on the wings, back and corners of the tail, red flanks and a white belly. The female may be the same or more gray and the juvenile is brownish and heavily streaked, and lacks the red flanks. The Spotted Towhee forages on the ground for insects, spiders, seeds and berries.

CALIFORNIA TOWHEE

Scientific name:	*Pipilo crissalis*
Length:	9 inches
Habitat:	Chaparral, parks, gardens
Identification:	Stocky ground-dwelling bird with long tail and rounded wings. Brownish overall, buffy beneath, throat bordered with line of dark brown spots, cinnamon-brown undertail coverts
Similar species:	Canyon Towhee paler and grayer, reddish crown, whitish belly patch with blurry dark spot above

The California and the Canyon Towhee were once considered to be one species, known as the Brown Towhee. The California lives mainly in the chaparral, parks and gardens of western California, spreading south into Mexico and with a few birds in southwest Oregon. It nests on or just above the ground, building a cup of grass, twigs and stems, in which it lays 3 or 4 bluish-green eggs lightly spotted with brownish-black. These are incubated by the female for 9-11 days and the young are ready to leave the nest around 8 days after hatching, often making way for a second or third brood. The adult is a stocky bird with a long tail and rounded wings. It is brownish overall and buffy beneath, the throat is bordered with a line of dark brown spots, and it has cinnamon-brown undertail coverts. The juvenile is streaked beneath and has faint wing bars. The California Towhee forages quietly under cover, scratching the ground for seeds, grain and insects. On overcast days it may come out onto lawns to feed.

CANYON TOWHEE

Scientific name:	*Pipilo fuscus*
Length:	8 inches
Habitat:	Arid hills, desert canyons, brushy areas
Identification:	Stocky ground-dwelling bird with long tail and rounded wings. Gray-brown overall, reddish crown, paler beneath, throat bordered with line of dark brown spots, whitish belly patch with blurry dark spot above, cinnamon-brown undertail coverts
Similar species:	California Towhee darker and browner, lacks reddish crown, whitish belly patch and blurry dark spot

Once known as the Brown Towhee, along with the California, the Canyon Towhee is now accepted as a separate species. The Canyon lives mainly in arid, hilly areas and desert canyons across the far southern states and south into Mexico. It nests on or just above the ground, building a cup of grass, twigs and stems, in which it lays 3 or 4 bluish-green eggs lightly spotted with brownish-black. These are incubated by the female for 9-11 days and the young are ready to leave the nest around 8 days after hatching, often making way for a second or third brood. The adult is a stocky bird with a long tail and rounded wings. It is gray-brown overall with a reddish crown, paler beneath, the throat is bordered with a line of dark brown spots and it has a whitish belly patch with blurry dark spot above, and cinnamon-brown undertail coverts. The Canyon Towhee forages quietly for seeds, grain and insects.

ABERT'S TOWHEE

Scientific name:	*Pipilo aberti*
Length:	9½ inches
Habitat:	Desert woodland, riverside thickets, dense underbrush
Identification:	Stocky ground-dwelling bird with long tail and rounded wings. Black face, warm brown above, paler beneath, buffy belly, cinnamon undertail coverts
Similar species:	Similar to Canyon and California, but black face distinctive

Common within its limited range, Abert's Towhee is a very shy and secretive bird that hides in dense thickets and is difficult to spot - although its loud and frequent calls can easily be heard. It also sometimes lives in suburban backyards and orchards, but prefers to be near water. It is very similar to both the Canyon and California towhee and their ranges overlap, but it does not interbreed. It nests close to the ground, building a cup-shaped mass of bark strips, stems and other plant fibers, in which it lays 3 or 4 pale blue-green eggs spotted with brown. The adult is a stocky bird with a long tail and rounded wings. It has a black face and is warm brown above, paler beneath, with a buffy belly and cinnamon-brown undertail coverts. Abert's Towhee forages quietly for seeds and insects.

CHIPPING SPARROW

Scientific name:	*Spizella passerina*
Length:	5½ inches
Habitat:	Backyard lawns, grassy fields, woodland edges
Identification:	Medium-size sparrow with longish tail. Rust-red crown above white eyebrow and black eyeline, gray cheeks, collar and underparts, brown back with dark streaking, two white wing bars
Similar species:	Rufous-winged Sparrow larger and more secretive. Fall birds have less sharp coloring and may suggest Clay-colored or Brewer's sparrow although they have brown rump instead of gray

Widespread and common across most of North America in summer, the Chipping Sparrow is often seen in backyards and gathers in flocks in the south in winter. It nests up to 40 feet above the ground in a bush or tree, building a neat cup of plant fibers lined with animal hair, in which it lays 3-5 pale blue eggs, marked with brown, black and purple mainly at the rounded end. These are incubated by the female for up to 2 weeks and the young leave the nest after around 9-12 days. The adult is a medium-size sparrow and has a longish, slightly notched tail. It has a rust-red crown above a white eyebrow and black eyeline, plain gray cheeks, collar and underparts, a brown back with dark streaking, and two white wing bars. The juvenile is similar, but has some streaking below. The Chipping Sparrow often feeds in the open and eats insects and seeds.

CLAY-COLORED SPARROW

Scientific name:	*Spizella pallida*
Length:	5½ inches
Habitat:	Brushy fields, groves, riverside thickets
Identification:	Medium-size sparrow with longish tail. Brown crown with black streaks and white central stripe, whitish eyebrow, brown cheek with dark outline, dark mustache mark, buffy breast, whitish belly, gray nape, brown back with dark streaking, brown rump, two light wing bars
Similar species:	Chipping Sparrow has gray rump. Brewer's Sparrow lacks central crown stripe and has whitish eye ring and less contrasting head markings

In summer, the Clay-colored Sparrow is common across central North America in brushy areas; it migrates across the central states to spend the winter in Mexico - although a few birds remain in southern Texas. Although its habitat has been destroyed in some areas, deforestation has extended it in others, so its range has increased. It nests on the ground or just above in a dense shrub, building a well-constructed cup of grass and twigs lined with animal hair, in which it lays 3-5 bluish eggs, which may be marked with brown. These are incubated by both birds for up to 2 weeks and the young leave the nest after around 8-10 days. The adult is a medium-size sparrow and has a longish, slightly notched tail. It has a brown crown with black streaks and a white central stripe, a whitish eyebrow, brown cheeks with a dark outline, a dark mustache mark, and a buffy breast and whitish belly. Its nape is gray and its back brown with dark streaking, and it has a plain brown rump and two light wing bars. The Clay-colored Sparrow eats insects and seeds.

AMERICAN TREE SPARROW

Scientific name:	*Spizella arborea*
Length:	6½ inches
Habitat:	Tundra, open areas with groves of trees, brushy fields
Identification:	Large sparrow with long tail. Chestnut cap and eye stripe, gray head and nape, gray underparts with dark spot on center of breast and chestnut patch at side, red-brown back with dark streaking, two white wing bars
Similar species:	Chipping and Field sparrows smaller and lack breast spot

A bird which prefers colder climates and can tolerate subzero temperatures, the American Tree Sparrow spends the summer in the tundra zone and winters across central North America. It nests on or very near the ground, building a cup of plant fibers lined with feathers, in which it lays 4 or 5 pale blue eggs, speckled with brown. These are incubated by the female for just under 2 weeks and the young leave the nest to start fending for themselves after around 9-11 days. The adult is a large sparrow and has a long, slightly notched tail and a bill that is dark above and yellow below. It has a chestnut cap and eye stripe, a gray head and nape, gray underparts with a dark spot at the center of the breast and a chestnut patch at the side, a red-brown back with dark streaking, and two white wing bars. Birds in the west tend to be paler than those in the east. The American Tree Sparrow mainly eats seeds, but will also take insects and spiders.

VESPER SPARROW

Scientific name:	*Pooecetes gramineus*
Length:	6¼ inches
Habitat:	Dry grassland, forest clearings, sagebrush, open prairie
Identification:	Large sparrow with long tail. Streaked brown above and on throat and breast, pale narrow eye ring, dark ear patch outlined in white below and behind, creamy-white belly, white outer tail feathers, chestnut spot on shoulder may not be evident
Similar species:	Savannah Sparrow has bold eyebrow and white central crown stripe

Common in the west but less so in the east, the Vesper Sparrow prefers to spend the summer on prairies and other open, dry areas. On its southern wintering grounds, it may gather into flocks with other sparrows. It nests on the ground, building a cup of plant fibers lined with grass hidden in dense vegetation, in which it lays 3-6 creamy-white eggs, spotted with brown. These are incubated for 12-14 days by the female and the young leave the nest some 7-12 days later. The adult is a large sparrow with a long tail and a stout bill. It is streaked brown above and on the throat and breast, with a pale, narrow eye ring, a dark ear patch outlined in white below and behind, a creamy-white belly and white outer tail feathers. It also has a chestnut spot on the shoulder, but this may not be evident. The Vesper Sparrow eats seeds, insects and grain.

BREWER'S SPARROW

Scientific name:	*Spizella breweri*
Length:	5½ inches
Habitat:	Mountain meadows, sagebrush flats, open desert
Identification:	Medium-size sparrow with longish tail. Brown crown with black streaks, grayish-white eyebrow, whitish eye ring, brown cheek with darker outline, dark mustache mark, whitish breast and belly, gray nape, brown back with darker streaking, brown rump, two light wing bars
Similar species:	Chipping Sparrow has gray rump. Clay-colored Sparrow has central crown stripe, more contrasting head pattern and lacks whitish eye ring

Brewer's Sparrow is common in the west in summer but has two distinct breeding areas - one on the sagebrush flats of the west and the other in the Canadian Rockies. It is thought that the Canadian birds may be a separate species. It nests on the ground in sagebrush or just above in a cactus, building a cup of grass in which it lays 3-5 bluish, brown-spotted eggs that are incubated for up to 2 weeks. The adult is a medium-size sparrow and has a longish, slightly notched tail. It has a brown crown with black streaks, a grayish-white eyebrow, distinct whitish eye ring, brown cheeks with a darker outline, a dark mustache mark, and a whitish breast and belly. Its nape is gray and its back brown with darker streaking, and it has a brown rump and two light wing bars. Brewer's Sparrow can survive long periods without water and eats insects and seeds.

FIELD SPARROW

Scientific name: *Spizella pusilla*
Length: 5¾ inches
Habitat: Open brushy woodland, overgrown fields
Identification: Large sparrow with long tail. Gray face, reddish crown, whitish eye ring, pale rust eyeline, bright pink bill, brown streaked back, plain gray-brown rump, two white wing bars, buffy breast and sides, grayish-white belly, pink legs
Similar species: American Tree Sparrow larger and has central breast spot. Chipping Sparrow has dark eyeline and darker bill

Fairly common on open, brushy ground, the Field Sparrow spreads across most of the east in summer, but retreats back to the southeast in winter. It nests on or up to 10 feet above the ground in a bush or low tree, building a cup of grass and leaves, in which it lays 3-5 pale blue-green eggs, very densely speckled with red-brown. These are incubated for 12-17 days by the female and the young leave the nest to start fending for themselves after around 7-9 days. The adult is a large sparrow with a long, slightly notched tail, a stout, bright pink bill and pink legs. It has a gray face with a reddish crown, a distinct whitish eye ring and a pale rust eyeline, a brown streaked back with a plain gray-brown rump, two white wing bars, a buffy breast and sides, and a grayish-white belly. The Field Sparrow mainly feeds on seeds, but it will also take insects and spiders.

SAVANNAH SPARROW

Scientific name:	*Passerculus sandwichensis*
Length:	5½ inches
Habitat:	Marsh, fields, grassy beaches
Identification:	Neat sparrow with small crest, short notched tail and pointed wings. Coloring variable, but generally streaked brown above, heavily striped beneath, white belly, light central crown stripe and eyebrow, pale pink legs
Similar species:	Vesper Sparrow has pale eye ring, lacks bold eyebrow and white central crown stripe

A common and widespread bird across much of North America, the Savannah Sparrow can often be seen perching in the open on marshes, fields or grassy beaches. It nests on the ground, building a cup of grass and plant stems hidden in vegetation, in which it lays 4-6 whitish eggs spotted with brown and purple. These are incubated for 10-12 days by both birds, and the young are ready to begin fending for themselves around 2 weeks later. The adult is a neat and compact bird with a small crest, short, notched tail and rather pointed wings. Its coloring is very variable, ranging from very dark and heavily streaked to light brownish or rufous, depending on its range, but it is generally streaked brown above, heavily striped beneath, with a white belly, a light central crown stripe and eyebrow, and pale pink legs. The Savannah Sparrow usually lives in loose flocks and eats seeds and insects.

LARK SPARROW

Scientific name:	*Chondestes grammacus*
Length:	6½ inches
Habitat:	Prairie edges, open brushy woodland, farmland
Identification:	Slender sparrow with long, rounded tail and pointed wings. Chestnut ear patches and crown stripes outlined in black, white cheek and central crown stripe, black mustache mark, streaked brown above, plain buff beneath with central black spot on breast, black tail with white sides and corners
Similar species:	Head pattern is distinctive

Common in the west in summer, but rarer in the east, the Lark Sparrow is found on open ground near brush for cover and can often be spotted in small flocks. It nests on or near the ground, building a cup of grass lined with fibers and hair, hidden in grass or in a low bush, in which it lays 3-5 white eggs spotted with brown and black. These are incubated for 10-12 days by the female, and the young are ready to begin fending for themselves around 10 days later. The adult is a slender bird with a long, rounded tail and rather pointed wings. It has chestnut ear patches and crown stripes outlined in black, a white cheek and central crown stripe and a black mustache mark, and is streaked brown above and plain buff beneath with a central black spot on the breast and a black tail with white sides and corners. The juvenile is duller and streaked below. A very sociable bird, the Lark Sparrow flocks together when feeding, even in the nesting period. It can often be seen perching in the open and eats seeds and insects.

FOX SPARROW *(below)*

Scientific name:	*Passerella iliaca*
Length:	7 inches
Habitat:	Coniferous and mixed woodland undergrowth, chaparral
Identification:	Large, stocky, round-headed sparrow with heavy bill. Coloring very variable, either gray, dark brown or streaked rufous above, heavy triangular spots beneath arranged in stripes and merging on breast, white belly, reddish rump and tail
Similar species:	Hermit Thrush has white eye ring, lacks heavy streaking below

The Fox Sparrow is one of the largest sparrows in North America and is fairly common in many areas, but it lives in dense thickets and so it may be difficult to spot. It nests on or just above the ground, building a neat, solid cup of plant fibers lined with feathers hidden in a thicket or low in a bush. It lays 4 or 5 pale green eggs speckled with brown, which are incubated for up to 2 weeks by the female bird. The adult is a large, stocky sparrow with a round head and a heavy bill. Its coloring is very variable, either gray, dark brown or streaked rufous above, with heavy triangular spots beneath arranged in stripes and merging on the breast, a white belly, and a reddish rump and tail. Gray-headed birds are found in the west, dark brown in the northwest and rufous in the east. The juvenile of each is similar to the adult, but duller. The Fox Sparrow scratches at the ground under bushes with both feet, hunting for seeds and insects.

BACHMAN'S SPARROW

Scientific name:	*Aimophila aestivalis*
Length:	6 inches
Habitat:	Dry brushy fields, palmetto stands, pine woods
Identification:	Large, long-tailed sparrow. Gray above heavily streaked chestnut-brown, buffy-gray cheeks, long dark eyeline, breast and sides buff or gray, belly whitish
Similar species:	Closely resembles Botteri's Sparrow, but no overlap in range

Rather uncommon and declining still further in some areas of its range, Bachman's Sparrow is a bird of dry, open woodland that tends to stay fairly close to the ground in long grass. Except when the male perches in the open to sing in the breeding season, it may be difficult to see. It nests on the ground, building a woven cup of grass and stems well-concealed under a tuft of grass, in which it lays 3-5 white eggs. These are incubated for up to 2 weeks by the female and the young birds are ready to start fending for themselves some 2 weeks later. The adult is a large sparrow with a long, rounded tail, a flattish forehead and a sturdy bill. It is gray above, heavily streaked with chestnut-brown, and has buffy-gray cheeks, a long dark eyeline, buff or gray breast and sides, and a whitish belly. Birds in the west are brighter colored and more rufous overall, while those in the southeast are grayer and darker. The juvenile has more streaking, which lingers into the second summer, and a distinct pale eye ring. Bachman's Sparrow eats insects, spiders and seeds.

BLACK-THROATED SPARROW

Scientific name:	*Amphispiza bilineata*
Length:	5½ inches
Habitat:	Rocky desert slopes
Identification:	Medium-size sparrow with long tail. Gray above, black face and bib, white eyebrow, mustache mark and spot below eye, whitish below, black tail with white sides and corners
Similar species:	Sage Sparrow lacks black bib and white on tail, has central dark breast spot, streaked sides

A desert bird, the Black-throated Sparrow can tolerate extremes of heat and drought and is common in the desert areas of the southwest, spreading north across Nevada, much of Utah and parts of Colorado in summer. It nests just above the ground, building a loosely-constructed cup of plant fibers lined with animal hair, well-hidden in a low bush or cholla cactus, in which it lays 3 or 4 bluish-white eggs. The adult is medium-size with a long tail and a small, stout bill. It is gray above and whitish below, with a black face and bib, a white eyebrow, mustache mark and spot below the eye, and a black tail with white sides and corners. The juvenile lacks the black bib and has a finely streaked breast. The Black-throated Sparrow is sometimes known locally as the "desert sparrow". It forages on the ground in pairs or small groups and eats seeds, plants and insects - which usually also give it all the moisture it needs.

SAGE SPARROW

Scientific name:	*Amphispiza belli*
Length:	6¼ inches
Habitat:	Sagebrush & saltbush flats, mountain chaparral
Identification:	Large sparrow with long tail. Gray above, white beneath with central dark spot on breast, streaked back and sides, dark gray head and cheek, white eye ring and spot before eye, black mustache mark, black tail
Similar species:	Black-throated Sparrow has black bib, no streaking and white on tail

The Sage Sparrow prefers barren country, particularly sagebrush flats and coastal chaparral. It nests around 4 feet above the ground, building a loosely-constructed cup of sagebrush lined with animal fur, well-hidden in sagebrush or low scrub, in which it lays 3 or 4 bluish-white eggs speckled with brown and black. These are incubated for just under 2 weeks, and there is often a second brood. The adult is a large sparrow with a long tail and a small, stout bill. It is gray above and white beneath with central dark spot on the breast, and has streaked back and sides, a dark gray head and cheek, a white eye ring and spot before the eye, a black mustache mark, and a plain black tail. The juvenile is browner with a white throat and fine dark streaking on a buffy breast and belly. Birds on the Pacific Coast are generally darker with more contrast in pattern. The Sage Sparrow often runs on the ground with its tail held upwards, but wags and dips its tail when perched. It eats both seeds and insects.

LINCOLN'S SPARROW

Scientific name:	*Melospiza lincolnii*
Length:	5¾ inches
Habitat:	Brushy bogs, mountain meadows, dense thickets
Identification:	Stocky sparrow with round head, short tail and small pointed bill. Streaked brown-gray above, buffy breast finely striped with brown, white belly, brown cheeks and crown, gray central crown stripe and eyebrow, white eye ring, buffy mustache mark, pinkish legs
Similar species:	Song Sparrow has heavier streaking below and central breast spot

Although it is common in brushy bogs and mountain meadows in the west in summer, Lincoln's Sparrow is much rarer in the east. It spends the winter along much of the Pacific coast and across the south, where it prefers to live in thickets. In the breeding season it nests on the ground, building a cup of dry grass well-hidden in vegetation, in which it lays 4 or 5 greenish-white eggs heavily spotted with brown. These are incubated by the female for around 2 weeks, and the young are ready to leave the nest around 3 weeks later - there is sometimes a further brood in the season. The adult is a stocky bird with a rounded head, a short tail and a rather small, pointed bill. It is streaked brown-gray above, with a buffy breast finely striped with brown, a white belly, brown cheeks and crown, a gray central crown stripe and eyebrow, a white eye ring, buffy mustache mark, and pinkish legs. Lincoln's Sparrow is a wary and secretive bird, which is usually only spotted when singing. It eats seeds, grain and insects.

SONG SPARROW

Scientific name:	*Melospiza melodia*
Length:	5½-7½ inches
Habitat:	Dense riverside thickets, parks, backyards
Identification:	Stocky sparrow with round head, long tail and stout bill. Coloring variable, but generally streaked red-brown above, heavily striped beneath with distinct central breast spot, white belly, light gray central crown stripe and eyebrow, pinkish legs
Similar species:	Lincoln's Sparrow more buffy with narrow streaks beneath and no central breast spot. Savannah Sparrow lacks central breast spot and has shorter tail

The Song Sparrow is the most widespread sparrow in North America, but it hides in dense cover - although it also lives in suburban gardens and parks, where it can become quite tame. It nests on or just above the ground, building a cup of grass and plant stems well-hidden in vegetation, in which it lays 3-6 greenish-white eggs heavily spotted with brown. These are incubated for around 2 weeks by the female bird, and the young are ready to begin fending for themselves around 10 days later - there are often several further broods in a season. The adult is a stocky bird with a rounded head, a long tail and a rather short, stout bill. Its coloring is very variable geographically, but it is generally streaked red-brown above, heavily striped beneath with a distinct central breast spot, a white belly, a light gray central crown stripe and eyebrow, and pinkish legs. The Song Sparrow usually lives in family groups or pairs and is rarely seen in flocks. It eats seeds, grain, berries and insects.

GOLDEN-CROWNED SPARROW

Scientific name:	*Zonotrichia atricapilla*
Length:	7 inches
Habitat:	Tundra, dense woodland, brush
Identification:	Large, heavy sparrow with long tail and two-tone bill. Brown streaked darker above, gold crown with wide black stripe on each side, gray cheek, gray-brown breast, sides and flanks, whitish throat and belly, two narrow white wing bars. Winter plumage duller
Similar species:	White-crowned Sparrow has pink or yellow bill, lacks gold crown

Fairly common in the tundra bogs of the northeast in summer, the Golden-crowned Sparrow winters in the west in dense woodland and undergrowth. In the breeding season it nests on or near the ground, weaving a neat cup of grass, stems and leaves well-hidden in vegetation or in a bush, in which it lays 4 or 5 bluish, brown-speckled eggs. The adult is a large, heavy sparrow with a long tail and a bill that is dark above and pale beneath. It is brown, streaked with darker brown above, and has a gold crown with a wide black stripe on each side, a gray cheek, gray-brown breast, sides and flanks, a whitish throat and belly, and two narrow white wing bars. The winter plumage is duller with less distinct and extensive black stripes on the crown. The Golden-crowned Sparrow often joins flocks of other sparrows in winter, but forages under bushes rather than out in the open. It eats seeds, buds, flowers and insects and will visit feeders in winter.

WHITE-CROWNED SPARROW

Scientific name:	*Zonotrichia leucophrys*
Length:	7 inches
Habitat:	Woodland edges, grassland, thickets
Identification:	Large, heavy sparrow with long tail. Gray-brown streaked above, black and white striped crown, pink or yellow bill, white eyebrow, thin black line behind eye, gray cheek and breast, white throat and belly, two narrow white wing bars
Similar species:	White-throated Sparrow is browner with dark bill

Abundant in the west but uncommon in the east, the White-crowned Sparrow is seen in flocks at the edges of woodland and in hedges across the south in winter and spends the summer in the north and northwest. In the breeding season it nests on or high above the ground, weaving a neat cup of grass hidden in vegetation or in a tree, in which it lays 3-5 pale blue eggs spotted with red-brown. These are incubated by the female for 12-17 days, and the young are ready to leave the nest around 10-12 days later. The adult is a large, heavy sparrow with a long tail. It is gray-brown streaked above, with a black and white striped crown, a pink or yellow bill, a white eyebrow with a thin black line behind the eye, a gray cheek and breast, white throat and belly, and two narrow white wing bars. The juvenile has a brown and buff striped crown and streaked underparts. The White-crowned Sparrow eats seeds, grain and insects and often visits feeders in winter.

WHITE-THROATED SPARROW

Scientific name:	*Zonotrichia albicollis*
Length:	6¾ inches
Habitat:	Woodland undergrowth, brush, backyards, parks
Identification:	Large, heavy sparrow with long tail. Chestnut-brown above, black and white striped crown, bright yellow spot behind dark bill, either white or tan eyebrow, gray cheek and breast, white throat, two narrow white wing bars
Similar species:	White-crowned Sparrow is grayer with pink or yellow bill

The White-throated Sparrow is commonly seen in flocks in woods, parks and gardens in the southeast in winter, but is rare in the west. It spends the summer in the cool forests of the north and northeast. In the breeding season it nests on the ground, weaving a cup of moss, grass, rootlets and bark strips, lined with fine grass and hidden in vegetation, in which it lays 3-5 greenish-white eggs heavily spotted with brown at the rounded end. These are incubated by the female for up to 2 weeks, and the young are ready to leave the nest around 10-12 days later. The adult is a large, heavy sparrow with a long tail. It is chestnut-brown above, with a black and white striped crown, a bright yellow spot behind a dark bill, either a white or tan eyebrow, a gray cheek and breast, white throat, and two narrow white wing bars. The juvenile is brown and buff, with fine streaking on the breast. The White-throated Sparrow is usually found on the ground, where it forages for seeds, berries and insects - often in flocks with juncos and other sparrows.

BAIRD'S SPARROW (*above*)

Scientific name:	*Ammodramus bairdii*
Length:	5½ inches
Habitat:	Marsh, fields, grassy beaches
Identification:	Medium-size, flat-headed sparrow with a short tail. Streaked or scaled brown above, mustard-yellow tinge to head, whitish beneath with necklace of dark streaks on chest
Similar species:	Savannah Sparrow has a bold eyebrow and pale central crown stripe

An uncommon and elusive bird, Baird's Sparrow is hard to find both in winter and during migration, although it may be spotted singing during the breeding season. It nests on the ground on dry prairie, building a cup of grass and plant stems well hidden in tall vegetation, in which it lays 4 or 5 white eggs blotched with brown and lilac. These are incubated for 11-14 days by the female bird alone, and the young are ready to begin fending for themselves just over a week later. The adult is a medium-size bird with a rather flat head and a short tail. It is streaked or scaled brown above, with a mustard-colored tinge to the head that may appear as a broad ochre-yellow stripe across the crown, and whitish beneath with a necklace of dark streaks across the chest. Baird's Sparrow is extremely reluctant to fly and tends to either run away through the grass like a mouse when disturbed, or fly up very briefly and stay low. It eats seeds, spiders and insects.

GRASSHOPPER SPARROW

Scientific name:	*Ammodramus savannarum*
Length:	5 inches
Habitat:	Pasture, dry grassland, palmetto scrub
Identification:	Long-billed sparrow with flat head, short tail and pointed wings. Dark brown crown with buffy central stripe, white eye ring, chestnut and black striped back, plain buffy breast, whitish belly
Similar species:	Le Conte's Sparrow has buffy-orange eyebrow and pale gray ear patch. Savannah Sparrow may be similar in some color variations but usually has heavy striping beneath

Shy and secretive, the Grasshopper Sparrow usually lives on its own and hides in tall, dense grass so it is easily overlooked. It is declining in the east, due to destruction of its habitat. It nests on the ground, building a neat cup of grass lined with soft fibers and hair, concealed under a clump of tall grass, in which it lays 4 or 5 creamy-white eggs spotted with brown. These are incubated for 10-12 days by the female, and the young are ready to fend for themselves around 9-10 days later. The adult is a small sparrow with a large, flat head, a relatively long bill, a short tail and rather pointed wings. It has a dark brown crown with a buffy central stripe, a white eye ring, a chestnut and black striped back, a plain buffy breast and a whitish belly. The juvenile has pale streaks on the belly. The Grasshopper Sparrow eats seeds, grain, spiders and insects.

SEASIDE SPARROW *(above)*

Scientific name:	*Ammodramus maritimus*
Length:	6 inches
Habitat:	Grassy tidal marshes
Identification:	Stocky, rounded sparrow with short spiky tail and long bill. Coloring variable but usually dark olive-gray above, yellow patch above and in front of eye, white throat, whitish mustache mark, buffy-white underparts streaked dusky
Similar species:	Coloring and long bill distinctive

Only found in tidal saltmarsh grass along the Atlantic and Gulf coasts, the Seaside Sparrow is common within its range, which does not extend very far inland. The darkest color variation became extinct in 1987, due to destruction of its habitat. It nests on the ground, weaving a cup of grass and rushes concealed and often attached to marsh grass stems, in which it lays 3-5 greenish-white eggs spotted with brown. These are incubated for 10-12 days by the female, and the young are ready to begin fending for themselves around 9-10 days later. The adult is a stocky, rounded sparrow with a short spiky tail and a long, stout, very pointed bill. Its coloring is very variable within its range, but it is usually dark olive-gray above, with a yellow patch above and in front of the eye, a white throat, a whitish mustache mark and buffy-white underparts streaked dusky. Juveniles are duller and rather browner than the adult. The Seaside Sparrow eats small crustaceans, snails, insects, spiders and seeds.

LE CONTE'S SPARROW

Scientific name:	*Ammodramus leconteii*
Length:	5 inches
Habitat:	Wet fields, shallow marsh edges
Identification:	Small-billed sparrow with short spiky tail. Gray cheek, orange-buff eyebrow and stripe below cheek, black crown with white central stripe, gray nape with fine pink stripes, chestnut and black striped back, buffy breast with sharp black streaks on sides, white belly
Similar species:	Grasshopper Sparrow lacks buffy-orange eyebrow and pale gray ear patch

A shy and very secretive bird, Le Conte's Sparrow hides in tall, dense grass in wet fields and shallow marshes and is common but easily overlooked. If disturbed it will fly up briefly, but does not go high and soon drops back down into the grass. It nests on the ground, building a small cup of grass well-concealed amidst tall grass or sedges, in which it lays 4 or 5 white eggs speckled with brown that are incubated for 12-14 days by the female. The adult is a small sparrow with a rather small bill and a short spiky tail. It has a gray cheek, with an orange-buff stripe below and eyebrow above, a black crown with a white central stripe, a gray nape with fine pink stripes, a chestnut and black striped back, a buffy breast with sharp black streaks on the sides and a white belly. The juvenile is paler and has heavy streaks on the breast. Le Conte's Sparrow eats seeds and insects.

CHESTNUT-COLLARED LONGSPUR

Scientific name:	*Calcarius ornatus*
Length:	6 inches
Habitat:	Damp upland prairie, dense tall grass
Identification:	Stocky, short-tailed ground-dwelling bird with short rounded wings and small bill. Breeding male has chestnut nape, buffy-brown above, black below with white lower belly, black cap and eyeline, white cheek, buffy-white throat and ear stripe. In flight shows black triangle on white tail. Female and juvenile gray-brown
Similar species:	Female similar to female McCown's Longspur, but darker

The range of the Chestnut-collared Longspur overlaps that of McCown's, but it prefers taller grass and is more common. The male is easier to spot, as it flies up singing, or perches in the open on a tall stalk. The Chestnut-collared nests on the ground, lining a scrape next to a stone or bush with grass and laying 3-5 greenish-white eggs with brown-black speckles, which hatch within 11-14 days. The adult is a stocky, rather short-tailed bird with short, rounded wings and a small bill. The breeding male has a chestnut nape, and is buffy-brown above and black below, with a white lower belly, a black cap and eyeline, a white cheek, and a buffy-white throat and ear stripe. The female and juvenile are gray-brown and rather sparrow-like, but in flight all birds show a distinctive black triangle on a white tail. The Chestnut-collared Longspur forages on the ground and eats insects and seeds.

LAPLAND LONGSPUR

Scientific name:	*Calcarius lapponicus*
Length:	$6\frac{1}{4}$ inches
Habitat:	Arctic tundra, grassy and plowed fields
Identification:	Slender ground-dwelling bird with long pointed wings and stout bill. Breeding male has black head, throat and bib, chestnut nape, white eyebrow and border between nape and bib, brown streaking above, white belly with black streaks on flanks, dark tail with white outer feathers. Winter male and female have brown striped head, indistinct dark breast band, buffy flanks, chestnut wash at nape
Similar species:	Summer plumage distinctive, winter plumage rather like other longspurs or sparrows

In summer, the Lapland Longspur lives on Arctic tundra, but it winters on the Great Plains and is common in surrounding areas, often in large flocks with Horned Larks and Snow Buntings. In its breeding area, it nests on the ground in the shelter of a small bush, lining a depression with feathers, and laying 4-7 pale olive-green or buffy-brown eggs with brown speckles and blotches. The adult is a slender, quite long-tailed bird with long, pointed wings and a stout bill. The breeding male has a black head, throat and bib, a chestnut nape, a white eyebrow and border between the nape and bib, brown streaking above, a white belly with black streaks on the flanks, and a dark tail with white outer feathers. The winter male (*right*) and female have a brown striped head, an indistinct dark breast band, buffy flanks, and a chestnut wash at the nape. The Lapland Longspur forages on the ground in flocks, running or walking rather than hopping, and eats insects and seeds.

McCown's Longspur

Scientific name:	*Calcarius mccownii*
Length:	6 inches
Habitat:	Short-grass plains, dry lake beds, plowed fields
Identification:	Stocky, short-tailed ground-dwelling bird with short thick bill. Streaked brown and buffy above, whitish below, gray ear patch, white throat and eyebrow, rusty wing bar. In flight shows inverted black T on white tail. Breeding male grayer with black crown and mustache mark, dark crescent on central breast
Similar species:	Female similar to female Chestnut-collared Longspur, but paler

Although its range is fairly limited and has shrunk considerably over the last century, McCown's Longspur can be quite common locally. It spends the winter on open ground with short grass and plowed fields, often with flocks of Horned Larks, but in the summer it prefers dry open plains. It nests on the ground, lining a depression in the bare earth with grass and laying 3 or 4 white or pale green eggs with brown and purple streaks and spots. The female incubates the eggs for 11-14 days and the young birds are ready to begin fending for themselves around 12 days after hatching. The adult is a stocky, rather short-tailed bird with a short, thick bill. It is streaked brown and buffy above and whitish below, with a gray ear patch, a white throat and eyebrow, and a rusty wing bar which may not be very evident. In flight it shows a distinctive inverted black T on a white tail. The breeding male is grayer, with a black crown and mustache mark, and a dark crescent patch across the central breast. McCown's Longspur eats insects and the seeds of weeds.

YELLOW-EYED JUNCO

Scientific name:	*Junco phaeonotus*
Length:	6¼ inches
Habitat:	Coniferous and pine-oak mountain slopes
Identification:	Slender ground-dwelling bird with long tail. Gray head, sides and flanks, rust-red on back and wings, pale throat, two-tone bill, whitish belly, dark tail with white outer feathers
Similar species:	Female "Oregon", "Gray-headed" and "Red-backed" Dark-eyed Junco have less red on back and dark eyes

Only found in the far south of North America and extending down into Mexico, the Yellow-eyed Junco lives in coniferous and pine-oak forests. It nests on the ground, building a compact saucer of rootlets and fine grass lined with horsehair, situated under a fallen log or protected by vegetation. It lays 3 or 4 blue-white eggs spotted with brown, which are incubated for around 12 days by the female bird; the young birds are ready to leave the nest about 2 weeks later. The adult is a slender bird with a relatively long tail. It has a gray head, sides and flanks, rust-red on back and wings, a pale throat, a dark bill with a pale lower mandible, a whitish belly, and a dark tail with white outer feathers. The Yellow-eyed Junco forages on the ground, moving around slowly and deliberately and walking rather than hopping. It eats seeds, insects and berries.

DARK-EYED JUNCO

Scientific name:	*Junco hyemalis*
Length:	6¼ inches
Habitat:	Coniferous and mixed woodland, thickets
Identification:	Slender ground-dwelling bird with long tail. Distinct color variations geographically, all have white belly, dark tail with white outer feathers
Similar species:	Female "Oregon" can look like "Pink-sided". "White-winged" paler than "Slate-colored", has two white wing bars. "Gray-headed" distinguished from female "Oregon" and "Pink-sided" by gray sides and flanks. "Red-backed" similar to "Gray-headed" but has paler throat, darker bill. Yellow-eyed Junco has more red on back and yellow eyes

The Dark-eyed Junco has at least six different color variations, which tend to have different summer ranges but which may flock together in winter. The "Slate-colored" in the east has a dark gray head, back and sides; the female and juvenile are slightly browner. The "Oregon" is common in the west, the male has a solid blackish hood, chestnut-brown back and sides; the female is paler with a gray hood. The "Pink-sided" summers in the northern Rockies and has a pale blue-gray hood, pinky-cinnamon flanks and a brown back. The "White-winged" breeds in South Dakota and has a pale gray head, back and sides, two white wing bars and more white in tail. "Gray-headed" breeds in the central Rockies and has pale gray hood, sides and flanks, reddish patch on back. The "Red-backed" lives in northern Arizona and New Mexico and has gray head, sides and flanks, reddish back, pale throat and dark bill with pink lower mandible. The Dark-eyed Junco nests on the ground building a compact cup of plant material to hold 3-6 blue-white eggs spotted with brown. It eats seeds, insects and berries.

SNOW BUNTING

Scientific name:	*Plectrophenax nivalis*
Length:	$6\frac{3}{4}$ inches
Habitat:	Tundra, rocky shores, sand dunes, beaches, barren fields
Identification:	Stocky ground-dwelling bird, with short tail and pointed wings. Black central tail feathers and wing tips, variable black patch at shoulder. Breeding male white with black back, winter male white with buffy crown, ear patch, collar and back. Female white with rusty-tan crown, ear patch, collar and back
Similar species:	Plumage distinctive

The Snow Bunting is fairly common across central North America in winter, and spends the summer on Arctic tundra, but is also often seen in various open habitats during migration. It nests in a crevice or a depression in the ground among rocks, lining the hollow with moss and feathers to hold 4-6 blue-white eggs, very heavily spotted with brown and lilac. These are incubated by the female for about 2 weeks and the young are ready to fend for themselves around 11-18 days after hatching. The adult is a stocky bird, with a short tail and pointed wings and has black central tail feathers and wing tips and a variable black patch at the shoulder. The breeding male is white with a black back, the winter male is white with a buffy crown, ear patch, collar and back. The female is white with a rusty-tan crown, ear patch, collar and back. The Snow Bunting is often seen in large flocks along with Horned Larks and longspurs. It eats insects, seeds and spiders.

LARK BUNTING

Scientific name:	*Calamospiza melanocorys*
Length:	7 inches
Habitat:	Dry plains, prairie, sagebrush
Identification:	Large, stocky ground-dwelling bird, with short tail and short rounded wings. Breeding male black with large white wing patch. Female and winter male streaked brown-buff above, white streaked brown below, white wing patch, white-tipped tail
Similar species:	Plumage of breeding male distinctive, otherwise rather sparrow-like

Very common in the central states just east of the Rockies in summer, the Lark Bunting winters in large flocks across the south and down into Mexico. The distinctive plumage of the male is very conspicuous in summer but the female may be harder to spot. It nests in a deep scrape in the ground hidden in vegetation, lining the hollow with loose grass to hold 4 or 5 light blue-green eggs, sometimes lightly spotted with brown. The adult is a rather large and stocky bird, with a short tail and short, rounded wings. The breeding male is black overall, with a large white wing patch. The female and winter male are streaked brown-buff above, white streaked with brown below, with a white wing patch that may not be visible on the resting bird. All plumages show a white-tipped tail. The Lark Bunting eats insects, seeds and grain.

PAINTED BUNTING

Scientific name:	*Passerina ciris*
Length:	5½ inches
Habitat:	Low thickets, brushy streams, woodland edges
Identification:	Stocky ground-dwelling bird, with short tail and rounded bill. Male has indigo-blue head, bright green back, bright red underparts and rump, dusky wing and tail. Female lime green above, lemony-green below
Similar species:	Coloring distinctive

Despite its bright and distinctive coloring, the Painted Bunting can be difficult to spot since it hides in foliage even when singing. The male was once a popular caged bird, but now its capture is illegal. It nests not far above the ground, building a woven cup of grass and plant fibers lined with fine grass and hair, low in a low tree, or in a thick bush. It lays 3 or 4 gray-white eggs, spotted with brown, which are incubated by the female for about 11-13 days; the young are ready to leave the nest and begin fending for themselves around 2 weeks after hatching. The adult is a stocky bird, with a short tail and a rounded bill. The male has an indigo-blue head, a bright green back, bright red underparts and rump, and dusky wings and tail. The female is lime green above and a lemony yellow-green below. The juvenile resembles the female. The Painted Bunting sings all year round, except when it molts in late summer. It forages on the ground, looking for insects, spiders and seeds.

VARIED BUNTING

Scientific name:	*Passerina versicolor*
Length:	5½ inches
Habitat:	Thorny thickets, canyons, near water
Identification:	Stocky ground-dwelling bird, with short tail and rounded bill. Breeding male purple-red with bright red patch on nape, browner in fall. Female plain light brown
Similar species:	Female Varied Bunting resembles female Indigo but lacks streaking on breast

Locally common within its limited range, the Varied Bunting prefers thorny thickets and canyons near water and is seen in the far south along the Mexican border in summer, spreading down into Mexico. It nests up to 10 feet above the ground, building a woven cup of grass, stems and plant fibers in a low tree, thick bush or tangle of vines to hold 3-5 plain pale blue-white eggs. These are incubated by the female for about 11-13 days and the young are ready to leave the nest and begin fending for themselves around 2 weeks after hatching. The adult is a stocky bird, with a short tail and a rounded bill. The breeding male is purple-red with a bright red patch on the nape, but sometimes appears black at a distance. The fall male is browner and the female is plain light brown. The Varied Bunting forages on the ground, looking for insects and seeds.

INDIGO BUNTING

Scientific name: *Passerina cyanea*
Length: 5½ inches
Habitat: Woodland clearings, farmland, brushy pasture
Identification: Stocky ground-dwelling bird, with short tail and stout bill. Breeding male indigo blue overall. Female and fall male brown with fine streaks on chest and blue tint to tail
Similar species: Male Blue Grosbeak is bigger with bigger bill and has wide cinnamon wing bars. Female Indigo lacks obvious wing bars of female Lazuli

Common in the east in woodland clearings and on farmland in summer, the Indigo Bunting is rarely seen in the west although part of its range overlaps with that of the Lazuli Bunting, and the two sometimes interbreed. It nests up to 15 feet above the ground, building a neatly-woven cup of grass, leaves and bark strips in a tree or bush to hold 3-5 plain pale blue-white eggs. These are incubated by the female for about 11-14 days and the young are ready to begin fending for themselves around 9-11 days after hatching. The adult is a stocky bird, with a short tail and a stout bill. The breeding male is indigo blue overall. The female and fall male are brown with fine streaks on the chest and a blue tint to the tail. The Indigo Bunting mainly forages on the ground in flocks, looking for insects and seeds, but it also takes berries in fall.

LAZULI BUNTING

Scientific name: *Passerina amoena*
Length: 5½ inches
Habitat: Deciduous and mixed woodland, chaparral, brush near water
Identification: Stocky ground-dwelling bird, with short tail and stout bill. Breeding male has bright turquoise hood, back and rump, cinnamon breast and sides, white belly, dark wings with two white wing bars. Female is gray-brown above, warm buffy below with paler throat and belly, blue tint to wing tips, rump and tail, two buffy wing bars
Similar species: Bluebirds have thinner bills, lack wing bars. Female has more obvious wing bars than female Indigo

Wintering in Mexico, but fairly common across the west in summer, the Lazuli Bunting prefers deciduous woodland and brushy areas near water. Part of its range overlaps with that of the Indigo Bunting, and the two species sometimes interbreed. It nests up to 10 feet above the ground, building a neatly-woven cup of grass in a tree, bush or vine to hold 3 or 4 plain pale blue eggs. These are incubated by the female for about 10-12 days and the young are ready to begin fending for themselves around 2 weeks after hatching. The adult is a stocky bird, with a short tail and a stout bill. The breeding male has a bright turquoise hood, back and rump, cinnamon breast and sides, a white belly, and dark wings with two white wing bars. The winter male is duller and more brownish. The female is gray-brown above and warm buffy below with a paler throat and belly, a blue tint to the wing tips, rump and tail, and two buffy wing bars. The Lazuli Bunting mainly forages on the ground for insects, caterpillars, beetles and seeds, but sometimes flies up to catch its prey in the air.

PYRRHULOXIA

Scientific name:	*Cardinalis sinuatus*
Length:	8¾ inches
Habitat:	Thorny brush, mesquite thicket, desert, dry woodland edges
Identification:	Crested, long-tailed bird with large, rounded stubby bill. Male gray, with crimson crest, rosy-red stripe down middle of breast and belly, dark red flashes in wings and tail. Female buffy with red spot in front of eye and red on crest, wings and tail. Bill yellow in summer, pale gray-yellow in winter
Similar species:	Coloring distinctive. Female Northern Cardinal has longer red bill

Fairly common across the south near the Mexican border, the Pyrrhuloxia prefers thorny brush, mesquite thickets and other dry habitats. It nests up to 15 feet above the ground, building a compact cup of twigs, bark and plant fibers in mesquite or a thorny bush, in which it lays 2-4 grayish-white eggs with brown spotting. These are incubated by the female for around 2 weeks, while the male provides food and helps feed the nestlings after they have hatched. The adult is a crested bird with a long tail and a large, rounded stubby bill. The male (*right*) is gray, with a crimson crest, a rosy-red stripe down the middle of the breast and belly, and dark red flashes in wings and tail. The female is buffy with a red spot in front of the eye and red on the crest, wings and tail. The bill of both birds is yellow in summer, and pale gray-yellow in winter. The Pyrrhuloxia feeds on seeds and insects and is particularly welcome in cotton fields, where it eats cotton worms and weevils.

DICKCISSEL

Scientific name:	*Spiza americana*
Length:	6¼ inches
Habitat:	Open meadows, prairie
Identification:	Stocky, short-tailed open-country bird with long bill and pointed wings. Gray-brown above, buffy-white beneath, with yellowish eyebrow, chestnut shoulder patch. Breeding male has black bib, white chin, bright yellow breast. Female has some yellow on breast. Winter male has less distinct bib
Similar species:	Female similar to House Sparrow, but has yellow on breast and chestnut shoulder

The range of the Dickcissel varies quite a bit in different years, but it is generally fairly common and abundant in the midwest in summer and migrates in dense flocks to South America for the winter. In its breeding area it nests on the ground or up to 15 feet above, building a cup of grass and plant fibers concealed in vegetation or in a bush or tree. It lays 2-5 plain pale blue eggs, which are incubated by the female for around 2 weeks; the young birds leave the nest some 9 days after hatching. The adult is a stocky bird with a short tail, a relatively long bill and pointed wings. It is gray-brown above and buffy-white beneath, with a yellowish eyebrow and chestnut shoulder patch. The breeding male has a black bib, a white chin, and a bright yellow breast; the winter male has a less distinct bib and the female (*right*) has some yellow on the breast. The Dickcissel feeds on seeds, grain and insects and will come to backyard bird feeders in fall.

NORTHERN CARDINAL

Scientific name:	*Cardinalis cardinalis*
Length:	$8\frac{3}{4}$ inches
Habitat:	Forest, swamps, thickets, parks, suburban backyards
Identification:	Crested, long-tailed woodland bird with large triangular bill. Male bright red, with black face and throat and red bill. Female olive-buff with reddish crest, wings and tail, juvenile reddish-buff
Similar species:	Coloring of male distinctive. Pyrrhuloxia has shorter, dull yellow bill

The Northern Cardinal is common both in the east and the southwest in a wide variety of habitats, even city parks and backyards as long as there is sufficient cover. The Cardinal not only returns to the same breeding area, pairs mate for life. It nests up to 12 feet above the ground, building a loosely-woven cup of twigs and plant fibers in a shrub or thicket, in which it lays 3 or 4 pale green eggs with brown-lilac spots. These are incubated by the female for just under 2 weeks, while the male provides food and helps feed the nestlings after they have hatched. The adult is a crested bird with a long tail and a large triangular bill. The male (*above*) is bright red, with a black face and throat and a red bill. The female is olive-buff with a reddish crest, wings and tail, and the juvenile is reddish-buff with a black bill. The Northern Cardinal feeds mainly on the ground, out in the open. It eats fruits, seeds and insects and regularly comes to bird feeders in winter, particularly for sunflower seeds.

ROSE-BREASTED GROSBEAK

Scientific name:	*Pheucticus ludovicianus*
Length:	8 inches
Habitat:	Woods along streams
Identification:	Stocky, large-headed woodland bird with very large triangular bill. Breeding male has black head and back, rose-red breast, white underparts and rump, white wing bars and spots, black tail with white outer feathers, rose-red wing linings in flight. Winter plumage is browner. Female dark brown above, whitish streaked brown beneath, white eyebrow, yellow wing linings
Similar species:	Female almost identical to female Black-headed Grosbeak, but has heavier streaking beneath

Common in woods alongside streams in the east in summer, the Rose-breasted Grosbeak is rarely seen in the west even during migration. It nests high above the ground, building a flimsy-looking shallow cup of twigs, plant fibers and grass in a shrub or tree, which holds 3-5 pale blue eggs, spotted with brown. The adult is stocky and large-headed with a big, triangular bill. The breeding male has a black head and back, a rose-red breast, white underparts and rump, white wing bars and spots, a black tail with white outer feathers and rose-red wing linings in flight; its winter plumage is browner. The female is dark brown above, whitish streaked brown beneath, with a white eyebrow and yellow wing linings. The Rose-breasted Grosbeak stays high in the trees, but sometimes forages on the ground or comes to bird feeders. It eats fruit, seeds and insects.

BLUE GROSBEAK

Scientific name:	*Guiraca caerulea*
Length:	$6\frac{3}{4}$ inches
Habitat:	Overgrown fields, riversides, woodland edges
Identification:	Stocky, large-headed open-country bird with very large triangular bill. Breeding male dark blue with two cinnamon wing bars. Female tan above, lighter buff beneath, faint blue tint on wings and rump, pale cinnamon wing bars
Similar species:	Male Indigo Bunting is smaller with smaller bill and lacks cinnamon wing bars

The Blue Grosbeak is found across the south in summer, in brushy fields, woodland edges and roadsides, and it is fairly common in most areas. It nests up to 15 feet above the ground, building a loose cup of twigs, plant fibers and stems in a low shrub or tree, which holds 3 or 4 plain pale blue eggs. These are incubated by the female for 10-12 days, with the young leaving the nest just under 2 weeks after they have hatched. The adult is a stocky, large-headed bird with a very large, triangular bill. The breeding male is dark blue with two cinnamon wing bars, but in winter is brownish. The female (*right*) is tan above, lighter buff beneath, with a faint blue tint on wings and rump, and pale cinnamon wing bars. The Blue Grosbeak gathers in small flocks after breeding, sometimes along with finches and sparrows, to forage for fruit, seeds, spiders and insects - particularly grasshoppers in open fields.

BLACK-HEADED GROSBEAK

Scientific name:	*Pheucticus melanocephalus*
Length:	8¼ inches
Habitat:	Open woodland, forest edges
Identification:	Stocky, large-headed woodland bird with very large triangular bill. Breeding male has black head and back, rusty-orange collar, breast and rump, yellow belly and wing linings, white wing bars and spots, black tail with white outer feathers. Winter plumage is browner. Female brown above, buff finely streaked brown beneath, white eyebrow, yellow wing linings
Similar species:	Female almost identical to female Rose-breasted Grosbeak, but has lighter streaking beneath

Very common across the west of North America in summer, but rarely seen in the east, the Black-headed Grosbeak prefers oak woods and dense woodland along rivers. It will sometimes breed with the Rose-breasted where their territories meet, creating hybrids. Unlike some other species, it is the female bird that stakes out a territory and defends it. It nests quite high above the ground, building a loose, shallow and rather flimsy cup of twigs, plant fibers and rootlets in the fork of a shrub or tree, which holds 3-5 pale blue eggs, spotted with brown. These are incubated by both birds for just under 2 weeks, with the young leaving the nest 10-12 days after they have hatched. The adult is a stocky, large-headed bird with a very large, triangular bill. The breeding male has a black head and back, a rusty-orange collar, breast and rump, yellow belly and wing linings, white wing bars and spots, and a black tail with white outer feathers; its winter plumage is browner. The female is brown above, buff finely streaked brown beneath, with a white eyebrow and yellow wing linings. The Black-headed Grosbeak eats fruit, seeds and insects, and sometimes comes to bird feeders - particularly for sunflower seeds. Its large beak is perfectly adapted to crush large, hard seeds, which enables it to take some foods that the other birds are unable to tackle.

RED-WINGED BLACKBIRD

Scientific name:	*Agelaius phoeniceus*
Length:	8¾ inches
Habitat:	Freshwater marshes, open fields, farmland
Identification:	Stocky marshland bird with fairly short tail and rounded wings. Male black with bright red and buff-yellow shoulder patch. Female and juvenile streaked brown with buff eyebrow
Similar species:	Male Tricolored Blackbird has dark red and white wing patch, but is only found in a limited area. Female is browner than Tricolored female, with heavier streaking. Also resembles a sparrow, but has spike-shaped bill, darker belly

Widespread and abundant, the Red-winged Blackbird is found on all kinds of wet ground across most of North America. Except in the breeding season, it forms huge flocks - often with other blackbird species. It nests near the ground, weaving a sturdy cup of grass attached to marsh reeds or in a low bush, in which it lays 3-5 pale blue-green eggs, heavily marked with brown and black. These are incubated by the female for around 10-12 days and the young birds begin to fend for themselves just under 2 weeks after hatching. The adult is a rather stocky bird with a fairly short tail and rounded wings. The male is black with a bright red and buff-yellow shoulder patch, the female and juvenile are streaked brown with a buff eyebrow. In central California, the males may have an all-red shoulder patch. Although the Red-winged Blackbird may be considered a pest for eating grain in spring, it catches large quantities of crop-damaging insects during the nesting season. It also eats seeds and spiders.

TRICOLORED BLACKBIRD

Scientific name:	*Agelaius tricolor*
Length:	8¾ inches
Habitat:	Marshland, rice fields, open country
Identification:	Stocky marshland bird with fairly short tail and rather pointed wings. Male black with dark red and white shoulder patch. Female and juvenile gray-brown with faint streaking and pale eyebrow
Similar species:	Red-winged Blackbird has bright red and buff-yellow wing patch. Female Red-winged is browner, with heavier streaking

Although it is found only in limited areas mainly in California, the Tricolored Blackbird is often seen in large numbers because it breeds in dense, crowded colonies and travels in flocks. It nests near the ground, weaving a sturdy cup of grass attached to reed stems or in a low vine, in which it lays 3 or 4 pale green eggs, heavily marked with brown scrawls. These are incubated by the female for around 10-12 days and the young birds leave the nest just under 2 weeks after hatching. The adult is a rather stocky bird with a fairly short tail and rather pointed wings. The male is black with a dark red and broad white shoulder patch, the female and juvenile are gray-brown with faint streaking and a pale eyebrow. The Tricolored Blackbird feeds on grasshoppers in late summer and on insects and seeds in rice fields and marshes in winter. Its population is declining, due to the draining of its marshland habitat.

YELLOW-HEADED BLACKBIRD

Scientific name:	*Xanthocephalus xanthocephalus*
Length:	9½ inches
Habitat:	Freshwater marshes, reedy lakes, farmland
Identification:	Large, heavy-billed marshland bird with fairly short tail and rather broad wings. Male black with yellow head and breast, in flight shows white wing patch. Female brown-black with dusky-yellow chest, throat and face, plain wings. Juvenile dark with buffy-yellow head
Similar species:	Coloring distinctive

The Yellow-headed Blackbird is very distinctive on the marshland of the west and ranging east across the prairie states in summer, but it retreats south to spend the winter along the border and down into Mexico. In the breeding season the male (*above*) puts on a courtship display to attract the female, fanning its tail and spreading its wings before making a deep and courtly bow. After pairing, it nests in large, crowded colonies in tall marsh plants over water - the water deters predators such as raccoons and skunks, while hawks and crows are mobbed by the colony until they retreat. Its nest is a sturdy basket of grass woven between several reed stalks, in which it lays 3-5 whitish eggs, speckled with brown. These are incubated by the female for around 2 weeks; the juveniles leave the nest 10-12 days after hatching. The adult is a large bird with a fairly short tail and rather broad wings. The male is black with a yellow head and breast, and shows a white wing patch in flight. The female is brown-black with a dusky-yellow chest, throat and face, and plain wings. The juvenile is dark with a buffy-yellow head. The Yellow-headed Blackbird often mixes with other species of blackbird outside the breeding season. It feeds on insects, small snails, grain and seeds.

BOBOLINK

Scientific name:	*Dolichonyx oryzivorus*
Length:	7 inches
Habitat:	Damp meadows, hayfields
Identification:	Slender open-country bird with pointed wings and pointed tail feathers. Breeding male mostly black with buffy nape, white patches on shoulder and rump. Female and winter male buffy with dark streaks on back, rump and sides, buff and black stripes on crown
Similar species:	Breeding male distinctive

In summer the Bobolink is fairly common in meadows and hayfields across the northern states and into Canada, but its population appears to be declining. In fall it migrates across the southeast, east of the Great Plains, to spend the winter in South America. It nests on the ground in hayfields and grass meadows, creating a flimsy cup of grass hidden in a dense tuft of vegetation, in which it lays 4-7 pale gray eggs, blotched with lilac-brown. These are incubated by the female for around 2 weeks and the young birds leave the nest a further 2 weeks or so after hatching. The adult is a slender bird with rather pointed wings and pointed tail feathers. The breeding male is mostly black with a buffy nape and white patches on shoulder and rump. The female and winter male are buffy with dark streaks on the back, rump and sides, and buff and black stripes on the crown. The Bobolink often mixes with other species of blackbird in fall to form large, mixed flocks. It feeds on insects, grain and seeds.

WESTERN MEADOWLARK

Scientific name:	*Sturnella neglecta*
Length:	9½ inches
Habitat:	Roadsides, grassland, open ground
Identification:	Heavy-bodied open-country bird with short tail and long bill. Dark gray-brown above with darker streaks and bars, buff-white stripes on black crown, cheek partly gray, yellow underparts with black V-shaped breast band, white outer tail feathers
Similar species:	Eastern Meadowlark almost identical and the two interbreed

Almost identical to the Eastern, the Western Meadowlark can sometimes be distinguished by range and call, although where the ranges overlap they learn each other's call and interbreed. The Western Meadowlark tends to prefer low vegetation and is often seen on roadsides. It nests on the ground, building a cup with a dome-shaped roof of grass hidden in dense vegetation, in which it lays 3-7 white eggs, heavily spotted with brown. These are incubated by the female for up to 2 weeks and the young birds begin to fend for themselves a further 10-12 days after hatching. The adult is a heavy-bodied bird with a short tail and a long, pointed bill. It is dark gray-brown above with darker streaks and bars, has three buff-white stripes on a black crown, gray on the upper cheek, yellow throat extends round onto lower cheek, yellow underparts with a black V-shaped breast band, and white outer tail feathers. Its song is a bubbling, flute-like and complex series of phrases speeding up towards the end and its call is a low-pitched *chook*. The Western Meadowlark eats insects, spiders, grain and seeds.

EASTERN MEADOWLARK

Scientific name:	*Sturnella magna*
Length:	9½ inches
Habitat:	Fields, meadows
Identification:	Heavy-bodied open-country bird with short tail and long bill. Dark gray-brown above with darker streaks and bars, buff-white stripes on black crown, gray cheek, yellow underparts with black V-shaped breast band, white outer tail feathers
Similar species:	Western Meadowlark almost identical and the two interbreed

The Eastern and the Western meadowlarks are almost identical and although they can sometimes be distinguished by range and call, where their ranges overlap they learn each other's call and interbreed. The Eastern Meadowlark tends to prefer taller vegetation. It nests on the ground, building a grass cup with a dome-shaped roof of grass stems hidden in dense vegetation, in which it lays 3-7 white eggs, spotted with brown. These are incubated by the female for up to 2 weeks and the young birds are ready to leave the nest to fend for themselves a further 10-12 days after hatching. The adult is a heavy-bodied bird with a short tail and a long, pointed bill. It is dark gray-brown above with darker streaks and bars, has three buff-white stripes on a black crown, a gray cheek, yellow underparts with a black V-shaped breast band, and extensive white on the outer tail feathers. Its song is a clear, whistled *te-seeyou see-yeeer*, its call is a high buzzy *drezzt*. The Eastern Meadowlark eats insects, spiders, grain and seeds.

BRONZED COWBIRD

Scientific name:	*Molothrus aeneus*
Length:	8¾ inches
Habitat:	Open country, farmland, wooded mountain canyons
Identification:	Stocky, short-tailed open-country bird with long, heavy bill and thick ruff of feathers at neck. Male black with iridescent bronze sheen, glossy blue-black wings and tail, red-orange eyes. Female dull black or dark gray-brown with red eyes
Similar species:	Red eyes distinctive at close range

Although its range in North America is rather limited, the Bronzed Cowbird is locally common in open country in summer, and gathers round farmland and feedlots in winter. Outside the breeding season, it often forms huge flocks with its own species and blackbirds. It does not build its own nest, but lays its pale blue-green eggs in the nest of an oriole, blackbird or sparrow or other songbird of similar size, one egg per nest. These are incubated by the host bird and the young bird leaves the nest some 11 days after hatching. The adult is a stocky, short-tailed bird with a long conical bill and a thick ruff of feathers at the nape that gives it a hunched look. The male is black with an iridescent bronze sheen, glossy blue-black wings and tail and red-orange eyes. The female and juvenile are dull black or dark gray-brown with red eyes. The Bronzed Cowbird picks ticks from livestock, hence its name. It also eats grain and insects.

BREWER'S BLACKBIRD

Scientific name:	*Euphagus cyanocephalus*
Length:	9 inches
Habitat:	Open ground, urban areas
Identification:	Slender, long-tailed open-country bird with short, straight bill. Breeding male black with iridescent purple head, green-violet glossy body, yellow eyes. Winter male less glossy. Female light gray-brown with brown eyes
Similar species:	The Rusty Blackbird has longer, thinner bill, plumage duller, breeding male has overall green sheen, female and juvenile rust-brown

Brewer's Blackbird is very common in the west and is not only seen regularly in open country but also in suburban parks and sometimes even in city areas. It is a gregarious bird, and outside the breeding season often flocks with other blackbirds and the Brown-headed Cowbird. It nests in small, loose colonies, building a bulky bowl of twigs and grass plastered with mud or cow dung and lined with finer material, in which it lays 4-6 light gray eggs blotched with brown and gray. These are incubated for around 2 weeks by the female and the young leave the nest some 2 weeks after hatching. The adult is a slender, long-tailed bird with a short, straight bill. The breeding male is black with an iridescent purple head, a very glossy green-violet body and yellow eyes; in winter it retains the basic coloring but is less glossy. The female and juvenile are light gray-brown with brown eyes. Brewer's Blackbird forages on the ground and eats seeds, grain and insects.

BROWN-HEADED COWBIRD

Scientific name:	*Molothrus ater*
Length:	7½ inches
Habitat:	Open woodland, farmland near cattle, suburbs
Identification:	Slender, short-tailed open-country bird with pointed wings. Male black with metallic green sheen and coffee-brown head. Female light gray-brown, juvenile gray-brown with scaled upperparts
Similar species:	Male distinctive, but female drab and confusing

The Brown-headed Cowbird is very common across most of North America and its population has increased with the clearing of forests so that it now threatens the existence of many smaller birds. It does not build its own nest, but lays its white eggs speckled with brown in the nest of a finch, warbler or vireo or other songbird of similar size, one egg per nest. These are incubated by the host bird, and after hatching the young cowbird crowds and starves out the other nestlings. The adult is a slender, short-tailed bird with pointed wings. The male is black with a metallic green sheen and a coffee-brown head. The female is light gray-brown and the juvenile is pale gray-brown with scaled upperparts. The Brown-headed Cowbird often feeds near livestock, walking on the ground with its tail held upward, and outside the breeding season it will often flock with other blackbirds in fields and pastures. It eats grain, seeds, berries and insects.

RUSTY BLACKBIRD

Scientific name:	*Euphagus carolinus*
Length:	9 inches
Habitat:	Wet woodland, swamp, trees near water
Identification:	Slender, square-tailed swampland bird with thin pointed bill. Breeding male black with dull metallic green sheen, yellow eyes. Breeding female slate-gray with yellow eyes. Winter adults and juvenile light rust-brown, finely barred beneath
Similar species:	Brewer's Blackbird has shorter, thicker bill, plumage more glossy, male has purple sheen to head, female and juvenile gray-brown

Although it is sometimes still seen in large flocks, the Rusty Blackbird is not as common as it was and populations are still declining. It prefers wet habitats and is rarely found far from water. It nests on or near the ground in boreal woodland, building a bulky bowl of twigs and grass sheltered in vegetation or low in a shrub or tree, in which it lays 4 or 5 light blue eggs blotched with brown. These are incubated for around 2 weeks by the female and the young leave the nest some 2 weeks later. The adult is a slender, square-tailed bird with a thin pointed bill and yellow eyes. The breeding male is black with a dull metallic green sheen and the breeding female is slate-gray. Winter adults are light rust-brown, finely barred beneath, and the female has a gray rump. The juvenile resembles the winter adult, but has dark eyes. The Rusty Blackbird often forages in shallow water, catching small crustaceans, tadpoles and aquatic insects. It also eats seeds, grain and berries.

COMMON GRACKLE

Scientific name:	*Quiscalus quiscula*
Length:	12½ inches
Habitat:	Open fields, woods, swamps, parks, suburban lawns
Identification:	Medium-size long-billed open-country bird with long tail and yellow-white eyes. Male black with bronze sheen, blue gloss to head and breast, purple gloss on tail. Female smaller and duller. Juvenile dusky-brown, with brown eyes
Similar species:	Great-tailed and Boat-tailed larger and more evenly colored

East of the Rockies, the Common Grackle is found in a wide variety of habitats - even walking on suburban lawns. It is gregarious, traveling in huge, noisy flocks, sometimes with other blackbirds, and breeding in colonies. It nests high above the ground in an evergreen tree, building a bulky and sturdy cup of twigs and grass, lined with finer stems, in which it lays 4-6 greenish eggs marked with brown. These are incubated by the female for around 2 weeks; the young birds leave the nest just under 3 weeks after they have hatched. The adult is a medium-size, long-billed bird with a long, keel-shaped tail and yellow-white eyes. The most common male, the "Bronzed Grackle", is black with a bronze sheen to the body, a blue gloss on the head and breast, and a purple gloss to the tail. The "Purple Grackle" male is black with a bronze sheen, a dark green glossy back, a purple gloss on the head and breast, and a blue gloss to the tail. The female is smaller than the male and is less glossy. The juvenile is dark brown, with brown eyes. The Common Grackle feeds on the ground and eats almost anything, including grain, insects, small fish, salamanders, seeds and eggs and young of small birds.

GREAT-TAILED GRACKLE

Scientific name:	*Quiscalus mexicanus*
Length:	15 inches (female), 18 inches (male)
Habitat:	Open farmland, freshwater marsh, riversides
Identification:	Large long-billed open-country bird with long tail. Male black with iridescent purple-blue gloss and yellow eyes. Female and juvenile brown, with buff eyebrow and underparts, dark eye
Similar species:	Boat-tailed almost identical, but usually has dark eyes, rounder head and shorter tail. Common Grackle smaller, less evenly colored

A long-tailed blackbird, the Great-tailed Grackle is numerous in the southwest and its range is extending both north and westward. It is a social bird, traveling in flocks and breeding in colonies. It nests either on the ground or quite high above it, building a bulky mass of twigs and grass, lined with finer stems, amongst marsh reeds or in a tree or bush. It lays 3-5 bluish eggs covered with purple-brown scrawls, which are incubated by the female for around 2 weeks; the young birds leave the nest around 3 weeks after they have hatched. The adult is a large, long-billed bird with a very long tail. The male is black with an iridescent purple-blue gloss and yellow eyes. The female is smaller than the male, with a shorter tail, and is brown, with a buff eyebrow and underparts and a dark eye. The juvenile resembles the adult female but may have some streaking beneath. The Great-tailed Grackle feeds on the ground and will eat a wide variety of things, including fruit, grain, insects, garbage, offal and small birds.

BOAT-TAILED GRACKLE

Scientific name: *Quiscalus major*
Length: 14½ inches (female), 16½ inches (male)
Habitat: Coastal saltwater marshes, inland lakes and streams
Identification: Large long-billed open-country bird with long tail. Male black with iridescent green-blue gloss and brown eye. Female and juvenile tawny-brown, with buff eyebrow and underparts, brown eye
Similar species: Great-tailed almost identical, but usually has yellow eyes, flatter head and longer tail. Common Grackle smaller, less evenly colored

The Boat-tailed Grackle is found along the southeast coastline and prefers saltwater marshes - although it does go inland in

Florida. It is gregarious, traveling in flocks and breeding in small colonies. It nests on the ground amongst marsh reeds or high in a tree or bush, building a bulky mass of twigs and grass, lined with finer stems. It lays 3-5 blue-white eggs marked with purple-brown, which are incubated by the female for around 2 weeks; the young birds leave the nest around 3 weeks after they have hatched. The adult is a large, long-billed bird with a very long tail. The male is black with an iridescent green-blue gloss and brown eyes - but at the eastern end of its range some birds have yellow eyes. The female is smaller than the male, with a shorter tail, and is tawny-brown, with a buff eyebrow and underparts and a brown eye. The juvenile resembles the female but may have some streaking beneath. The Boat-tailed Grackle feeds on the ground and eats grain, insects and small birds.

HOODED ORIOLE (above)

Scientific name:	*Icterus cucullatus*
Length:	8 inches
Habitat:	Palm trees, riverside woods, parks, suburbs
Identification:	Small, slender woodland bird, with long down-curved bill and long tail. Male is orange with a black throat, back and wings, two white wing bars. Female is olive-yellow above, yellow beneath with dusky wings and two white wing bars
Similar species:	Male distinctive. Female and juvenile Orchard Oriole almost identical but have shorter tail, Baltimore and Bullock's orioles have orange tones or whitish belly, straighter bill

The Hooded Oriole is common during the summer in parks, suburbs and woods near rivers across the southwest. If possible, it prefers to nest in a palm or eucalyptus tree, weaving a hanging basket of plant fibers suspended from a palm frond or branch, with the entrance at the top. It lays 3-5 pale blue or gray eggs, spotted with brown and lilac, which are incubated for about 13-15 days by the female; the young birds are ready to leave the nest around 2 weeks after hatching. The adult is a small, slender bird, with a long, down-curved bill and a long tail. The male is orange with a black throat, back and wings, and two white wing bars. The female is olive-yellow above, yellow beneath with dusky wings and two white wing bars. The juvenile resembles the female, but the male soon has a black bib as it begins to acquire its adult plumage. The Hooded Oriole forages slowly through the trees hunting for insects. It also takes nectar from flowers and will often visit garden hummingbird feeders.

ORCHARD ORIOLE

Scientific name:	*Icterus spurius*
Length:	$7\frac{1}{4}$ inches
Habitat:	Stands of trees, woodland edges, suburbs
Identification:	Small, compact woodland bird, with thin, down-curved bill and short tail. Male is chestnut with a black hood and wings, two white wing bars. Female is olive above, lemon-yellow beneath with dusky wings and two white wing bars
Similar species:	Male distinctive. Female and juvenile Hooded Oriole almost identical but have longer tail, Baltimore and Bullock's orioles have orange tones or whitish belly, straighter bill

The smallest North American oriole, the Orchard Oriole is found across the eastern states in summer at the edges of woodland or in small stands of trees. It is most common in the southeast, but rarer towards the northern parts of its range. It nests up to 20 feet above the ground, weaving a hanging cup of plant fibers suspended from a tree branch, in which it lays 3-7 pale blue-gray eggs, spotted with brown and lilac. These are incubated for about 2 weeks by the female, and the young birds are ready to leave the nest around 13-15 days after hatching. The adult is a small, compact bird, with a thin, down-curved bill and short tail. The male is chestnut with a black hood and wings, and two white wing bars. The female is olive above, lemon-yellow beneath with dusky wings and two white wing bars. The juvenile resembles the female, but the male soon has a black bib as it begins to acquire its adult plumage. The Orchard Oriole forages in trees and eats insects and fruit, but it also takes nectar from flowers and may visit hummingbird feeders.

ALTAMIRA ORIOLE

Scientific name: *Icterus gularis*
Length: 10 inches
Habitat: Tall riverside trees, willow, mesquite
Identification: Large woodland bird, with thick bill and long tail. Orange with a black throat, back and wings, orange shoulder bar, white wing bar. Juvenile duller with yellow shoulder patch
Similar species: Hooded Oriole has longer, thinner bill, and white rather than orange wing bar

Only found in North America in the Rio Grande valley in south Texas and down into Mexico, the Altamira Oriole is locally common throughout the year. When looking for a nesting site it tends to prefer tall, riverside trees, weaving a long, hanging basket of plant fibers suspended from a branch, with the entrance situated at the top. It usually lays 3 or 4 white eggs, spotted with brown, and raises two broods a year, but the exact details of incubation and nestling periods are currently unknown. In the breeding season it is a frequent victim of the Bronzed Cowbird, which often chooses to lay an egg in its nest. The adult is a large bird with a shortish, thick, slightly down-curved bill and a long tail. Its plumage is orange with a black throat, back and wings, an orange shoulder bar and a white wing bar. The juvenile is duller than the adult bird, with a yellow shoulder bar, but it soon develops a black bib as it begins to acquire its mature plumage, a process that is complete by its second fall. The Altamira Oriole eats insects and berries.

BALTIMORE ORIOLE

Scientific name:	*Icterus galbula*
Length:	8¼ inches
Habitat:	Deciduous woodland
Identification:	Medium-size woodland bird, with long straight bill and short square tail. Male has black hood and back, bright orange rump and underparts, orange shoulder patch, white wing bar, large orange patches each side of tail. Female is olive-brown above, orange beneath with variable black on head and throat, dusky wings and two white wing bars. Juvenile like female but yellow breast and whitish belly
Similar species:	Female and juvenile Bullock's Oriole can look almost identical to juvenile Baltimore. Orchard and Hooded orioles are more yellow, with down-curved bill

The Baltimore and Bullock's orioles are very similar and sometimes interbreed, so they are often considered to be one species, the Northern Oriole. The Baltimore is found mainly to the northeast and prefers deciduous woods. It nests high above the ground, weaving a hanging basket of plant fibers suspended from the tip of a branch, in which it lays 3-6 whitish eggs, with brown scrawls. The adult is medium-size, with a long, straight bill and a short, square tail. The male (*right*) has a black hood and back, a bright orange rump and underparts, an orange shoulder patch, white wing bar, and large orange patches on each side of the tail. The female is olive-brown above and orange beneath, with variable amounts of black on the head and throat, dusky wings and two white wing bars. The juvenile is like the female but has a yellow breast and whitish belly. The Baltimore Oriole eats insects and fruit.

SCOTT'S ORIOLE

Scientific name:	*Icterus parisorum*
Length:	9 inches
Habitat:	Arid grassland with yuccas, junipers, oak woods
Identification:	Medium-size woodland bird, with long, thin, down-curved bill and long tail. Male has black hood, back, and breast, bright lemon-yellow underparts, rump and upper tail, black lower tail and wings, yellow shoulder bar, one white wing bar. Female is dusky-yellow above, yellow beneath with dusky wings and two white wing bars
Similar species:	Male is distinctive, female is larger and darker than Hooded or Orchard orioles

In the dry grassland and semi-arid woods of the southwest, Scott's Oriole is fairly widespread but rather uncommon. It nests high above the ground, weaving a hanging pouch of plant fibers suspended from the leaves of a yucca or the branch of a tree, with the entrance at the top. It lays 3-5 blue-white eggs, unevenly spotted with brown, which are incubated for 13-15 days by the female; the young birds are ready to leave the nest around 2 weeks after hatching and there is usually a second brood. The adult is a medium-size bird, with a long, thin, down-curved bill and a long tail. The male (*right*) has a black hood, back, and breast, bright lemon-yellow underparts, rump and upper tail, a black lower tail and wings, a yellow shoulder bar, and one white wing bar. The female is dusky-yellow above, yellow beneath with dusky wings and two white wing bars. The juvenile resembles the female, but the male soon develops black marks at the throat as it begins to acquire its adult plumage. Scott's Oriole forages in trees for insects. It also eats fruit and takes nectar from flowers.

BULLOCK'S ORIOLE

Scientific name:	*Icterus bullockii*
Length:	$8\frac{1}{4}$ inches
Habitat:	Riverside treetops, lowland woods
Identification:	Medium-size woodland bird, with long straight bill and short square tail. Male has black crown, nape and back, narrow black eyeline, bright orange rump and underparts, large white wing patch, black inverted T on orange tail. Female and juvenile olive-brown above, yellow throat and breast and whitish belly, dusky wings and two white wing bars
Similar species:	Female and juvenile Bullock's Oriole can look almost identical to juvenile Baltimore. Orchard and Hooded orioles are more yellow, with down-curved bill

The ranges of Baltimore and Bullock's orioles were once separated by treeless plains, but now these have been broken up by towns and other settlements, the Baltimore has spread west and Bullock's east. Where they now overlap they will often interbreed freely, so they are sometimes considered to be one species, the Northern Oriole. Bullock's Oriole is found mainly to the southwest in summer and prefers trees along rivers and lowland woods. It nests high above the ground, weaving a hanging basket of plant fibers suspended from the tip of a branch, with the entrance at the top. It lays 3-6 blue-white eggs, with gray or black scrawls, which are incubated for about 2 weeks by the female; the young birds are ready to leave the nest about 13-15 days after they have hatched. The adult is a medium-size bird, with a long, straight bill and a short, square tail. The male (*above*) has a black crown, nape and back, a narrow black eyeline, a bright orange rump and underparts, a large white wing patch, and a black inverted T on an orange tail. The female and juvenile are olive-brown above, with a yellow throat and breast and a whitish belly, dusky wings and two white wing bars. Bullock's Oriole forages in the trees for insects and also eats fruit.

GRAY-CROWNED ROSY-FINCH

Scientific name:	*Leucosticte tephrocotis*
Length:	5¾ inches
Habitat:	High mountains
Identification:	Slender, long-winged open-country bird with long tail and short legs. Dark brown back and underparts, black forehead, gray nape and crown, pink shoulder and rump, face gray or brown. Female duller
Similar species:	Black Rosy-Finch has similar coloring but with more contrast

In summer the Gray-crowned Rosy-Finch lives high in the mountains, but in winter it descends to lower elevations - although it rarely comes right down onto the plains. It breeds on alpine tundra and high snowfields, building a bulky nest of grass, feathers and moss in a rock cavity, in which it lays 3-6 white eggs. These are incubated by the female for around 2 weeks and the young birds leave the nest to begin fending for themselves about 3 weeks after hatching. The adult is a slender, long-winged bird with a long tail and rather short legs. It has a dark brown back and underparts, a black forehead, a gray nape and crown, and pink on the shoulder and rump. Birds near the coast have a gray face, inland birds have a brown face. The female is similar, but duller and the juvenile more gray. The Gray-crowned Rosy-Finch feeds mainly on alpine plant seeds and insects at lower elevations.

EVENING GROSBEAK *(below)*

Scientific name:	*Coccothraustes vespertinus*
Length:	8 inches
Habitat:	Mixed woods, suburban backyards
Identification:	Medium-size, short-tailed woodland bird, with short pointed wings and massive bill. Male dark olive-brown head, neck and breast, yellow forehead and eyebrow, yellow body, black wings and tail with large white wing patch. Female and juvenile grayish-gold, black wings and tail marked with white
Similar species:	Goldfinches smaller, with much smaller bill

A wandering nomad, both range and numbers of the Evening Grosbeak vary a great deal from year to year. It is often seen in large, noisy flocks, which may visit feeders to eat sunflower seeds. It breeds in woodland, building a loose, flimsy bowl of small twigs and rootlets near the tip of a branch in dense foliage - several pairs may nest quite near one another. It lays 3 or 4 bluish-green eggs with fine markings, which are incubated for up to 2 weeks by the female bird; the young birds leave the nest around 2 weeks later. The adult is a medium-size, short-tailed bird, with short, pointed wings and massive, conical bill that is yellow-green in breeding birds and ivory in winter. The male has a dark olive-brown head, neck and breast, a yellow forehead and eyebrow, yellow body, and black wings and tail with a large white wing patch. The female and juvenile are grayish-gold, with black wings and tail marked with white. The Evening Grosbeak forages high in trees in flocks, for seeds, berries, buds or fruit - it also sometimes eats insects.

BLACK ROSY-FINCH

Scientific name:	*Leucosticte atrata*
Length:	6 inches
Habitat:	High altitude areas, mountain towns
Identification:	Slender, long-winged open-country bird with long tail and short legs. Dark brown-black back and breast, black forehead, gray nape and cap, pink shoulder, belly and rump. Female browner, may lack gray cap
Similar species:	Gray-crowned Rosy-Finch has similar coloring but with less contrast

The Black Rosy-Finch lives high in the Rocky Mountains during the summer, but when winter comes it spreads down to the lower elevations and sometimes forms mixed flocks with the Gray-crowned. The breeding grounds of the Black Rosy-Finch are high in the mountains, where it builds a bulky nest of grass, feathers and moss in a cliff cavity, in which it lays 3-5 white eggs. These are incubated by the female for around 2 weeks and the young birds begin fending for themselves about 3 weeks after they have hatched. The adult is a slender, long-winged bird with a long tail and rather short legs. It has a dark brown-black back and breast, a black forehead, a gray nape and cap, and pink on the shoulder, belly and rump. In its fresh plumage, the male may have some silver-gray scaling. The female is very similar to the male, but is rather grayer or browner and has less pink. The Black Rosy-Finch forages on the ground, hunting for the seeds of alpine plants. At lower elevations it will also eat insects, and it may come to visit the bird feeders in alpine towns.

RED CROSSBILL

Scientific name:	*Loxia curvirostra*
Length:	$6\frac{1}{4}$ inches
Habitat:	Coniferous woods
Identification:	Stocky woodland bird with short tail and large bill with crossed tip. Male mottled brick-red with dark wings and tail. Female mottled olive-gray with darker wings, dull yellow rump and underparts. Juvenile orange-tinted with dusky streaks
Similar species:	White-winged Crossbill has two broad white wing bars

The unique bill of this species has developed to allow it to open pine cones and extract the seed. The Red Crossbill lives in coniferous forests but wanders around in flocks in search of pine cones and breeds in any season when food is plentiful - even in the depths of winter. It nests well above the ground in a conifer, building a neat, shallow cup of twigs, rootlets and moss lined with lichens and fur in which it lays 3-5 bluish eggs spotted with brown at the rounded end. The female bird incubates the eggs for around 2 weeks and the young leave the nest around 15-17 days after they have hatched. The adult is a stocky bird with a short tail and a large bill with the tips of the mandibles crossed. The male is mottled brick-red above and below, with dark tail and wings. The female is mottled olive-gray with darker wings, and a dull yellow rump and underparts. The juvenile is orange-tinted with dusky streaks. The Red Crossbill eats pine nuts and insects.

WHITE-WINGED CROSSBILL

Scientific name:	*Loxia leucoptera*
Length:	$6\frac{1}{2}$ inches
Habitat:	Coniferous woods
Identification:	Plump woodland bird with short notched tail and large bill with crossed tip. Male pink-red with dark tail and wings with two broad white wing bars. Female olive-gray with yellow rump, dark tail and wings, two white wing bars. Juvenile heavily streaked with narrow white wing bars
Similar species:	Red Crossbill darker and lacks white wing bars

Like the Red Crossbill, the White-winged Crossbill lives within coniferous forests but wanders around in flocks in search of cones and breeds whenever food is plentiful - even in the depths of winter. It nests well above the ground in a conifer, building a deep cup of twigs, rootlets, bark strips and moss lined with fine grass and feathers. It lays 3 or 4 greenish-white eggs spotted with brown, which are incubated for around 2 weeks. The adult is a stocky bird with a short, notched tail and a large bill with the tips of the mandibles crossed. The male is pink-red, with a dark tail and wings and two broad white wing bars. The female is olive-gray with a yellow rump, dark tail and wings, and two broad white wing bars. The juvenile is heavily streaked and has narrower wing bars than the adults. The White-winged Crossbill has a smaller, slimmer bill than the Red, so it is much better adapted for spruce cones rather than pine. It also eats other seeds, fruit and insects.

PINE GROSBEAK

Scientific name:	*Pinicola enucleator*
Length:	9 inches
Habitat:	Spruce and fir woods, deciduous woods, orchards, mature suburban trees
Identification:	Large, plump woodland bird with long notched tail and stubby rounded bill. Male mostly rose-pink with dark streaking on back, gray tail, dark wings with two white wing bars. Female gray with mustard head and rump, dark wings, two white wing bars. Juvenile similar to female but russet head and rump
Similar species:	Red and White-winged crossbill much smaller, with longer bill

Mainly found in the conifer forests of the far north, the Pine Grosbeak can be quite common. In winter it is also found in deciduous forests, sometimes coming well down into the south in search of food and seen in orchards and suburban trees. It nests up to 12 feet above the ground, usually in a conifer, building a bulky cup of grasses, rootlets and moss lined with hair in which it lays 2-5 pale greeny-blue eggs spotted with brown and gray. The female bird incubates the eggs for around 2 weeks and the young leave the nest around 3 weeks after they have hatched. The adult is a large, plump bird with a long notched tail and a stubby, rounded black bill. The male (*below*) is mostly rose-pink above and below, with dark streaking on the back, gray under the tail, a dark tail and wings and two white wing bars. The female is gray with a mustard head and rump, dark wings and two white wing bars. The juvenile is very similar to the adult female but has a russet head and rump. The Pine Grosbeak eats seeds, buds, berries, nuts and insects.

PURPLE FINCH

Scientific name:	*Carpodacus purpureus*
Length:	6 inches
Habitat:	Coniferous and mixed woodland, suburbs, parks, wooded canyons, orchards
Identification:	Stocky woodland bird with short, notched tail and stout bill. Male mostly dusky rosy-red, with brown streaked back, white belly, brown wings and tail. Female streaked brown above, white streaked brown beneath, bold brown and white stripes on head, broad white eyebrow, brown cheek with white mustache mark
Similar species:	Male darker than Cassin's or House finch, female has heavier streaking on breast

Despite its name, the Purple Finch is pink rather than purple. It is fairly common across most of its range and can be seen in large flocks in orchards and parks during fall and winter. It breeds in the north, building a neat, shallow nest of twigs, bark strips and rootlets lined with grass, up to 60 feet above the ground on the horizontal branch of a conifer. It lays 4 or 5 pale bluish-green eggs, spotted and scrawled with brown and black, which are incubated by the female for 12-14 days; the young birds leave the nest to start fending for themselves some 2 weeks after hatching. The adult is a stocky bird with a short, notched tail and a stout bill. The male is mostly dusky rosy-red, with brown streaks on the back, a white belly and brown wings and tail. The female is streaked brown above, and white heavily streaked with brown beneath, with bold brown and white stripes on the head, a broad white eyebrow, and a brown cheek with a white mustache mark. The juvenile is like the female. The Purple Finch eats seeds, fruits and also insects.

HOUSE FINCH

Scientific name:	*Carpodacus mexicanus*
Length:	6 inches
Habitat:	Open woods, deserts, canyons, backyards, cities
Identification:	Stocky open-country bird with long, slightly notched tail and short, stout bill. Male has red or orange-yellow eyebrow, forehead, breast and rump, brown cap, brown streaked back, white belly with dark streaks on sides, brown wings and tail. Female streaked gray-brown above, buffy with blurred brown streaks beneath, indistinct patterning on head
Similar species:	Male browner with longer tail than Purple or Cassin's finch, and shorter, more rounded wings. Female plainer than Cassin's or Purple finch

Common and abundant over most of North America, the House Finch lives in a wide variety of habitats up to elevations of about 6000 feet. Native to the west, it was introduced around New York in 1940 and has now also spread across the east. It breeds almost anywhere, building a neat, compact nest of grass, stems and leaves high above the ground in a tree, bush or on a building, in which it lays 3-5 bluish eggs. The adult is a stocky bird with a long, slightly notched tail and a short, stout bill. The male has a red or orange-yellow eyebrow, forehead, breast and rump, a brown cap, brown streaked back, a white belly with dark streaks on the sides, and brown wings and tail. The female is streaked gray-brown above, buffy with blurred brown streaks beneath, and has indistinct patterning on the head. The House Finch is a social bird and often forages in flocks; it eats almost anything, including seeds, buds, fruits and insects.

CASSIN'S FINCH

Scientific name:	*Carpodacus cassinii*
Length:	$6\frac{1}{4}$ inches
Habitat:	High mountain forests, evergreen woods
Identification:	Stocky woodland bird with short, notched tail and stout bill. Male has bright red crown and breast, brown streaked back washed pink, white belly, brown wings and tail. Female streaked gray-brown above, white finely streaked brown beneath, brown and white stripes on head, pale eye ring, brown cheek with faint white mustache mark
Similar species:	Male larger than Purple or House finch, red on head brighter, otherwise rather paler. Female has lighter streaking on breast than female Purple but it extends under tail, head markings less distinct. Female House Finch has plainer head

Cassin's Finch is quite common in conifer woods in the mountain areas of the west - although it sometimes ranges further north in summer and in winter may stray down into Mexico. It builds a neat cup of twigs and rootlets lined with grass and horsehair, up to 50 feet above the ground on the horizontal branch of a conifer, in which it lays 4 or 5 pale bluish-green eggs, spotted with dark brown. The adult is stocky with a short, notched tail and a stout bill. The male has a bright red crown and breast, a brown streaked back washed with pink, a white belly, and brown wings and tail. The female is streaked gray-brown above, white finely streaked with brown beneath, with brown and white stripes on the head, a pale eye ring, and a brown cheek with a faint white mustache mark. Cassin's Finch eats seeds, buds, fruits and also insects.

PINE SISKIN

Scientific name:	*Carduelis pinus*
Length:	5 inches
Habitat:	Open coniferous and mixed woods, fields
Identification:	Small woodland bird with short forked tail, long pointed wings and slender bill. Brown-gray above, buffy beneath, finely streaked overall, in flight shows yellow bars across wings and yellow tail with black tip. Female has slightly less yellow
Similar species:	Goldfinches have more yellow, sparrows lack yellow and have thicker bill

Found in open coniferous forests, the Pine Siskin is fairly common across much of its range and is often seen in large flocks with goldfinches during the winter. It breeds in the north in loose colonies, building a large nest of twigs and rootlets lined with grass, usually 10-20 feet above the ground on the horizontal branch of a conifer. It lays 3-6 pale blue eggs, spotted with lilac-black, which are incubated by the female alone for just under 2 weeks; the young birds leave the nest just over 2 weeks after they have hatched. The adult is a small bird with a short forked tail, long pointed wings and a slender bill. It is brown-gray above and buffy beneath, finely streaked overall, and in flight it shows yellow bars across the wings and a yellow tail with a black tip. The female has slightly less yellow. The Pine Siskin feeds in flocks, often hanging upside down to reach the seeds in hanging catkins and pods. It also eats insects and will visit bird feeders in winter.

HOARY REDPOLL

Scientific name:	*Carduelis hornemanni*
Length:	$5\frac{1}{2}$ inches
Habitat:	Open ground above Arctic tree line
Identification:	Small open-country bird with long, slightly notched tail and small yellow bill. Light gray-brown above with pale brown streaks, white rump, black chin, red cap, dark wings with white wing bars. Male has pink breast, female white. Juvenile lacks red and is streaked beneath
Similar species:	Common Redpoll is darker, but females can be difficult to tell apart

The Hoary Redpoll generally lives further north than the Common and rarely comes very far south in winter. Although their ranges overlap, they do not interbreed. The Hoary Redpoll builds a nest of grass and fine rootlets lined with feathers on the ground or very low down in a tree or bush, in which it lays 3-6 pale green eggs, lightly speckled with brown. These are incubated by the female for about 10-12 days; the young birds leave the nest some 9-15 days after hatching. The adult is a small bird with a long, slightly notched tail and a small yellow bill. It is light gray-brown above with pale brown streaks, and has a white rump, a black chin and red cap, and dark wings with white wing bars. The male has a pink-washed breast, the breast of the female is white. The juvenile lacks any red and is streaked beneath. The Hoary Redpoll is a gregarious bird and is sometimes seen in flocks with the Common Redpoll. It eats the seeds of trees and also insects.

COMMON REDPOLL

Scientific name:	*Carduelis flammea*
Length:	5¼ inches
Habitat:	Subarctic forests, tundra, birch and willow scrub
Identification:	Small open-country bird with long, slightly notched tail and small yellow bill. Gray-brown above with brown streaks above and below, black chin, bright red forehead, dark wings with white wing bars. Male has deep pink breast, female white or buffy. Juvenile lacks red and is heavily streaked beneath
Similar species:	Hoary Redpoll is paler, but females can be difficult to tell apart

An Arctic bird, the Common Redpoll often sleeps in tunnels in the snow to keep warm during the long northern nights and only comes further south during the winter. It breeds on Arctic tundra, building a nest of grass and rootlets lined with feathers on the bare ground or low in a tree or shrub, in which it lays 3-6 pale blue-green eggs, lightly spotted with brown. These are incubated by the female for about 2 weeks; the young birds leave the nest some 12-15 days after hatching. The adult is a rather small, plump bird with a long and slightly notched tail and a small yellow bill. It is gray-brown above with brown streaks above and below, a black chin, a bright red forehead, and dark wings with white wing bars. The male (*above*) has a deep pink breast, the breast of the female is white or buffy. The juvenile lacks any red and is heavily streaked beneath. The Common Redpoll is an extremely social and a very active bird and is usually seen in large flocks; if one takes flight, the rest will immediately follow. It eats the seeds of trees such as birch, alder and willow and also insects. It will often visit feeders in winter and can appear very tame.

LESSER GOLDFINCH

Scientific name:	*Carduelis psaltria*
Length:	$4\frac{1}{2}$ inches
Habitat:	Dry brushy fields, woodland edges, streamsides
Identification:	Small, stocky open-country bird with short forked tail, short rounded wings and large bill. Male has black crown, white patches on black wing and tail, bright yellow underparts, back either black or green. Female and juvenile olive above, duller yellow beneath, lack black cap
Similar species:	Male distinctive. Female American Goldfinch has white undertail coverts

Common in dry and brushy habitats and along the edge of woodland, the Lesser Goldfinch is also often seen in backyards across its range. It sings almost constantly, and in the Old World its relatives were kept as caged birds. It nests in a bush or low tree, building a cup of fine twigs and plant fibers lined with grass and plant down, usually around 20 feet above the ground. It lays 4 or 5 plain pale blue eggs, which are incubated by the female alone for around 11-14 days. The adult is a small, stocky bird with a short forked tail, short, rounded wings and a relatively large bill. The male has a black crown, white patches on black wings and tail, and bright yellow underparts. The color of the back varies from black in eastern birds to green in the west. The female and juvenile are olive above and a duller yellow beneath, and they lack the black cap. The Lesser Goldfinch mainly eats seeds and is particularly fond of dandelion seeds.

AMERICAN GOLDFINCH

Scientific name: *Carduelis tristis*
Length: 5 inches
Habitat: Weedy fields, open second-growth woods, suburbs
Identification: Small, stocky open-country bird with short forked tail, short rounded wings and large bill. Breeding male bright yellow with black cap, white rump and undertail coverts, yellow shoulder, white bars on black wings, white edges to black upper tail feathers. Female and winter birds dull olive above, yellow below, white undertail coverts, lack black cap. Juveniles mainly pale tan
Similar species: Breeding male distinctive. Female Lesser Goldfinch lacks white undertail coverts

The American Goldfinch is fairly common across most of North America, except in the far north. It is a very gregarious bird, and often forages in mixed flocks with other species. It breeds within the central and northern areas of its range, building a small, tightly-woven cup of grass and plant fibers lined with plant down, usually high above the ground in a bush or tree. It lays 3-6 plain blue-white eggs, which are incubated by the female alone for around 2 weeks; the young leave the nest to start fending for themselves around 12-17 days after they have hatched. The adult is a small, stocky bird with a short, forked tail, short, rounded wings and a relatively large bill. The breeding male (below) is bright yellow with a black cap, a white rump and undertail coverts, a yellow shoulder, white bars on black wings, and white edges to black upper tail feathers. The female and winter birds are a dull olive above and yellow below, with white undertail coverts, and no black cap. The juvenile bird is brownish overall, with dark wings and tail. The American Goldfinch mainly eats seeds - especially thistle seeds - but it will also take small insects and berries. The nestlings are fed on seeds that have been shelled and partly predigested by the parent birds.

HOUSE SPARROW *(opposite)*

Scientific name: *Passer domesticus*
Length: 6¼ inches
Habitat: Urban areas
Identification: Plump, short-tailed open-country bird, with short wings and stout bill. Breeding male has gray crown, brown and black striping on wings and back, chestnut nape, white face, large black bib. Chestnut and black markings concealed with grayish feathers in winter. Female streaked brown-gray above, buffy eyebrow, plain buffy-gray beneath
Similar species: Native sparrows have longer legs, thinner bills

An Old World species, the House Sparrow was first introduced in Central Park, New York City, in 1850 and has spread and adapted so it is now found across most of North America. It is often considered to be a pest as it sometimes drives out native birds, but it also thrives in urban environments, where few other birds care to live. It nests in a cavity in a tree, building, lamp post or similar place, lining the hole with an untidy mass of straw and grass and laying 5 or 6 pale greenish-white eggs, speckled with brown. These are incubated for up to 2 weeks by the female bird alone and the young birds leave the nest to make way for a second brood around 2-3 weeks after they have hatched. The adult is a plump, short-tailed bird, with short wings and a stout, blunt bill. The breeding male has a gray crown, brown and black striping on the wings and back, a chestnut nape, white face, and a large black bib. The chestnut and black markings are concealed under grayish feathers in winter, which gradually wear off to reveal the breeding plumage. The female is streaked brown-gray above and plain buffy-gray beneath, with a buffy eyebrow. The House Sparrow gathers in noisy flocks and eats a wide variety of things, including insects, spiders, caterpillars, seeds, berries, grain and bread crumbs.

EURASIAN TREE SPARROW *(above)*

Scientific name: *Passer montanus*
Length: 6 inches
Habitat: Parks, suburbs, farmland
Identification: Plump, short-tailed open-country bird, with short wings and small bill. Rufous crown, white collar, brown and black striping on wings and back, black ear patch on white face, small black bib. Juvenile streaked brown-gray above, dark spot on whitish cheek, plain buffy-gray beneath
Similar species: House Sparrow has gray crown and larger black bib. Native sparrows have longer legs, thinner bills

An Old World species, the Eurasian Tree Sparrow was first introduced in St Louis in 1870 and has spread into parks and farmlands in the region and into western Illinois and southeastern Iowa. It avoids urban environments, but does live in the suburbs. It nests in a sheltered cavity in a tree, building or cliff, lining the hole with feathers and grass and laying 2-6 pale gray-white eggs, speckled with brown. These are incubated for up to 2 weeks by both adults and the young birds leave the nest around 2 weeks after they have hatched. The adult is a plump, short-tailed bird, with short wings and a small bill. It has a rufous crown, white collar, brown and black striping on the wings and back, a black ear patch on a white face, and a small black bib. The juvenile is streaked brown-gray above, plain buffy-gray beneath, with a mottled crown, a gray throat and a gray ear spot on a whitish cheek. The Eurasian Tree Sparrow gathers in small flocks and eats insects, seeds, berries, grain and bread crumbs.

INDEX OF COMMON NAMES

INDEX OF LATIN NAMES

PICTURE CREDITS

208B - John Brown; 209 - Robert R Tyrrell; 210 - E R Degginger; 211 - Robert R Tyrrell; 212 - Michael Fogden; 213 - Wendy Shattil & Bob Rozinski; 214T - Tom Ulrich; 214B - Tom Ulrich; 215 - Richard Day; 216 - Joanne Huemoeller; 217T - Alan G Nelson; 217B - Richard Day; 218T - Eric Woods; 218B - Richard Day; 219 - Paul Berquist; 220T - G W Willis; 220B - Jack Wilburn; 221 - Tom Ulrich; 222 - Alan G Nelson; 223T - C C Lockwood; 223B - Richard Day; 224T - Tom Ulrich; 224B - John Gerlach; 225T - Tom Ulrich; 225B - Alan G Nelson; 226 - Joe McDonald; 227T - Breck P Kent; 227B - Mike Price; 228T - Tom Edwards; 228B - Patti Murray; 229 - Bill Beatty; 230 - Tom Ulrich; 231 - Ted Levin; 232T - Dale & Marian Zimmerman; 232B - Frank Schneidermeyer; 233 - Patti Murray; 234T - Eric Woods; 234B - Stan Osolinski; 235 - Tom Ulrich; 236T - Jack Dermid; 236B - Joe McDonald; 237 - John Gerlach; 238 - C M Perrins; 239 - Maresa Pryor; 240 - Richard Day; 241T - Joe McDonald; 241B - Patti Murray; 242 - David Tipling; 243 - Charles Palek; 244 - Ron Willocks; 245 - James H Robinson; 246T - John S. Dunning/Ardea, London; 246B - Richard Day; 247 - John S Dunning/Ardea, London; 249 - Tom Ulrich; 250 - Mike Price; 251T - Len Rue Jnr; 251B - Stan Osolinski; 252 - Tom Ulrich; 253T - Leonard Lee Rue III; 253B - James Robinson; 254 - Tom Ulrich; 255T - Mark Hamblin; 255B - Arthur Gloor; 256 - Breck P Kent; 257T - Richard Packwood; 257B - Jim Zipp/Ardea, London; 258T - Ken Cole; 258B - Tom Ulrich; 259 - Vicki J Anderson; 260T - Tom Ulrich; 260B - Terry Andrewartha; 261T - Terry Andrewartha; 261B - G A Maclean; 262 - Bates Littlehales; 263 - Ken Cole; 264 - Wendy Shattil & Bob Rozinski; 265 - Robert H Armstrong; 266 - N V Howell; 267 - Joe McDonald; 268 - John Anderson; 269T - Paul Berquist; 269B - Paul Berquist; 270T - John Gerlach; 270B - Jack Dermid; 271 - Tom Ulrich; 272T - Scott Smith; 272B - Donald D Burgess/Ardea, London; 273 - Bill Beatty; 274T - Richard Day; 274B - Noah Satat; 275 - Marty Cordano; 276T - Frank Huber; 276B - Bates Littlehales; 277T - Niall Denvie; 277B - Dennis Green; 278T - Michael Habicht; 278B - James H Robinson; 279 - T C Nature; 280T - Robert H Armstrong; 280B - Doug Wechsler; 281 - Richard Day; 282T - Michael Habicht; 282B - John Trott; 283 - Richard Day; 284 - Patti Murray; 285 - Tom Ulrich; 287 - Richard Reinhold; 288T - Richard Day; 288B - John Gerlach; 289 - Tom Ulrich; 290T - Tom Ulrich; 290B - Stan Osolinski; 291 - Stan Osolinski; 292T - Dale & Marian Zimmerman; 292B - Jack Wilburn; 293T - Tom Ulrich; 293B - John Gerlach; 294 - Tom Ulrich; 295- Marty Cordano; 296 - Alan G Nelson; 297 - David Tipling; 298 - Tom Ulrich; 299T - E R Degginger; 299B - Mark Hamblin; 300 - Patti Murray; 301T - John Trott; 301B - Richard Day; 302T - Bates Littlehales; 302B - G W Willis; 303T - Adam Jones; 303B - Ted Levin; 304T - David M Cottridge; 304B - Phyllis Greenberg; 305 - Kenneth Day; 306 - Robert Lubeck; 307 - Patti Murray; 308T - Tom Lazar; 308B - Richard Day; 309 - Robert Lubeck; 310T - Tom Lazar; 310B - John Trott; 311T - Robert Lubeck; 311B - Ken Carmichael; 312 - Patti Murray; 313 - Edward Robinson; 314 - Tom Ulrich; 315 - John Mitchell; 316 - G W Schwartz; 317 Robert Lubeck; 318 - John Mitchell; 319T - Daniel J Cox; 319B - John Trott; 320 - John Gerlach; 320 - Richard Day; 322 - Lon Lauber; 323 - Ken Cole; 324 - Tom Edwards; 325 - James H Robinson; 326 - Frank Schneidermeyer; 327 - Joyce & Frank Burek; 328 - Tom Ulrich; 329T - Frank Schneidermeyer; 329B - Stan Osolinski; 330 - Tom Ulrich; 331T - Tom Ulrich; 331B - Terry Andrewartha; 332T - Tom Ulrich; 332B - Noah Satat; 333 - John Gerlach; 334T - Tom Ulrich; 334B - Jack Willburn; 335 - Michael Habicht; 336T - Jack Wilburn; 336B - Jack Wilburn; 337T - R H Armstrong; 337B - Chris Sharp; 338 - Frank Schneidermeyer; 339T - Daniel J Cox; 339B - Daniel J Cox; 340 - Bates Littlehales; 341 - Joe McDonald; 342T - Tom Ulrich; 342B - David Tipling; 343 - Tom Ulrich; 344T - Joe McDonald; 344B - Tony Tilford; 345T - Tom Leach; 345B - Tom Ulrich; 346T - Tom Ulrich; 346B - Tony Tilford; 347T - Tony Tilford; 347B - Tony Tilford; 348T - Tom Ulrich; 348B and back jacket - Richard Day; 349 - Tom Ulrich; 350T - Tom Ulrich; 350B - Richard Day; 351 - Tom Ulrich; 352T - Frank Schneidermeyer; 352B - Jack Wilburn; 353 - Stan Osolinski; 354 - John Gerlach; 355T - Frank Schneidermeyer; 355B - John Harris; 356T - Maresa Pryor; 356B - Stan Osolinski; 357T - Richard Packwood; 357B - Bates Littlehales; 358T - Richard Day; 358B - Frank Schneidermeyer; 359 - Eric Woods; 360 - Frank Schneidermeyer; 361 - Leonard Lee Rue III: 362T - Richard Day; 362B - Alan G Nelson; 363 - Frank Schneidermeyer; 364 - Alan G Nelson; 365 - John Gerlach; 366T - Hans Reinhard; 366B - Erwin & Peggy Bauer; 367 - Tom Ulrich; 368 - James Robinson; 369T - Michael Habicht - 369B - Tom Ulrich; 370T - Tom Ulrich; 370B - Alan G Nelson; 371 - John Gerlach; 372 - Stan Osolinski; - 373 - Alan G Nelson; 374 - Hans Reinhard/Okapia; 375 - Mark Hamblin.

Front jacket Bald Eagle - Lon E Lauber and back jacket Dicksell - Richard Day

ACKNOWLEDGEMENTS

Thank you to all the research staff at Oxford Scientific Films and Sophie Napier at Ardea, London. Thanks also to Richard Betts, David Clarke, Marie Clayton, John Dunne, Eric Good, Judy Linard, Anthony Linden, Carol Salter, Cliff Salter, Jenny Salter, Simon Taylor and Stephanie Young.